lr/24n

ROBERT E. KRIEGER
PUBLISHING COMPANY INC.

MALABAR
FLORIDA 32950

LIBERTY AND EQUALITY IN THE EDUCATIONAL PROCESS

LIBERTY AND EQUALITY IN THE EDUCATIONAL PROCESS
A COMPARATIVE SOCIOLOGY OF EDUCATION

REMI CLIGNET

A WILEY-INTERSCIENCE PUBLICATION

JOHN WILEY & SONS, New York · London · Toronto · Sydney

Library of Congress Cataloging in Publication Data:

Clignet, Remi.
  Liberty and equality in the educational process.

  "A Wiley-Interscience publication."
  Includes bibliographical references.
  1. Educational sociology. 2. Education—Economic
aspects. 3. Educational equalization. I. Title.

LC191.C54   370.19'3   74-9737

ISBN 0-471-16057-1

Printed in the United States of America

10 9 8 7 6 5 4 3 2 1

ACKNOWLEDGMENTS

In this book I show the influence that the past exerts on educational institutions and roles. Thus it is only fair to indicate how the present venture itself has been affected by my previous experiences and encounters. I am French; I have both studied and taught in the schools of that country. Also I have worked and taught in several African countries before coming to the United States. Hence my experiences are European, African, and American.

Clearly, this alone is not sufficient reason to justify the following undertaking. In this book, I have attempted to translate all the wisdom of the "significant others" who preceded me in the field, notably C. Arnold Anderson, Howard Becker, Ronald Corwin, Philip Foster, John Kitsuse, Malcolm Spector, Ivan Vallier, and Walter Wallace, who have been more than generous in their comments, suggestions, and encouragements. Similarly, I have done my best to incorporate the numerous suggestions of the students who were patient enough to see the project develop and grow. In this respect, I am particularly indebted to Mrs. Jeanne Nash, Gail Thieman, and to Miss Jennifer O'Day who had the courage to tell me that my ideas were not always as clear as they could be and as I thought they were. I am also indebted to Miss Barbara Teising who, with a warm smile, typed successive versions of the manuscript.

To be faithful to tradition, I must claim that all the errors and weaknesses that persist in this manuscript are not theirs but my own misdeeds. As it stands, I dedicate this book to Sara and Marion.

REMI CLIGNET

April 1974
Northwestern University
Evanston, Illinois

CONTENTS

PART TWO   THE SCHOOL AS A MICROCOSM

Variety of Utopian Responses to These Contradictions

TABLES

xi

FIGURES

INTRODUCTION

University student agitation, high school riots, teacher strikes, boycotts of integrated or segregated schools both by parents and their offspring, defeats of referenda designed to alter educational policies or to increase the resources of educational institutions—the list of the diseases affecting educational systems keeps increasing. And the symptoms do not appear to be culturally relative; they manifest themselves in one form or another in nation-states throughout the world.

Many political leaders expect social scientists not only to find a satisfactory explanation of the turmoil affecting educational institutions but also to identify the panacea that will eliminate both the symptoms and the roots of the malaise. Some social scientists might be inclined to defer to such a request, but their attempt at a solution necessitates preliminary analyses. These scientists must identify the grievances of the variety of individuals and groups participating in the educational process (students and their parents, teachers and administrators, taxpayers and other interest groups). They must also determine whether the malaise has the same meaning, the same causes, and the same implications in various parts of the world or types of institutions and whether it is similarly experienced across and within the main categories of individuals and groups involved in the educational process. The first step of the relevant analysis deals with the "action meanings" individuals and groups develop to justify their perceptions and behaviors, and the second step involves the identification of the relevant "act meanings" and hence the integration of the perceptions and rationalizations held by educational actors into a unifying sociological form of explanation.[1]

1

In fact, the current discomfiture reflects increasingly divergent views about the functions of formal schooling and the definition of the policies designed to implement these functions. Are educational experiences supposed to "liberate" the individual from the constraints imposed upon him by familial, economic, political, and religious organizations? Conflicts do occur because of disagreements about the meaning and desirability of these "liberating" effects of educational experiences. Formal schooling may be viewed as liberating insofar as it enables an individual to achieve a better understanding of current social arrangements and thus to claim a privileged position in the various arenas in which he participates. Conversely, formal schooling may be viewed as liberating, only insofar as it enables individuals or groups to alter critical aspects of the overall social structure. Further, the liberating functions of education are sometimes defined in broad and diffuse terms and are sometimes viewed as fundamentally specific.

For a first group of parents, students, teachers, administrators, and certain segments of the population at large, the liberating functions of formal schooling are primarily economic. This group challenges schools because rewards fall short of expectations, and they raise questions about curricula or pedagogical techniques because schools apparently are unwilling or unable to provide their graduates with the jobs they anticipate or which their predecessors preempted too easily. A second group defines the liberating functions of schools in political terms and criticizes educational institutions because they do not foster a sufficient political mobilization and favor a mindless perpetuation of the existing political order. For a third group, the liberating functions of educational experiences refer primarily to individual creativity. The increased bureaucratization of educational institutions prevents students from "doing their own thing" and finding an authentic meaning to their existence. Far from being liberating, educational experiences are viewed as oppressive.[2] In short, people discuss whether schools can and should free individuals or limited social groups from all or from selected institutional constraints.

Against these perspectives, however, the liberating functions of schooling also may be primarily defined in collective terms. From this particular viewpoint the main function of schools is to cater to the needs of the *community* as a whole and to train the personnel needed for ensuring the survival and growth of local economic, political, and social organizations. Current educational conflicts also reflect divergent assumptions about the preeminence of individual over local or national aspirations. But what are the legitimate boundaries of a community?

Are these boundaries territorial or are they based upon the sharing of common beliefs and attitudes? Perhaps the liberating functions of education consist merely in enhancing the number of alternative solutions to the problems raised by the interaction between the individual and his surroundings.

However, the current challenges confronting educational institutions focus not only on their functions but also on the implementation of the relevant policies. Thus the main groups of actors interested in the educational processes often protest against the economic and social costs of formal schooling, which does not alleviate but rather perpetuates current inequities. Educational crises do not result from lacks or excesses in the influence schools are supposed to exert on the liberation of individuals, but from their contributions to the current patterns of inequalities. Oppressed minorities (women, lower classes, religious or ethnic groups) do not obtain their fair share of educational amenities. Not only are they kept out of the most prestigious types of schools, or of the schools which lead to the most rewarding types of job, but the institutions they attend lack the social, material, and human resources needed to enhance the attractiveness of learning activities. Inequality characterizes not only patterns of *access* to schools but also patterns of *interaction* between various categories of students and teachers or administrators.

Individuals and groups have increasingly divergent views of both the optimal functions to be performed by schools and of the strategies most appropriate for reaching the goals.[3] What is the ideal nature of educational activities and what is their contribution to liberty? Who profits most from educational amenities and what is the contribution of schools to equality? As the title of the book suggests, one of the tasks of sociology is to evaluate the convergences and divergences of liberty and equality as they manifest themselves on the educational scene.

"It is not so much by offering a solution to my reader that I can render him a real service as in actually forcing him to think for himself about these problems."[4] The purpose of this book is not to solve conflicts in the concepts of liberty and equality as they affect the educational process. It is to highlight the substantive educational issues underlying the dilemma between liberty and equality and to define the particular sets of methodological rules likely to facilitate the study of this particular dilemma.

The Dilemma Between Liberty and Equality in Education. Current educational conflicts reflect both divergences in the meaning to be attached to the concept of liberty and contradictions between this ideal and the ideal of equality. Philosophers involved in the critical examination of values are necessarily interested in assessing the ethical dimensions of the contradictions between liberty and equality and in proposing universal and hence abstract models of an educational enterprise.

While the training of a philosopher often requires him to deal with the *absolute* or *ideal* aspects of the educational dilemma between liberty and equality, the sociologist is more likely to stress the cultural *relativity* of such a dilemma. As a prerequisite to this undertaking, however, he must first achieve an accurate definition of the concepts as they apply to the educational process. Insofar as the concept of liberty refers to the control that individuals or groups of individuals exert over their own fate, the underlying issue is to identify which actors or groups of actors have the power to define the functions of educational institutions, their organization, and their clientele and to control the resources necessary for attaining the corresponding objectives. In this perspective the liberties of individual actors or groups of actors are liable to be mutually exclusive. The autonomy teachers enjoy in the exercise of their occupation, and hence their professionalization, parallels the restrictions imposed upon students' behavior and learning activities. Similarly, the professionalization of teachers is incompatible with the control that administrators and—more generally—the public would like to exert upon the functioning of schools. Further, the degree to which the various categories of actors in education are able to control the purposes and the functioning of educational processes is likely to reflect the differential positions they occupy in the society at large. Hence their relative liberty is influenced by social and cultural inequalities. The liberty enjoyed by students during or after their educational experiences is perhaps directly affected by the inequalities governing access to the institutions they have attended and varies with the characteristics of the population which is excluded from their schools. Similarly, the liberty enjoyed by teachers in the definition of their teaching activities and hence the power they hold over administrators or over the public might vary with the extent to which these teachers are able to prevent "undesirable" candidates from entering this occupation. Historically, educational liberty precedes educational equality; early educational reformists were primarily concerned with the idea of enhancing the social, economic, and cultural privileges of teachers and students without simultaneously challenging the multiple forms of alienation experienced by uneducated and illiterate masses.

Inconsistencies in the concept of equality itself are similar to contradictions between the concepts of liberty and equality. This concept has rarely been defined as absolute, and few societies have proposed, for example, that all individuals should be entitled to own equal shares of property. William Faulkner argued that there is no such thing as equality per se, but only equality to; "equal right and opportunity to make the best one can of one's life within one's capacity and capability without fear of injustice or oppression or violence." [5] The concept of equality of opportunities that emerges indicates that, while it is up to the individual to seize opportunities, they might be refused to him because of social affiliations and, more generally, because of ascriptive traits (e.g., sex, age, social, cultural, and ethnic origin).

An increasing number of governments have passed equal-opportunity legislation in at least four areas of social participation. Equality of opportunities affects matrimonial choices, and potential conjugal partners are increasingly chosen independently of social, religious, or ethnic affiliations. This equality also affects patterns of production and of consumption; and sex, ethnic, social, or cultural discrimination is unlawful in labor as well as in housing markets. More recently, equality pertains also to the use of educational facilities. Yet the concept of equality of educational opportunities remains problematic. Does this concept mean that all schools should be accessible to *all* children? Does the fulfillment of this condition require children to attend schools characterized by equal human, material, and social resources? Fifty years ago F. Thomson answered this question by asserting that "schools cannot bestow an equality of benefits through the *same* ministrations to all children" and that "children equipped with lesser gifts by nature must be given more by nurture." [6] Does the fulfillment of equality require then that schools take into account prior inequalities so that graduates have equal chances to participate successfully in familial, economic, political, and religious institutions, regardless of initial differences in the positions these graduates or their family occupy in the social structure? Thus, while initial conceptions of equality have stressed the importance of minimizing contrasts in the opportunities offered to school-aged populations and hence in the educational treatment to which they were to be subjected, more contemporary scholars and reformists have emphasized the necessity of achieving equality of results rather than equality of opportunities. This should minimize contrasts in the income, prestige, and power that various individuals derive from an identical educational experience.

In addition, the interaction between educational liberty and equality has always remained problematic. Ideally the terms are complementary, since individuals should enjoy an *equal* amount of liberty—that is, control over their lives. Historically, however, conflicts between these two facets have existed. Insofar as the liberty enjoyed by individuals or groups of individuals has often been acquired at the expense of other segments of society, it stimulates the perpetuation or the systematization of inequalities. Alternatively, while the pursuit of a greater equality has often entailed a growing centralization of economic and political power in the educational sphere, it has been associated with a sharp decline in the educational liberty of various groups.

These contradictions are manifested differentially during various phases of the educational process. They pertain to the relative *access* of various categories of the population to educational roles and the underlying issue is to determine who becomes a student, a teacher, or an administrator. At the same time, these contradictions pertain to the communications taking place *within* educational institutions, and the underlying issue is to determine the nature and consequences of the restrictions on teachers, students, and administrators in the exercise of their activities within the school situation.

But is the conflict between liberty and equality confined to the school scene, or is it a particular manifestation of more diffuse tensions present in the whole society? Does such a conflict take its roots in the educational scene, or are its educational manifestations the mere by-products of broader societal processes? [7]

The initial step of the analysis is to delineate the interaction between educational and other societal institutions. However, since the examination of such interactions requires the two sets of institutions to be analytically distinct, Chapter 1 is devoted to an examination of the processes by which educational enterprises become differentiated from other segments of a society, and notably from religious and familial institutions. Until this differentiation is made, educational and socializing activities are exclusively geared to the fulfillment of societal needs, and individuals cannot experience the educational specificity of the dilemma between liberty and equality. It is only after this differentiation is completed, that the definition of educational goals and processes becomes problematic. Correspondingly, Chapter 2 is an assessment of the network of reciprocal influences between educational and familial, political, economic, and religious structures and processes. Before deciding whether the dilemma experienced by individuals or groups between liberty and equality is specific to education, it is necessary to determine the degree to which the current profile and dynamics of educational roles and institutions reflect the cross-pressures emanating from other arenas of social participation; and conversely, the degree to which participation in educational enterprises is a force modifying forms of participation in familial, political, economic, or religious structures. Thus the theme underlying Part One pertains to the problem of assessing whether the dilemma between liberty and equality has a specific educational meaning, or whether its educational manifestations are related to what goes on in the society at large.

In Part Two a marked dependence of schools toward other institutions is assumed. This makes necessary an exploration of the external constraints that weigh on schools' organization and functioning. Thus, Chapter 3 is an analysis of the variety of pressures members of other institutions exert on schools, their rationale for doing so, and the mechanisms by which such pressures are manifested. Parents, taxpayers, the clergy, businessmen, government officials, have a vested interest in maximizing the predictability of educational processes, for this predictability enhances the continuity of social patterns of interaction, guarantees perpetuation of the existing order, and minimizes the costs of schooling. Since schools are not *equally free* to choose the content of the courses they offer, the techniques they use, the personnel they hire, and the students they enroll, I identify in Chapter 3 both the mechanisms by which their activities are controlled and the strength of the pressures to which they are subjected.

However, the liberty of teachers may be acquired at the expense of students or administrators as well as at the expense of the remaining segments of society. In fact, the relative power teachers are able to exert over students and their parents or over educational administrators, and hence the relative liberty these teachers can exercise, depends upon the patterns of access into that particular occupational group. The narrower such a pattern (and hence the larger the representation of privileged social and cultural groups in the teaching force), the easier it should be for teachers to claim a privileged status and to enjoy a greater amount of occupational freedom. Thus, the relative power held by teachers and administrators varies with their social and cultural origin and hence the degree to which their recruitment can be characterized by significant social and cultural inequalities. This power, however, depends also upon the solidarity among the individual practitioners and hence upon the patterns of socialization into these occupational groups as well as upon the conditions under which they perform their daily activities. In Chapter 4, I show how the educators' liberty (and thus their lack of vulnerability to external influences) depends upon their professionalization—that is, upon their recruitment, their socialization, and the organization of their daily routines.

Yet, the educational liberty of teachers and administrators also depends upon the organizational structures within which they operate. While these two groups vie to obtain a maximum amount of occupational autonomy in the contemporary world, formal schooling is nevertheless expected not only to act as an *equalizing* factor among social classes, ethnic and religious groups, between generations and sexes, but also to provide the individual with equal chances to move in the social and occupational hierarchy. Independently of their equalizing functions, educational institutions are also influenced by bureaucratic models, which induce a growing standardization of educational processes and hence a growing equality in the status assigned to individuals performing similar sets of educational activities. Thus, although as professionals, teachers and administrators strive to achieve a status that *differentiates* them from the remaining population, their endeavors in this respect run against the *generalizing* principles underlying both the functions assigned to schools and their organizational profiles. Correspondingly, the dilemma resulting from the professionalization and the bureaucratization of school personnel is associated with the development of a number of significant educational tensions. Chapter 5 is devoted to an analysis of their manifestations and outcomes as well as of their implications on the conflict between liberty and equality.

However, the educational process does not depend solely upon the pressures that communities exert on their schools or upon the dominant characteristics of school administrators and their teaching force. It depends also upon the characteristics of the school clientele, whose social profile we examine in Chapter 6 and 7. Again, the underlying issue is to determine the conditions under which schools open their doors to broad categories of the population or restrict their admission to particular categories, and whether schools represent a democratic system advocating education for all or an elitist organization whose function is to perpetuate existing social arrangements and hierarchies. I show that increasing societal complexity is associated with a corresponding differentiation of the mechanisms by which different types of educational institutions attract various segments of the school-aged population. In Chapter 7, I examine the determinants of current inequalities characterizing patterns of access to various types of schools.

After this description of the major actors involved in the educational process, I discuss the interaction between teachers and students, and more specifically, the extent and determinants of variations in teaching (Chapter 8) and learning styles (Chapter 9). The dilemma between equality and liberty affects not only the relative characteristics of students, teachers, and administrators—and hence their patterns of access into their roles—but also their mode of communication. Teachers as well as students use assimilation to organize *inwardly* their modes of interaction; that is, they use their past experiences and patterns of action as a generalizing principle around which they articulate their current activities. But they also use accommodation as a principle of differentiation, which leads them to change *outwardly* the premises on which they build their communications. Insofar as teachers or students adopt an assimilation-oriented teaching or learning style, they give preeminence to their own generalized framework and in so doing, they affirm the liberty they believe to enjoy in their educational activities. Alternatively, when teachers or students adopt an accommodation-based teaching or learning style, they differentiate their own perspective from that used by their interlocutors, and since they stress the relativeness of their own viewpoint, they assert the significance of equality in their pedagogical communications. Yet, to analyze separately the mode of adaptation retained by teachers and students is insufficient. In these chapters, I suggest indeed that an examination of the liberty and equality achieved by these two groups of actor in their activities requires an understanding of their very *interaction*. The liberalizing and equalizing effects of the communications between teachers and students are contingent upon the *linkage* between the prevailing mode of adaptation retained by each. While students may adopt an assimilation oriented learning style, independently of the teaching style adopted by their instructors, they may also adopt this particular mode of adaptation as a response to an assimilation or alternatively accommodation oriented teaching style. The outcome of this type of learning is not the same in the three situations; in addition, it also varies with the organizational climate of the schools and the orientations specific to each discipline.

Teachers are expected not only to provide their students with the legitimate cognitive emotional and social skills required for the performance of adult roles, but also to certify that these students have acquired such skills. In this sense, teachers act as agents of control over the liberty of students. Therefore, we must examine variations in the mechanisms by which this control is exerted and analyze how such variations in turn affect interactions between teacher and student. This is the theme of Chapter 10.

After this analysis of the various phases of the life cycle of students and teachers, Chapter 11 is an analysis of the influence exerted by educational experiences on occupational achievement; that is, of the degree to which educational experiences modify the modes of individual participation in the labor force and, alternatively, of the degree to which the role of formal schooling is strictly epiphenomenal.

Finally, Chapter 12 is a summary of the contrasts and similarities between the various facets of the equality and liberty processes. By isolating consistencies and inconsistencies in our quest toward educational equality and liberty, the implications of the underlying myths are evaluated. Are our longings self-defeating, or can they help us to give new forms and new meanings to our daily experiences?

Methodological Considerations.   Regularities in educational processes and structures can be defined within three distinct perspectives. First, these regularities have both an historical and a social meaning. The profile of schools is simultaneously determined by the legacy of the past and current social forces. Second, these regularities are not "mechanical" and the relationships among the internal functions of schools or between such functions and the outside world rarely are linear. They are more likely to follow complex patterns because there are discontinuities in the influence exerted by the determinants of educational activities or because the responses of such activities occur only after the pressures to change exceed a critical threshold. Third, these regularities are not simple. Each determinant of educational roles, functions, and institutions operates in conjunction with a number of varying forces.

The Concurrent Influences of the Past and the Present on Educational Roles and Institutions.   Because schools transmit the cultural heritage of a particular social system, they are not independent of the history of that system. History affects not only the nature of the curriculum offered but also the definition of educational roles and functions. For example, the expression "community of scholars" reveals the persistence of the values forged during the Renaissance when intellectuals aspired to live in monasteries dedicated to the pursuit of Platonic ideals.[8] Similarly, the initial preeminence of religious forces in the development of educational institutions and roles continues to affect the standards used to evaluate educational activities around the world.

The influence of historical factors may be more specific. In this book, for example, I sketch the numerous implications attached to the contrasts between centralized and decentralized school systems. Yet the meaning of centralization varies with the specific historical circumstances under which educational enterprises have been controlled by central political agencies. In France centralization reflects the fear of a weak government confronted with the centrifugal forces corresponding to the initiatives taken earlier by private individuals and institutions; [9] and the actions of the government took place only after private institutions had been able to establish a broad network of schools. In Italy centralization results from the leading role played by a particular region (Piedmont) and a particular segment of the social structure (the industrial bourgeoisie) in the economic and political development of the country, and the organization of such networks has been the result of government investments.

The current profile of schools, however, is not only a function of the internal history of the countries examined but also the result of past international relationships. The current organization of African schools reflects both the variety of colonial models imposed upon them and the resistance displayed by local authorities against the corresponding forms of cultural imperialism. In black Africa traditional institutions often have been unable to maintain their formal socializing roles. As a result, current disparities in the organization or the functions of Senegalese, Ghanian, Angolan, and Congolese schools reproduce differences both in the colonial systems of France, Great Britain, Portugal, and Belgium and in the organization and functions of the past metropolitan educational enterprises of these European countries. [10]

In contrast, Morocco has been able to perpetuate two educational systems, one turned toward the teaching of Islamic culture and the other aimed at the diffusion of a French life style. [11] This duality has been possible because of the intense competition opposing European colonial powers to one another at the turn of the century and because of the limitations experienced by French colonizers in Morocco. It also results from the political integration achieved by Morocco at the eve of its colonization and from the resistance that it was able to muster against the ambitions of French educators.

Yet the references to historical, internal, or international models are not global. Through processes of selectivity, past elements are retained in the current organization of educational systems. Although the existence of educational enterprises is often justified on the basis of historical precedents, past experiences are reinterpreted by reference to the perceived requirements of a current situation. While the concept of community control, for example, is often defined as a faithful translation of the American ideal of grass-roots democracy, it is still selectively used by those who hope to derive more rewards from the power *they think they have mustered* at the local level. The exploitation of the theme of community control cannot be alike for blacks living in the

urban ghettos of northern states, for well-established white-dominated
rural communities of New England, and for black sharecroppers of the
Deep South. Similarly, one also can expect that two countries with parallel histories but distinctive current political, economic, and social organizations will not necessarily have similar educational institutions.
Legacies of the past do not fully explain the profile and the dynamics
of educational institutions or the views held by individuals in this
regard. Structural constraints as much as historical precedents shape
interactions between schools and society or between schools and their
actors.

Reciprocally, however, similarities in both the current profile and the
dynamics of schools and societies are not necessarily associated with
corresponding parallels in the values attached to formal schooling or in
the form taken by educational tensions. Such values and tensions are
dependent also on the particular historical development of the societies
examined. Although the functions that American and French universities perform today are somewhat similar, teacher status varies because
of the decentralized tradition of the first country and the centralized
tradition of the second. Students of these two countries do not anticipate either the same rewards from their experiences and do not complain about the same things with the same intensity.

This first approximation of the regularities in which sociologists are
interested (the role of historical and functional forces in shaping educational institutions) involves a discussion of the diffusionist and structuralist approaches.[12] The first emphasizes the transmission through
time or space of certain significant elements of the educational scene.
For example, a number of political leaders argue that the current educational malaise has diffused from a particular starting point, either as
a result of mass-media influence or as a result of an international con-
spiracy. They are likely to interpret the tragedy of Kent State University in 1970 as the by-product of the outbursts that occurred two years
before at Columbia or in Paris. They are similarly prone to view the activism of French high school students as the result of the disorders advocated by their elders. Such a view is limited. It does not explain the
sequential order in which the educational crisis has spread from one
country to another. The researcher still must identify which elements
of existing economic, political, social, and educational structures facilitate or impede the diffusion of particular forms or themes of protest
among student populations. Further, he must isolate the factors explaining why certain societies are likely to borrow an entire pattern of

action while others initially break down such patterns and select certain components.

Conversely, the structuralist approach emphasizes the synchronic and hence immediate response of educational institutions and roles to the demands of their environment. The universal educational crisis is supposed to reflect the simultaneous and universal emergence of objective conditions likely to foster student discontent in a variety of countries. There should be, for example, widespread strains in the current system of interaction among students, teachers, and administrators or between these educational actors and members of other social groups. But this is unlikely to happen because the schools of various countries have had different histories, have catered to different clientele and have served different functions.

Analysis of the cultural relativity of the educational dilemma between liberty and equality requires an evaluation of the relative validity of the diffusionist and structuralist approaches and an assessment of the conditions under which each holds true. This involves an investigation of convergences and divergences in patterns of educational development as well as an examination of similarities and dissimilarities in educational roles and institutions.

Relationships among Educational Variables.   Often there are sharp discontinuities in the intensity and the direction of educational patterns.[13] Certain aspects of educational development follow a pattern of lawful acceleration. The later a social system starts toward modernization, the higher will be its rates of development. For example, rise in the incidence of literacy is more marked in contemporary Africa than in the European countries of the nineteenth century.

Variations in the magnitude of the association between educational variables may be due also to the initial lack of responsiveness of educational institutions to external stimuli. Like all bureaucratic organizations, schools are characterized by a certain amount of inertia, particularly salient in the case of a highly centralized school system. In France, for example, the mechanisms of self-protection developed by teachers have impeded change in the size of classrooms, the functions assigned to examinations, and the nature of the curriculum offered to various categories of pupils despite an increase in the size of the population attending schools or expecting to do so. Such changes took place only after the increase in the size of the school population had reached a critical threshold. Similarly, changes in the organization of French universities have occurred only since student discontent reached a critical value and culminated in the uprise of May 1968.

While there are discontinuities or changes in the magnitude of the association between educational variables, there are also discontinuities or changes in the forms of their association. Initially negative, this association may become positive or vice versa. For example, while an initial rise in the proportion of educated women often is associated with a parallel increase in the level of their participation in the labor force, subsequent rises in the former proportion may be accompanied by a decrease in the relative number of working females. Frequently enough, the functions assigned to the formal schooling of women change with the relative scarcity of educated females. Similarly, the relationship between the educational achievement of the African adult male population and the incidence of polygyny is curvilinear in nature.[14] In Abidjan, the capital city of the Ivory Coast, illiterate male adults are monogamous because their lack of formal schooling prevents them from gaining access to the resources necessary for maintaining more than one wife. The incidence of monogamy declines conversely among individuals who have completed up to 10 years of formal education, because their moderate participation in educational structures has increased their resources without changing their systems of aspirations and expectations. Plural marriage is conversely less frequent among individuals with more than 10 years of formal schooling because their academic experiences have changed both their means and their ends.

Finally, variations in the direction of the association between educational variables may reflect the mere completion of a particular cycle. In many institutional contexts we often view organizational patterns, norms, and values as paired alternatives. Centralization and decentralization, environment and heredity offer two instances of paired alternatives particularly relevant to education. Emphasis on one of these alternatives does not necessarily dispel or dismiss its counterpart, and successive but unsuccessful attempts to increase compliance with the alternative currently viewed as the rule often lead to a restoration of its counterpart. Thus the administrators of many school systems, after having looked at centralization as a bureaucratic ideal, currently favor decentralization, and the changes they have introduced in this regard turn out to be cyclical in nature. Decentralization has been stigmatized in the recent past as the cause of the dull parochialism and attenuated totalitarianism characterizing American public education but tends to be currently perceived as a mechanism enabling individuals to recapture a sense of cultural identity.

Similarly, schools were deemed to be a significant factor of change during the 1960s as long as the influence of environment on individual behavior was deemed to be absolute, but the role attributed to schools in this regard has become more modest when an increasing number of scholars have become more convinced of the influence of heredity factors on individual behavior. Thus, examination of the cultural relativity of the educational dilemma between liberty and equality necessitates an identification of the various forms of association between educational variables.

Determinants of Educational Roles, Functions, and Institutions in Conjunction with Others. The significance attached to associations between educational variables cannot be assumed to remain constant in a variety of cultural contexts. For example, the schools of European communist and noncommunist countries are socially selective in their modes of recruitment and, in both instances, draw a disproportionate number of students from the nonmanual segments of the population.[15] Yet social selectivity does not have the same meaning in these two cases. In Western Europe, the transmission of educational inequalities across generational lines depends upon the uneven access of the various social classes to cultural stimuli (museums, mass media, books), upon their uneven access to sources of information regarding educational opportunities, and upon their differing financial resources and hence their distinctive abilities to meet the costs of an additional amount of schooling. In eastern European countries, the origin of educational inequality is more limited, and governments have tried to modify the social composition of the incoming flow of students in institutions of higher learning or in secondary schools, either by legally fixing the number of students from each social group or by giving positive or negative financial inducements to individuals from various backgrounds who want to go on with their studies. In the latter case disparities in the levels of the participation of various groups in educational structures reflect only contrasts in the cultural heritage of each social segment.

To analyze only the relationship between social class and academic achievement is thus insufficient. Because this relationship is not unidimensional, it is necessary to investigate how the educational implications of social stratification vary with the society's cultural, political, and economic profile. If in this book I extend an invitation to travel through the educational systems of a variety of countries and a variety of times, it is not in order to familiarize the reader with the charms and shortcomings of exotic countries, but rather in order to help him identify the nature and the variability of the most significant determinants of the educational scene. The greater the sample of school systems surveyed, the more accurate should be the reader's assessment of the available choices and limitations.

Objectives and Limitations of a Crosscultural Approach. To indicate the kinds of regularities that interest me and to sketch the outline of a crosscultural approach does not provide the reader with a sufficient understanding of the "sociological glasses" he is invited to wear. This involves a description of the rules, the objectives, and the limitations of the method I use.

Rules and Objectives of the Crosscultural Method. The crosscultural method is an attempt to assess the extent and the determinants of variations in a particular phenomenon. Such variations are threefold. First, crosscultural comparisons might pertain to variations in the qualitative traits of educational roles or institutions. Thus schools might be compared in terms of their organizational profile and more specifically in terms of whether they are centralized or decentralized. Similarly teaching and learning styles can be determined to be based upon assimilation or accommodation—that is, upon inward- or outward-oriented processes of adaptation.[16]

Second, comparisons may deal with a more quantitative evaluation of schools. Not all educational systems are the same size. Nor do all individuals attend similar types of institutions and spend similar amounts of time at school. School systems can be therefore compared in terms of the relative chances that various social groups have to attain the highest rungs of the academic ladder.

Third, the object of the comparison may be to establish interrelationships among two or more qualitative traits or quantitative measurements. Herein I determine whether there is an association between the relative enrollments of various social groups and the organizational nature of the schools attended, specifically whether selectivity in the recruitment of students is more pronounced in decentralized or centralized systems. Similarly, I explore whether there is a correlation between the organization of an educational institution and the teaching style of its educators.

Comparisons are based upon the use of two models.[17] The first, an *anthropological model,* is developed in terms of dichotomies (presence or absence of a particular trait). The researcher examines, for instance, whether centralized educational systems are characterized by the *pres-*

ence of particular types of students or teachers. The second, a *sociological model*, circumscribes the educational universe in terms of relative differences (more or less). The researcher examines how often variations in the relative centralization of a school system are associated with parallel differences in the relative number of students or teachers with specific characteristics.

To isolate associations between selected characteristics of an educational system is nevertheless insufficient. The problem remains to identify the conditions under which the association takes place.[18] The identification of such conditions requires four tests. First, the researcher must establish that variations in one of the variables chosen as an explanans are always accompanied by corresponding variations in the other variable, retained in the analysis as explanandum. To illustrate, one might hypothesize that the organization of a school (the independent variable or explanans) determines the extent of the social selectivity characterizing its recruitment patterns (the dependent variable or explanandum) and that—other things being equal—centralization reduces disparities in the relative number of individuals with various social origins enrolled in institutions of higher learning. Hypothetically, the offspring of a social elite will have a greater chance of reaching the highest rungs of the academic ladder in a decentralized rather than in a centralized system. For example, one might assume that upper-class children will be relatively less numerous in French centralized universities than in the corresponding American universities. Or one might hypothesize that the relative social selectivity of a particular school system (the dependent variable) will vary as a function of the amount of social differentiation (the independent variable). The more significant the contrasts in the income earned by various social categories as well as in their respective life styles, the sharper the inequalities in the enrollments of their children. To observe that this is the case and that distributions of the dependent and independent variables follow similar patterns, however, does not constitute an acceptable evidence of a causal relationship between the two phenomena.

The second test for evaluating the validity of the proposition consists in establishing that an absence of variations in the first variable is accompanied by a similar lack of variations in the other variable. To return to the two examples discussed, the researcher must prove that societies whose school systems are similarly organized (the independent variable) also are characterized by a similar amount of social selectivity in the recruitment of their students (the dependent variable). Similarly he also must prove that when societies have similar forms of social dif-

ferentiation—that is, when the income of their various groups are analogous and when there are no differences in their life styles—the relative enrollments of the children of the various groups of these societies
also will be similar. While the first test aims at establishing *positive evidence* of the association between independent and dependent variables,
the evidence brought about by the second test is *negative.* In fact,
should the researcher fail to demonstrate that similarities in the organization of schools or in the extent of social differentiation (the two independent variables) are also associated with comparable similarities in
the selectivity underlying the recruitment of students (the dependent
variable), he then should suspect that the association between variations
in the organizational profile of schools or in the social stratification of
the societies investigated, and in the social composition of student bodies is spurious or the result of chance.

   This leads to the third test required by comparative sociology. It is
insufficient to establish that there is a significant association between
the organizational profile of schools or the extent of social differentiation prevailing in a society and the recruitment patterns of students,
for it also must be established that the distribution of such patterns
across societies is not affected by any other factor. The third test consists of examining whether variations in the recruitment patterns of
students (the dependent variable) are independent of variations in
other characteristics of the societies and schools being studied. For example, the researcher may suspect that variations in the recruitment
patterns of schools, and hence in the composition of their student
body, depend not only upon their organizational profile and upon the
social stratification of the society in which they are located, but also
upon the religious orientation or the political regime of that society.
Accordingly, the researcher must determine whether inequalities in the
enrollments of various social groups are independent of the particular
faith embraced by these groups or by the society at large, of the ideological orientations of such groups, and of the type of government to
which they are subjected. In brief, the purpose of this third test is to establish whether these particular educational inequalities are universal.

   Should the researcher demonstrate, for example, that religious and
political factors influence social inequalities in patterns of access to
school, he must undertake the fourth test of the comparative strategy.
This test is a determination of the conditions under which independent
and dependent variables are associated and thus an identification of the
variables likely to intervene in the corresponding equation. To return
to the two examples, both the direction and the magnitude of the rela-

tionship between the social selectivity of a school (the dependent variable) and its organization or the social stratification of the society at large (the independent variables) may vary with the political regime or the religion of that society (the intervening variables).

Even though a sociologist does not necessarily make these tests in this order, only after their completion can one isolate the necessary and sufficient conditions for explaining the extent and the forms of educational inequalities. The purpose of crosscultural studies is, however, double in this respect. When *synchronic,* such studies are an attempt, for instance, to identify the extent and the determinants of educational inequalities at a single point in time. Further, they are functional insofar as they determine how the current level of educational inequalities is linked to other immediate properties of a social system. When *diachronic,* cross-cultural studies are an attempt to identify, for example, how the extent and the determinants of these inequalities change over time. Thus the first type deals with comparison of levels of inequalities, but the second pertains to a comparison of their rates. Synchronic studies are concerned with a comparison of enrollments in the primary or secondary schools of distinct nations *today,* and the researcher uses static photographies and still shots of the phenomena under study in order to establish a typology of the most crucial educational dimensions and of their determinants. Conversely, diachronic studies compare changes in these enrollments at two or more points in time, and a cumulative and dynamic image of that phenomenon is obtained in order to evaluate the responsiveness of schools to the pressures of social change.

However, the study of this responsiveness raises some difficulties. I have emphasized the sensitivity of educational roles and institutions to both historical and social factors. Yet the nature of historical factors remains equivocal. The time within which educational roles and institutions evolve may be sociological in nature—that is, made up of homogeneous, reversible, and additive elements. For example, we may argue that the actors of a school system who have participated in educational enterprises for more than 20 years share similar traits, regardless of the particular historical dates at which this particular experience has been completed or regardless of the specific age at which these actors have entered educational enterprises.[19] But the time within which educational roles and institutions evolve also is historical and, as such, is made up of discontinuous and irreversible elements. To have taught for 20 years does not necessarily have the same meaning for individuals who begin their career when they are 20 years of age and for those who start such a career after their fortieth birthday. Similarly, the implications of this form of seniority were not necessarily the same in 1939 as they are now.

Thus the purpose of diachronic crosscultural comparisons is to determine the extent to which the history of educational phenomena reveals continuities and discontinuities in their developmental processes. For example, many observers of the current student agitation are tempted to compare it to the unrest that plagued medieval institutions and later, European universities during the first half of the nineteenth century.[20] Insofar as such a comparison highlights striking similarities among these three crises, there are apparently certain structural regularities in the conditions underlying the emergence of student rebellion which thus can be examined in the context of a sociological time. Whether in the fifteenth, nineteenth, or twentieth century, whether they involve high school or university students, whether these students have similar backgrounds, these rebellions are always the products of factors that are symbolically equivalent to one another. In this context, history is defined as a permanent repetition of identical mechanisms. Insofar as such a comparison reveals the revolutionary nature of such outbursts and shows at least three basic and specific ruptures in the forms of linkage between educational roles or institutions and other aspects of the social structure, it suggests conversely that "the wheel of time does not only turn on itself, but also proceeds on a changing terrain." [21] In this latter perspective, student rebellions must also be studied in the context of an historical time.

The function of diachronic crosscultural studies is to reconcile the generalizing views of the sociologists and the differentiating perceptions of the historian on the dilemma between liberty and equality. It is more specifically to evaluate the relative significance of the two types of time.[22]

Limitations of the Crosscultural Method. Since the comparisons evoked here require the use of many data, sociologists must rely upon the researches of other scholars. Yet the validity of these comparisons depends upon the theoretical and methodological choices made by researchers.

Many studies are influenced by the application to education of the assumptions used to evaluate the productivity of economic enterprises. Because productivity often is equated with rationality, many of such studies rank-order the educational systems of various countries in terms of their relative rationality—that is, in terms of the degree to which they produce the maximum number of most useful graduates in the minimum amount of time, use to that end the most adequate and pedagogical tools and techniques, and recruit for that purpose their students and teachers from the broadest spectrum of the current social system after a complete elimination of the class, sex, ethnic, and cultural barriers in patterns of access to educational institutions.[23]

Insofar as these studies consider *all* educational systems to be equally responsive to a same definition of rationality, they often underestimate the role of the particularistic forces at work in the elaboration and execution of educational programs. They treat societies as undifferentiated entities and do not take into account the possible educational implications of power struggles among social groups.

The recognition of the social and psychological factors affecting educational choices, however, raises other theoretical dilemmas. In addition to recognizing that educational institutions have changing functions and profiles, scholars also must determine whether these changes are preceded or followed by parallel ideological changes. While this involves an assessment of the relative impact of ideologies on the emergence of new educational systems or strategies and vice versa, the corresponding analyses often are dictated by a priori assumptions on the relative importance of economic, political, or psychological forces. Scholars who hold functionalist, conflict, or tension-management theories, for example, do not ask the same questions from educational data.

Functionalists are eager to stress the network of interdependences between educational roles or institutions and structures or processes prevailing in the society. T. Parsons, for example, emphasizes a number of correspondences between the functions and values of American primary or secondary schools and those of the entire American social system.[24] In the two contexts he stresses the significance of social processes based on principles of universalistic achievement. The stratification of youth groups (cliques and gangs with differing subcultures) acts in educational institutions as a bridge to the achievement-based system of stratification at work in the adult society. Similarly the patterning of heterosexual relations in both the youth and the school culture clearly foreshadows patterns of marriage and family formation in the adult American context. Functionalist scholars view the dominant features of a particular school system as being parallel to the dominant features of the entire social structure. Further, they view educational institutions as serving both the needs of society and the aspirations of each individual teacher or student.

In contrast, conflict theorists tend to perceive the tensions observable in education as duplications of the conflicts among social groups. A Marxist analysis of western European school systems shows, for example, how both the mechanisms of recruitment of their students and the courses taught by their teachers reflect the changing principles through which the privileged classes assert their dominance upon the masses. The extent and the form of inequalities in the recruitment of school populations and the distinctive nature of the courses offered to these various populations are deemed to reflect not only the mechanisms of division of labor prevailing in the society at large, but also and more specifically the particular modes of oppression of current rulers. For example, during the early stages of industrialization in western Europe, entrepreneurs tried to prevent working-class children from gaining access to any type of education, primarily because they were afraid of losing access to the unlimited reservoir of unskilled laborers needed for their economic activities. As the schooling of the working classes became a political necessity and as industrialization required higher skill levels, the same entrepreneurs emphasized the need of differentiating the curricula of schools catering to various clientele. Thus the institutions of working-class communities were supposed to teach basic skills but above all to stress religion in the courses they offered and hence to induce poor children to accept their fate in this "worldly valley of tears." [25]

Finally, tension-management theorists are most concerned with isolating both the conditions under which educational institutions reinforce the overall current social order and the conditions under which they are significant places where a variety of social tensions are reenacted. This leads such theorists to examine the degree to which the development of educational roles and systems of interaction is independent of processes at work in other institutional contexts.[26] It also leads them to analyze the extent to which the relationships most characteristic of school systems act as mechanisms designed to alleviate some of the conflicts among sex, age, or social groups.

Yet the validity of the studies undertaken in sociology of education is dependent not only upon the theoretical choices made by their authors, but also upon the methodological decisions made by such scholars. Insofar as many current studies rank educational systems in terms of "rational" criteria, the relative rationality of the indicators used for comparative purposes should be similarly defined both by each society and by its educational institutions. Further, these indicators should have the same meaning in a variety of societal contexts.

For example, insofar as the rationality of a school system is evaluated in terms of the openness of its recruitment, it is relevant to compare educational systems in terms of the relative sex ratio of their students— that is, to examine the extent to which the ratio of male to female students departs from the corresponding ratio observed for the totality of the relevant age group. Yet this is meaningful only insofar as the number and significance of biases introduced in the enumerating of the two populations are identical. This condition is not in fact likely to be easily met, for the pressures exerted on census takers and on educational administrators are not the same.

In addition, the sex ratio of student populations does not necessarily reflect exactly the degree to which access to elite positions is independent of restrictions attached to sex roles. Variations in the sex ratio of student populations are not necessarily associated with corresponding contrasts in the level of female participation in the most rewarding sectors of employment.[27] The relatively easy access of French women to institutions of higher learning is not perceived as incompatible with the perpetuation of the traditional role imposed upon them, and many of the females graduating from French universities have never joined the labor market. Conversely in Algeria, where the post-primary schooling of women is limited and mainly results from the differential erosion of traditional structures, no less than 70 percent of the women who have completed primary education are engaged in nonmanual activities, and very few graduates are unemployed. The meaning to be attached to the sex ratio of the student populations of the two countries is probably not the same. In France female schooling is often viewed as an important mechanism of mate selection; in Algeria it is more significantly associated with changes in the occupational aspirations held by women.

Thus, the cultural relativeness of the dilemma between liberty and equality in the educational context is twofold: This dilemma is relative insofar as its manifestations, determinants, and implications vary over time and through space. It is also culturally relative insofar as the conceptual and methodological tools used by social scientists have only a limited validity and reflect the constraints to which they are subjected as members of their particular society.[28]

Conclusions.   The idea of this book is born from the observation that an increasingly large number of countries currently are plagued by an educational malaise. Does this mean that the determinants and the implications of the current crisis are universal? Does the dilemma between liberty and equality, as it affects the educational process, remain the same in a variety of cultures and historical times, in the different sub-parts of the educational systems of the world, and for the different categories of actors involved in the educational process?

To test the validity of this hypothesis, I argue that it is necessary to identify the form and the extent of the linkage between educational and other societal institutions. If the autonomy of schools is limited and their influence on churches, political processes and structures, businesses, and familial groups are restricted, the forms of the dilemma between liberty and equality in educational structures and processes should be culturally relative. Thus, the manifestations of this dilemma should not be similarly experienced by teachers, administrators, or the public at large and we must hence examine how interactions between and among these groups reflect particular facets of the dilemma. However, conflicts between liberty and equality also influence not only the relative access of school-aged populations to various types of schools but the kind of interaction they develop with teachers and educational administrators. Thus we also must assess how such conflicts evolve throughout the life cycle of students, before, during, and after their careers in the various types of institutions they are entitled to attend.

An appropriate methodology is required to evaluate the influences exerted by the past and present on the current profile of educational structures, processes, and roles. Accordingly, I have sketched the rules and the limitations of the crosscultural method I will use in the following chapters. Finally, two caveats are in order. First, the literature summarized is not necessarily representative of the field labeled sociology of education. Although the researches I cite tend to be classics of their own gender, they do not necessarily represent the full range of theoretical perspectives used in the field. Further, my exploitation of data pertaining to foreign countries is not necessarily complete, for there are obstacles in the patterns of diffusion of the pertinent literature. For example, I present very little data on the structures and functioning of Asiatic or Australian educational institutions. Similarly, while I may hope that my treatment of American and French educational phenomena is sufficiently rich, valid, and to the point, I cannot make the same claim with regard to Germany or Scandinavia. Language barriers— networks of communication among sociologists—are not evenly distributed and sociologists have not only an uneven access to crosscultural educational data, but they also are not equally interested in the same problem. While there is a mine of crosscultural information concerning patterns of access into educational institutions, it is more difficult to undertake a comparable treatment of variations in learning or teaching styles or in patterns of interaction between teachers and administrators. As a result, some chapters are more speculative than others.

Thus the propositions I derive from the body of historical and sociological data to which I had access do not represent ultimate truths. While I use them to identify linkage among various types of institutional arrangements or between social structures and individual attitudes and behaviors, they merely constitute invitations to further research. Indeed, sociology of education is never complete.

NOTES AND REFERENCES

1. A. Kaplan, *The Conduct of Social Enquiry* (San Francisco: Chandler, 1964) pp. 139–140

2. For an initial development of this subjective theme, see A. Zijderveld, *The Abstract Society* (Garden City: Doubleday, 1970), notably, Chapter Four.

3. For an initial definition of functions allocated to schools, see P. Bourdieu, "Le système des fonctions du système d'enseignement," in M. A. Matthijsen and C. E. Vervoot, *L'Education en Europe: recherches sociologiques* (Paris: Mouton, 1969), p. 181. See also *infra* my Part Two, Chapter 3.

4. A. Gide, *The Journal of the Counterfeiters* (New York: Random House, 1955), p. 413.

5. W. Faulkner, "On Fear: Deep South in Labor: Mississippi," J. Meriwhether ed. *Essays, Speeches and Public Letters by W. Faulkner* (New York: Random House, 1965) p. 105.

6. As quoted by L. Fein in *The Ecology of the Public Schools* (New York: Pegasus, 1973).

7. In fact, the *normative* dilemma between liberty and equality is paralleled by a *logical* dilemma between differentiation and generalization. The stress on liberty rests upon the principle of *differentiation* because it aims at guaranteeing individual autonomy. By contrast, the emphasis placed on equality suggests the development of rationally organized bureaucracies that deliver the same goods and services through uniform processes to distinct categories of the population at large. As such, the emphasis on equality involves the principle of *generalization*. In Part One of this book, however, the dilemma between generalization and differentiation presents another facet, since we must determine whether the educational contradictions between liberty and equality are merely by-products of more diffuse or general societal tensions, or whether these contradictions present aspects which are specific to the school scene.

8. Such was, for example, the mythical abbey of Thelème extolled by Rabelais in *Pantagruel*.

9. Indeed, to a large extent the centralization of the French Catholic Church enabled it to achieve early a tight control on the educational institutions that had spread widely over the French territory. The centralization of political institutions and hence of public schools was achieved much later. Throughout French history champions of decentralization have always been recruited from among the ranks of the nobility or of the Church who saw in this pattern of organization a guarantee for the perpetuation of their privileges. For a discussion of the contrasts between various types of centralization, see R. Castel and J. C. Passeron, eds., *Education, Développement et Démocratie* (Paris: Mouton, 1967). See also in the same volume, P. Bourdieu and J. C. Passeron, "La comparabilité des systèmes d'enseignement," pp. 21–48.

10. For a more general discussion of this theme, see R. Clignet, "Inadequacies of the Notion of Assimilation in African Education," *Journal of Modern African Studies,* Vol. 8, 1970, pp. 425–444.

11. See P. Bourdieu and J. C. Passeron, *op. cit.,* p. 33.

12. For a discussion of these approaches, see R. Clignet, "A Critical Evaluation of Concommitant Variations Studies," in R. Cohen and R. Naroll, eds., *A Handbook of Methods in Cultural Anthropology* (New York: Natural History Press, 1970), pp. 579–619.

13. This entire section is derived from W. Moore, "Predicting Discontinuities in Social Change," *American Sociological Review,* Vol. 29, 1964, pp. 331–338.

14. See, for example, R. Clignet and J. Sween, "Type of Marriage and Social Change," *American Journal of Sociology,* Vol. 75, 1969, pp. 123–145.

15. For a discussion of this example, see R. Castel and J. C. Passeron, eds., *op. cit.*

16. For a full discussion of this last theme see Chapter 8, 9.

17. For a presentation of these models see C. Levi Strauss, "La notion de structure en ethnologie," *Anthropologie Structurale* (Paris: Plon, 1958), Chapter XV.

18. For a discussion of the strategies, see R. March, *Comparative Sociology* (New York: Harcourt and Brace, 1967), pp. 39–40. For a more general review of the problems raised by comparative studies in education, see M. Eckstein and M. Noah, *Scientific Investigations in Comparative Education* (London: Mullen, 1969), pp. 3–66.

19. For a distinction between historical and sociological time, see C. Levi Strauss, *loc. cit.*

20. That the number of books dealing with historical accounts of student agitations at various points in time has markedly increased after the events of May 1968 is certainly not accidental. For example, there has been a reediction of J. Michelet, *L'etudiant* (Paris: le Seuil, 1970). For a discussion of

the conflicts between medieval universities and other institutions of the same period, see N. Schachner, *The Medieval Universities* (London: Allen and Unwin, 1932).

21. W. Moore, *loc. cit.*

22. For a further elaboration of the distinctive tasks to be performed by historians and sociologists, see G. Gurvitch, *Dialectique et sociologie* (Paris: Flammarion, 1962).

23. See P. Bourdieu and J. C. Passeron, *op. cit.*, pp. 23–24.

24. See T. Parsons, "The School Class as a Social System: Some of Its Functions in American Society," *Harvard Educational Review*, Vol. 29, 1959, pp. 297–318.

25. The materials presented in E. P. Thompson, *The Making of the English Working Class* (New York: Knopf, 1963) provide good illustrations of such views.

26. Although to my knowledge they have not written about issues directly concerned with the field of education, W. Moore and A. Feldman are the most significant representatives of this last school of thought. Insofar as M. Trow shows both the multiplicity of external influences exerted on American education and the forces emanating from it, one could enter M. Trow in this last category. See M. Trow, "Two Problems in American Public Education," in H. Becker, ed., *Social Problems, A Modern Approach* (New York: Wiley, 1966).

27. See P. Bourdieu and J. C. Passeron, *op. cit.*, pp. 26–27.

28. See R. Aron, "La Société Américaine et sa sociologie," *Cahiers internationaux de sociologie*, Vol. 29, 1959, pp. 55–56. See also P. Bourdieu and J. C. Chamboredon, *Le métier de sociologue: Sociologie de la connaissance et épistémologie* (Paris: Mouton, 1968). For a more narrow treatment of the ways in which sociological analyses of patterns of recruitment into educational institutions are affected by ideological considerations, see Scofford Archer, "Egalitarianism in French and British educational sociology," *Archives Europeennes de sociologie*, Vol. 11, 1970, pp. 116–129. It could be easily demonstrated that studies of school personnel are more numerous and more significant in the United States than in France. In the first country, the decentralization of educational institutions implies a large variability in the conception and the performance of educational roles, with the consequence that educational functions are necessarily viewed as problematic. In contrast, France's high centralization is perceived to limit the range of variations in educational structures and processes. Accordingly, there are virtually no studies of the relations developed among the various echelons of the French educational hierarchy (and, e.g., of the relations between teachers and *proviseurs, censeurs* and other administrators of high schools).

Part One

SCHOOLS AND SOCIETIES

1

THE EMERGENCE OF AUTONOMOUS EDUCATIONAL INSTITUTIONS

While the current crisis in education strikes primary and secondary schools as well as universities thoughout the world, there are divergent opinions as to its origins. Some people view all educational institutions as centers of innovation in all arenas of social participation and hence as places where new life styles, techniques, norms, and values are to be discovered and tried. Correspondingly, the current malaise is mainly defined in terms of the resistance to change displayed by the society at large. There is a crisis because schools are prevented from according as much liberty to their students as they would like to enjoy.

According to other experts, however, schools should serve primarily as mechanisms of social and economic placement. In this context current disturbances are defined as the product of failures inherent to the educational system itself. Both the inappropriate nature of the rules concerning the admission or the graduation of high school or university students and the obsolescence of the material presented to them are deemed to be the cause of the present discontent. "We want to be able to understand what is going on in the real world, and we want schools to really prepare us to the realities of an ever-changing technological environment." These were the demands of some French high school students in 1971.[1] The crisis arises because schools have failed to *equalize* the chances that individuals from various backgrounds should have to gain access to the most desired amenities of the occupational and social world.

31

In one case educational institutions are seen as more responsive to change than the society at large; in the second case they are defined as the very sources of resistance to a necessary but peaceful revolution.

A third concept is that academic experiences constitute privileged moments in the life cycle of an individual, during which children and adolescents must be accorded all the leeway necessary for a successful development of their personalities. In this perspective the current malaise is but a single manifestation of the growing conflict between the repressive character of an impersonal and ubiquitous bureaucratic order and the demands of a highly subjective individualism.[2] While the first two interpretations focus our attention on the problems associated with the existing linkage between educational and other societal institutions, the third interpretation highlights the more diffuse difficulties resulting from the current patterns of interaction between individuals and their environments.

The diversity of all these positions and the growing distance separating each category of educational actors (parents, students, teachers, administrators), both from one another and from the public at large reflect the complexities and cleavages of the "Abstract Society" in which we live.[3] Under such conditions, to decide that current academic experiences are irrelevant and that there is a need for alternative educational structures is perhaps to place the cart before the horse. Whether placed in the splendors of the wilderness or at the center of the community, schools are not social islands independent of the remaining parts of society. Before suggesting appropriate remedies to the current crisis, and before criticizing schools for what they do and do not, it seems therefore appropriate to identify the constraints to which they are subjected. Are differences in the overall organization and goals of various social systems associated with parallel contrasts in the organization and the orientation of their respective educational activities?

Further, because a social system is always multifaceted, what is the interaction between the structures and processes of educational institutions and those of the other four basic societal institutions—families; economic enterprises; legal, political, or military organizations; and churches?

Prior to an examination of this interaction, our initial task is to retrace briefly the most significant stages of development of educational institutions. In contrast to the views held by many radical educators in the United States, I believe that to be free from the past does not consist of ignoring it but rather of assessing the continuing constraints that the past imposes on the expectations and aspirations of today.

This chapter is divided into two sections. In the first I examine the circumstances under which the roles of students and teachers become analytically distinct from the positions attached to other basic institutions. Initially, learning and teaching activities are mere by-products of the stations occupied by individuals in familial or religious structures. As long as socialization and formal schooling exclusively take place within familial, political, or religious institutions, the reciprocal dependence of schools and other basic societal institutions cannot be evaluated. Accordingly we must first identify the conditions under which schools emerge as autonomous sub-parts of a social system.

In the second section of this chapter I examine the processes by which the functions and structures of educational enterprises become internally differentiated, each one serving the needs of the society at large or of a particular subgroup.

To sum up, initial patterns of educational differentiation involve the establishment of schools as institutions distinct from other basic social agencies. In subsequent stages, the role of schools becomes more specialized and the functions assigned to high schools and to universities are increasingly differentiated both from one another and from those attached to elementary schools. Further, the relations that these schools maintain both with other educational institutions and with outside agencies become narrower and more functionally specific.

Influence of Emerging Societal Complexity on Educational Roles. To identify the conditions under which socializing and educational functions become independent of other basic societal institutions requires a comparative analysis of educational phenomena among societies with differing levels of complexity. Among the most traditional societies, socialization hardly necessitates specialized agencies. It simply involves participation in the activities deemed crucial to the survival of the society at large, and it only requires members of the oncoming generation to imitate the actions of individuals already occupying central positions in the social structure. The dyad teacher–student has no existence in itself; rather, it is a correlate of the relationship between parents and children because, among noncomplex societies, all or almost all basic societal functions are performed by familial groups.

In these highly functional groups the child is always assigned to the position of student, while there are variations in the identity of familial actors invested in the roles of teachers. These variations reflect disparities in the rules underlying division of labor along sex lines, in the rules of descent, and in the rules of residence. For example, among societies where agricultural tasks incumb upon women and where men are engaged in herding, hunting, or gathering, all children regardless of their sex often are uniformly exposed to the teaching activities of adult female actors. It is only later that socialization becomes specialized along sex lines. Similarly, in patrilineal societies, teaching functions tend to be monopolized by fathers but in matrilineal organizations, these functions are shared by fathers and maternal uncles.[4]

It is not sufficient merely to show that among societies with a minimal complexity familial groups carry the totality of socialization functions. The main task remains to identify the processes by which socializing responsibilities are transferred from familial institutions to specialized agencies. Winch and Freeman suggest that this transfer cannot take place until the society at large has reached a certain level of complexity.[5] The goal of these authors is to determine whether societal complexity is easily measurable and whether it is appropriate to treat this characteristic as unidimensional. Taking a sample of 48 traditional societies, they demonstrate that it is possible to place them into seven categories. At the lower end of the continuum one finds cultural units with none of the traits presented below and which are therefore defined as characterized by a *minimal* level of complexity. As one moves toward the other extremity, the following characteristics appear in the following order: (1) money is substituted for barter as a mechanism of economic transaction, (2) crimes against persons or property cease to be punished through private groups and are prosecuted by central governments, (3) religious functions are performed by full-time priests, (4) teaching emerges as a full-time occupation, (5) administrative activities are carried out by full-time bureaucrats constituting a group distinct from the rulers, and (6) communication involves the circulation of written documents.

The study suggests that societal complexity is unidimensional. All societies placed in the sixth category (in which, communication between groups and persons involves the circulation of written documents) have necessarily all the characteristics of the five preceding groups. Such units have also full-time bureaucrats, full-time teachers, and full-time priests, and are characterized also by a system of integrated justice as well as by the use of monetary symbols in their economic organizations. More important for my purpose, this study identifies the prerequisites for the emergence of distinct educational roles and institutions. This emergence presupposes an accentuated specialization of economic roles, the integration of these roles into larger political entities, and the incorporation of the expectations attached to economic specialization and to legal integration into a consistent religious and ideological framework.

As money is substituted for barter in economic transactions, producers and consumers cease to be in direct face-to-face contacts. Trading activities take place within a larger physical space and require the services of specialized brokers. The use of money induces an increase both in the physical and social distance separating buyers and vendors. It is also conducive to the emergence of new specialized economic roles—those of brokers and traders.

The institutionalization of long-range and large-scale commercial transactions is not possible as long as producers, consumers, and brokers are not subjected to uniform and standardized sets of contractual and penal rules.[6] The more diverse the categories of persons interacting with one another and the larger the social and physical space within which these interactions take place, the more pressures there are toward the transfer of judicial processes from private and particularistic institutions into public and more encompassing agencies. Legal integration is conducive to the emergence of specialized judicial roles.

Individuals are torn between the centrifugal forces resulting from economic specialization and the centripetal principles associated with legal integration. As a result, they are likely to experience role conflicts which can be alleviated only through the formulation of religious or ideological prescriptions reconciling the conflicting demands of economic specialization and legal standardization. This requires the services of full-time priests whose function is to legitimize the apparently contradictory requirements of existing institutions.

Thus, the study of Winch and Freeman suggests that educational developments are the consequences of prior economic, legal, and religious changes. The emergence of autonomous educational roles and institutions seems to be the result of prior interaction between mechanisms of specialization and integration in the fields of economy, law, and religion. There are no teachers as long as there are no brokers, no judges, and no priests. In turn, the emergence of full-time teachers commands further political development. It also contributes to enhance the physical and social space within which human interaction takes place, through the systematic use of written documents.

But to order societies in terms of their relative complexity and to suggest that *all* societies with full-time teachers are necessarily also characterized by the use of monetary symbols in commercial transactions, a public rather than a private system of punishment for crimes against persons and property, and a body of full-time priests, in this very order, does not say anything about the developmental trajectory of each one of the societies included in the sample. Educational development is not necessarily uniformly linear. Distinctions should be made between synchronic and diachronic researches, for differences among a *number* of societies at one single point in time may be independent of the differences among the profiles of *each one* of these societies at various points in time. To observe that a society with a currently maximal complexity has not only the same traits as those cultures with lower rank but also uses a system of written communications is not the same as to observe that this particular society successively experienced a transformation of its economic, legal, religious, educational, and bureaucratic organization—in that order.

Because the range of variables used by Winch and Freeman is limited, we are able to determine only whether educational roles are distinct from others. Anthropological in nature, the model underlying the analysis is based upon a simple dichotomy of the "yes-or-no," "presence-or-absence" type, and is appropriate only for treating societies occupying positions in the lower part of the world-wide distribution of complexity. Since the existence of a written language is not a legitimate indicator of maximal societal complexity, it is also appropriate to examine variations in rates of literacy and to assess the impact of such variations on the relative differentiation of educational roles. As a society exceeds a certain level of complexity, the use of a sociological rather than of an anthropological model should yield more convincing results.

Educational Roles in Societies with Low Levels of Literacy. Initially the emergence of distinct teaching roles was restricted to special fields of human knowledge. Whereas socialization into most adult occupational roles was still ensured by the practitioners themselves through "on-the-job" training programs, the teaching of religion and law was in the hands of a specialized personnel.[7] The power of teachers in such disciplines was directly affected by the scarcity of written documents. Specifically, their power was maximal whenever little use was made of the storage capability of books. In both religion and law, this use was initially limited and the exclusive function of written documents was to support the verbal learning of a body of knowledge deemed to be immutable. Even today Muslim schools in Africa or Asia or schools concerned with the diffusion of the Vedic tradition in India are characterized by the stress placed upon sheer memorization. Pupils learn the precepts of the Koran but are hardly expected to reinterpret their meaning. Nor are they able to transfer their knowledge of Arabic to fields other than religion. In this context the power of teachers also results from the fact that written documents serve to preserve the monopoly of power and are surrounded with an aura of secrecy, as was the case of ceremonial texts in Egypt or of the principles of Pythagoras in ancient Greece.

The early creation of seminaries and law schools in Europe similarly explains why their organization has acted as models for other educational institutions. In England writing was taught one year after the pupil learned to read, and learning to read religious texts was deemed more desirable than learning to communicate with others.[8] Similarly, the function of "little schools," which were widespread in France toward the end of the Middle Ages, was to teach the Latin of the Church and thus to train altar boys and religious chorists. French was introduced relatively late in the curriculum and for a long time followed Latin in the course of studies. The teaching of writing was a prerogative of the scribes (the equivalents of our contemporary printers) who usually traveled from city to city.[9]

The influence of religious factors is equally evident in the early patterns of educational development in the United States. This was to be expected in view of the religious motivations underlying the migrations of the early Pilgrims. The first textbook used by the children of migrants to New England was the "horn book" which included the doctrine of the Trinity and the Lord's Prayer. Similarly the curriculum of early grammar schools included "liberal doses of classical Latin" usually taught by teachers licensed by the Church.[10]

The power of teachers, initially derived from the monopolistic access of some of them to written documents, was further enhanced by the immutable character assigned to knowledge. It also was increased by the close association of teachers with lawyers and priests, the most prestigious and powerful social groups in societies with low levels of literacy.

At the same time, little differentiation was given to the role of pupils. To be sure, women were excluded from educational institutions (the idea of providing girls with a suitable education did not appear in France before seventeenth century.[11]) Yet there was no age–grade system in early institutions. It was common to find nine- and 19-year-old students in the same classroom, and there were large variations in the age distributions of the entire student population enrolled in a French college of the seventeenth century. (Table 1) Only at the beginning of the nineteenth century, did French schools begin to group pupils by

Table 1. Age Composition of the Student Population of the College of Caen, 1692. Percentage Distributions of Students with Differing Ages Enrolled in Various Classes [a]

Class [b]	Age											Total	N
	9	10	11	12	13	14	15	16	17	18	19		
Fifth	2	9	18	23	16	14	12	5	1	0	0	100	104
Fourth	1	2	9	15	26	18	14	11	2	2	0	100	133
Third	0	1	2	12	14	20	24	14	9	4	0	100	171
Second	0	0	0	1	4	14	26	29	21	4	1	100	72

[a] Pere de Rochemonteix, *"Le Collège Henri IV de la Flèche"* Paris, 1889 as quoted by P. Aries, *L'Enfant et la Vie Familiale sous l'Ancien Régime,* p. 240.

[b] Note that the French reverse the sequential numbering of classes and that the French fifth form is therefore the equivalent of the United States seventh grade.

age rather than by level of knowledge and to organize curriculum along age lines.

   Access to early educational institutions remained open to a variety of social groups. Despite the rigid system of social stratification characterizing French society of the seventeenth century, Jesuit high schools were attended by a substantial number of lower-class children. In the eighteenth century the idea developed to provide distinct social classes with distinct subject matters and to teach them in distinct institutions. "The lower classes should be guided, not educated," wrote Voltaire to La Challotais.[12] Finally, there was little differentiation in the curriculum offered to students by various teachers. Some students repeated the same set of courses under the authority of several schoolmasters.

   The combination of geographic barriers and of ethnic, linguistic, and religious differences in the immigrant populations was associated with an earlier and a more significant differentiation in the composition of the student body of American educational institutions. The Quakers were eager to create schools where "poor children were to be educated and taught in good literature until they be fit to be apprentices or masters or workers in such schools." [13] In New Amsterdam and in Virginia, girls were not necessarily excluded from educational institutions. Yet slaves as well as the "servant class" were barred from school and only the offspring of a narrow segment of the elite was provided with a postprimary education.[14]

Progressively, teachers became a particular occupational group in certain privileged disciplines. Only after the emergence of an autonomous teaching force was completed did students begin to cluster into a variety of distinct subgroups which were homogeneous in terms of both age and social class.

Increase in Scale and Differentiation of Educational Roles.

Definition of the Concept of Increase in Scale. Variations in literacy rates and school enrollments do not constitute isolated trends. Such increases are parts of what many sociologists call the increase in scale of social systems.[15] Increase in scale represents an extension of the control system prevailing in the societies under study. Initially the extension of this control system is territorial. It involves the amalgamation of heterogeneous ethnic groups into a single superordinate political unit. It also involves massive migrations toward centers of economic surplus. Thus increase in scale implies both increases in the overall volume of migrations and in the average distance between places of destination and of origin of migrant populations. In the United States, for example, this increase in scale has manifested itself in the extension of the federal control over an even larger number of territories or colonies. It also has manifested itself in a substantial increase of the number of migrants derived from different sections of Europe and from the Far East.

In the sphere of economic activities, extension of control systems is associated with the emergence of large-scale organizational networks. The number of productive associations declines while their size grows. As a result there is an increase in the number of wage earners and salaried personnel. By 1950, for example, the usually accepted indicator of the size of productive associations was $3 \cdot 25$ in the United States as against only $1 \cdot 44$ in Venezuela.[16] In other words, whereas American salaried employees and manual workers were 3 times 25 more numerous than self-employed individuals and employers, salaried employees and manual workers were only 1 times 44 as many as self-employed workers in Venezuela. Increase in scale is associated with a vertical and horizontal concentration of economic enterprises.

Similarly this extension also involves an increase in both the content and the flow of exchanges within and without the system. Within the system, there is an accentuated division of labor and a widening in the range of occupations constitutive of the labor force. To illustrate, the American working populations are spread among a large number of branches of activity and of occupational categories than their counterparts in less developed parts of the world. By 1950, for example, the indicator of division of labor among industries was .813 for the United States but only .509 for Guatamala. Similarly the overall intra-industry degree of division of labor among occupations was .605 for the United States but only .031 for Guatamala. This accentuated division of labor takes place both at the level of the entire society and of its territorial components, which become specialized and engaged in economically complementary activities. Exchanges with the outside are equally affected and there is a corresponding increase in the volume and the distance of international trade.

The territorial and economic extension of a control system demands an accentuated coordination among its various subgroups. This coordination is twofold. First, it involves the implantation of control functions at points which are fixed in space; increase in scale is therefore associated with the spatial redistribution of populations and more specifically with massive urbanization. In the United States, for example, the proportion of individuals residing in urban areas has increased from 57 percent in 1940 to 64 percent by 1950 to 70 percent by 1960. Second, it is associated with a rise in the level of communication skills of the populations investigated. This rise implies increases both in educational and occupational levels. Thus with an increase in the scalar position of the United States, the proportion of persons 14 to 17 years of age attending secondary schools has climbed from 11 percent for the academic year 1899–1900 to 73 percent in 1939–1940 and 87 percent in 1959–1960. This increase in educational level has been accompanied by an increase in the relative size of the labor force employed in the tertiary sector of the economy—and hence in activities of coordination (transportation, banking, insurance, tourism). For the above periods of time, the proportions of gainfully employed workers in the tertiary sector has increased from 23 percent to 41 percent by 1940 to reach 51 percent in 1960.[17]

Educational Consequences of Increase in Scale.   The increase in scale of a particular social system presents three important consequences for our examination of the changes in the definition of educational roles.

First, extension of control systems implies a corresponding decline in the flexibility of individual behavior. In the economic sphere the requirements of mass production are associated with a standardization of tasks. Mass production also requires a standardization of the attitudes and orientations characteristic of consumers—a condition that is fulfilled through the exploitation of potential markets by mass media.

In education the number and importance of the constraints imposed upon students keeps increasing. Among societies with a lower scalar position, the child is placed in a situation of dependence and submission. But this situation characterizes a circumscribed locale and lasts a limited period of time. Among societies with a high scalar position, socialization is no longer exclusively carried out by specialized agencies such as familial groups and educational institutions. In fact, as a society increases in scale, there is a rise in the geographic level at which political agencies impose control upon educational institutions. As early as 1779—even though there was still hardly any sign of industrialization in the New World—Jefferson attempted to establish a state-controlled system of educational facilities. Even though this attempt reflects the importance that Jefferson attached to liberty, the fact remains that the early stages of political development in America were associated with deliberate—albeit unsuccessful—attempts to impose a centralized system of support and control upon educational institutions.[18]

While increase in scale should thus be associated with a spatial concentration of educational processes and structures, it also should be associated with change in the *duration* of the educational experience. In fact, it is not only the overall experience of socialization which lasts longer, but also the daily amount of time during which pupils are exposed to socializing influences. Social control invades their entire daily routine since the educational activities of schools and familial groups are reinforced and made more homogeneous by the intervention of mass media, themselves regulated by centralized and hence generalizing mechanisms.[19]

Second, extension of control systems is associated with increased social differentiation. The various segments of the population do not enjoy comparable access to the resources and rewards of their environment. In the educational sphere, social groups do not enjoy even access to distinctive types of schools. Further, these institutions are characterized by the accentuated differentiation of their organizational profile. Thus as a society increases in scale, there are increased contrasts among its schools in terms of their level (the populations attending primary, secondary, and postsecondary schools do not have the same size or profile nor are they socialized to the same norms and requirements), the types of knowledge that they diffuse [20] (as the scalar position of a society increases, there are accentuated differences in the characteristics and the experiences of students and teachers involved in the social sciences, the natural sciences, and in the fine arts [21]), and of their organization (access to public and private institutions or to day and

evening schools does not necessarily depend upon the same set of criteria, does not characterize the same populations, and is not necessarily
conducive to the same sets of attitudes and expectations).

Third, and as a corollary, extension of control systems is associated
with shifts in the nature of significant social tensions. As a society increases in scale, the problem of communications and coordination becomes more salient and difficult to solve. As a result the most significant social tensions which previously prevailed in the secondary sector
of the economy (that of manufacturing activities) decline in significance
whereas those characterizing the tertiary sector have more long-term
and serious implications.

> The central social conflict of contemporary societies opposes
> technocrats to the salaried employees of large-scale organiza-
> tions who, although able to escape the control of such organi-
> zations owing to their educational level, are nevertheless ma-
> nipulated through their status, their career aspirations, and
> other forms of integration. New technicians and experts
> know (especially if they are young) that the majority of stu-
> dents, far from being expected later on to exert activities of
> leadership, will have to content themselves with functions of
> organization, of coordination, and communication without
> any participation in the real decision-making processes.[22]

Thus the increased salience of communications in the contemporary
world leads student movements to be somewhat similar to the workers
movements of the nineteenth century. They represent the attempt of a
special category of producers to fight against the loss of a formerly
privileged position and against the growing obsolescence of the models
underlying their socialization. It is certainly not by chance that French
students of 1968 received a warmer welcome among journalists, news-
casters, and engineers (particularly in the branch of electronics) than
among the union leaders of the more classic working class. Nor is it accidental that the dominant political theme of our period is that of par-
ticipatory democracy.[23]

Conclusions.   Although the schools of different cultures do not necessarily respond similarly to the increasing complexity of social arrangements, the data examined here suggest that:

1.   Initially limited to certain privileged disciplines, the differentiation
of educational roles and structures from other institutions is the result
of the interplay between the centrifugal effects of specialization and the

centripetal effects of integration in the economic, legal, and religious spheres.

2. The differentiation of the roles of students can take place only after the roles of teachers are themselves made distinct.

3. As these two forms of differentiation develop, contrasts appear among various categories of teachers and pupils. University professors neither enjoy the same rights nor face the same duties as primary school teachers. Similarly the patterns of recruitment and of socialization of primary and secondary school students do not follow the same logic.

While there is an increase in the number of factors influencing access to educational amenities, formal schooling itself becomes an increasingly significant determinant of the differential individual placement in both physical and social space.

Although all educational institutions act as important mechanisms of social differentiation, they nevertheless perform significant functions of social communication, for they are expected to facilitate a more equitable allocation of human resources and to establish bridges not only between the children of distinct social groups but also between the past and present elements of a national culture. Correspondingly they are at the very center of the centrifugal and centripetal forces at work in the entire social system.

NOTES AND REFERENCES

1. See J. Alia, "Les nouveaux lyceens," *Le nouvel observateur,* No. 330, March 1971, p. 39. See also C. F. Jullien, "La fabrique d'ouvriers," *Ibid.,* No. 336, March 1971, p. 41.

2. See A. Zidjerveld, *The Abstract Society* (Garden City: Doubleday, 1970), Chapter 4.

3. *Ibid.,* Chapter 3, 4.

4. Among matrilineal societies the lines of authority of familial groups run through males but lines of descent run through females. From this principle it results that maternal uncles (i.e., mother's brothers) claim a position of authority toward the children of their sisters. This position cannot be exerted before the children reach a certain age and cease to be subjected to the control of their fathers. For a general discussion of the implications of matrilineal organization on the style of interaction between parents and children, see D. Schneider and K. Gough, eds., *Matrilineal Kinship* (Berkeley: University of California Press, 1961), Introduction.

5. See R. Winch and L. Freeman, "Societal Complexity—An Empirical Test of a Typology of Societies," *American Journal of Sociology,* Vol. 62, 1957, pp. 461–466.

6. It is quite clear in this respect that the centralization of criminal law is accompanied also by an increase in the relative importance of the laws underlying contractual relations. For a full treatment, see E. Durkheim, *The Division of Labor in Society* (Glencoe: The Free Press, 1960).

7. For a more complete treatment of this question, see J. Goody, ed., *Literacy in Traditional Societies* (Cambridge: Cambridge University Press, 1968).

8. This point is raised by P. Schofield, "Measurement of Literacy" in J. Goody, ed., *ibid.,* pp. 311–325. For a further description, see also E. P. Thompson, *The Making of the English Working Class* (New York: Random House, 1963), pp. 375–378.

9. For a full treatment, see P. Aries, *Centuries of Childhood* (New York: Knopf, 1962).

10. See C. Lucas, *Our Western Educational Inheritage* (New York: Macmillan, 1972), Chapter 8.

11. Fenelon is the first French author to suggest a curriculum of studies especially adapted to the needs of women or more specifically to the social conceptions of the women's role in society. Later the need to give women a special education is found in the *Emile* of Rousseau.

12. As quoted by P. Aries, *op. cit.,* pp. 310–311.

13. C. Lucas *op. cit.* p. 481.

14. See ibidem, *op. cit.*

15. For a general presentation of the notion of increase in scale, see G. and M. Wilson, *The Analysis of Social Change* (Cambridge: Cambridge University Press, 1945). See also E. Shefki and W. Bell, *Social Area Analysis* (Stanford: Stanford University Press, 1955).

16. For a full treatment, see J. Gibbs and H. Browning, "The Division of Labor, Technology and Organization of Production in 12 Countries," *American Sociological Review,* Vol. 31, 1966, pp. 91–92.

17. Data derived from R. Havighurst and B. Neugarten, *Society and Education* (Boston: Allyn and Bacon, 1962), pp. 415, 418. For a more general statistical analysis of the relationship between increase in scale and educational development, see D. McElrath, "Social Differentiation and Societal Scale," in S. Greer et al., eds., *The New Urbanization* (New York: Saint Martin's Press, 1968) pp. 39–51.

18. See C. Lucas, *loc. cit.*

19. For a discussion of this theme, see A. Touraine, *Le mouvement de Mai ou le Communisme Utopique* (Paris: Le Seuil, 1968); see also H. Lefebvre, *La vie quotidienne dans le monde moderne* (Paris: Gallimard, 1968), Chapter 2.

20. Interrelationships between specialization of knowledge and social dif-

ferentiation begin at an early stage of scalar development. For a general discussion, see J. Goody and I. Watt, "The Consequences of Literacy," in J. Goody, ed., *op. cit.*, pp. 57–68.

21. This differentiation is related not only to the processes of increase in scale and the resulting forms of social interaction but also to cultural forces and more specifically to the form of bureaucratic action prevailing in a particular society. On this question, see M. de Saint Martin, "Les Facteurs de l'élimination et de la sélection différentielles dans les études de sciences," *Revue francaise de sociologie,* Vol. 9, 1968, pp. 152–184; P. Bourdieu and J. C. Passeron, "L'examen d'une illusion," ibid., pp. 225–253; M. Crozier, *The Bureaucratic Phenomenon* (Chicago: Chicago University Press, 1968), pp. 237–244.

22. See A. Touraine, *op. cit.*, p. 177. (Translation is mine.)

23. The notion of participation politically coined in France by De Gaulle seems to indicate his deep understanding of the most crucial problems of our times. There is however an interesting contradiction between his appreciation of the significance of participation and his desire (resulting from his background) to give unilaterally this participation rather than to bargain about it. It is also interesting that in the second half of the 1960s the vice president of the United States focused his political attacks on mass media and on universities, the two institutions within which the problems of participation are the most acute.

2

EDUCATION AND THE
FOUR OTHER BASIC
SOCIAL INSTITUTIONS

To assess the educational determinants and implications of the dilemma between liberty and equality, it is necessary to determine the relative interdependence of educational structures or processes and of the overall organizational profile of societies as well as of their distinct subparts. An evaluation of this interdependence is in effect twofold. First, I summarize briefly how general educational orientations appear to vary with the overall profile of distinct social systems. Then I examine successively the network of reciprocal influences between the schools and the four other basic institutions of a particular social system. To the extent that this social system exists, its various subparts should not be independent of one another.

In the last century, Durkheim showed how contrasts in the political or economic profile of ancient Greek communities were paralleled by similar disparities in the relative emphasis that each of these communities placed upon the teaching of military, literary, or musical arts. He also showed how the definition of the physical education imposed in each of these communities varied with the specific social symbols they attached to the human body. Thus physical education was meant to train warriors in belligerent Sparta while in Athens it was aimed at the formation of Appolinian artists.[1] Panofski demonstrates that during the Middle Ages, the teaching of arts—specifically, architecture—was aiming at the graphic translation of the scholastic philosophy that permeated the organization and the value systems of the societies of that period.[2]

Similarly Michael Katz shows how variations in the economic activities and in the religious orientations of early American communities have affected both the organizational patterns of local schools and the ideal conceptions of their functions.[3] In the contemporary world, Touraine suggests (though indirectly) that the overall concern of social systems with the problems of communication affects and shapes the daily patterns of interaction taking place in the schools.[4] Thus the themes dominating the overall orientations of a particular society are likely to be directly and indirectly translated in the curriculum taught in its schools as well as in the patterns of interaction that develop both among and between students, teachers, and other segments of the population. Schools seem to reflect the major preoccupations and orientations of a society.

Social influences on educational enterprises also are more specific. It is important to assess both the relative influence that familial, economic, political, and religious institutions exert on schools and their actors and the reciprocal impact of academic experiences on the functioning and the organization of these same societal institutions. If it is true that the current profile of educational enterprises reflects the double impact of the past and the present, it is equally true that from the patterns of interaction prevailing among students, teachers, and administrators will emerge the types of parents and children, managers and workers, judges, administrators and voters, priests and worshippers of the society of tomorrow.

The perpetuation of any society requires the fulfillment of five basic prerequisites:[5]

1. Recruitment and reproduction of members. The perpetuation of any society requires its members to renew themselves either naturally (this raises the question of fertility) or by attracting new persons from the outside (this raises the question of migrations). Therefore, each society has familial organizations.

2. Economic production. Social systems can survive as independent entities only insofar as they are able to ensure the subsistence of their members. Accordingly, all societies are characterized by the institutionalization of economic production patterns and hence by the formulation of specific rules regarding both division of labor and circulation of economic goods and services. Each society has its specific economic organization.

3. Socialization and education. The two preceding conditions are insufficient to ensure the perpetuation of a particular society. It also

depends upon the degree to which a society is able to ensure an optimal continuity of its norms, values, and practices. This requires individuals of each new generation to fit the roles allocated to them. The
fulfillment of this requirement is mediated mainly through the activities of educational institutions.

4.   Maintenance of order. A social system must protect its integrity by
maintaining its physical boundaries and hence by preventing aggres-
sions from the outside. It also must cope with potential internal disruptions and it must develop appropriate mechanisms to alleviate the
. strains and conflicts which oppose individuals and subgroups to one
another. Social systems cannot survive without military, political and
judicial institutions.

5.   Sense of purpose. This function concerns the emotional commitment of each individual toward the social system in which he participates. Individuals internalize their social affiliations only insofar as they
share a common set of moral beliefs, orientations, and expectations.
Thus, in all societies there are religious institutions (in the broad sense
of the term), the main role of which is to formulate the ideological
framework which binds all individuals together.

The modes of interaction among these institutions are problematic
and they have been treated in a variety of ways by contemporary sociologists.[6] Some have underlined differences between societies where the
dominant social order is markedly influenced by primary group ties
and hence by familial institutions, and those societies where this order
is predominantly shaped by the bureaucratic interaction prevailing in
political, economic, educational, and eventually religious institutions.
Other sociologists have emphasized the distinctive functions of these
basic institutions; for instance, they have been keen to show that certain
functions performed by the family or by a Church could not be performed in another institutional context. A third group of scholars
seems to be more anxious to examine the joint functioning of these
various institutions and to analyze variations in the mechanisms that coordinate their activities.

In the following sections of this chapter I show how contrasts in the
profile of familial, economic, political, and religious roles and institutions affect various aspects of the educational scene; and reciprocally
how differences in the outlook of educational roles and institutions are
paralleled by similar cleavages in the nature of the four other basic
functions. The analysis uses alternatively, schools and their populations
as dependent and then as independent variables. The analysis of the
corresponding linkage is made within both synchronic and diachronic

frameworks. Because schools are prisoners of the past as much as of the present, the main purpose of this chapter is to establish the limits within which the reciprocal linkage between schools and other basic societal institutions operates.

Education and the Family.   In education, as in other fields, individual and collective actions are organized after consciously imitated models.[7] Conscious educational models—that is, the rules underlying the functioning of schools as well as the interpretations that actors give of their activities within the educational scene—reflect the strong influence of familial ideologies. Thus a university is called an alma mater (this institution is considered to be the mother of arts and sciences; indeed, schools are viewed as "giving birth" to desired members of the community). It is no wonder that school authorities often are expected to act toward students in *loco parentis,* even when the family has ceased to play as significant a socializing role as the expression would lead us to believe. Undoubtedly, the models underlying our actions do not necessarily fit reality and are characterized by varying degrees of obsolescence. In fact the importance of the familial model in educational interaction is particularly paradoxical when one analyzes, with Dreeben, contrasts in the number, the sex and, the age composition of the actors participating in these two institutional contexts.[8]

Yet the relationships between educational roles and familial institutions are not only conscious and ideological but they also reflect the intervention of unconscious and objective factors. In a first step I examine the impact of familial structures, functions, and roles on academic behavior and educational institutions. Specifically I demonstrate that individual educational behaviors are influenced by family size, by sibling position, and by the networks of institutionalized as well as non-institutionalized communications between generations. Thus I demonstrate that the dilemma between liberty and equality in the educational context is affected by familial structures. In a second step I reverse the approach and examine how educational experiences modify the profile of familial groups; that is, I show how formal schooling is conducive to a reinterpretation of familial roles and hence to a greater individual sense of liberty in this particular institutional arena. Thus I treat educational experiences alternatively as dependent and independent variables.

Influence of Familial Groups on Schools.   The main function of familial groups is to ensure a sufficient reproduction of the members of a particular society. Current research evidences the existence of a negative correlation between this particular function (as measured by family size) and educational achievement (as measured by performances on intelligence tests, by academic grades, or by enrollment rates in the upper echelons of secondary institutions). Although moderate (values of the corresponding coefficient range between −.20 and −.30), this negative association seems to hold true both for a variety of samples and in a variety of countries (Scotland, Great Britain, France, Italy, Greece, and the United States).[9] This suggests the existence of potential strains between the reproductive and socializing functions of familial institutions.

The origin of these contradictions remains problematic and while some of these contradictions exist independently of the perceptions that groups and individuals hold about familial functions, others result from the divergent conscious models that individuals elaborate as rationalizations of such functions.

Influence of family size on educational roles. Modes of interaction among the various members of large-sized families exert a negative influence on the academic behavior and aspirations of children. Yet the largest families of industrialized nations are most frequently found among lower social classes which hold negative attitudes toward formal education and maintain a system of values and of rewards and punishments at variance with that of most school systems. Can we say then that the relationship between familial size and educational behavior is spurious and masks a more significant association between social class and academic performances?

In fact, the association between family size and educational achievement tends to hold true for a variety of social classes and occupational subgroups. Regardless of their position in the social structure, large families are characterized by a system of relationships between adults and children which discourages the explorative behavior demanded of pupils. The more children in a family, the less interaction develops between adult actors and each child and the less exposed is each child to adult vocabulary, syntax, and system of logic. Available evidences show the negative affects of family size to be maximal on verbal performances.

The negative effects of family size on academic performances are however differential and vary with the position the child occupies in the familial group.[10] The demands imposed upon the oldest, youngest, and intermediate children are not alike, with corresponding contrasts in their respective role patterns. Despite his privileged contacts with his

parents, an oldest child must learn how to face alone the requirements
of the adult world; intermediate children are less exposed to parental
influences and must learn the significance of being an important
member of the familial group by imitation of their siblings; while last
born children are confronted with the task of overcoming the consequences of their position and hence of avoiding being regarded as inferior. Such factors are believed to account for the differential performances obtained by British pupils on tests as well as for their respective
abilities to negotiate the hurdles encountered during their academic career. Table 2 shows that while eldest children are proportionately most

**Table 2. *Percentage Distribution of British Students in the Secondary
System (Midland Borough), by Sibship Position* [a]**

Sibling Position	Years 1–4	Fifth Form	Sixth Form
Only	19	17	31
Eldest	43	37	31
Intermediate	17	19	11
Youngest	21	27	27
Total	100	100	100
N	674	161	81

[a] Lees and Stewart, "Family or Sibship Position and Scholastic Ability," *Sociological Review*, Vol. 5, 1957, p. 188.

numerous in the classes examined, their relative share declines as they
move up the academic ladder. By relative terms, only children and
youngest siblings are more likely than elder or intermediate children to
overcome obstacles to their academic progress. These results are parallel to those reported by Blau and Duncan: "It is less of a disadvantage
for a child to have many older than many younger siblings." [11]

Yet the influence of sibship position on academic performance does
not seem to be the same for boys and girls. Girls seem to be higher
achievers than boys when they are the youngest of the families but the
opposite is true when one considers children with higher rank order.
The influence of sibship position does not seem to be independent of
the sex of children with a higher rank order. For example, regardless
of their own sex, sibs with brothers seem to exhibit higher performance
on achievement tests than sibs with sisters. However this observation is
indirectly at variance with the research of Brim in the United States

who suggests that male children with older sisters are more likely to obtain higher academic performances than those with elder brothers.[12]

The potential role played by the sex of siblings as an intervening factor in the association between family size and various aspects of academic behavior suggests that the contradictions between the socializing and reproductive functions of familial groups are not independent of cultural factors, specifically of the cultural definition of the role allocated to women. The studies reported here, however, were undertaken among industrialized societies where upward mobility (as mediated through formal schooling) is deemed to be incompatible with familism (as measured by family size) and where the socializing roles of women are seen as hindered by their childbearing activities.

Similar results are not likely to be obtained in African new nations. In that context adult individuals often tend to believe that the larger the number of children they have, the more chances at least one of their children has to reach the upper rungs of the social ladder. They deem a large family to be the most appropriate channel for upward mobility. For example, the full census of Douala shows that among the households whose heads are derived from an urban origin and are employed in the modern public sector of the economy, one finds the highest incidence of polygyny, the largest number of children, and (most important for us) the highest number of students over 16 years of age.[13]

Influence of the cultural aspects of familial life on educational roles.   Thus the contradictions between family size and academic behavior or educational experiences are culturally relative. This is because to a large extent, such contradictions reflect the particular models underlying the functions of social placement that familial groups are expected to perform for their children, and hence, variations in the degree to which academic experiences are intended to confirm or correct the position ascribed to a child. There are at least three mechanisms by which familial groups "place" their children in the social structures of the community; these are rules of inheritance and, in some particular cultural contexts, type of marriage as well as type of descent. In the following I show the conditions under which schools are intended to correct or confirm the position ascribed to a child as a result of the rules of inheritance, of descent, and of marriage that are adopted by the society to which he belongs.

Participation in educational structures is not independent of rules of inheritance. In prerevolutionary France, for example, it was customary for noble families to transmit the rights and duties of the title to the eldest son while the second male child was destined to a military career and the third son was expected to enter a religious occupation. Insofar as formal schooling was initially most closely associated with religious and military functions, we can suspect the educational level of lastborn children always to have been higher than that of their elders. In an article dealing with the relationship between familial arrangements and industrialization in central Europe, Habbakuk demonstrates that the industrial development of Bohemia, Moravia, and Silesia was accelerated by the single heir rule, which induced the junior members of a familial group to migrate permanently toward emerging industrial urban centers and to acquire the secondary or university education necessary for gaining access to the major rewarding occupations of the urban labor market.[14] In contrast the rules of partible inheritance which prevailed in Slovakia impeded permanent emigrations from rural areas as well as transfers from agriculture to other types of occupations. In countries similar to the first type, school enrollments should vary positively with family size and thus should also increase with migrations. In countries of the second type, conversely, school enrollments should develop much slower while individual educational attainment should be more independent of sibship position. In the first context schools may be viewed ultimately as mechanisms designed for equalizing the economic chances of children with differing rank order within their familial groups; in the second context the functions assigned to schools are more independent of the internal organization of familial groups.

Even in the United States, the rule of primogeniture is probably of relevance to account for the differential academic and social behavior adopted by individuals with various sib-positions. Up to the college level, firstborn girls, for example, tend to be conservators of the "traditional culture" more often than laterborn females. Thus the former are more likely than the latter to follow a curriculum deemed to fit the subservient and expressive role expected of women.[15] Insofar as the American society is comprised of a variety of ethnic groups with distinct cultural traditions and rules of inheritance, one might also wonder whether there are ethnic variations in the association between academic success (measured, for instance, in terms of rates of college attendance or of grade average in high school) and sibship position. Whenever familial groups control significant economic assets and whenever such groups transmit those assets to the elder son, this particular child should have less reason to do well at school than his younger brothers and sisters.

As long as one segment of the population is expected to be committed to the preservation of traditional roles and as long as such a segment is defined—at least in part—in terms of familial positions, one can expect significant differences in the academic behavior of individuals with differing familial rank orders. Either schooling is seen as congruent with the requirements of traditional values and the children who are in the position of potential "heirs" should be more likely to attend an educational institution and should be induced to be higher achievers than their younger siblings; or schooling is defined as inconsistent with the demands of tradition and the children most motivated both to attend school and to do well by academic standards should be those with junior positions.

In nonwestern societies it has generally been admitted, after the research of Dr. McClelland, that polygynous societies are uniformly characterized by a lower need for achievement (and hence indirectly by a lower level of participation in educational activities) than monogamous cultures.[16] Because the main function of polygynous arrangements is to increase family size, these arrangements are seen as reducing the contacts of a child with his or her father, hence as limiting the exposure of this child to images of excellence which are necessary for the building of achievement orientations. In addition, the existing literature on plural marriage would induce us to assume that insofar as senior co-wives and their offspring are entitled to an ascribed higher status, it is primarily the children of junior co-wives who are the most likely to view formal schooling as a mechanism of upward mobility.

Nevertheless Clignet and Foster, in their study of Ivory Coast secondary students, tentatively demonstrated that children from polygynous families are proportionately as numerous in the quite selective school system of the country as their counterparts derived from monogamous groups.[17] Further, Clignet suggests that in rural areas, the co-wives of patrilineal polygynous mates place more relative emphasis on the academic achievement of their male children than the spouses of monogamous males, while the pattern is reversed among a rural sample of matrilineal monogamous and polygynous families.[18] In addition, although the actual academic achievement of students coming from families characterized by differing types of marriages are similar, children of rural polygynous patrilineal families have frequently higher occupational aspirations than those of rural monogamous patrilineal parents.[19]

It is therefore impossible to draw generalizations from the contrasts between the socialization functions of monogamous and polygynous familial groups. This is because, regardless of type of marriage, the educational role of familial institutions varies primarily with type of descent. Among patrilineal peoples, the rewards to which a married woman can aspire are extensively controlled by her husband's family and often depend upon the position that her own offspring achieves within that kin group. This induces a high degree of competition among patrilineal co-wives who entertain particularly high expectations with regard to the formal schooling of their children. In contrast, among matrilineal peoples the rewards that a married woman can hope to obtain depends upon her own family of origin. This reduces both the interaction she has with her husband and the competition which may oppose her to other co-wives. Thus variations in type of marriage are not prime determinants of variations in the educational behavior of African familial actors. In fact polygynous arrangements accentuate the contrasts opposing the orientations, attitudes, and behaviors of familial groups organized along distinctive lines of descent.

The dichotomy between patrilineal and matrilineal organizations is certainly a more basic determinant of the socializing functions performed by African adult familial actors. Among patrilineal societies, lines of descent and of authority run through male actors. This ensures a certain degree of congruence in the demands exerted by adult actors on members of the oncoming generation. In turn this congruence facilitates the adaptation of the educational goals and techniques of familial groups to a changing environment.

Among matrilineal societies lines of authority run through male actors, whereas lines of descent run through women. Thus a child belongs to the familial group of his mother and is hence ultimately subjected to the authority and control of his maternal uncle, whereas his father remains responsible for his early socialization without enjoying commensurate power and rewards. As a result, there are recurrent conflicts between the educational objectives and techniques of the father and the maternal uncles. These conflicts are both inter and intra roles, since the father of a child is the maternal uncle of another. Both types of conflicts are likely to be exacerbated by social change and more specifically by the consequences of educational development. Fathers are reluctant to become financially and emotionally involved in the formal schooling of their offspring as long as familial structures are not changed and made more consistent with the consequences of the individualization of economic rights. They argue that tradition does not oblige them to participate in the formal schooling of their own children and that new obligations along these lines can only follow sharp modifications of existing social structures. At the same time maternal uncles believe that the costs of the formal education of their nephews should be supported by the fathers. They do not themselves have particular incentives to adopt positive attitudes toward an institution that makes their heirs more rebellious to the demands of tradition and more anxious to acquire individualized roles and status in a changing environment. Mothers are thus the only familial actors interested in the schooling of the oncoming generation, but their ability to finance educational experiences depends upon their gainful employment and hence upon the extent to which they are able to achieve economic autonomy.

Thus social change seems to exacerbate conflicts between the socialization and placement functions of matrilineal groups. Latent in the traditional context, the tensions which oppose fathers and maternal uncles with regard to their respective socializing responsibilities have built up with the introduction of a western type of formal schooling. Such tensions cannot but slow down the rates of educational developments of many new African nations where matrilineal peoples frequently are found.

Inequalities in a child's chances for access to higher education are markedly affected by the cultural models underlying the placement functions of familial groups. Depending on the culture under study, schooling is likely to confirm or to modify the differential status ascribed to children with differing rank orders.

Influence of familial orientations on academic orientations and behaviors. Educational development depends not only upon the strains between the reproductive and socializing functions of the familial group but also upon that group's power structure. Consensus between parents is thus often shown to heighten individual academic achievement.[20] Bowerman and Elder remind us however that domestic power structures are differentiated and that significant distinctions should be entered between the power exerted by conjugal partners in their reciprocal dealings, the initiatives that each spouse takes with regard to the upbringing of children, and the nature of the authority that each parent manifests toward their offspring.[21] Although these three forms of domestic power are interrelated, there are significant variations in the influence that each one exerts on academic behavior and attitudes. Parental role patterns (that is, the extent to which socializing responsibilities are shared or exerted by either parent) and child rearing structures (that is, the extent to which parents are authoritarian, democratic, or permissive toward their children) prove to be more important in this regard than conjugal relations per se.

However the effects of imbalances in these various facets of domestic power structure appear to be uncertain. Thus Strodtbeck shows that among Italian and Jewish families living in the United States, a decline in the traditional dominance exerted by fathers induces both mothers and sons "to believe that the world can be rationally mastered and that the son should risk separation from the family." [22] Strodtbeck indicates that a relative decrease in the power held by fathers and husbands towards their sons and wives enhances the initiatives that the sons are willing to take, especially in the academic field. In fact, other authors have also suggested that youth from wife-dominant families display a usually high level of achievement and aspiration.[23] Using a large sample of slightly under 20,000 adolescents enrolled in junior high and high schools, Bowerman and Elder demonstrate conversely that regardless of their social class, the democratically reared adolescents coming from husband-dominated families are the most likely to pursue their formal schooling beyond high school. Wife dominance in conjugal relations, or autocratic paternal control in child rearing, or both in combination are most likely to deflate the educational aspirations of the pupils interviewed. Among middle-class pupils, for example, no less than 70 percent of those coming from a family dominated by husbands who act democratically as fathers, expect to go to college, as against only 29 percent of those coming from a family which is dominated by the wife-mother and in which the paternal socializing style is autocratic in nature. Among their lower-class counterparts, the corresponding figures range from 36 to 18 percent respectively and reveal a similar (although less visible) contrast in the relative impact of distinctive power structures on academic aspirations.

These data suggest that academic aspirations depend upon the relative consistency of the following:

1. The various facets of the domestic power structure. The greater the disparities in the models of action offered to a child by his parents, the more deflated will be his own ambitions.

2. The value system of each family and the immediate social environment. The literature gives conflicting evidences on the influence that

wife-dominance exerts on academic ambitions. In fact the effects of this dominance may vary with the stereotypes that various segments of the American society hold about domestic matriarchy. The effects of wife dominance along these lines are probably more beneficial when such stereotypes are positive than when the particular group studied resents the fact that women "wear the britches."

3. The demands imposed upon students in the context of their home and of their school. The data discussed above have shown the differential impact that variations in both power structure and child rearing practices exert on the plans for college of students with distinctive social origins. Even in the best cases, the plans of lower-class students are less optimistic and this results from the conflicts opposing their familial value system to that of the majority of educational institutions.

However domestic power structure affects not only individual academic aspirations and orientations but the entire system of interactions which develop between students and teachers. It is possible to argue, for example, that pupils transfer to their teachers the emotional responses they have built toward their parents. Such a transfer is made easier when primary school teachers share the same age characteristics as the parents of the children they teach. The variety of forms of dependence displayed by pupils toward teaching personnel is thus often seen as resulting from the diverse forms of identification that children develop toward their parents. There are differences between male and female students in this regard. If both fathers and male teachers are unavailable as models, many male children may experience difficulties in the way they solve role identification problems, and such difficulties are reinforced by the frequently negative nature of the admonishments to which they are subjected. In class and at home they are told that they should not be sissies without being precisely shown what they should be.[24] Thus the difficulties they experience in the classroom often are seen as the reenactments of the difficulties they experience in achieving an acceptable performance of their role within the family.

Symmetrically, the teaching style of teachers and the set of attitudes and behaviors that they develop toward students might reflect their basic orientations toward parental roles. Some teachers appear to be anxious to maintain their students in a situation of dependence for as long a period of time as possible; this anxiety might be attributed to an unconscious desire to retaliate against the emotional repression to which they were subjected during their childhood. Other teachers seem to maintain cold and impersonal contacts with their pupils; this is sometimes interpreted as resulting from the particular defense mechanisms they built up during their own childhood.

If it is true that "the child is the father of the adult," it is equally true that the familial group is the mother of all formal and informal associations in which individuals participate. In the same way that the conflicts experienced by individuals in their dealings with strangers often are seen as replications of the unsolved conflicts characterizing their personal relations in the family, the dominant characteristics of the interactions prevailing in schools (and for that matter in all human organizations) should parallel the most salient features of familial bonds.[25]

Influence of Formal Education on Familial Structures and Roles. Educational experiences also influence the orientations that individuals entertain toward familial institutions. Specifically, the extent and the form of formal schooling affects patterns of mate selection, patterns of domestic power, and behaviors and attitudes concerning both child-bearing and child-rearing activities.

Initially, educational attainment influences patterns of marriage; indeed formal schooling is a major determinant in defining the field of eligible mates. In all countries similarity of educational experiences increases both the chances of interaction between two individuals of the opposite sex and the likelihood of their sharing similar attitudes and beliefs. Conjugal partners tend to share similar educational backgrounds. The extent of this educational homogamy varies however with the educational development of the societies studied. In countries with a high level of enrollments in primary, secondary, and postsecondary institutions, the relative numbers of male and female students do not differ significantly. Both male and female students are similarly able to find partners with analogous educational attainments. However in countries with lower educational enrollments, the number of male students is higher than that of their female counterparts. The sex ratio of the student population of such countries is very high. As a result educational homogamy is more characteristic of the female than of the male population. In Yaounde, the capital city of the Cameroon, only 30 percent of literate monogamous husbands have literate wives. In contrast no less than 95 percent of the literate monogamously married female populations have husbands who are literates.[26] In that case educated women can be more demanding of their future partners than their male counterparts. The situation is the same in Yugoslavia.[27] Regardless of their religious background, female university students view educational homogamy more favorably than their male classmates. No less than 69 percent of the women raised within a Communist oriented family want their partner to have an equal level of education to their own as against only 45 percent of their male counterparts. Even though educational homogamy is not as strongly stressed by students coming from religious families, the trends are the same and half of the women coming from Muslim, Catholic or Orthodox families want to marry a university student while less than one third of their male counterparts would like their future partners to have the equivalent of a college degree. The attitudes these women display in this respect correspond to the patterns of behavior actually adopted by the adult female population. In 1956 almost two-thirds of the female married population with a postsecondary educational attainment had husbands who also had attended an institution of higher learning. By contrast, only one-fourth of the male married population having attended a university had a spouse with the same educational characteristics.

The importance attached to educational homogamy varies with the religious or cultural background of the populations studied. There are marked disparities in the attitudes adopted toward educational homogamy by Yugoslavian students with differing cultural backgrounds. Only one-third of the students with a Catholic, Muslim, or Orthodox origin favor educational homogamy as against almost one half of their peers coming from atheist or Communist families. Cultural variations in the importance attached to educational homogamy seem nevertheless to be independent of the level of complexity of the society at large. Thus only 49 percent of the American Catholic males (interviewed by Hollingshead in New Haven) who had at least 13 years of education married women with a similar educational attainment; but among Protestants and Jews the corresponding figures were as high as 64 and 76 percent respectively.[28]

Yet individual levels of formal schooling determine the width of the field of eligibles; that is, the higher the educational level of a person, the less importance he or she attaches to religious or cultural factors in his or her pursuit of the ideal mate. In Yugoslavia the students interviewed were quite clearly less inclined than the adult population at large to practice religious or cultural endogamy. Whereas 90 percent of the Serbian males had married Serbian women, ethnic endogamy was of primary importance in the selection of a mate for only 6 percent of the university students interviewed. However in the United States a higher education does not seem to increase the number of interfaith and intercultural marriages and hence to enhance the liberty of individuals toward familial institutions.[29]

Educational attainment also influences matrimonial status and specifically age at marriage. Among societies characterized by a low level of educational development and hence by marked disparities in the relative size of male and female enrollments, the age at marriage of women tends to increase directly with their level of formal schooling. Their marriage is often delayed because educated males remain conservative in their matrimonial expectations and are unwilling to meet the expectations of their female counterparts toward matrimonial relations. As a result educated women are not anxious to enter marriage at an early age. Among societies with a higher level of educational development, conversely, the relationship between level of formal schooling and age at marriage tends to be curvilinear in nature (Table 3). Individuals with

Table 3.   Median Age at Marriage of American Males and Females with Differing Educational Attainments [a]

	Number of Years Elementary		Number of Years High School		Number of Years College	
Sex	Less Than 8	8	1–3	4	1–3	4
Males	24.7	24.9	22.8	24.0	24.7	26.0
Females	20.2	20.4	19.7	20.7	21.8	23.8

[a] Based on the number of marriages occurring between January 1947 and June 1954. Derived from National Office of Vital Statistics, *Vital Statistics–Special Reports* Vol. 45, no. 12, September 9, 1957 tables 24 and 27, as analyzed by R. Winch, *The Modern Family* (New York: Holt, Rinehart and Winston, 1967), p. 350.

a low educational level marry late because their lack of occupational and social skills prevents them from being attractive partners. At the other end of the educational continuum, persons with university training are inclined to defer their matrimonial choices until they have entered the labor force and have eventually enlarged the field of their potential eligible partners. Accordingly the individuals with a high school training are the most likely to marry early. In their case the various definitions of social maturity coincide; the age at which one leaves school is also the age at which one both enters the labor market and forms an independent household.[30]

Yet in an historical perspective, the age at marriage of students in highly educated societies keeps declining, for the large number of students reduces the marginality of their status. In the United States, for example, the growing number of scholarships enables individuals and their families to transfer to the community at large the costs attached to a higher education. As a result, individuals use a broader time scale in planning their lives and this enhances the importance of anticipatory socialization—that is, the extent to which students learn a matrimonial role before being in a position to really perform it. Correspondingly there is a relative decline in the age of marriage of highly educated young populations.

Educational attainment also affects the distribution of power and authority within familial groups. In view of the small age differences between conjugal partners with highest educational achievements, it is not surprising that they tend to maintain equalitarian relations. W. Goode, however, warns us against possible confusion between verbal and actual behavior in this respect.[31] He argues that individuals with high levels of schooling tend to describe themselves as more liberal in their domestic power dealings than they actually are, while individuals with a minimal educational attainment are more egalitarian in fact than their expressed ideology would induce us to believe. Regardless of these remarks, the high education of women often tends to facilitate their continuing participation in the labor force even after their marriages.

Educational attainment also influences attitudes toward the reproductive functions of the family. Fertility is negatively associated with educational status because familism is frequently perceived as incompatible with upward mobility. Educated females are more prone than illiterate females to perceive such a contradiction and to control family size. However the development among educated women of hostile attitudes toward fertility is neither universal nor permanent. Among industrialized societies, for example, the negative relationship between education and fertility holds true only for women who marry early.[32] Females who marry late tend to exert a tighter control on all the aspects of their matrimonial life and hence on their reproductive activities—and this regardless of their educational attainment. Conversely among developing societies still dominated by traditional prescriptions, familism is perceived as the most appropriate mechanism of upward mobility. Thus in industrial nations, educated individuals believe that a child's success is a function of the intensity of the care that he receives; but their counterparts living in a more traditional society often believe that chances of success are evenly distributed among the individuals of a particular age group. Accordingly the more children there are in a family, the more the family believes that at least one of them will get ahead and will in turn facilitate the upward mobility of his siblings.

Finally, educational attainment modifies both childbirth techniques and child rearing practices. In the United States the mothers most likely to use new child delivery methods are those exposed to the most diverse sources of knowledge and hence those with the highest levels of formal schooling.[33] Similarly formal education transforms the attitudes that women entertain toward breast feeding. Usually there is a negative association between the length of nursing period and the educational level of a woman.[34] However this relationship is not stable. In more general terms, studies show that maternal demands in the United States vary both with social class and the level of formal schooling achieved by mothers. Among American middle classes, educated women attach more importance to formal schooling than their less educated counterparts. Among lower classes, mothers graduating from high schools and higher institutions place more emphasis than mothers with low academic qualifications upon the self-control of their male children and upon the consideration as well as the curiosity of their female offspring.[35]

In conclusion, there are a variety of interrelations between educational and familial experiences. While familial structures affect *inequalities* of access to educational amenities or of educational performances, educational experiences influence the *liberty* of individuals toward the constraints of familial roles and structures. However interaction between liberty and equality, as it results from the interplay between educational and familial institutions, varies across cultures. These variations reflect not only contrasted conceptions of the functions to be performed by these two institutions, but also differences in the mechanisms that actually coordinate their activities.[36]

Education and the Economy.   Influence also is exerted on educational development by economic concepts and ideologies. Indeed the dilemma between equality and liberty is not independent of the significance attached to production and consumption in the economic realm.

Early economists viewed schooling as a private venture; Adam Smith claimed that educational enterprises should not be endowed and that in education parents should act as responsible counterparts of the independent entrepreneurs in business.[37] For a long time schooling remained an item of private consumption and the existence of many educational institutions was entirely dependent upon the gifts of munificent individuals or groups. During the sixteenth and seventeenth centuries in England, one-fourth of all charitable bequests went to schools.[38] Similarly in the pre-Meiji Japan many schools were supported by the patronage of wealthy individuals and by private contributions. Motivations underlying the financing of educational enterprises seemed to have been comparable in these two countries. Religious forces, concern over appalling rates of pauperism, fear of the populace, and desire to establish a significant clientele contributed to this particular form of sponsorship.

Educational institutions began to be treated as national investments much later. The emergence of this particular concept was concomitant with the exploration and identification of the role played by human factors in industrial organizations. As a result schools have been increasingly defined as factories of knowledge. Scholars concerned with education became anxious to examine interrelations between educational inputs and outputs and to identify indicators that measured efficiently the productivity of educational enterprises.

The models initially developed to explain the economic organizations of the society at large also account for variations in patterns of educational development. A school that depends upon the charitable bequests and the goodwill of the existing elites corresponds to a feudal system of social organization. Within an industrial society the structures of school systems often are derived from those of industrial organizations. Yet insofar as the modern world is increasingly organized around the concepts and the tensions surrounding means of communication, there should be parallel changes in the models accounting for educational activities. In fact many researchers currently analyze the difficulties faced by educational organizations in terms of shortcomings in their communication and information networks.

Thus the conceptions that individuals and groups hold about the dilemma between equality and liberty, as it influences the educational scene, are affected by conscious models derived from the field of economics; but answers to the problems of educational inequalities also depend upon the degree to which schooling is regarded as a common good or as a productive instrument concerning the welfare of an entire community. In the first instance, justice is the relevant underlying value, while in the second instance, the underlying issues are those raised by the rationality and the productivity of the system.

Economic ideologies however influence not only the tools of analysis used to explain educational activities but also the content of the curriculum deemed to be the most appropriate to the needs of society. Thus both A. Smith and Hume urged educators to convert their pupils to the merits of competition.[39] American schools today are expected to extol the virtues of free enterprise while their Soviet counterparts are supposed to celebrate the contribution of socialism. Interestingly however, there has apparently been no attempt to evaluate the impact of such ideologies on the attitudes developed by students. Specifically, no distinction seems to be made between the differential influence exerted by the teaching of ideologies destined to facilitate the survival of a social system and by the teaching of the skills needed to facilitate its functioning. Yet our task is not so much to measure the degree to which economic ideologies shape the functions performed by educational activities as to identify forms of interdependence between economic and educational organizations.

Influence of Economic Organizations on Schools. Variations in technology and hence in division of labor are associated with variations in the composition of the school population, the type of education provided by the schools, and the profile of educational development. Specifically contrasts both in types of economic organization and in levels of economic development are associated with differences (*a*) in the extent and the form of inequalities in the composition of school populations and of teaching forces, (*b*) in the definition of school functions and hence in the curriculum as well as in the pedagogical methods to be used by educational institutions, and (*c*) in the mechanisms of allocation of educational resources.

Economic development and types of school populations. Societies with a low level of economic development and hence a low division of labor also have limited school enrollments. However the problem remains to determine whether the corresponding scarcity of educational facilities is always conducive to inequalities in access to such facilities. In effect these inequalities vary both with the prevailing modes of economic exploitation and with the rigidity of the existing systems of social stratification.

Thus segments of the population whose wealth was dependent upon extensive rather than intensive work and hence upon an abundant unskilled and cheap labor force were negatively predisposed toward the formal schooling of the masses. In preindustrial southern United States, "Circumstances imposed a prohibition on the formal education of slaves, as a luxury beyond their condition or an acquirement incompatible with domestic quiet." [40] In Alabama a statute was passed in 1832 (the year following Nat Turner's insurrection) making it a crime to instruct a Negro freeman or slave in the arts of reading and writing,[41] and in 1918 Mississippi was the last state to adopt a law concerning compulsory attendance.[42] Although unable to pass such a legislation, most European industrialists of the early part of the last century were at least as intensely hostile to the diffusion of formal schooling among the strata of the population from which they were drawing the cheap labor force needed by their industrial activities. Closer to contemporary times, French planters in the Ivory Coast were able to limit the development of educational budgets by imposing appropriate pressures upon local politicians. They viewed formal education as likely to promote aspirations toward upward mobility and thus as a force likely to deprive them of the masses of unskilled laborers needed in a plantation economy.

Access to educational amenities was likely to remain open among preindustrial societies whose wealth was determined by individual productivity. Thus the political and economic individualism prevailing in the preindustrial urban centers of France and of Great Britain facilitated the opening of local schools to a variety of social groups. Similarly in some Japanese schools of the pre-Meiji era, adult commoners were permitted to sit once a month among the two sword-bearing samurai.[43]

Although there are thus some contrasts in the size and the social composition of the schools of preindustrial societies, economic development has remained uniformly associated with an increase in school enrollments. This increase reflects a variety of economic, social, and political forces. First, the growing complexity of industrial organizations requires the services of a highly skilled—and therefore highly educated—labor force. The more rapid the rates of technological changes, the richer the body of knowledge that the oncoming generation is expected to acquire. As this body of knowledge becomes more diverse, student populations are required to stay longer in school as if there was a necessary and high correlation between the length of formal studies and their complexity. In addition, technological changes usually are associated with a decline in the significance of age as a determinant of division of labor. Accordingly there is a decline in the potential economic contributions of children and adolescents and a parallel decrease in the forces pushing students out of school. Such a decrease also is accentuated by the fact that technological changes enable the adult generation to stay longer in the labor force. As older elements of the adult population postpone retirement, they are anxious to limit the pressures exerted on the labor market and hence to lengthen the period of compulsory school attendance. Finally, economic development usually is accompanied by changes in the economic power of the adult labor force. Such a population is able to support for a longer period of time a larger number of dependents and hence of students.

The combination of all these factors affects the nature of regulations pertaining to formal schooling. As a society reaches a certain level of economic complexity, it is likely to pass laws which define the duration of the minimal formal schooling that all children and adolescents must acquire. For example, in France school attendance was not defined as compulsory before the completion of the first phase of the industrial revolution in the last part of the nineteenth century. Initially placed at ten years of age, compulsory attendance was raised to fourteen years after World War I and to sixteen by 1959. In the Soviet Union the duration of the compulsory attendance period was raised from seven years before World War II to eight years after 1945.[44] In most instances a legal lengthening of this period has been associated with a broadening of the curriculum to be taught during that time and with an aggravation of the punishments meted to individuals who fail to comply.

In the United States differences in the relative economic development of the various states are quite closely related to the extent and the forms of the control exerted upon formal schooling. While compulsory attendance laws were not adopted before 1918 by rural states, such laws were adopted as early as 1852 by the more industrialized state of Massachusetts. In addition, the significance of such laws depends upon the degree to which state agencies have the resources necessary for enforcing them.[45] In 1929 only two states had departments of education—which is not surprising in view of the dominant *laissez faire* ideology dominating the American educational scene. Today there are still marked variations in both the definition and the enforcement of such laws among the various states of the union. In Illinois, for example, the text is broad enough to allow parents to enroll their children in any institution of their choice, including free schools.

Economic development changes not only the size but also the social composition of school populations. Although the populations of larger school systems should be socially more diverse, the relationship between the size of an educational system and the openness of its recruitment is not always linear. Thus whereas the schools of many preindustrial European countries were in a position to recruit their pupils from a broad spectrum of the population, the emerging industrialization and urbanization of such countries has induced marked cleavages in the educational experiences of their various social classes. In Great Britain, for example, the rapid growth of industrial centers has necessitated the massive and rapid displacement of rural populations toward newly created urban slums. This uprooting of emerging urban lower classes prevented them from maintaining their earlier formal and informal educational associations. The negative effects of their growing powerlessness in this respect were accentuated by the transformation of the economic basis of the urban centers toward which they were attracted. This transformation led to changes in local leadership and to declines in the commitment to the local community that had earlier fostered a number of schools attended by the offspring of all the social groups present in the city.

As economic development proceeds, there are corresponding changes in the types of educational inequalities. Initially, the most significant educational inequalities oppose urban to rural populations. While their respective school enrollments differ significantly from one another, such contrasts are more limited among their respective components. But as social differentiation becomes localized and affects most strikingly the urban environment, school enrollments are the most disparate among the urban subpopulations characterized by differing occupational roles and thus by uneven resources. As social differentiation changes in character and becomes more complex, so do the most significant types of educational inequalities. The "have nots" are not the same in countries with differing levels of economic development. In developing societies, the children of rural populations still engaged in subsistence activity are the most unlikely to have access to schools, for their parents have neither the resources nor the orientations appropriate for their schooling. In industrialized societies the children of the urban poor should be the most frequently deprived of such access.

Variations in levels of economic and educational development also affect the forms and the timing of educational inequalities. Among school systems limited in size, social minorities (women, blacks, the poor) have a limited level of participation in *overall* educational structures. Yet as primary schooling becomes compulsory and as the rewards attached to formal education become more visible, all segments of the population are evenly represented at the bottom of the educational hierarchy and almost all children of primary school age attend an elementary institution of some sort. In industrialized nations however, there are still differences among social and cultural groups in terms of the duration and the nature of the studies undertaken by their children. Social and cultural minorities are not fairly represented in institutions of higher learning nor in the secondary schools leading most directly to such institutions.

Thus economic development implies both a greater diffusion of formal schooling and an accentuated differentiation of the selection processes of students. As a society becomes more complex, there are sharper discrepancies in the educational aspirations, abilities, and resources of its various social and cultural components and the types of educational inequalities become proportionately more diversified. The more complex a society, the longer students will wait before dropping out of schools or before engaging in the specialized studies of their choice. In this sense economic development also affects the timing and the forms of educational selectivity.

While economic changes influence access of students to educational institutions, they also influence the recruitment of teachers. As economic development proceeds, male teachers are increasingly drawn from marginal segments of the population for which access to this particular career represents a first step toward upward mobility. Economic development modifies also the sex composition of the teaching force and there is an increasing competition between women derived from fortunate circumstances and men with more modest origins, for entering and moving ahead in that particular occupation.

The role performed by economic development in this respect is yet unclear. Thus Hodge, Treiman, and Rossi compare the prestige positions—and hence the desirability—ascribed to a number of occupations (including teaching) in a variety of countries with differing degrees of economic complexity. Observing that in the 23 nations studied, teaching in primary schools enters in the second fourth of the hierarchy, these authors also demonstrate that occupational status rankings are independent of economic development as measured by gross national product.[46] Dividing the 23 nations into two groups—those whose gross national product was lower than $300 and those whose gross national product never fell below $450—they suggest that these two groups are similar to the United States in prestige evaluations. Many new nations seem to have achieved a structure of occupational evaluations similar to that observed in the most industrialized societies; and there seems to be few variations in the status assigned to teaching. Regardless of their relative economic development, all societies require the services of similar major institutional complexes (hospitals, schools, churches, public and private bureaucracies), which results in similarities in the white-collar prestige hierarchy (doctors, scientists, clerks, teachers). These findings suggest that variations in the hierarchical evaluation of occupations—and hence in the relative desirability of teaching as an occupation—are not necessarily the direct and immediate consequence of variations in economic development.

The relative status of teaching depends in fact upon the number of perceived alternative channels for upward mobility and hence upon patterns of political development. To illustrate, among African students, the declining attraction of teaching jobs results both from economic and political forces. Before independence, such jobs were most highly regarded. Offering the same economic and social rewards (in terms of pay, security of employment, and prestige) as other bureaucratic positions, they also provided individuals with a greater sense of independence from colonial pressures. An African teacher was much more a king in his own classroom than a bureaucrat was in his office. But at the eve of independence, a number of political offices and positions became open to Africans. This resulted in a decrease of the perceived additional rewards attached to teaching positions. After independence, private European concerns became increasingly anxious to hire African supervisory and executive personnel in order to avoid accusations of colonialism; and this particular political force also contributed to the declining value attached to teaching.[47] Although the desirability of teaching as an occupation diminishes with an increase in the number of perceived alternative channels for upward mobility, in turn such a number is not exclusively determined by patterns of economic development but also by political and historical factors.

Economic development and the content of educational roles. Economic changes are associated with changes not only in the recruitment patterns of those actors present in education but also in the functions ascribed to teachers. Changes in technology are necessarily conducive to parallel changes in teaching techniques. As long as the number of books effectively used in a society remains limited, a teacher is the unique mediator of universal knowledge. Written documents are treated as a benchmark against which teachers can evaluate the verbal conformity of their pupils. With the diffusion of printed material these teachers lose their monopoly over access to knowledge. Their role tends to be limited not only to the teaching of a particular discipline but also to the repetition of the materials included in the relevant textbooks; and the power they hold over their students tends to decline accordingly. At this stage of educational development the crucial pedagogical goal is to teach a maximal number of individuals with as limited a teaching force as possible. Clearly the underlying pedagogical question pertains to the difficulties raised by the corresponding depersonalization of the teacher-student relations. The development of other technological changes—specifically the introduction of mass-produced audio-visual materials—has confronted teachers with a set of new dilemmas. While earlier "radical" educators were concerned over the increased dependence of teaching and learning upon mere visual perception, the introduction of audio-visual materials and of computers alters the role ideally assigned to face-to-face communications. Technological development modifies the form of personalization deemed to be most important in the contacts established between students and teachers.

Economic changes also are associated with parallel variations in curricula. Among societies characterized by low patterns of division of labor, schools tend to adopt curriculum aiming at specific and narrowly defined vocational objectives. In Czarist Russia the main function of schools was to train individuals derived from specific segments of society for leadership positions in the Army, the Navy, or in mining and armament industries. In pre-Meiji Japan many schools were aiming at the formation of able samurai whose training had to differ from that imposed upon those with lower social ranking. Indeed many higher samurai looked down upon the teaching of arithmetic as fit only for merchants. In Europe the learning of Latin and of humanities was a privilege reserved to the elites, whereas the acquisition of specific manual and industrial techniques was a responsibility exclusively incumbing upon the children of lower classes.

But with economic development, curriculum must aim at reconciling the conflicting demands of a growing universalism and of the increasing specialization of knowledge. As division of labor becomes more marked, it becomes difficult to determine how much common knowledge teachers should teach to their classes and to what degree they should prepare their students for a particular occupational niche. Is a school of generalists preferable to a school of specialists? [48]

But the question is also to determine "preferable for whom?" Undoubtedly the longer an individual can afford to wait before being engaged in specialized studies, the longer his occupational choices remain open and the freer he is. But such a postponement is increasingly costly for the community; and the enhanced liberty fostered by a general type of education is in fact acquired at the expense of the working population who must support the additional burden. In addition, is this postponement of vocational studies equally relevant for all students? To impose a uniform curriculum can be construed as alienating because it ignores the variety of cultural and social segments from which students are derived. To illustrate, champions of black studies programs in the United States are likely to argue that to delay the exposure of children to the conflicts and tensions resulting from their status as blacks limits rather than enhances the individual liberty of these children. In fact the underlying question is to assess whether uniformities in the courses offered by schools foster a greater equality among the social segments of a particular society or whether they ultimately induce perpetuation of existing inequalities.

Table 4. Percentage of Gross National Product Affected to Education, Health, and Defense in Selected Countries (Expressed in local currency) [a]

	Education	Health	Defense	Year
Europe				
Great Britain	4.6	3.3	6.2	1963
	5.7	3.9	6.0	1967
Portugal	1.3	0.7	4.8	1963
	1.1	0.6	5.1	1966
Asia				
Thailand	2.7	0.5	2.6	1963
	2.3	0.4	2.4	1966
Malaysia	4.5	1.5	2.3	1963
	6.0	2.1	4.7	1967
Africa				
Sudan	1.1	1.0	1.8	1963
	1.2	0.5	2.0	1964
America				
Dominican Republic	1.7	1.3	3.5	1963
	2.5	1.5	3.0	1966
Brazil	0.7	0.3	1.2	1963
	1.4	0.7	2.7	1966

[a] Derived from *United Nations Statistical Yearbook 1968* (New York, Statistical Office of the United Nations, 1969), Tables 155, 186. Our selection is based on variations in levels of economic and political developments.

Economic development and the financing of education.   Economic development commands the resources allocated to educational enterprises; there is a close relationship between the growth of gross national product (GNP) and the growth of educational facilities. In fact educational expenditures vary with the rate of increase of GNP per head, and in Europe, for example, the percentage of GNP spent on education has doubled in the past fifty years.[49] Yet an increase in national resources accentuates the pressures to spend more not only in the field of education but also in other competing fields such as health and defense (Table 4). Further, available evidence suggests that as a nation develops, the costs of higher education decline relatively to those of primary schooling and this casts some doubt on the validity of the educational policies pursued by developing nations which tend to stress the significance of universities at the expense of lower institutions.[50]

While the economist evaluates how governments actually divide national resources among a variety of public services, the sociologist's task is to analyze the social determinants of the underlying choices. Such choices are not necessarily dictated by sheer economic considerations. High educational costs in French-speaking Africa, for example, are moderately related to indicators of economic development.[51] In this case political more than economic factors were the prime determinants of the growth of educational institutions. African political leaders often have been obliged to fulfill the promises they made during the colonial period and to allocate all resources available to the financing of massive educational programs.

Examination of the relationship between economic and educational developments also necessitates an analysis of the mechanisms by which financial resources are allocated to educational activities and of the social factors underlying the nature of those mechanisms.

A centralized educational system is primarily financially supported by national taxes. But among societies where the creation of schools was initially dependent upon local initiatives, educational expenditures were—and are—often covered by local property taxes which mirror the differential wealth acquired by various subgroups. Despite significant changes in economic activities and in sources of wealth and despite the corresponding increased mobility of individual social and economic rights, educational financing often has remained based upon the same system of property taxes. In the United States around 1965, for example, although the major form of wealth was already made of liquid assets, stocks, and bonds, no less than 54 percent of the overall costs of education were still supported by property taxes which accounted for only 8 percent of all governmental resources.[52]

This reflects the differential rates of change undergone by the various institutions of the American society. New conceptions of economic rationality affect perhaps the functioning of public and private industrial or commercial concerns but they have hardly influenced the mechanisms underlying the allocation of educational funds. Such mechanisms remain shaped by the weight of historical precedents rather than by the demands of the current national economic organization. This lag in the patterns of diffusion of new economic conceptions reflects probably the differential scale at which a variety of institutions operate. Whereas competition enlarges the scope of interaction of most public and private economic concerns and makes them respond to economic innovations, the local character of educational enterprises makes them more immediately sensitive to the perceived social order. Correspondingly, changes in the modes of financing educational activities are more likely to result from crises than from a gradual and peaceful evolution. The current rejection of many referendums to increase the taxes earmarked for education suggests the imminence of such a crisis and the necessity to redefine the financial basis of school structures.[53]

But are variations in the mechanisms by which educational resources are allocated associated with corresponding contrasts in the resources effectively spent for educational purposes? The relevant comparisons are difficult to undertake because actual prices differ not only among regions but also among districts and because many authors do not distinguish school revenues from school current expenditures. With the differential patterns of economic and political development of the various states, there are nevertheless growing contrasts in both the amount and the origin of funds allocated to primary and secondary educational enterprises. In 1970 annual current expenditures per student capita in the United States varied between a minimal of $489 for Alabama and a maximal of $1370 for the State of New York.[54] By 1969 only 32 percent of public primary and secondary schools funds in the South were of a *local* origin and hence were derived from property taxes, whereas in the Great Lakes areas 61 percent of corresponding funds had such an origin. The contribution of local taxes seems in fact to be maximal in many of the states where agriculture is both a long-established and lucrative activity. The contributions of *state* funds varied for the same year between a high of 56 percent in the southeast and a low of 26 percent in New England. The *federal* contribution was only 5 percent in the mideast and Great Lakes area but 12 percent in the southeast.

But do the disparities characterizing both the overall resources of the basic government units and the relative importance as well as the origin of the resources they allocate to primary and secondary schools prevent the elimination of inequalities in per pupil expenditure? This erosion requires specific sets of actions on the part of federal, state, and local governments. Data available suggest that the degree to which federal funds erode existing inequities remains limited. Michelson argues that these funds "have only been 21 percent as equalizing as they could have been," and that this equalizing influence varies among regions but does not change markedly over time.[55]

At the state level two distinct strategies can be used to minimize existing inequalities in per pupil expenditure. States may standardize the procedures that basic governmental units use to establish and levy property taxes and they may also impose differential ceilings upon the rates used by districts characterized by varying levels of wealth. But states may also use their own resources to equalize inequalities among districts. Available data suggest however that the equalizing actions of states differ from one another and inequalities in school finances are thus greater among the districts of New England states than in the South. This is because, although the equalizing influence of states varies with the importance of their contributions, it is more closely dependent upon the procedures used to distribute such subsidies. In many cases this equalizing power is limited by the fact that state educational aid involves a floor level (a certain amount of dollars flows unconditionally to all districts) above which the amount of additional funds allocated depends on the performance of pupils—a condition which favors wealthier districts.

There also are intradistrict variations in the mechanisms of resources allocation. Thus in Chicago a complaint presented in 1970 before the United States District Court, Northern District of Illinois, states that instructional expenditures per pupil vary between $413 for the schools with a predominantly nonwhite population and $459 for those where the majority of pupils is white. In Detroit the per pupil cost of the total personnel of elementary schools varies between $495 in institutions where less than 10 percent of the students are black and $430 in those having more than 90 percent black population.

These differentials are in turn associated with contrasts in amenities offered and notably in the quality of teaching (as measured by the verbal ability of teachers or by the teacher student ratio).[56] But can we prove that variations in the amount of educational resources or in their modes of allocation are associated with parallel contrasts in students' educational attainments? Initial analyses of the Coleman report seem to suggest that school resources have little effect on student achievement (although this conclusion is challenged by an increasing number of scholars). Further, available data suggest that variations in the modes of financing education do not necessarily affect enrollments. Despite contrasts in the centralization of French and British educational structures there are no differences in the growth rate of their respective enrollments in institutions of higher learning.

To indicate variations in both allocation mechanisms and their implications is however insufficient. Educational expenditures depend also upon the needs and the relative power of other local agencies. In the same way that at the national level schools compete financially with the military services and other governmental departments, their resources at the local level also vary with the profile of the community and with its commitment to other services. Thus American central cities spend one-third more per capita for welfare and two times more per capita for public safety than suburbs—which are alternatively able to spend nearly twice as much of their total budget upon education as inner cities (Table 5).

**Table 5.   *Expenditures for Public Services in Central Cities and Suburbs in the United States, 1957* ** [a]

	Units	Central Cities	Suburbs
Average per capita expenditure for fire and police	$	27.5	13.0
Proportion of average general expenditure	%	12.6	7.0
Average per capita expenditure for welfare	$	18.2	11.6
Proportion of average general expenditure	%	8.3	6.2
Average per capita expenditure for education	$	58.1	85.9
Proportion of average general expenditure	%	31.3	53.8

[a] Derived from *Racial Isolation in the Public Schools, A Report of the United Commission on Civil Rights, 1967,* p. 26.

Disparities in levels of economic development are associated with parallel contrasts in the recruitment of students and teachers as well as in the definition assigned to their respective roles. As economic development proceeds, so does the extent and the form of social differentiation. As a consequence, the social or cultural minorities most intensely deprived of access to educational amenities do not remain the same and there are parallel changes in the timing and the forms of the mechanisms of social selectivity. Thus, as economic development proceeds, educational inequality tends increasingly to pertain to the duration and the nature of the studies undertaken. Similarly economic changes modify the number of channels of upward mobility available to a particular age group entering the labor force. In turn, variations in that number influence the relative popularity of teaching jobs and hence the selectivity in recruiting teachers. Finally, changes in the economic organization of a society modify the system of interaction between teachers and students. The material used, the number of individuals to be catered to, as well as the definition of the educational enterprise lead pedagogical communications to oscillate between personalization and depersonalization.

Changes in the profiles of teachers and students or in the definition of their roles reflect however both the *amount* of the financial resources devoted to education and the legal mechanisms by which these resources are allocated. Variations in such mechanisms reflect the weight of specific historical antecedents and affect the extent to which formal schooling perpetuates, aggravates, or alleviates existing social inequalities. Thus economic factors influence who *learns* what and who *teaches* what. In this sense economic forces affect the educational manifestations of the dilemma between equality and liberty.

Influence of Education on Economic Organization. In the following pages, I reverse the approach and analyze the influence of educational development on economic patterns of organization and processes, and more specifically on economic attitudes and orientations, individual placement in productive structures and placement in residential structures. In short, I show how formal schooling affects the liberty that individuals and groups enjoy toward economic structures and processes.

Education and economic attitudes. Associated with the use of more rational devices to measure time and space—the two basic categories of human experiences—literacy leads to the division of years, months, and days in exact and systematic sequences.[57] This division facilitates a more systematic distribution of economic activities and thus an enhanced productivity. Literacy also is accompanied by the introduction of more universalistic and more standardized yardsticks in economic transactions. The growing systematization of economic arrangements combined with an emerging specialization of knowledge constitutes a first step toward further division of labor and further economic development.

But does formal schooling itself exert a comparable influence on economic innovations? This speculation is particularly important because of the significance attached to educational planning in the overall development of emerging countries. Evidence available in Africa shows that participation in educational structures does not necessarily induce more positive orientations toward economic innovations.[58] In the Ivory Coast secondary school students attach more importance to security of employment than to opportunities for the promotion they expect to accompany their educational experiences. An overwhelming majority of them prefer to work for large-scale organizations rather than to start independent businesses or enterprises. Since economic development is allegedly a function of entrepreneurship, these observations tend to suggest that the economic future of African countries remains bleak. We must still decide whether the relationship between economic development and individual economic orientations holds true in a variety of geographic and historical contexts. Even if it is true that the economic development of Europe was mainly stimulated by individual entrepreneurs (and it would still remain necessary to compare their educational status with that of both their unsuccessful peers and of the society at large), it does not follow that Africa and the Third World must develop along an identical path. The current development of emerging nations depends upon the economic organization of highly industralized nations and upon the models underlying their current international transactions more than it is affected by references to a somewhat mythical set of historical precedents.

These skeptical views do not only concern Africa. In a study of the problems raised by the economic development of Sardinia, Barberis shows that educational achievement has enabled its rural populations to enter occupations other than agriculture rather than to improve traditional methods of farming.[59] Taking a sample of 120 farmers with differing levels of education, he establishes that individuals with only two years of primary schooling obtain better financial results from their farming activities than their counterparts who have spent five years in primary institutions. Controlling for the areas cultivated, the net returns obtained by the first subgroup are higher than those of the second one. Further, while these returns increased by 25 percent over a period of four years in the first case, they decreased by 9 percent during the same amount of time among the more educated farmers.

The author suggests that a variety of forces account for the absence of relationships between the formal schooling of farmers and their economic productivity. First, it is not sure that the depth of knowledge acquired in school varies as a direct function of the time spent in that institution. Second, it is not sure that the knowledge so acquired is easily transfered into the daily routines and activities of an agricultural enterprise. Third and most important, the returns obtained from educational investments in this respect remain conditioned by historical and cultural factors—notably by the prevailing modes of agricultural exploitation. Thus these returns appear to be influenced by the land tenure systems and by the ownership status of the farmers included in the sample.

The influence of academic experiences on economic attitudes and behaviors is not direct. Further, such an influence probably varies with the functions assigned by the majority of the population to formal schooling, and parents as well as children do not necessarily expect academic experiences to enhance technological innovation. Finally, this influence varies with each specific field of economic activity taken into consideration; academic experience is not evenly relevant to a number of occupations.

Education and economic placement. Nevertheless formal education is not only expected to affect economic orientations but also to influence individual placement in occupational structures. There is undoubtedly a relatively close association between education and occupation. Figure 1 shows that the educational background of workers varies for jobs requiring different skills. While workers with less than an elementary education are rarely skilled, those with a higher educational level are consistently concentrated at the upper rungs of the occupational hierarchy. As economic development becomes more evident, education becomes a prime determinant of occupational placement. Thus while the correlation between the distributions of aggregate educational and occupational scores throughout the census tracts of two West African cities, Accra and Abidjan, does not exceed .500, such a correlation approximates .800 for San Francisco or Rome, in more industrialized and bureaucratic countries.[60] Analysis of individual data in an historical perspective reveals the same trends. While one-fourth of the eighteenth century British scientists had no formal educational background, the corresponding proportion has certainly dropped considerably today.[61]

Yet the influence exerted by educational achievement in this respect should not be exaggerated. First, far from being necessarily direct, the association between education and occupational placement may be indirect. Insofar as education affects the demographic composition of the labor force by influencing birth rates and the length of period during which an age group is out of the labor force, its impact upon the labor market is indirect.[62]

The extent of this influence also varies with the employment sectors

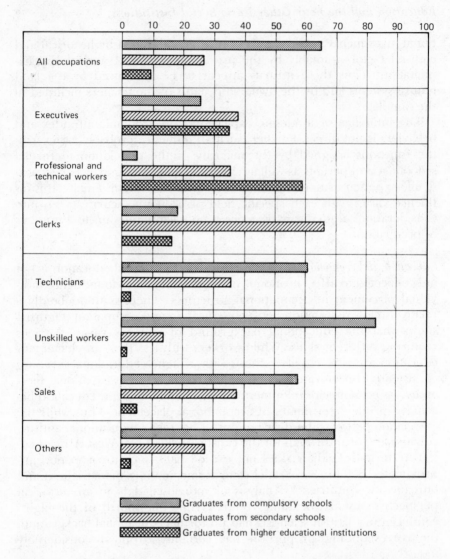

Figure 1. Educational background of various categories of Japanese workers. Derived from *Education in Japan* (Tokyo: Ministry of Education, 1964) as quoted by J. Vaisey, *Education in the Modern World* (New York: McGraw-Hill, 1967), p. 59.

considered. It tends also to be more marked in the initial than in the later stages of individual occupational histories. Undoubtedly formal schooling determines both the point of entry in the labor force as well as the level of initial occupational success; but the relative weight of this particular factor declines as the individual gets older.

For example, Clignet demonstrates that while the overall educational score of the nonmanual workers in the private Camerounian economy is higher than that of their manual counterparts, this particular variable is not necessarily the prime determinant of mobility experienced by these two categories. As time passes the skill level ultimately achieved also depends upon the duration and the diversity of the occupational experiences acquired.[63] Yet the role played by formal schooling as a determinant of upward mobility remains more important for nonmanual than for manual workers. The effects of formal schooling on occupational success are cumulative in the first instance but not in the second. This is because the market structures are more perfect in the case of nonmanual than in the case of manual wage earners. The former have more control of their own occupational history than the latter.

The influence of educational attainment on occupational placement also depends upon the relative discrepancies between rates of educational and economic development. Because it is easier for many governments to open schools than to create jobs, a situation may arise where the number of school graduates exceeds that of openings in the labor market. In a recent study on urban unemployment in Douala, the economic capital of the Cameroun, Clignet and Sween demonstrate that a distinction should be entered between deemployed individuals (that is, individuals who have been displaced out of the labor force) and unemployed individuals (that is, individuals who have never entered the labor market).[64] The former—usually older than the latter—are pushed out of the labor force because of their insufficient educational qualifications. In contrast unemployed individuals do not enter the labor market because this market offers them positions which are not as rewarding as those they hoped to obtain in view of their qualifications. As the number of graduates of African primary and post-primary institutions increases, the significance of the rewards attached to a particular level of academic achievement decreases and graduates are accordingly obliged to modify the expectations inspired by the experiences of their predecessors. Thus differences in the educational attainment of younger Camerounian manual and nonmanual workers are more limited than those observed in their elders.

Further, the relationship between education and employment varies with cultural factors and hence with both the contrasted structures of the local economies and with the different expectations that distinct societies hold toward the returns of formal schooling. Available data show that in both Ceylon and Iran rates of unemployment by education follow a curvilinear pattern and are higher among secondary schools than among primary school leavers and university students; while in the Philippines, in Kenya and in Columbia these rates tend to decline with additional years of schooling. In brief, the returns from schooling are not alike for societies with similarly low levels of development.[65]

Finally, the role played by education on intergenerational mobility varies with the level of economic development achieved by the society at large. Among developing nations (Ghana, the Ivory Coast, Kenya) the recent character of both educational and economic developments enables the sons of farmers not only to be relatively well represented in the local secondary institutions but also to obtain occupational rewards more directly related to their educational attainment than to their parental background.[66]

Among highly industrialized nations the relationship between occupational level and parental backgrounds becomes more complex. Thus Anderson reminds us that in the United States two-thirds of individuals with an occupational status identical to that of their fathers had nevertheless a higher educational level.[67] Similarly 57 percent of those individuals with an occupational level lower than that of their fathers had nonetheless a better education. Chances of downward mobility become as frequent as chances of upward mobility and educational attainment ceases to be the only determinant of access to the most rewarding slots of the occupational market. In the United States less than half of the mobility experienced by the most schooled populations is explainable by their relative formal schooling. This is partly because educational currency does not remain the same for all social or cultural groups. While a black between 24 and 27 years of age with 15 years of formal education and more has a .24 probability to reach an income of $6000 in northern states, his white counterpart has a probability of .52 to earn the same income. For the group 40 to 45 years of age the probability is .42 for the first population but .82 for the second. Thus the combined effects of age and education on income are greater for whites than for blacks.[68]

To conclude, the liberating effects exerted by formal schooling on occupational experiences is differentiated and does not remain the same throughout time. This effect is not the same in societies with differing levels of complexity, nor is it the same for different age groups with differing occupational experiences; nor for the various employment sector considered; nor for various cultural groups within a same society.

Education and residential placement.   Education affects individual placement in consumption structures as well. For example, it influences individual residential placement. Among developing nations individuals with longer academic experiences and better scholastic abilities are more anxious to live in urban than in rural environments. Insofar as they are able to fulfill these aspirations, they contribute to accentuate disparities in the relative development of rural and urban subareas.[69]

Among developed nations education also influences the residential choices of urban populations. Feldman and Tilly argue that in the United States such choices are affected both by economic competition and by cultural factors.[70] The relative income earned by individuals determines the *range* of options available to them in this regard, while their educational and occupational levels shapes the very *nature* of such options. In order to share identical residential amenities, urban subpopulations must share a same educational as well as financial and occupational status. Yet even though manual workers and nonmanual workers with similar incomes are likely to be similarly isolated from those groups who do not enjoy the same resources, their differential occupational subcultures or educational backgrounds lead them to adopt distinctive life styles and to be also isolated from one another.

Educational status affects not only patterns of residential choices but also the entire gamut of individual modes of consumptions. It stimulates responses to innovations and hence responses to the introduction of new products in the market. It also positively influences modes of anticipatory socialization—that is, the extent to which individuals are able to project themselves into their future roles and thus the extent to which they are able and willing to purchase goods and services beyond their current financial abilities.[71] Finally, it also shapes the nature of the decision-making processes in the field of consumption.

To conclude this section, I caution against the views which tend to consider educational experiences as leading to overall and undifferentiated changes in the value systems adopted by individuals. Many educational planners seem to believe that the participation of individuals in specific educational institutions automatically alters their economic orientations and aspirations. Yet to attend an agricultural school in a developing nation where the yields of export cultures (coffee, cocoa, rubber) keep declining does not necessarily induce students to experience an agricultural vocation. Regardless of their training, the students of developing nations tend to be attracted toward the careers they deem to be the most economically and socially rewarding. Similarly to attend a specific institution in such a context does not necessarily lead students to adopt the same attitudes as their counterparts in industrialized nations toward the additional resources to be gained from further education. The influence of schooling on modes of economic decision and participation is not necessarily linear and direct; rather it is likely to be filtered through the main characteristics of the immediate environment in which individuals participate. Educational attainment does not free uniformly all individuals from the constraints of their economic surroundings. It is perhaps a necessary condition in this regard but certainly not a sufficient one.

Education and the Polity.   Undoubtedly political ideologies influence the social definition of educational institutions and roles. "What you want in the state, you must put in the school." This stance reflects the concern that politicans feel toward the characteristics of the school personnel as well as toward the curriculum they should use.[72] Yet political leaders often are disappointed in their expectations and academia—the cradle of intellectual life—has always been the object of strong feelings on the part of the community (often because intellectuals always have dreamt to be the most significant focus of social influence). Throughout history academic institutions have attempted to exemplify ideal forms of liberty and to work out successful experiments of democratic forms of government. The use of expressions such as "community of scholars" or "faculty senate" reflects both the strong political preoccupations and the particular orientations of teachers and school administrators. Nor is there doubt that universities have always been anxious to provide their members with a privileged status, protecting them with a special judicial and police system, with a monopoly over certain types of training programs, and offering them substantial guarantees with regard to freedom of expression and of thought—symbolized in the tenure of teachers. Such claims have stirred the envy of many segments of the society at large, and it is not surprising that teachers often are viewed as eggheads unable to understand the necessities of "Realpolitik."

Influence of Political Factors on Education.   The political importance of educational institutions is reflected in the fact that variations in political arrangements are associated with parallel contrasts in educational settings.

Interaction between the relative centralization of political and educational organizations. In France formal schooling is an inalienable right guaranteed by central authorities to all children living within the boundaries of the national territory. This conception has developed from the centrifugal forces exerted on central institutions and specifically from the fear that Church schools are more concerned with the development of loyalties toward the interests of the clergy or of the Holy See than toward those of the nation. But in many Anglo-Saxon countries formal schooling is considered as an individual privilege to be exerted privately through voluntary agencies or through local communities. Two opposite conceptions of liberty or of democracy lie behind these two distinctive forms of educational development. In the French tradition democracy is supposed to require a certain amount of egalitarianism and stress is placed upon the positive effects of a centralized bureaucracy. But in the British tradition democracy can take place only at the grass root level and its perpetuation necessitates supposedly loose ties among self-centered and self-contained communities.

The implications of this distinction are manifold. First, the perceived dependence of educational equalities upon the centralization of educational institutions leads to uniform and standardized curricula and regulations. French Ministers of Education often boasted to be able to know offhand what pupils of all French classes were doing at a particular hour on a particular day of a particular year. In contrast there are marked variations in the curriculum offered by English or American schools to the students of a same age. Indeed the stress placed upon liberty implies an increase in the choices that students and their parents can make with regard to curriculum. As a result American political scientists have often considered that political structures or processes have no effect on schools.[73]

Second, the centralization of educational institutions leads to marked uniformities in the prerequisites for access to the teaching profession. The French equivalents of the teaching certificate are national rather than local in application and this limits variations in the background and the qualification of teachers. The stress thus placed upon the teachers' homogeneity limits competition among both institutions and individual teachers. There is a monolithic hierarchy of institutions and teachers whose apex is at the very center of the system—that is, Paris. As a result French teachers are able to enjoy a marked liberty toward students and other educational actors. In contrast there are more variations in the background and qualifications of the teaching force of decentralized systems (e.g., in Great Britain or in America). The quality of teachers varies with the resources and the orientations of each community. This situation favors competition among schools and individual teachers. In turn this competition accentuates inequalities in the opportunities offered to children from various social backgrounds. The schools of poor districts have teachers who are less qualified than those of wealthy communities. As a result the chances that students have to gain access to the top of the educational ladder are more limited in the first case.

Third, the centralization of educational systems facilitates a better coordination between schools and labor markets. Depending on the perceived needs of the economy, schools control entry into the labor market by increasing or decreasing the rates of "doubling" (repeats) or of failures in the final examinations. Schools also can control the occupational destination of their graduating populations by orienting them toward courses of study deemed appropriate not only to their abilities and aspirations but also to the needs of the labor market. Centralization enables therefore a government to avoid the multiplication of unemployed graduates and to aim at a universalistic definition of the interaction between educational and economic planning. Centralization however lowers the sensitivity of teachers and educational administrators to the demands of public opinion. French parents participate very little in the elaboration of crucial educational decisions, which are primarily influenced by the objectives of the central bureaucracy. In centralized countries, educational development is often much more a function of the needs experienced by the government to modernize particular sectors of the society, than a function of the aspirations of individuals at the grass root level.

Decentralized systems are less in a position to exert a high control on the quality of their students. The more limited size of each school system fosters a more personalized system of interaction between students and teachers, the latter being also more vulnerable to the community's demands and expectations. Because of this vulnerability, educational development is more often determined by parental demands for education than by the views held by political authorities in the economic sphere. As a corrolary schools should be less responsive to the needs of the labor market than in the French context. The strategies they can use along these lines are more limited, and their dependence upon their clientele makes it difficult to use examinations and guidance as means of adjusting school outputs to the labor market.

Finally, contrasts in the organizational profile of educational institutions are associated with parallel disparities in styles of interaction. Such styles in fact tend to be characteristic of the entire social structure. Thus Crozier demonstrates that there are equivalences in the dominant features of French political, labor, and educational organizations. In these areas the centralized organization of social interaction fosters intense rivalry among individuals in subordinate positions who are unable to unite for constructive activities.[74] This fact characterizes not only French workers who encounter difficulties in organizing effective unions or members of political assemblies who have been unable to constitute efficient and stable majorities, but educational actors as well.

Lack of solidarity limits the face-to-face relations of this variety of actors with one another in these distinctive institutions. There is a marked distance between students and teachers, between teachers and administrators, between workers and managers, and more generally between actors differentially placed in the social, economic, or political hierarchy. Thus most subgroups of French communities hold authoritarian and absolute beliefs, yet adopt routinized and bureaucratic daily life styles. French students and teachers, managers and workers, civil servants of various executive branches—while entertaining a permanent hope for the emergence of "singing mornings"—are obliged to confirm strictly to formal and impersonal rules. This contradiction makes compromises particularly difficult and tends to reinforce the conservatism associated with a centralized administrative pattern. The characteristics of French educational institutions—far from being isolated phenomena—are the by-products of the particular bureaucratic patterns prevailing in the entire French system.

The style of interaction prevailing in decentralized societies is quite different. Thus authority tends to be uniformly functionally limited in scope and individual actors enjoy a larger amount of leeway. Although there is a large number of impersonal rules, they are more likely to cover procedural matters than substantive issues. This facilitates the mobilization of a variety of human resources which would remain untapped under other circumstances. Heightening individual participation and face-to-face contacts, decentralization raises however innumerable problems as to the jurisdictional competence of each decision-making unit. In the United States such problems were manifested during Summer 1969 in the conflict opposing the superintendent of the school system in Evanston to the members of the Board, and the California school system to the Mayor of San Francisco as to control over educational materials. The same jurisdictional conflict has plagued American labor unions and was rampant in the variety of urban crises recently experienced in New York City.

The uniformities characteristic of the French educational system may limit the significance of inequities but alienate individuals and induce them to believe they have little control upon their own fate. But in the United States, even though decentralization facilitates the mobilization of individuals and subgroups, it is nevertheless not evenly spread among all the segments of society and this accentuates inequities in the quantity and the quality of the education to which they have access. The original character of such dilemmas is important at a time when French society is slowly moving toward decentralization and certain segments of the American society are struggling toward a greater centralization. In France what will be the long-term implications associated with the opening of universities amidst communities which are not necessarily centers of political decision? Will this decentralization introduce a desired diversity in styles of interaction prevailing among individuals and institutions or will it alternatively reinforce the preexisting monolithic hierarchy, because newer units are often doomed to enjoy a marginal position or status?

In the United States initial steps toward centralization have involved not only the consolidation and merging of school districts but also the direct delegation of authority by the state to boards operating independently of local control. This strategy intended allegedly to limit competition between educational and other public services and to remove education from partisan politics. Although school efficiency was initially believed to be inversely related to the dependence of the board upon external agencies, more recent research shows that the relative efficiency of dependent and independent school systems depends both upon their relative size and upon the severity of the competition among groups vying for control of the system.[75] Thus data collected from roughly 1200 school districts in 1962–1963 suggest that while *small* school districts independent from municipal governments are able to spend more per pupil than those districts attached to local authorities, there are no such differences between large districts. Further, whether dependent or not, large-sized school districts tend to have rigid institutional arrangements which often enable professionals (teachers and supervisory personnel) to form effective barriers against the changes they deem undesirable.

Centralization of American school systems has induced a rise in the relative power of teachers and administrators. This rise in power is important to understand the conflicts that divided New York City residents in 1968 as to the relative merits of educational centralization. Attitudes toward centralization and decentralization depend in fact upon the relative control that social groups currently hold both toward other social categories at the same societal level (other interest groups—for example, unions, taxpayers' associations) and toward higher institutions of the society at large (legislatures). These attitudes depend thus upon the gains social groups expect to acquire by enlarging or reducing the scope of their interactions with other social groups. Contrast along these lines the orientation of blacks in the large urban centers of the North and in the Deep South. The former tend to assume that centralization accentuates the negotiating power of teachers but does not enable the inhabitant of ghettos to reap the rewards to be derived from mobilizing militants. But blacks in the Deep South have seen decentralization as a mechanism designed to diversify the oppressive strategies of white communities and to reinforce their own political powerlessness.

Thus in the United States—as elsewhere—the outcome of variations in the stress placed upon further centralization or decentralization of educational institutions remains markedly influenced by relevant historical legacies. While French views toward decentralization are contaminated by the notion that this organizational pattern has been long enough advocated by counterrevolutionary forces, the word "centralization" evokes in the United States the arbitrariness of a remote and irresponsible government. Educational organizational patterns cannot escape the weight of historical precedents.

Political development and educational roles.   Political conceptions underlying systems of control influence the curriculum as well as the organizational outlook of educational institutions. Thus there is certainly a relationship between the intensity of nationalism and the content of courses offered. Many studies show how historical studies in French and German schools varied relative to the hostility between these two countries.[76]

In many African countries the few African individuals able to follow a "European-like" academic career before or immediately after World War II were assimilated into metropolitan structures and were supposed to learn at the same rate the same material offered to their European counterparts. There are definite difficulties associated with this particular set-up. For example, French-speaking Africans obliged to learn about the innumerable virtues of French civilization—notably in Africa—did not necessarily perceive their academic experience as rewarding and justified.[77] With independence, many African political leaders whose platform was most often based on the educational short-comings of colonialism became most anxious to free school curricula from too obvious European influences.[78] Their desires were reinforced by the notion that to build a nation requires massive emotional mobili-zation, which in turn can only be achieved through a celebration of Af-rican traditions and the actualization of potential nationalist orienta-tions. Yet the success of nation building also requires new states to maintain administrative practices and norms as congruent as possible with those of modern states. This last requirement implies that local elites must be trained according to "universalistic" orientations—or at least to orientations compatible with those prevailing among the indus-trial states likely to give them assistance. Thus African new nations are confronted with a difficult dilemma. While mobilization of the masses necessitates a definite rejection of the colonial past and an "Africani-zation of the curriculum," the second requirement leads to a reinforce-ment of European-oriented courses and standards.

The same dilemma seems to be currently experienced by Afro-Americans in the United States. The teaching of Afro-American courses will not give any additional jobs to unemployed blacks who most urgently need courses that will enable them to acquire desirable skills. Yet black nationalists counterargue that hiring in the United States is not only an economic but also a political act and that the chances for blacks to find employment increase with the intensity of the pressures imposed upon white employers. These pressures cannot be exerted as long as blacks are not highly organized and mobilized; and mobilization can be achieved only through courses celebrating the merits and virtues of black cultures. To paraphrase W. E. B. Dubois, "only a color organization may be successful against a color line." Al-though the motto "Black is beautiful" is perhaps only one moment in the dialectic of the relations between black and white, this moment is nonetheless necessary to achieve an integration which would be based on the mutual acceptance of plurality rather than on the assimilation of blacks by the white majority. For African as well as American blacks the dilemma is thus to identify the circumstances under which educational process should "liberate" students as individuals or as members of op-pressed minorities. Indeed schools should not offer the same curricu-lum when liberty is defined in individual as opposed to collective terms.

Influence of Education on Political Arrangements. Whereas differing political structures induce variations in the definition that individuals and subgroups hold of educational liberty and equalities, educational experiences also modify both the placement of individuals in political structures and the set of attitudes and orientations they adopt in this respect. The main question is then to determine what kinds of political attitudes and behaviors are influenced by formal schooling. It is also to determine the intensity, the duration, and the universality of such an influence.

Influence of education on political attitudes.   A number of studies show that the scope of interaction developed by an individual varies as a direct function of his level of formal schooling. As this level becomes higher, the spectrum of political topics in which the individual is involved becomes broader. The higher this level, the wider is also the range of persons with whom this individual is willing to discuss political matters. Finally, the higher this level, the more the individual is likely to entertain optimistic feelings about the control he seems to be able to exert on his immediate surroundings. These three forces tend to affect the level of tolerance that individuals show toward social events. Education tends to foster a liberal approach toward political and social issues.[79]

However, education is a necessary but insufficient condition in this regard and its effects are not independent of the dominant features of the environment. In his study of attitudes toward communism and civil liberties Stouffer shows that variations in the levels of education attained by Northern and Southern segments of the American population or by metropolitan and rural residents are not sufficient to account for the differential amounts of tolerance displayed toward these issues.[80] The overall educational, economic, and political outlook of the Northern metropolitan populations makes it easy for the educated individual to be liberal, whereas his Southern counterpart is more likely to be viewed and treated as a deviant. Liberalism is a form of conformity in the first instance but a deviance in the second context.

If the effects of formal schooling on individual political attitudes vary among the various components of a same social system, they are likely to vary even more significantly crossculturally. The intensity of these effects depends upon the distance separating socializing institutions from one another. Thus while in highly developed and integrated countries schools complement the influence of families, churches, and mass media, their role in new nations is to counterbalance the more conservative impact of familial groups or of traditional institutions.[81] Under such conditions it is one thing to assert that the socializing burden of schools weighs heavier in developing than in developed nations

but it is another to evaluate the differential effectiveness of the two
types of educational institutions.

Further, the direction of the socializing effects of formal schooling
depends upon the conceptions that different cultures hold of both political processes and the role that intellectuals may play in such processes.[82] For instance, although education uniformly enhances individual access to political informations and stimuli, the effects of education
in this regard are more marked in the United States than in France.[83]
The difference between these two countries probably results from contrasts both in the significance attached to French and American mass
media and in the relative position occupied by intellectuals in the two
social systems. The decentralized nature of American institutions enables individuals not only to take frequent initiatives in a variety of
social arenas but also to quickly evaluate the efficiency of such initiatives. The ensuing visibility of political institutions enhances the potential relevance and hence the consumption of political information, particularly among the educated segments of society. This high
consumption of political information is reinforced by the fact that the
American society tends to view mass media as one variety of economic
enterprise and treats the products of such media like those of any other
market. In contrast the centralization of French political institutions
not only limits private initiatives but also makes such initiatives more
difficult to evaluate. Further, the history of centralization in France has
led governments as well as private citizens to evaluate the products of
mass media in strict political terms and hence to consider political information as a mechanism by which a government attempts arbitrarily
to maintain its control or, alternatively, by which the opposition tries to
overthrow the existing social order. Under such conditions incentives
to absorb political information are fewer in France than in the United
States, particularly in the case of educated persons who are afraid of
being manipulated. Thus the association that Lerner claims to exist between educational development and the degree of empathy of a population (as measured by its consumption of newspapers and radio and
television programs) is more likely to characterize English-speaking and
decentralized cultures than their French-speaking and centralized
counterparts.[84] In the latter case education is as likely to induce political skepticism as to enhance the degree of control that individuals believe to exert on their private political destiny.

Influence of education on political participation.   Education affects not only
political orientations but political participation as well. A number of

studies in the United States show that participation in voluntary associations increases with level of schooling.[85] There is in fact a chain of interdependences between (a) social background—which facilitates participation in educational structures, (b) schooling—which mediates participation in voluntary organizations, and (c) membership in such associations—which leads to a better integration of the individual in his social surroundings and eventually facilitates his further upward mobility. Correspondingly it has often been suggested that political office holders are always characterized by a higher level of formal education than the population at large.

Yet political participation is not only influenced by the level of formal schooling attained but also by the kind of studies undertaken. Etzioni notes, "Mobilizers are more likely to come from subgroups concerned with synthetising rather than analytical work (with a training in the liberal arts rather than in the professions), and from groups which are relatively immune or invulnerable to political and economic pressures, such as faculty or students." [86] Indeed mobilizers have been philosophers, historians, priests or pastors, and more recently sociologists. Sensitive to the mobilizing power of French students in social sciences, Lefebvre has observed that it had been a serious political mistake to transfer the school of social sciences rather than the schools of engineering or of sciences from Paris to Nanterre, a shantytown area of uprooted immigrants.[87] Whereas future physicians or chemists are not supposed to be sensitive to the physical conditions of their surroundings, French students in social sciences saw in the slums surrounding their new university the very symbol of the degenerating social order they were so anxious to denounce as a characteristic of the society at large. Thus Lefebvre hints that the ill-conceived transfer of that school into a delapidated part of the Paris metropolitan area was instrumental in the uprising of May 1968.

In the same way that we have suggested that the relationship between education and political attitudes varies crossculturally, it is easy to demonstrate that the association between formal schooling and political participation varies among the distinctive subcultures of a particular society. Thus Greer hypothesizes and then verifies that the use an individual makes of his educational assets in the urban context depends upon the social composition of the area in which he lives.[88] Residential areas differ from one another in terms of their social rank (that is, the occupational and educational level of the adult population), their life style, and their ethnic composition.

The extent to which a person translates his educational experiences into a form of political participation depends on the relative similarity of the educational experiences acquired by his or her neighbors and hence on the social rank of the local area. The form of this translation is likely to vary also with the dominant life style of the neighborhood. Individual and collective dependence upon immediate surroundings cannot be the same in areas characterized by a familistic or, alternatively, an urban life style. Thus the population of highly urbanized areas is characterized by a high proportion of active women, a low fertility rate (hence a low proportion of large-sized families), and a high sex ratio (that is, a disproportionate number of males as compared to that of females). Such a population is characterized also by a low level of neighboring, a low level of participation in locally-based voluntary associations, and a low propensity to read community-oriented journals, magazines, or newspapers. In contrast the large number of inactive women with many children living in those urban environments characterized by a familistic life style enhances the dependence of all individuals upon their immediate surroundings, and hence their level of neighboring and of participation in locally-based social movements.

In turn such contrasts are associated with parallel disparities in the form of political participation adopted by the educated residents of these two types of urban milieux. Educated persons living in highly urbanized areas are more likely to be cosmopolitan in their orientations and are therefore more likely to participate in associations interested in national and international issues. Further, the low level of immediate pressures exerted on them makes them more prone to be political voyeurs—that is, more prone to maintain an open access to communication flows without getting committed to a particular mode of political action.

The notion that the relationship between individual levels of formal education and of political participation varies with the social context is verified at the international level as well. Thus it varies with the rigidity of the prevailing systems of social stratification. The influence exerted by educational attainment on both voting and active political participation is greater in the United States where each political party recruits its membership from a variety of social groups than in the case of many West European countries where the social composition of political parties is narrower and more closely follows class lines.[89] The openness of political parties to all segments of society obliges each one of them to court the favors of the most educated individuals. Alternatively the high dependence of these parties on particular social classes leads them to minimize the influence they attach to education as a valid criteria for holding a political office. In addition the association between schooling and participation in political offices is not independent of the rate of educational development of the country as a whole. A high rate of development tends often to restrict the political mobility of new generations and is hence associated with an accentuation of tensions between incumbents and aspirants.[90]

To conclude, the political implications attached to the educational status of a person—far from being universal—vary with the nature of the environment. As a result it becomes particularly important for the social scientist to identify the limits within which the politically liberating influence of participation in educational structures remains constant.

Education and Religion. Of all basic societal functions, religion is the one most closely associated with education and socialization. This results mainly from historical factors. The first documents to be printed were of a religious nature and the main role of early teachers was to act as middlemen between written texts considered to be sacred—and hence immutable—and children who were supposed to memorize these texts. Reading was justified only insofar as it accelerated the internalization of religious and moral beliefs. This happened in Muslim schools, in Indian institutions of the Vedic tradition, and in the medieval schools of the Catholic Church in many countries of western Europe as well as early Protestant schools. In his study of the British working class E. P. Thompson notes, "Under the influence of the Evangelicals the function of education began and ended with the moral rescue of the poor. Not only was the teaching of writing discouraged but many Sunday school students left the schools unable to read." This, adds Thompson, was perhaps a blessing in view of the material that they were supposed to read.[91] Thus the first type of formal education to develop is often religious in nature. Administered by the clergy, it aims primarily at a proper ethical socialization of the individual.

The historical influence of churches on education explains the persisting conflict between those who hold that the prime function of educational institutions is to teach morality and those who view schools as centers of diffusion of cognitive skills and knowledge. At the institutional level this dilemma underlies the conflicts pertaining to the relative educational responsibilities of the church and the state. Champions of an educational philosophy stressing the preeminence of morality over cognitive skills are likely to favor parochial or private institutions. The power historically held by such champions explains the severity of the conflicts which have opposed French public and private teachers during the nineteenth and the first half of the twentieth centuries. Similarly, in American society, the constitutionality of the rules obliging children to attend religious ceremonies in the context of educational institutions is repeatedly challenged.

If it is thus difficult to assess the relative preeminence of political over religious factors in education, it is equally difficult to evaluate the relative importance of religions as opposed to economic forces. Although a classical Marxist analysis tends to see the endeavors of churches in the educational process as dictated by economic considerations, an analysis of the early development of American schools reveals divergences in economic and religious orientations and suggests that religious divisiveness may have more serious educational implications than convergent economic interests.[92]

But the problem of the relationship between church and state, or between morality and knowledge is differentially perceived by the various religions. American Jews are the least concerned; in his sample of the Detroit Area Study Lenski notes that three-quarters of his Jewish respondents do not think of necessary incompatibilities between the teachings of science and those of their religion.[93] The situation is more complex among white Protestants. Schools located in states where fundamentalist sects prevail are religion oriented, and in a sample of Kentucky schools examined in 1960, 100 percent of the institutions visited engaged in programs of bible reading, 87 percent of them had Christmas programs, 44 percent gave religious materials to their students, and 27 percent let churches use their property.[94] On the other hand, the Methodists have established distinctions between various types of intellectual enquiry, and have valued the acquisition of useful knowledge as godly and full of merit. "In the early Victorian culture," writes Thompson, "there is the non-conformist parson with his hand on the Old Testament and his eye on the microscope." [95] Although half of the Protestants included in the sample of Lenski view the possibility of conflicts between the teachings of their religion and of science, only 23 percent of them perceive this conflict as potentially serious. More important, the perceived intensity of the conflict declines as one moves up the educational ladder.

This conflict is experienced most acutely within the Catholic church. This is not surprising in view of its centralizing tendencies which discourage unorthodox research. European philosophers and scientists of the period preceding 1789 (such as Galileo Galilei) learned it the hard way. The notion of a collective truth controlled at the very center of the system through the Holy Office probably contributes to make individual research an anxiety raising activity. For this reason Catholic students in the United States are believed often to experience intense conflict between science and religion. For similar reasons American Catholic colleges and universities have been said to produce far less than their fair share of scientists.

Yet the influence of churches along these lines is not independent of the larger social context in which they operate. When other factors are held constant, European Catholic countries probably have produced their fair share of scientists. In other words the intensity of the conflict experienced between the teachings of science and of religion probably varies as an inverse function of the number of Catholics in the overall society and of the social position that they have achieved in the general structure. Pressures toward Catholic conformity and the ensuing fear of betraying cannot take the same form in Catholic-dominated countries (e.g., France or Italy) and traditionally Protestant countries (for example, Sweden or the United States).

Influence of Religion on Education. Potential discrepancies between the orientations of various religious and educational institutions raise two kinds of questions:

1. Are variations in the religious backgrounds of individual students associated with parallel contrasts in their levels of academic achievement? The influence exerted by religion is not necessarily independent of that played by socioeconomic and cultural variables.

2. Are discrepancies in the definitions that public and private educators give of morality and knowledge associated with variations in the effectiveness of the socialization of their respective students? An examination of differences in the political and social attitudes of students with the same religious background but enrolled in distinctive types of institutions may give an answer to this question.

Religion and educational achievement. It can be anticipated that where there are discrepancies in the cognitive and emotional style of a particular religion and of a public school system, there will be fewer children of that religion in the public school system and their academic performances will be less adequate. Thus, in Anglo-Saxon countries dominated by Protestant ideologies, Catholic families usually do not get a proportionate share of educational facilities. But in the American sample studied by Lenski, there are no significant differences in the overall educational distributions of the various white denominational groups. Yet the rates of dropouts are much higher among Catholics (only 48 percent of them completed the cycle of studies they had begun) than among Protestants (the corresponding proportion is 61 percent) or among Jews (71 percent). These differences persist when socioeconomic variables are taken into consideration. The problem remains to explain such disparities.

Initially it appears clearly that obedience to the Catholic faith favors much more intellectual heteronomy—that is, obedience to the dictates of others—than intellectual autonomy. Regardless of their social class the Catholic respondents in the Detroit sample used by Lenski attach more importance to this demand than their white Protestant counterparts.[96] The stress placed by Catholics upon this particular value and upon the corresponding style of interaction is at variance not only with the style that schools attempt to impose upon children but also with the mechanisms of upward mobility prevailing in the present American society. As a result rates of upward mobility are significantly lower among American Catholics than among their Protestant counterparts.

Yet at the same time the higher dropout rates observed among Catholics could be attributed to the particularly large size of most American Catholic families. Insofar as a large family often reflects a low level of aspirations toward upward mobility, Catholic children are unlikely to acquire within their familial environment the drives which supposedly underlie academic achievement. Since all large-sized families prevent frequent interactions between adults and children, Catholic children, like those of all large-sized families, are unable to anticipate the demands which are going to be imposed upon them by their teachers. Thus the negative influence exerted by Catholicism on academic achievement is eventually spurious since it is the *demographic* characteristics of American Catholics rather than their *beliefs* which are at stake.

Similarly the effects of Catholicism on academic achievement are likely to vary both with the ethnic and the socioeconomic characteristics of the populations investigated. The interpretations that Poles, Irish, Italians, and Mexicans give of Catholicism are not necessarily identical, and one might expect marked differences in the discrepancy between the cognitive and emotional styles of these ethnic groups and those prevailing in the official school system. The importance of ethnicity is indirectly suggested by Lenski when he observes that Catholic students enrolled in Catholic-controlled schools are more likely to entertain high educational aspirations than their counterparts enrolled in public schools.[97] Indeed in New Haven the Catholics with higher IQ and higher motivations are enrolled in parochial schools while public schools tend to be the dumping grounds for the less gifted and problem Catholic children who usually come from particular ethnic minorities.[98] The situation seems to be somewhat analogous in Bay City, Massachusetts where the parochial school of French Canadian neighborhoods caters primarily to the needs of the most gifted French Canadian children.

Finally, the negative effect of Catholicism on educational attainment varies with the dominant characteristics of the public school system as a whole. In the Ivory Coast, Clignet and Foster show that while the various religious groups of the country tend to be evenly represented in the postprimary system, Catholics are proportionately more numerous than any other group in the more prestigious classical high schools—that is, those that teach humanities, Latin, and Greek.[99] In this case affiliation with the Catholic church is an excellent mirror of the overall modernization achieved by individual families and hence of their abilities to transfer to their children the modern skills demanded by European-dominated schools. In addition it could be suggested that in this context, both the local Catholic church and the French-dominated school system attach a similar high value to intellectual heteronomy. In both institutions, dependence upon others is a prerequisite rather than an obstacle to individual achievement and upward mobility.

While the influence of Catholicism on academic achievement is thus positive in the Ivory Coast school system, that exerted by Islam is negative. The overall representation of Muslim students in postprimary institutions as well as their general level of academic performance is lower than that of the remaining local society. This is predictable in view of the sharp discrepancies opposing the traditional teaching styles of Islam and those of a modernizing world. Yet contrasts between the educational achievements of Muslim and other students disappear when the socioeconomic level of the students' families is taken into consideration.[100] Hence the negative influence that Islam is deemed to exert on formal schooling is not necessarily attributable to this religion per se but rather to the dominant psychological outlook of subpopulations with a low level of participation in modern structures that tend to be particularly numerous in contemporary Islamic cultures. The impact of a particular religious system on educational participation is not independent of the position that the holders of this belief occupy in the general social structure.

Socialization in public and private schools.   The second problem raised by
potential disparities in the values of the church and the state concerns
the differential profile characterizing students with the same religious
background but enrolled in varying institutions. Various Catholic subpopulations do not necessarily experience the dilemma between morality and knowledge with the same intensity and there are significant
variations in the enrollments of various subgroups in private schools.
In France, for example, Catholic enrollments in Catholic schools vary
along regional lines and are substantially higher in the western and
eastern parts of the country than in the south where Catholicism is sub-
verted by marked anticlerical tendencies. These schools are similarly
more frequently attended by rural than by urban populations and by
middle classes rather than by lower segments of the population. In the
United States enrollments in Catholic institutions differ significantly
along ethnic lines. Almost one-half of the Catholics coming from
northwest Europe have attended parochial schools as against only one-
fourth of the migrants coming from southern or eastern Europe.
This difference may reflect variations in the relative anticlericalism of
these two populations. Italians are traditionally more anticlerical than
the Irish. It also reflects variations in the degree to which both ethnicity
and religion play a significant role in local social stratification. Rossi
thus argues that Irish enrollments in the private schools of New England result from the underdog status traditionally imposed upon this
group by the Bostonian Protestant elites. Private schools are less likely
to be popular in places or among ethnic groups where Catholics feel
themselves to be merely another Christian denomination.
    To attend a Catholic institution affects the familial, social, occupa-
tional, and political orientations of Catholic individuals. First, it favors
Catholic orthodoxy. American Catholics raised in Catholic institutions
are more likely than their counterparts educated in public institutions
to attend Mass regularly and to receive communion during Lent. They
are also more likely to believe that the Catholic church is the only
Church of God. Second, graduates of Catholic schools are stricter than
graduates of public institutions concerning the problems of domestic
morality. For example, the stand taken by the former against divorce
or birth control is more vigorous than that of the latter. In this sense
Catholic institutions contribute to the perpetuation of a Catholic morality. Third, attending a parochial school tends to reinforce the allegiance of the individual to the Church—particularly when its welfare
is at stake. The former students of parochial schools are more likely to
consider religious leaders as reference groups in elections. Fourth, al-

though it has been argued that Catholic populations enrolled in parochial elementary and secondary schools have later on a lower level of
educational and occupational attainment, recent data suggest that this
proposition is not tenable. In the past, individuals trained in parochial
schools often may have required more time to secure their higher academic degrees than their counterparts enrolled in other types of elementary and secondary schools. However among younger groups—
those under 25 years of age in 1960—individuals with a parochial
school background had neither a lower nor slower advancement than
those with other educational experiences. As differences between the
advancement of the two populations decline it becomes increasingly
clear that the effects of a parochial education cannot be interpreted
independently of economic factors. Academic creativity requires not
only a certain affluence but also the confidence that this affluence is
likely to last.[101]

Lastly, there is no evidence that parochial schools alienate individual
Catholics from their communities. Despite marked variations along ethnic and regional lines a Catholic education seems to predispose individuals to shift away from their traditional Democratic allegiances toward
Republicanism. Truly enough this shift is a response to the strong appeals toward traditional morality developed by so many Republican
candidates.

To conclude, the effects of a parochial education are not independent
of the ethnic or social composition of their population nor of the standing of this population in the society at large. With a decline in the
stigmas initially attached to Catholic populations, there should be parallel changes in the functions of parochial schools. In many instances
such institutions are no longer religious ghettos but act indeed as
centers of pedagogical innovation.

Influence of Education on Religion.   Insofar as a higher level of schooling enhances both knowledge and commitment, one can speculate
about its religious implications. Although increased knowledge should
be conducive to a greater level of tolerance and skepticism, increased
intellectual commitment may also exert an opposite influence. Positive
ecumenical orientations tend to prevail among persons with higher education. In countries with deep-rooted religious traditions (for example, Yugoslavia) university students attach less importance to the significance of religious endogamy than the population at large. More
intriguing is the apparent effect of higher education on the political
orientations of religious subgroups. In France highly educated Protes-

tants and Catholics took liberal positions during the Algerian war. Following the recommendations of Christian magazines (*Esprit, Réforme, Témoignage Chrétien*), many of them were prosecuted for the humanitarian assistance they gave to nationalist leaders. A similar trend exists in the United States with the influence of Christian magazines and the high participation of educated clerics against the war in Vietnam or against the infringements imposed upon the rights of black people.

Conclusions.   After this long trip through time and space it is time to summarize. First, although there is a network of reciprocal influences among the various components of a social system, each one of these components is also shaped by the history of its own development. The weight of history varies among institutional arenas and is probably maximal in the case of education. Although formal education allegedly serves the current needs of an entire society or its main subsegments, the definition given of those needs tends to take place in a retrospective rather than a prospective framework. This is because the main function of school is to ensure a maximal continuity of norms, values, and techniques. This is also because of age differences between students and teachers, and because the structures of educational institutions enable older age groups to maintain the *status quo*.

While social change tends to be associated with the emergence of convergent organizational patterns in a variety of institutional arenas, the weight exerted by history upon educational development limits such convergences in the educational sphere. Trajectories and rates of educational changes are likely to remain highly distinctive across cultural lines. This limits the extent to which educational institutions and experiences introduce drastic changes in the organization of familial, political, economic, or religious subsystems. Both the present and the past nature of these subsystems affect the current outlook of educational roles and institutions more than they are affected by it.

This analysis has enabled me to exemplify the various "regularities" that sociologists intend to isolate in the field of education:

1.   The first of these regularities pertains to the competing influences of social and historical factors on educational roles and developments. Increases in the level of formal schooling in Africa are not immediately associated with corresponding changes in familial patterns; and an increased educational attainment enables African individuals to restore or to maintain their faithfulness to their cultural history. Similarly the increase in the scale of the American economic system has not been

conducive to a similar increase in the scale of educational institutions which remain highly decentralized. History weighs heavier on educational than on economic organizations; therefore their rates of change are different.

2.   The second regularity pertains to the significance of the changes in the direction and the magnitude of the relationships involving educational variables. For example, the growth of educational institutions in contemporary developing nations is of greater magnitude than was the growth of similar institutions in nineteenth century Europe. Similarly the value attached to centralization oscillates: for example, blacks in Northern ghettos or in the Deep South do not expect to reap the same rewards from this particular organizational pattern.

3.   The final regularity pertains to the frequent nonlinear character of interaction between educational and other basic institutions. This is because specific links between education and each of the other societal institutions cannot be isolated from a more general context. The chances for educated women to be gainfully employed are not independent of their relative scarcity. Similarly the extent to which American Catholics attend Catholic institutions depends on their ethnic background and is maximal in areas with a history of ethnic-religious conflict.

Having stressed the relevance of comparative strategies I have indicated not only how the society at large affects the forms of the dilemma between equality and liberty in the educational field but also how formal education changes the meaning that individuals give to this dilemma in other arenas of social participation. Thus I have shown that the liberating effects of schooling and hence the quantity and the quality of the educational services to which a population has access depends upon (*a*) their familial backgrounds, (*b*) the amount and the allocation mechanisms of resources devoted to educational purposes, (*c*) the types of political control exerted on school structures, and (*d*) the religious orientations of the community at large. Alternatively I have suggested how variations in formal schooling affect the mechanisms by which individuals choose their mates and influence the style of their conjugal interaction as well as their child rearing practices. Similarly I have shown how variations in educational attainment provide individuals with distinct rewards and expectations in the fields of politics, of economics, and of religion. In this sense I have demonstrated that equality of educational opportunities is not an end in itself but rather a means necessary for gaining access to the good life.

Yet I have also shown the limits of the concept of equality of educational opportunities. First, a variety of cultures do not attach the same value to this particular type of equality; there are contrasts in the financial, political, and legal measures that governments edict in this regard. In addition, equality of educational opportunities acts perhaps as a necessary condition for enhancing individual liberty but it is not a sufficient condition. An individual's station in familial, political, economic, or religious structures does not depend exclusively upon his educational status and individuals with a *same* level of educational attainment may still enjoy differing economic or social rewards. This is because the relevant contributions of education to the dilemma between liberty and equality in other arenas are relative both in space (across cultures) and in time (throughout history).

NOTES AND REFERENCES

1. For a general discussion of these themes, see E. Durkheim, *Education and Sociology* (Glencoe: Free Press, 1956).

2. See E. Panofski, *Architecture and Scholasticism* (London: Lathrobe, The Archaeology Press, 1954).

3. See M. Katz "From Voluntarism to Bureaucracy in American Education," *Sociology of Education,* Vol. 44, 1971, pp. 297–332.

4. See A. Touraine, *Le mouvement de Mai ou le Communisme Utopique* (Pairs: Le Seuil, 1968).

5. See R. Winch, *The Modern Family* (New York: Holt, Rinehart and Winston, 1964), Chapter 1.

6. E. Litwak and H. Meyer, "A Balanced Theory of Coordination Between Bureaucratic Organizations and Community Primary Groups," *Administrative Science Quarterly,* Vol. 11, 1966, pp. 31–59.

7. For a general distinction between conscious and unconscious models, see C. Levi Strauss, *Anthropologie structurale* (Paris: Plon, 1958), Chapter 5.

8. R. Dreeben, *On What is Learned in School* (Reading, Mass.: Addison-Wesley, 1968), Chapter 2, 3.

9. For a general review of the literature on this question, see A. Anastasi, "Intelligence and Family Size," *Psychological Bulletin,* Vol. 53, 1956, pp. 187–209.

10. See Lees and Steward, "Family or Sibship Position and Scholastic Ability," *Sociological Review,* Vol. 5, 1957, pp. 173–190. For example, the authors show that it is among only older children that academic abilities are maximal. They also show that variations in abilities of sibship position are not alike for both sexes and that such variations are not necessarily associated

with corresponding variations in enrollments. For example, younger children have perhaps less aptitudes than their elders but they make a more effective use of them. See also B. Bernstein, "Social Class and Linguistic Development: A Theory of Social Learning," in A. Halsey, J. Floud, and C. Anderson, *Education, Economy and Society* (New York: Free Press, 1963), pp. 288–314.

11. P. Blau and R. Duncan, *The American Occupational Structure* (New York: Wiley, 1963), p. 314.

12. O. Brim, "Family Structure and Sex Role Learning of Children," *Sociometry*, Vol, 1958, pp. 1–16.

13. For a more general treatment, see R. Clignet and J. Sween, *Urbanization and Life Styles in Africa* (in preparation).

14. See J. H. Habbakuk, "Family Structure and Economic Change in XIXth Century Europe," *The Journal of Economic History*, Vol. 15, 1955, pp. 1–13.

15. K. Kammeyer, "Birth Order and the Feminine Sex Role Among College Women," *American Sociological Review*, Vol. 31, 1966, pp. 508–515.

16. See D. McClelland, *The Achieving Society* (Princeton: Van Nostrand, 1961), p. 374.

17. See R. Clignet and P. Foster, *The Fortunate Few* (Evanston, Ill.: Northwestern University Press, 1966), Chapter 3, 4. However, the study does not indicate whether there are variations in the school enrollments of children born of women with differing matrimonial ranks.

18. See R. Clignet, *Many Wives Many Powers* (Evanston, Ill.: Northwestern University Press, 1970), Chapter 8. Among the secondary school students from the matrilineal cluster of the Ivory Coast, 35 percent of those derived from rural monogamous families thought that academic success was the most important paternal demand, against 27 percent of those students belong to polygynous families. Among the patrilineal Bete students the corresponding percentages were 26 and 38 respectively. Correspondingly 66 percent of the patrilineal students coming from polygynous families entertained a high level of occupational aspirations, against 50 percent of their counterparts coming from monogamous households, whereas the pattern tended to be reverse among the students derived from a matrilineal background.

19. This observation presupposes that the patrilineal and matrilineal ethnic groups have a similar level of exposure to modernization.

20. For a review of the literature on the influence that domestic power structure exerts on academic achievement, see D. Lavine, *The Prediction of Academic Performance* (New York: Russell Sage, 1965), notably Chapter 6.

21. See G. Elder and C. Bowerman, "Adolescent Perception of Family Power Structure," *American Sociological Review*, Vol. 29, 1964, pp. 551–567.

22. See F. Strodtbeck, "Family Interaction, Values and Achievement," in R.

Winch and J. Goodman, eds., *Selected Studies in Marriage and the Family* (New York: Holt, Rinehart and Winston, 1958), pp. 364–383.

23. See for example B. Rosen and R. d'Andrade, "The Psycho Social Origins of Achievement Motivation," *Sociometry*, Vol. 22, 1959, pp. 185–218.

24. See for a further discussion D. Lynn, "The Process of Learning Parental and Sex-role Identification," *Journal of Marriage and the Family*, Vol. 28, 1965, pp. 466–470.

25. French sociologists J. and M. Van Bockstaele suggest that insofar as the psychoanalysis of an individual evolves around the revival of his early childhood, the therapy of formalized groups (such as in a classroom) should evolve around the revival of the familial relations experienced by members of the groups. See J. Van Bockstaele et al., "Quelques remarques sur le transfert sociologique et ses conditions d'observation," *Communication au VIe congrès mondial de sociologie,* 1966. See also by the same authors, "Nouvelles Observations sur la définition de la socianalyse, *L'Annee Sociologique,* Vol. 19, 1963, pp. 275–335.

26. R. Clignet and J. Sween, *op. cit.*

27. See A. Fiamengo, "L'Instruction et la choix du conjoint," in R. Castel and J. C. Passeron, eds., *Education, development et demoncratie* (Paris: Mouton, 1967), pp. 137–150.

28. A. Hollingshead, "Cultural Factors in the Selection of Marriage Mates," in R. Winch and J. Goodman, eds., *op. cit.,* pp. 486–496.

29. For a discussion of these results, see L. Barnett, "Research on International and Interracial Marriage," in *Marriage and Family Living,* Vol. 25, 1963, pp. 105–107. However, the author indicates variations in the results given by various surveys in this respect. Concerning interreligious marriages, Lee Burchinal indicates similarly variations in the educational characteristics of individuals contracting interfaith marriages. While a majority of students at the University of Minnesota seem to date partners from religious backgrounds other than their own, another study seems to indicate that favorable attitudes toward interreligious marriage vary as a reverse function of educational attainment. See L. Burchinal, "The Premarital Dyad and Love Involvement," in H. Christensen, *Handbook of Marriage and the Family* (Chicago: Rand McNally, 1964), pp. 652–653.

30. See R. Winch, *op. cit.,* pp. 339–354; and for a crosscultural study of this phenomenon, W. Goode, *World Revolution and Family Patterns* (New York: Free Press, 1963).

31. See W. Goode, *op. cit.,* Chapter 2 and Conclusion.

32. See P. Blau and R. Duncan, *op. cit.,* Chapter 11, notably pp. 358–380.

33. For a tentative exploration of this phenomenon, see B. Rayor, "The Effects of Preparation Classes for Childbirth on Birth Experience" (honors thesis, Department of Sociology, Northwestern University, 1968). It is interesting to note, however, that new techniques of childbirth have been

initially experimented by French lower classes. The attitudes and behaviors of educated women vary with the societal context within which they operate. For a discussion of the interaction between environment and innovation, see M. Becker, "Sociometric Location of Innovativeness: Reformulation and Extension of the Diffusion Model," *American Sociological Review*, Vol. 35, 1970, p. 258.

34. See R. Cavan, "Subcultural Variations and Mobility," in H. Christensen, ed., *op. cit.*, pp. 535–584. For another account of changes in the ideology adapted by educated women vis à vis breast feeding, see R. Winch, *op. cit.*, p. 456. For a portrait of the American educated women adopting a positive attitude toward lengthy breast feeding periods, see M. McCarthy, *The Group* (New York, Simon and Schuster, 1963).

35. See M. Kohn, "Social Class and Parental Values," in R. Winch and L. Goodman, eds., *op. cit.*, pp. 349–363.

36. E. Litwak and H. Meyer, *op. cit.*

37. See R. Storr, "The Growth of American Education," in C. A. Anderson and M. J. Bowman, eds., *Education and Economic Development* (Chicago: Aldine, 1965), pp. 135–136.

38. See C. A. Anderson, "Patterns and Variability in the Distribution and Diffusion of Schooling," in C. A. Anderson and M. J. Bowman, eds., *op. cit.*, pp. 314–344.

39. See J. Vaizey, *The Economics of Education* (Glencoe: Free Press, 1962), Chapter 1.

40. Bishop M'Tyeire, *Duties of Christian Masters* (Nashville: Douther Methodist Publishing House, 1859), p. 156.

41. See H. Mann Bond, *Negro Education in Alabama* (New York: Atheneum, 1969), Chapter 2.

42. See S. Michelson, "The Political Economy of Public School Finance," in M. Carnoy, ed., *Schooling in a Corporate Society* (New York: McKay, 1972), p. 150.

43. For a full treatment of this theme, see the articles of C. A. Anderson, *supra.* See also C. A. Anderson, "Literacy and Schooling on the Development Threshold: Some Historical Cases," *op. cit.*, pp. 347–362; H. Passim, "Portents of Modernity and the Meiji Emergence," *op. cit.*, pp. 324–421. See also H. Passim, *Society and Education in Japan* (New York: Teachers College, Columbia University, 1964).

44. See J. Piaget, *Psychologie et pédagogie* (Paris: Denoel, 1965), p. 124.

45. S. Michelson, "The Political Economy of Public School Finance, *op. cit.*

46. R. Hodge, D. Treiman, P. Rossi, "A Comparative Study of Occupational Prestige," in R. Bendix and S. Lipset, eds., *Class Status and Power* (New York: Free Press, 1965), pp. 309–321.

47. For an illustration of this decline, compare the occupational aspirations of the Congolese students examined by N. Xydias in the early 1950s and

those reported by Clignet and P. Foster, in *The Fortunate Few, op. cit.* For a presentation of the results of N. Xydias, see "Aptitudes et formation des noirs," *Aspects sociaux de l'urbanisation et industrialisation en Afrique au Sud du Sahara* (Paris: UNESCO, 1955), pp. 289–352.

48.   For a full treatment of this theme, see B. Clarke, *Educating the Expert Society* (San Fancisco: Chandler, 1962), Introduction, Chapter 2.

49.   For a full treatment of this theme, see J. Vaizey, *op. cit.;* see also J. Vaizey, *Education in the Modern World,* (New York: McGraw Hill, 1967), Chapter 9. At the international level, Muskin shows, however, that distinctive modes of financing secondary institutions are not necessarily associated with parallel variations in enrollments. See S. Muskin, "Financing Secondary School Expansion," *Sociology of Education,* Vol. 38, 1967, pp. 267–298.

50.   See M. Blaug, *Education and the Employment Problem in Developing Countries* (Geneva: International Labor Office, 1973), pp. 23ff.

51.   See R. Poignant and J. Hallak, *Les aspects financiers de l'enseignement dans les pays Africains d'expression Francaise* (Paris: Institute International de Plantification et l'Education: Monographies Africaines, 1966).

52.   As quoted by R. Corwin, *A Sociology of Education* (New York: Appleton-Century-Crofts, 1965), pp. 125ff.

53.   During the year 1970–1971 referendums to increase the financial resources of the local school systems were rejected in the suburban communities of Evanston and Wilmette (Illinois) which previously had attached a great value to the high status of their schools.

54.   For details on this point, see *Ranking of States* (Washington Research Division, National Educational Association, 1965). See also R. Corwin, *op. cit.,* and S. Michelson, *op. cit.* See also *Racial Isolation in the Public Schools, A Report of the United States Commission on Civil Rights* (Washington: U.S. Government Printing Office, 1967), p. 26ff. However Sacks and Ranney warn us that intersuburb variations are as important in this respect as the classical contrasts between suburbs and central cities; see S. Sacks and D. Ranney, "Suburban Education" in M. Gittell, ed., *Educating an Urban Population* (Beverly Hills: Sage, 1967), pp. 60–69.

55.   S. Michelson, *op. cit.,* pp. 155–174.

56.   For a discussion of such problems, see M. Carnoy, "Is Compensatory Education Possible," and S. Bowles, "Unequal Education and the Reproduction of the Social Division of Labor," in M. Carnoy, ed., *op. cit.*

57.   See J. Goody and R. Watts, *loc. cit.*

58.   See R. Clignet and P. Foster, *The Fortunate Few, op. cit.,* Chapter 6, 7.

59.   See C. Barberis, "L'influence de l'education sur le rendement des exploitations agricoles," in R. Castel and J. C. Passeron, eds., *op. cit.,* pp. 121–136.

60.   See R. Clignet and J. Sween, "Accra and Abidjan, A Comparative Examination of the Concept of Increase in Scale," *Urban Affairs Quarterly,* Vol. 4, 1969, pp. 297–324.

61. See N. Hans, *New Trends in Education in the Eighteenth Century* (London: Routledge, 1951), p. 33.

62. M. Blaug, *op. cit.,* pp. 84ff.

63. See R. Clignet, *Blue and White Collar Workers: the Modern Labor Force in the Cameroun* (forthcoming).

64. For a more complete description, see J. Sween and R. Clignet, "Unemployment as a Determinant of Political Unrest in West African Cities, the Case Study of Douala, Cameroun," *Canadian Journal of African Studies,* Vol. 3, 1969, pp. 463–487.

65. M. Blaug, *op. cit.,* p. 9. In industrialized nations the importance of education as a determinant of occupational placement or occupational success is not necessarily as high as some people believe. For a systematic analysis, see C. Jenks et. al., *Inequality: A Reassessment of Family and Schooling in America* (New York: Basic Books, 1973).

66. See R. Clignet and P. Foster, *The Fortunate Few, op. cit.,* Chapter 3, 4 for the Ivory Coast. For Ghana, see P. Foster, "Secondary Schooling and Social Mobility in a West African Nation," *Sociology of Education,* Vol. 37, 1963, pp. 150–171. For Kenya, see C. A. Anderson, "Patterns and Variability In Distribution of Schooling," in C. A. Anderson and M. J. Bowman, eds., *op. cit.,* pp. 327–328.

67. See C. A. Anderson, "A Skeptical Note on Education and Mobility," *American Journal of Sociology,* Vol. 66, 1961, pp. 560–570.

68. See S. Michelson, "Rational Income Decisions of Blacks and Everybody Else," in M. Carnoy, ed., *op. cit.,* p. 114.

69. See R. Clignet and P. Foster, *The Fortunate Few, op. cit.,* Chapter 7; R. Clignet, "Education et aspirations professionnelles," *Tiers monde,* Vol. 5, 1964, pp. 61–82.

70. See A. Feldman and C. Tilly, "The Interaction Between Physical and Social Space," *American Sociological Review,* Vol. 25, 1960, pp. 877–886.

71. See D. Riesman and H. Roseborough, "Careers and Consumer Behavior," in N. Bell and E. Vogel, eds., *A Modern Introduction to the Family* (New York: Free Press, 1968), pp. 199–218.

72. See J. S. Coleman, ed., *Education and Political Development* (Princeton: Princeton University Press, 1965), Introduction.

73. *Ibid.,* pp. 11–12.

74. M. Crozier, *op. cit.,* pp. 237–269.

75. For a full discussion, see T. Hollander, "Fiscal Independence and Large City School Systems," in M. Gittell, ed., *op. cit.,* pp. 103–116.

76. For another example of the disparities in the historical material presented to students of various countries, see B. Berelson, *Content Analysis* (Glencoe: Free Press, 1952), pp. 36–37 as quoted by B. Clarke,, *op. cit.,* p. 17.

77. See R. Clignet, "Inadequacies of the Notion of Assimilation in African Education," *Journal of Modern African Studies,* Vol. VIII, 1970, pp. 425–444.

78. For a development of the position of African leaders on this question, see A. Memmi, *Portrait du colonisateur suivi du portrait du colonisé* (Paris: J. J. Pauvert, 1967).

79. See S. Verba and G. Almond, *The Civic Culture* (Princeton: Princeton University Press, 1963), notably Chapter 10. Identical results are obtained when one limits the analysis to the college population. Seniors are more liberal and more oriented toward civil rights than are freshmen. See, for example, H. Selvin and W. Hagstrom, "Determinants of Support for Civil Liberties," *British Journal of Sociology*, Vol. 11, 1960, pp. 51–73.

80. See S. Stouffer, *Communism Conformity and Civil Liberties* (New York: Doubleday, 1965).

81. See R. LeVine, "Political Socialization and Cultural Change," in C. Geertz, ed., *Old Societies and New States* (New York: Free Press, 1963), pp. 282–301.

82. See J. S. Coleman, ed., *op. cit.*, Introduction.

83. See P. Converse and G. Dupeu, "Some Comparative Notes on Politicization of the Electorate in France and the United States," *Public Opinion Quarterly*, Vol. 26, 1962, pp. 1–23.

84. D. Lerner, *The Passing of Traditional Society* (New York: Free Press, 1958).

85. For a development of this theme, see L. Milbrath, *Political Participation* (Chicago: Rand McNally, 1965), pp. 56–59, 97, 122–132.

86. See A. Etzioni, *The Active Society* (New York: Free Press, 1968), p. 538. See also S. Verba and G. Almond, *op. cit.*

87. See G. Lefebvre, "Aller plus loin avec," *L'express*, No. 886, July 1, 1968.

88. See S. Greer, "The Social Structure and Political Process of Suburbia," *American Sociological Review*, Vol. 25, August 1960, pp. 514–526.

89. See S. Rokkan, "The Comparative Study of Political Participation, Notes Toward a Perspective on Current Research," in A. Ramney, ed., *Essays on the Behavioral Aspects of Politics* (Urbana: The University of Illinois Press, 1962), pp. 47–90.

90. J. S. Coleman, *op. cit.*, Introduction, p. 29.

91. See E. P. Thompson, *op. cit.*, p. 377.

92. M. Katz, *op. cit.*

93. G. Lenski, *The Religious Factor* (New York: Doubleday, 1961), Chapter 6.

94. R. Collier, "Education, Religion, and the Kentucky Court of Appeals," *Bulletin of the School Services*, Vol. 33, 1960, pp. 181–182.

95. See E. P. Thompson, *op. cit.*, p. 339.

96. See G. Lenski, *loc. cit.* In addition the methods of discipline used by Catholics differ from those used by Protestants.

97. For a more general discussion of this theme, see L. Rhodes and C. Nam,

"The Religious Context of Educational Expectations," *American Sociological Review,* Vol. 35, 1970, pp. 253–264.

98.　See R. and A. Rossi, "Some Effects of Parochial School Education in America," *Harvard Educational Review,* Vol. 27, 1957, pp. 168–199.

99.　See R. Clignet and P. Foster, "Un exemple d'assimilation la prééminence de l'enseignement classique en Côté d'Ivoire," *Revue Française de Sociologie,* Vol. 7, 1966, pp. 32–47.

100.　See R. Clignet and P. Foster, *The Fortunate Few, op. cit.,* Chapter 3, 4.

101.　See S. Warkov and A. Greeley, "Parochial School Origins and Educational Achievement," *American Sociological Review,* Vol. 31, 1966, pp. 401–410.

Part Two

THE SCHOOL AS A MICROCOSM

3

THE EXTERNAL CONSTRAINTS OF EDUCATIONAL INSTITUTIONS

The main function of all educational institutions is to ensure the exercise and the control of a particular form of communication.[1] This communication is twofold. Within the school scene teachers are expected to define and transmit the core of the culture's knowledge, practices, and values. Correspondingly they specialize in defining and ensuring the transmission of socially valued sets of attitudes, modes of thought, and actions and in perpetuating an appropriate teaching force. Outside of the school scene teachers are expected to facilitate the cognitive and emotional adaptation of individual students to the various social groups they enter after their graduation. In addition, the certification functions of teachers contribute to the legitimation of the existing social order.

Although all educational institutions engage in these activities, they do not attach a same preeminence to the external or internal aspects of their communications function. Nor do they similarly perform each one of those activities.

Variations result from the struggles that oppose social and cultural groups to one another as to the advantages which can be derived from education. The object of these struggles is twofold: the various segments of a society are anxious to impose upon others their own definition of education and formal schooling [2]; and they are anxious to obtain the means and resources necessary for reaching their goals. Such struggles, far from taking place in vacuo, are filtered and institu-

115

tionalized. As a society becomes more complex, there is an increased number of mechanisms designed both to limit the scope of educational struggles among social and cultural groups and to legitimitize the expression of the underlying social and emotional tensions. In this context both administrators and teachers are defined as being experts and this label allows them to hold "legitimate" views both as to the goals and purposes of educational activities and as to the means necessary for achieving those goals. Although teachers and administrators are thus entitled to a certain amount of liberty in the exercise of their occupation, the power they can muster is nevertheless limited because of the institutionalized systems of checks and balances imposed on their activities. In this chapter I identify the nature and the effectiveness of such systems.

Since the liberty of teachers and administrators is constantly threatened by a number of external pressures, I first identify the objects of such pressures. I show how these pressures pertain both to the means allocated to schools and to the functions they are supposed to perform. Second, I examine *who* exerts pressures on school personnel and who is legitimately expected to limit the power and hence the liberty that they claim. In other words, I examine variations in the institutional mechanisms of social control exerted on school personnel. Finally, while the actual liberty enjoyed by teachers and administrators ultimately depends on their vulnerability, it is also conditioned by the intensity, the form, and the nature of the pressures to which they are subjected. Correspondingly I analyze variations in the effectiveness of the mechanisms of control exerted on schools.

Objects of the External Pressures Exerted on School Personnel. Regardless of their overt functions, the functioning of schools requires both material and human resources. As competition develops among organizations serving both different and similar purposes, the prestige and hence the rank ordering of each one of these organizations depends in part upon the relative material resources they are able to obtain.[3] School administrators of American cities and suburbs compete with the administrators of hospitals, welfare agencies, and police and fire departments to obtain maximal resources from local governments. A similar competition takes place at the national level. Similarly school administrators also compete with one another to obtain more than their fair share of the resources allocated to education.

These administrators rationalize their demands by arguing that the quality of the services they render can be most appropriately measured by the quantity and the quality of the resources they have acquired. But the responses of adult members of the community to such demands are influenced by the role conflicts which they experience.[4] As parents they are keen to maximize the educational opportunities offered to their children. As taxpayers they are conversely interested both in maintaining the financial demands of school administrators within minimal limits and in making sure that the funds allocated to schools serve primarily their own interests and that of their offspring. In fact the conflicts over resources which oppose school administrators and other segments of the population raise two questions: How much liberty do administrators enjoy to define the needs of the enterprise of which they are responsible? How much inequality is there among schools as a result of the conflict between each administrator and the group of actors who control his wishes and his handling of the resources he is given?

Evidence shows that there are sharp disparities among American schools as to the educational materials to which they have access.[5] Only 53 percent of the elementary and high schools surveyed in the Coleman study are sheltered in buildings less than nineteen years old. Only 56 percent of those schools have more than 1500 books in their library, while only one-fourth of them support their own newspaper.

While there are thus sharp contrasts in the resources of American schools, there are also marked differences among them with regard to the diversity and the quality of the services they offer. Only 31 percent of these schools have one or more remedial teachers, 18 percent use the services of one or more guidance counselors, and only 29 percent offer special talents classes. Further the educational qualifications of their teaching and administrative personnel are not the same. Nor do they receive identical salaries.

The consequences of such differences remain unclear. Insofar as variations in the educational environment account for only a limited amount of the variance in the distribution of students' scores on verbal and mathematical tests, the resources of schools do not seem to affect their functions. Without effect on achievement, variations in environmental conditions may still influence job satisfaction and hence the meaning that teachers attach to their teaching activities or that students attach to their learning experiences.[6] Thus academic efficiency is probably an insufficient criteria to evaluate equality of educational opportunities.

Yet the pressures imposed upon administrators pertain not only to the amount of resources which they can use but also to the functions to be served by educational institutions. First, these pressures may reflect divergent views about the links between schools and the economy. As shown in *Small Town in a Mass Society,* an increase in the number of tracts offered to high school students might alter their occupational destination, induce corresponding pressures in the labor market, and change accordingly the economic profile of the community.[7] Administrators are accountable not only for the number of alternative routes they offer to students but also for the principles they use in order to allocate these students among the various tracts, streams, or branches of the system. For example, the systematic admission of lower-class students in the academic tracts deemed to be the most rewarding may be construed as an enterprise of subverting the existing hierarchy of social or ethnic classes.

These pressures also might reflect diverging views as to the political and religious functions of educational institutions. They concern the choice of the material to be taught, the books to be used, and the teachers to be hired. During the period following World War II, the teaching force of certain districts was advised not to teach materials concerning certain auxiliary organizations of the United Nations, such as UNICEF and UNESCO, which were perceived as forerunners of a communist invasion. In the same vein, by 1969 the governor of California attempted to renew a perennial—albeit illegal—veto against the hiring of Communist teachers by the state university system. The fear of seeing youth politically corrupted by teachers and their books is an old story. In ancient Greece Socrates incurred the fatal wrath of the Syracuse establishment because of the "pernicious" character of the doctrines and ideas he was teaching.[8]

In the religious sphere certain parts of the curriculum may be similarly viewed at variance with the fundamental religious and ideological beliefs of the community. For many years, schools in Tennessee were not permitted to teach evolutionary theories and doctrines which conflicted with a fundamentalist interpretation of the Bible. Similarly there is currently a strong resistance against the introduction of sex education programs in schools, either because the development of such programs is viewed as instrumental in the diffusion of erotism or because it is assumed that this constitutes an invasion of privacy and that sex education is the responsibility of individual parents. In the same vein, school administrators and parents may compete as to the limits of the control that the former are entitled to exert over students' behavior. The issue of hair length for males, of clothing for girls, and of the oath of allegiance for both are cases in point. What are the limits of the mandate given to teachers by the community and by parents? To what extent are teachers and administrators entitled to act as substitutes to parents deemed to be faulty? What is, in other words, the relative power and liberty that school personnel is entitled to enjoy vis a vis the definition of teaching activities?

As long as a community remains homogeneous, the power of teachers and administrators in this regard is unlikely to be challenged for there is a marked consensus both within the teaching force and between that force and the public at large as to the definition of educational activities. But with a decline in the cultural, social, and ethnic homogeneity of a community, the definition of what should be taught becomes increasingly problematic and some groups are likely to "assert that parts of the curriculum are offensive, harmful and otherwise undesirable, to publicize their complaints and to stimulate controversy in order to create a public or political issue over the matter." [9] Initially, at least, these groups often tend to view teachers and administrators as more progressive and liberal than they should be and it is only recently, as school systems reach a new phase in their development, that underprivileged segments of the population begin to challenge the activities of teachers and educational administrators. American political and religious conservatives have been active in this regard for longer periods of time than either blacks or members of political or religious associations with liberal or progressive orientations.

Insofar as the effectiveness of the corresponding complaints depends upon the approval of the largest part of the population, it is necessary to translate into appropriate terms the assertion that there is something questionable about the activities of teachers and about the books they use. Political challenges often are translated into a more popular moral framework; in the United States, for instance, the parts of the curriculum which are politically controversial often are challenged on the basis that they are obscene. The bans placed on books written by black authors offer frequent cases in point. There is a definite hierarchy in the perceived effectiveness of various complaints formulated against educational materials. Complaints about immorality are often deemed to be more effective than complaints about politics. Whereas during the 1950s charges of being "soft" toward communism or socialism had chances to stir controversy, the potential popularity of such assertions has declined—which obliges the conservative groups to mask their political challenges of educational material and to attack them on moral grounds.

As the controversy develops and spreads, official organizations, agen-

cies, or institutions are likely to recognize the initial assertion as legitimate. This may lead to an official investigation of the matter, to proposals for reform, and to the establishment of an agency designed to
respond to those claims and demands. The development of censorship
agencies often constitutes the response of state authorities to the
charges formulated against the use of some pedagogical material
deemed to be controversial.

However the development of censorship agencies does not necessarily lead to the end of the initial complaint. With the increased heterogeneity of a community, state authorities may be tempted to look for
compromises between the conflicting demands of associations involved
in educational matters. While the creation of censorship agencies may
placate the groups that started the controversy, their ineffectiveness
may alleviate the resulting frustrations experienced by teachers. Thus
the procedures followed and the decisions taken by censorship authorities are likely to vary with the differential perceptions that the political
personnel of the state or of the community hold about the power of the
groups involved in the initial issue and its subsequent development.
While in certain states controversial books will be banned altogether
from schools as a result of an administrative action taken by state cen-
sors, the authorities of other states will look for compromises (for instance, they will eliminate the controversial material from classrooms
but will allow its presence in school libraries).

Insofar as the attempts by some groups to "turn back the clock of educational activities" or more recently to "accelerate the liberating functions of schools" fail because of the perceived lack of appropriate response on the part of legitimate authorities, these groups are likely to
engage in activities designed to create alternative parallel or counter institutions as responses to the established procedures. Thus during this
particular stage of the development of educational censorship treated
as a social problem, groups dissatisfied with the current activities of
schools are likely to exert more direct pressures on publishers. There is
some evidence to suggest that conservative groups have been effective
in their endeavors to discourage the publication of textbooks deemed
to be offensive. For example, the history books provided to southern
and northern primary and secondary schools differed from one another for a long time. There also is some evidence to suggest that as
such endeavors are not completely successful, these groups will be
tempted to put there own pedagogical material on the market. Finally,
insofar as the recent activities developed along these lines by the militant segments of social or ethnic minorities have met a limited success,

they also are tempted to create their own schools to avoid the pressures of state authorities and to use their own curriculum and techniques.

Thus the pressures exerted on the functions assigned to educational institutions develop over time according to a definite sequence which involves different activities by various pressure groups and by legitimate political and educational authorities. Far from being unrelated, these differences in activities build on previous patterns of development. The development of "free schools" characterized by varying philosophies can take place only whenever the pressures previously exerted on public schools are deemed to have failed.

Yet, while it is pertinent to examine the pressures to which school personnel are subjected within a *specific* and short term time framework, it is also pertinent to analyze these pressures within a broader time perspective. The transformation of larger social structures affects both the perceived hierarchy of controversial issues and the profile of the groups engaged in a challenge of the activities currently defined as legitimate by teachers or educational administrators. Initially the politically and religiously conservative groups are most active in this regard, but administrators are increasingly obliged to cope with the demands of minorities (blacks, Indians, women) and of the most liberal-oriented segments of the population. In addition, the decisions of administrators concerning the materials and books to be used in classrooms are no longer influenced only by the conflicting forces of politically-oriented pressure groups but also by the more academically-oriented interventions of private foundations and federal or state agencies, whose purpose is to enhance the rationality of educational enterprises and hence to standardize the pedagogical treatment imposed upon students with differing backgrounds.[10]

Mechanisms of Social Control over Schools.   The concrete forms of the pressures exerted on school personnel depend upon institutional arrangements and notably upon the mechanisms through which teachers or educational administrators account for their activities to the society at large. The most important distinction is that between decentralized and centralized school systems.

Decentralization rests upon the belief that formal schooling is a privilege to be privately acquired—belief which in turn presupposes that the clientele of the schools should be able to communicate directly to educators what they expect from the educational process and what they would like their children to learn. This view minimizes the disruptive effects that conflicts among parents or between parents and teachers might have on their respective educational liberties. In fact decentralization often posits a marked interdependence between liberty and fraternity: It presupposes that all parents and teachers share a common definition of both what teaching methods and curricula should be. This presupposition is valid as long as there is a low degree division of labor and as long as familial groups remain engaged in similar sets of activity. But the system of beliefs justifying decentralization becomes problematic as soon as geographic and occupational mobility reach a critical threshold. Beyond this threshold the concept of community ceases to be territory-based and while certain social groups share a certain space because they have chosen to do so, other groups are passively confined within certain physical and social boundaries. Thus as the complexity of a particular society increases, decentralization ceases to enable all familial groups to enjoy *evenly* a same amount of control over their children's education. Changes in social conditions lower the validity of the premises on which decentralization is based. Indeed they lead decentralization to accentuate conflicts between educational liberty and equality.

The history of the organizational patterns of American educational institutions reveal the seriousness of such conflicts. During the nineteenth century the decentralization of American schools took three major forms.[11] A first form prevailing in many preindustrial and mercantile cities in New England consists in what Michael Katz calls *paternalistic voluntarism.* In this context, the obligation of noblesse oblige which goes with a system of stratification based on status and deference leads established elites to operate private institutions for the benefit of the less privileged. The function of such schools is to drill lower-class children and to socialize them into a system of values that induces them to accept their social station. This form came under attack when increased migrations entailed an increased heterogeneity in the religious orientations of American urban populations. This heterogeneity prevented schools from integrating the differing conceptions and orientations of various social classes into a same mold.

A second form of decentralization consists in recognizing to each ward the power of running its own school district. Labeled *democratic localism* by Katz, it tends to prevail both in rural areas and in the transitional neighborhoods of growing cities. It is based upon the notion that changes should be induced from within rather than from without local communities. The implementation of this form became challenged as soon as the growing differentiation of wards began to induce sharp inequalities in the financial resources allocated to education. Further, although this form of decentralization favored a conception of formal schooling which did not necessarily stimulate parochialism, it came under attack when the increased heterogeneity of the immigrating populations led elites to emphasize the melting-pot functions of schools and to stress the necessity of coordinating educational efforts at the national level.

A last form of decentralization labeled *corporate voluntarism* stimulates the development of private academies. In this perspective schools should be treated as educational corporations subject to the rules and principles governing competition within a free market. Clearly this last conception recognizes the limitations of territorially based patterns of decentralization. It emphasizes conversely the significance of communities based upon the sharing of orientations and hence of activities or of background rather than upon the sharing of a same space. In this context the survival of schools depends upon the extent to which they are able to attract a sufficient clientele. The difficulty of this conception however is that it minimizes the significance of variations in the organizational abilities of populations with differing means or differing political status. There are many imperfections in the educational market.

Current patterns of educational decentralization in the United States continue to reflect the divergent conceptions underlying the numerous initiatives taken by private persons and groups in the early stages of educational development. While early on, an educational bureaucracy was created to coordinate urban and rural education and to systematize rules designed to limit the economic exploitation of children, its power remained limited and the local school board has continued to be the key mechanism by which teachers and administrators are subject to the public at large. Because of the divergences underlying conceptions and forms of decentralization, there are sharp contrasts in the patterns of recruitment of school boards. In some communities members are appointed by the mayor, as is the case in Chicago. In other cases this procedure is made impossible by the fact that the boundaries of school districts have ceased to coincide with those of townships and other political basic units. School board elections however vary in form; in many communities they are indirect and are mere ratifications of the choices made by the members of caucuses representing "the most representative" voluntary associations of the community. Although variations in the legal procedures by which school board members are appointed should be associated with parallel contrasts in the relative power they can exert on school personnel, the extent of these contrasts should still remain limited, because of the regularizing function of the state which is the ultimate authority in educational matters.

However the power of these states is often weak. Only recently do all states have a personnel permanently appointed to cope with educational problems. In many instances appointments to such jobs result from political patronage, and civil servants do not have always the skills or the background necessary for checking and controlling the activities of local boards or teachers. In addition, the authority of the state is only indirectly exerted; state administrations expect boards to comply with minimal administrative and technical requirements, but the subsidies they offer to school districts—far from being uniform—vary often in proportion to the performance of local students or to the quality of the local teaching force. Similarly the federal government intervenes indirectly in educational matters by making grants-in-aid and subsidies contingent upon the fulfillment of certain conditions regarding the background of teachers and the ethnic origin and performance of students. In short, state authorities do not have the freedom nor the legal resources necessary for limiting contrasts in the wealth or the orientation of local school boards.

The situation is somewhat similar at the university level. Private institutions are placed under the control of a board of trustees who act as representatives of the most significant economic and social groups of a particular community, while state universities are placed under the tutelage of a board of regents appointed by governors or nominated by the electorate. As was the case at the level of lower educational institutions, variations in the procedures by which these boards recruit their members should be associated with relevant contrasts in the control they can exert on university personnel. But the extent of these contrasts should be somewhat attenuated by the indirect intervention of state and federal authorities. Subsidies offered to universities are contingent upon their meeting certain requirements defined by state legislatures or by Congress.

At the other end of the continuum, there are a number of highly centralized societies where the decisions concerning the hiring and promotion of teachers, the financing of school activities, or the development of new curriculum are administered at the very center of the educational and political system.

The champions of educational centralization justify their position on two counts. First, they view this organizational pattern as most efficient and productive. In addition, they see the traditional concept of community as a manifestation of the "dead hand of the past" and they argue that centralization frees the individual from particularism and enables him to achieve a higher rationality and universalism. While the champions of decentralization are in favor of a social structure comprised of organic compacts of individualized subgroups, proponents of centralization prefer a social system made up of an aggregate of independent individuals. In the first case, liberty is seen as contingent upon social affiliations and thus as dependent upon the degree to which an individual takes deep roots in a community; in the second case, there is the postulate that educational liberty depends upon individuals rather than upon groups, and champions of centralization define therefore the concepts of educational liberty and of community as mutually exclusive.

In brief, the contrast between decentralization and centralization mirrors diverging assumptions about the nature and the effectiveness of the external controls to be imposed upon educational activities. In the first perspective the effectiveness of schools is seen as contingent upon the degree and the form of social participation in the relevant decision-making processes. Conversely, in the context of centralization, the effectiveness of schools is viewed as determined by their rationality and universalism.

Centralization characterizes countries with as distinctive educational histories as France, the Soviet Union, and the Netherlands. In France the Ministers of Education bragged that they were able to know what part of the curriculum was treated at a particular hour of a particular day in all French classes. More recently, observers of the French scene have shown how the decision concerning student demands for parietal hours had to be made in Paris at the Ministry itself rather than in the particular university where such a demand had been initially formulated. Similarly responses to the occupation of the Sorbonne by students in May 1968 were influenced by the transmission of the relevant information to the Minister of Education who had to elaborate an adequate decision.[12] To be sure, the decisions taken by the Minister of Education are often preceded by discussions within advisory boards where a number of voluntary associations involved in educational issues are represented (teachers' organizations, parents' associations, churches, and religious groups). But most often the power of such boards remains limited and their voice is merely consultative.

Variations in the Effectiveness of the Educational Mechanisms of Social Control. Variations in the form, the object, and the intensity of

the pressures exerted on school administrators reflect organizational
arrangements and are not alike in decentralized and centralized school
systems. In fact, among each one of these two types of systems, pressures also are influenced by the overall political organization of the
society under study. Second, while the institutional mechanisms of social control are expected to channel the demands and the expectations
of various groups, the fact remains that their effectiveness varies with
the economic, demographic, and social characteristics of the community. In the United States, for instance, pressures exerted upon boards
and school administrators should vary with the economic profile and
the age of the district. Third, these pressures should depend upon the
background and the orientations of the local elites involved in educational matters. Finally, these pressures should vary over time and
should depend—at least in part—upon the complexity characterizing
educational bureaucracies.

Effects of Centralization and Decentralization. Decentralization enhances the vulnerability of school administrators and school board
members to the pressures of various interest groups. In his study of
American high schools Gross states that 92 percent of the superintendents interviewed and 74 percent of the school board members
under study report to have been exposed to the pressures of PTAs and
of individual parents.[13] No less than 49 percent of the superintendents
have been confronted with demands formulated by taxpayers' associations and 31 percent of the school board members have been in the
same position. Similarly 48 percent of the superintendents report to
have been exposed to the pressures of city councils, as against only
38 percent of the school board members interviewed. While the study
suggests that administrators are subject both to institutionalized and
noninstitutionalized pressures and that school boards are not necessarily acting as screens along these lines, the nature, the form and the intensity of these pressures vary with the characteristics of the community where they operate.

By contrast such variations are less evident in centralized systems. In
France, for example, the pressures exerted upon school administrators
are markedly influenced by the political trends prevailing at the national level. The effectiveness of these pressures depends primarily
upon the relationships between the executive and legislative branches of
government. Correspondingly regional or local variations in the implementation of educational policies are more limited. In fact local aspirations and orientations most often are channeled toward the center of

the political system through appropriate networks. Because of centralization, voluntary associations concerned with educational matters tend to be at least as sensitive to the vulnerability of central political institutions as they are to the expectations of their local constituency. Voluntary associations generally are prone to engage in radical ideological maneuvers aiming at changing the national rather than the local scene. For example, these associations have been active in the conflicts opposing various segments of French society with regard to the relations that the state should maintain with the church. Anxious to support or oppose state aid to parochial schools, they are on the whole less effective to obtain changes in the treatment accorded to students by the personnel of a particular school.

The strategies of these associations make it difficult for the common man to understand the chain of causal relations between his own local grievances, his own local actions, and the bureaucratic rules and laws that these actions will eventually engender at the national level. Because most often changes in the organization and the nature of educational activities affect the entire school system, and because such changes are most likely to come about, a long time after the initial expression of a particular grievance, individuals do not easily recognize the connection these changes and their own activities. As a result the level of participation observed in voluntary associations concerned with educational matters is low, and on the whole individuals experience a definite mistrust toward public or private initiatives taken in this respect. Thus L. Wylie in *Village in the Vaucluse* notes, "It is unreasonable to expect the adults of Peyrane [the small village he was studying] to organize spontaneously for forcing the hand of the government even for a just and an important issue such as the construction of a new school, for this would involve contacts with the government." [14]

In this centralized context both the scarcity of social and economic resources distributed by local powers and the restricted involvement of local communities in significant decision-making processes, limit the bargaining tools they may use in order to deal with educational tensions. Because of their lack of power, informal groups are often inclined to perceive city officials not as instigators of compromises over routine grievances but as petty tyrants prone to pursue personal vindicts. In *Bus Stop for Paris,* for example, the Andersons illustrate how the protests of the assistant mayor of Wissous against the administrative shortcomings of the local teaching force have been reinterpreted in terms of nonnegotiable local rivalries and have further isolated both local pressure groups and individual political actors. [15]

The centralized nature of the French educational system leads individual citizens to believe that their own grievances will be settled only through the outcome of a revolution which is yet to come and whose occurrence is made problematic by the difficulties that the same individuals encounter in organizing themselves at the grass root level. This situation enhances the autonomy of the teaching force toward the public. As a result the most significant conflicts taking place in the French educational system tend to pit various categories of educational bureaucrats against one another. At the national level, heads of the primary, postprimary, and university systems vie to obtain increases in the material and human resources allocated to them. Similarly these heads compete with representatives of teachers' organizations to obtain changes in the definition of teaching activities or of the treatment to be given students.

However there are variations in the implications of a bureaucratic and centralized educational structure. For example, the geographic stability of French teachers has long enough limited the social distance which separated them from the community they served.[16] Often returning to their village of origin, they frequently served as special assistants to the mayor and their main function was to act as a bridge between the demands of a centralized political order and the expectations of individuals or of local officials. Yet changes in the recruitment of primary teachers have induced a decline in the importance of their previous role in this respect. In Peyrane—as in most French communities—teachers are increasingly perceiving their job as a first step in a process of upward mobility. They consider their current assignment as temporary and their occupational aspirations predispose them to move toward larger and more impersonal structures.[17] This has accentuated the effects of centralization on the marginality of their role and their participation in local communities.

While the implications of educational centralization may vary over time, they also vary across cultures because of divergences in the origin of this particular pattern. Centralization may reflect the reactions of a weak state confronted with a number of significant centrifugal forces (as has been the case in France) or it may alternatively result from the absence of significant private initiatives (as was the case in Germany, Italy, Russia).[18]

Such contrasts are likely to be associated with variations in the relative autonomy enjoyed by school personnel. For example, in Germany teachers have all the rights but also all the obligations incumbing upon civil servants and they are supposed to take an oath of allegiance to the state, an obligation of which their French colleagues are exempted. Similarly variations in the origin of centralization are associated with parallel contrasts in the relative freedom that teachers enjoy as to the definition of their work loads. In Italy—where the educational system is born of the initiatives taken directly by the state acting under the strict pressures of the industrial middle class—the law defines the workload of the *incaricato* university professor (the professor endowed with a specific chair) who owes the state a minimal amount of three hours of lectures per week necessarily spread over a period of three days. By contrast, the only institutionalized duty of his French counterpart has been to grade his students at the end of the academic year.

Such contrasts also are likely to be associated with the control exerted by governments upon curricula and pedagogical methods. Thus while the liberal orientations of French centralization have been accompanied by a generalist-oriented curriculum, Russian students from an early date have been oriented toward specific branches of government. The curriculum of the best Russian *Lycée,* for instance, remained narrow in scope as late as 1848 and was supposed to prepare its students for careers within the Ministry of Interior.[19]

At the other end of the continuum, there also are variations in the degree and the form of decentralization experienced by various educational institutions. A comparison of British and American patterns of decentralization illustrates the differential consequences of this particular organizational structure.

Thus while American political authorities continue to delegate their educational responsibilities to a school board, such boards have been absorbed in England by all-purpose local authorities as long ago as 1902. These authorities maintain local education committees but the individuals serving on such committees have only a limited role. Their role is limited not only because—elected along national party lines—they must therefore pursue national rather than local policies, but also because the complexities of the tasks to be performed lead permanent local officials—and hence chief school officers—to exert a more decisive influence on the relevant decision-making processes. Both the recruitment patterns of local education officers and their expertise should make them less vulnerable to the pressures of local educational committees than their American counterparts—the local school superintendents—whose powers are entirely dependent upon the goodwill of the boards. In this sense the external control exerted on school administrators is more marked in the United States than in England.[20]

The situation is the same at the university level. In Great Britain the allocation of the funds for institutions of higher learning is controlled by the University Grant Committee manned mainly by university teachers.[21] The composition of this particular committee obviously limits the degree to which the British government may affect the policies of one particular or several institutions. Its only tool is to introduce variations in the overall "package deals" that university administrators are entitled to expect. By contrast in the United States the pressures exerted by the individual state on its public universities are more direct, and financial leverages enable them to intervene directly in the definition of university policies regarding the recruitment of teachers and students or the nature of the courses to be taught. (There are contrasts between American public and private institutions in this regard since it is only indirectly that state governments affect the organizational profile of the latter.)

Finally, the British Chief Officer has less power over principals and teachers than his American counterpart. Teaching methods, all matters related to curricula, relationships with parents, and control of teachers are recognized as matters for school heads to decide—and not only by local officials but by the central government as well. In this sense decentralization is more marked in Great Britain than in the United States because the personnel of each British school seems to enjoy more autonomy.

Thus British decentralization implies an enhanced autonomy of local educational administrators, while American decentralization is conversely associated with an accentuated dependence of school administrators upon external forms of local control. Contrasts between the two countries reflect in fact variations in the relative power held by educational actors in local community structures and hence divergences in their modes of recruitment and socialization. Initially at least, the orientations of the British educational system were more "elitist" and headmasters were frequently recruited from the ranks of narrow segments of the population. Expected to share the views of the trustees to which they were accountable, these administrators were therefore granted considerable leeway in the exercise of their activities. By contrast the more populist orientations of the early American educational system and the corresponding lowering in the prestige accorded to teaching or to educational administrative functions have in turn broadened patterns of access into these two types of jobs. Correspondingly contrasts in the forms taken by decentralization in British and American cultures reflect divergences in the hiring patterns of their educational officers. As British administrators belong to the elites, they should be more likely to use decentralization for their own profit.

Yet divergences between the two countries also result from the differential integration of political and religious institutions at the national level. The large autonomy that local officers of American churches, political parties, and economic organizations enjoy toward the relevant officeholders at the national level, obviously enhances the power they can claim on the local scene and notably in education. Their British counterparts are more dependent upon the decisions taken at the national level by political or religious representatives and this in turn lowers their "particularism."

To conclude, the contrasted definitions and implications of educational decentralization in England and the United States reflect variations both in the background of school personnel and in the relative integration of the economic, political, and social groups most likely to exert pressures on this personnel. More generally, the nature and the intensity of the pressures exerted on teachers and educational administrators differ both *between* and *within* centralized and decentralized systems. But on the whole, one can expect that in decentralized systems these pressures are more diffuse and vary more markedly in form and in intensity by region or by type of community.

Contrasts in the educational implications of centralization and decentralization are also culturally relative, insofar as their respective effects vary with the relative power that various components of the social system believe to hold over one another. In the United States centralization has often been viewed as the most appropriate means of limiting black educational exploitation and alienation. At times the federal government has been asked to exert control over the rules defining the educational treatment to be meted out to black pupils and in fact, to accelerate their integration into the mainstream of educational structures. In this context centralization has been conceived as the most appropriate mechanism for ensuring redistribution of societal assets along more equalitarian lines. Thus both the financial (through grants-in-aid) and judicial (through Supreme Court decisions) interventions of the federal government aimed at facilitating the access of black students to high quality educational institutions.

However recent developments in New York—and particularly the strike which plagued that city in 1969—suggests changes in the meaning attached to centralization. While teachers' unions are still anxious to maintain the centralized set-up characterizing the educational enterprises of the city, a number of black New Yorkers advocate a return to decentralization. This could indicate that black minorities living in

northern cities have achieved a sufficiently high level of mobilization at
the ghetto level to perceive centralization as limiting their own educational aspirations and orientations. But does the resistance of teachers
to decentralization reflect alternatively their fears of being unable to
protect their interests at the local level? Or does it more simply result
from the fact that the spatial and geographic level of mobilization
achieved by their unions is already higher than that attained by the
blacks and that decentralization is perceived as likely to lower the
bargaining positions of these unions by leading to a demobilization of
their rank and file members? [22]

Thus the gains to be acquired by a particular occupational, social, or
ethnic subgroup through centralization or decentralization vary over
time. Decentralization in the industrialized parts of the United States
cannot have the same meaning by 1970 as it had at the turn of the last
decade.[23] Nor has this pattern similar implications in the New York
ghettos and in the rural parts of New York State.

Demographic and Social Characteristics of the Communities.   Although
variations in the form, the nature, and the intensity of the pressures exerted on schools are more evident in a decentralized than a centralized
society, these variations still reflect disparities in the dominant characteristics of the communities.

Size of communities and school districts.   The extent of the pressures experienced by administrators or teachers should depend upon the size of
school systems; they should be most intense, most consistent, and most
tradition-oriented in small villages or towns. With urbanization and the
subsequent increase in the demand for schooling there has been however a concentration of educational facilities. In the United States, for
example (the number of small districts having decreased between 1947
and 1959 by one-half), 20 percent of local school systems currently ed-
ucate 80 percent of the school-aged children.[24] This concentration of
educational institutions should be associated with convergences in the
patterns of interaction between educational administrators and the
public. The object, the intensity, and the form of the pressures exerted
on school personnel should not only be increasingly uniform but also
less tradition-oriented and less internally consistent.

Economic profile of these communities.   Pressures also should be both more
intense, more direct and more consistently tradition-oriented in agricultural communities characterized by a low level of division of labor.

Further they should aim at a perpetuation of the current modes of economic activities. For example, the extensive nature of agricultural exploitations in the Ivory Coast has made all planters—Europeans and
Africans alike—wary of educational development since it limits their
access to the reservoirs of unskilled laborers needed to run their enterprises. For a long time these planters were effective in their efforts
to keep primary enrollments at a low level and to prevent the creation
of vocational training centers which would have increased the available
occupational alternatives.[25] The trend is similar in Springdale, the
small community in upstate New York studied by Bensman and Vidich.
The local school board has always been anxious to make decisions likely
to perpetuate the existing type of economic organizations. The board
strongly believed in the perpetuation of an agriculture-oriented curriculum and feared that industrial programs would modify the existing
structure of the labor market. In addition, bussing programs were primarily aimed at serving the needs and aspirations of agricultural families. Further, the board evaluated the purchases made by school authorities in terms of consequences on the local market, and its main
orientation was to protect local business rather than to investigate the
cheapest solutions in this respect. Finally, the board was anxious to hire
the services of preferably locally-born teachers or of persons born in
small communities to make sure that its tradition-oriented philosophy
would be correctly implemented.[26]

As the scale of the local economy increases, so does the relative
amount of division of labor and the diversity of the manpower needs of
community entrepreneurs. An increase in the scale of the local economy also enhances its needs for communication skills and hence for individuals able to occupy specialized positions in the tertiary sector of
the economy. As a result educational structures become more diversified and school boards tend to attach greater importance to the teaching of a variety of industrial skills than to the transmission of a fixed
cultural heritage.

This however is not the only contrast opposing communities with differing levels of economic complexity. Among communities characterized by a small economic scale, the homogeneous and stable nature of
elites reinforces the pressures that they can exert on educational institutions. The control they exert directly or indirectly upon local
churches, local associations, and the municipal government enhances
the demand they can impose upon school administrators. Whether in
a centralized or a decentralized societal context, monopolistic economic
organizations tend to participate in the financing of educational pro-

grams and are able therefore to shape the profile of schools according
to their own needs and orientations. In France, for example, the long-
established monopoly enjoyed by the Michelin tire industry in the economic and labor market of Clermont-Ferrand, has enabled the Michelin family to impose a strict control on the number and types of schools
to be open in the area. In the United States Corwin reports that in a
midwestern community dominated by one single mining operation, the
local school board submitted budget, school building plans, and other
special projects to the officials of the company who—even though they
lived in a different area—would still pay a substantial percentage of the
corresponding bills.[27]

But as the local economy becomes more complex, local power structures are more likely to be factional or coalitional than pyramidal.[28]
Elites interested in educational developments tend to differ from those
involved in political, cultural, religious, or economic issues. Further
there is large turnover in those various elites. Correspondingly, educational institutions follow patterns of change which increasingly depart from those characterizing other institutions; on the whole, pressures exerted on school personnel become more specific and the
outcome of such pressures is more uncertain.

Age of the communities.   The nature and the intensity of the pressures
imposed upon educational institutions also should vary with the age of
the communities studied. Significant contrasts should be apparent in
this respect when one compares new suburban developments and
townships with deeper roots in history. In the first case populations
have a low level of commitment to their new local area and are hardly
aware of the alternative solutions available to them in the various fields
of social participation. In Levittown, for example, the only thing that
was initially significant for those moving into the community was to see
the schools open on time.[29] The residents were unable to make more
specific educational demands for a variety of reasons. First, the energy
of new settlers tends to be geared to the solution of more urgent problems than the implementation of their own educational philosophies
(such as alleviating the difficulties associated with commuting to and
from their work or with their shopping). Second, the relative heterogeneity of their past residential experiences prevents them from establishing adequate channels of interaction and hence from identifying
the members of the community who share their own educational views.
Third, they are at a disadvantage in their initial dealings with school

authorities because the school district existed prior to their arrival and the school superintendent necessarily preceded them in that place and has therefore a better knowledge of the ropes to be pulled to achieve particular educational objectives.

At the other end of the continuum the school board and the various informal pressure groups of older communities do not necessarily have a higher commitment toward the local scene. As time passes and as the various segments of the community find their niche, control over educational activities becomes routinized and conflicts between school personnel and outside agencies become both more sporadic and more ritualized. At the same time, however, there is an increase in the number of reference groups used to evaluate the activities of the local teaching force and the various segments of the population compare their schools not only with those of other parts of the community but also with those of their counterparts elsewhere in the country.[30] There are, accordingly, greater inconsistencies in the pressures imposed upon schools. These pressures are nevertheless more complex and richer than those formulated by the persons moving in a new suburban development.

Stability of the communities. The consistency of the pressures exerted upon educational institutions also varies with the rates of mobility observable in the community. In America these pressures tend to be exerted through school boards, and the election of school board members is often directly or indirectly mediated through voluntary groups and associations with deep roots in the community. It follows that subpopulations recently moving into the local scene are unable to voice their educational aspirations. As noted, elections to the board often take place only after a "caucus" of the "representative" voluntary associations establishes a slate of candidates. Such associations are likely to be dominated by individuals or groups with a maximal amount of seniority in the community. Accordingly school boards tend to be packed with "old-timers" and with individuals particularly insensitive to the changes which may have taken place in the social and economic composition of the community. This is certainly one of the factors which underlies the bitter conflict that in 1969 and 1970 opposed the school board of Evanston, Illinois, to the local superintendent. The school board was perhaps representative of the more "provincial" and entrepreneurial interests of the city and of the older long-established citizens who viewed educational integration as costly and likely to threaten the high quality of local educational facilities. At the same time the board was less attuned to the orientations and aspirations of the younger residents usually employed in large-scale companies who on the whole supported the superintendent.[31]

Internal differentiation of local communities.   The intensity and the form of the pressures exerted on schools vary with the aggregate socioeconomic and cultural characteristics of the community. American communities are differentiated from one another in terms of the social rank, life style, and the ethnic status of their respective subpopulations. It is easy enough to show how variations in the overall *average* score obtained by these communities on each one of these three axes of differentiation as well as in their relative internal homogeneity affects their educational outlook.

First, variations in social rank and hence in the control that subpopulations exert on their immediate surroundings are associated with parallel variations in the modes of interaction developed between schools and their public. Analyzing manifestations of conflict in 48 suburban school districts of Cook County, Illinois, D. Minar has shown that both participation and dissent in the elections to school boards tend to decline with the social rank of the communities—that is, with their aggregate educational and occupational scores.[32] The author suggests that this is because communities with a high social rank are able to develop appropriate mechanisms for channelling educational pressures. In such communities caucuses play a mediating role between community and school decision makers, and are therefore both more frequent and more effective than in communities with low social ranks. Thus 15 of the 24 high social rank districts sampled use the caucus as a method for nominating candidates to school boards elections as against only nine of their 24 low social rank counterparts. Among high social rank districts there was only one instance where caucus candidates were opposed by independents, but among their low social rank counterparts the number of these instances rose to four. Finally, where caucuses were used as the method of nomination for school board candidates, only one of the 15 districts with a high social rank was characterized by a high level of dissent at the time of elections, but such a high level of dissent plagued no less than seven of the nine low social rank districts.

Contrasts in the use of the caucuses by high and low social rank communities reflect at least five factors. First, populations characterized by a high social rank tend to participate more often and more intensely in voluntary associations and particularly in those concerned with educational issues. Accordingly caucuses are necessarily more representative. Second, high social rank communities are probably more homogeneous and this homogeneity enhances the efficiency of caucuses. Third, better educated persons and individuals engaged in managerial or in professional activities (who constitute by definition the majority of high social rank populations) are more likely to "understand specialization and delegation since they see it in their own life routines." As a result, the nomination of candidates to the board is apolitical but tends rather to be based upon comparison of individual expertises. Fourth, populations of high social rank areas have broad educational perspectives and are unlikely to raise minor issues with regard to the functioning of the board and the educational institutions. Finally, a high social rank implies a minimum amount of dependence toward immediate social context and a maximal access to alternative educational solutions. Dissatisfied parents in such areas will send their children to private schools. This in itself lowers potential conflicts over educational issues and correspondingly enhances the effectiveness of the caucus system.

Similarly variations in the life style prevailing among the subpopulations of different school districts affect the magnitude and the consistency of the pressures exerted on educational institutions. The study undertaken by Minar established a positive relationship between life styles (as measured by fertility) and participation in school board elections, or between life style and dissent evident in such elections as well as in educational referendums. (The respective correlation coefficients were .30, .39, and .36, respectively.) This is because subareas with a high level of familism and hence with a large number of large-sized families tend to be communities of high liability. Local residents are highly dependent upon their immediate environment and hence upon local educational issues. In addition, the membership of the voluntary associations dealing with educational issues in areas characterized by high familism tends to be predominantly female because the large number of children present in such areas prevents women from participating in the labor force. This affects the nature and the intensity of the pressures imposed upon schools. As the number of housewives participating both in voluntary associations involved in educational matters and in school board activities increases, the control exerted over the daily routines of educational institutions becomes tighter. The timetable of these women enables them to maintain close tabs on what is going on in school.[33]

Finally, variations in the ethnic composition of a particular subarea should influence both the nature and the intensity of the demands im-

posed upon school authorities. In the United States the stress placed
upon introduction of Afro-American studies in the curriculum varies
probably with the size of the black minorities living in a particular district.[34] The situation was the same in Africa during the colonial period,
and regardless of their relative social rank, African families were often
unable to send their children to secondary schools, not only because the
colonizer deemed this type of schooling unfit to their orientations but
also because these families were concentrated in neighborhoods where
educational facilities were both limited in number and low in quality.[35]

Characteristics of School Board Members.   School board members on
the whole belong to upper- and upper-middle-class segments of the
American society and most of them are professionals as well as business
executives.[36] A study conducted by R. Cauchran in Illinois in 1956
shows that in addition many of them are at least middle-aged and
hence do not necessarily have children of school age.[37] Changes in the
definition of school district boundaries however are likely to be associated with parallel changes in the composition of the school boards.
Although a number of school boards are anxious to have representatives of social or ethnic minorities (and hence of labor or of blacks),
revivals of the decentralization issues and the development of cam-
paigns centered around the problems of community control could very
well be associated with even more significant changes in the social and
cultural origin of school board members.
     Yet it is not certain that variations in the composition of school
boards will necessarily be associated with corresponding contrasts in
their orientations and hence in the nature and the intensity of the pressures which individual board members are likely to exert on school administrators. The nature of this association remains doubtful for a
number of reasons.[38] A democratization in the patterns of access to
school boards is not necessarily conducive to a "democratization" of the
pressures exerted on school administrators. First, appointment to a
school board may be conceived as a first step toward upward mobility.
Hence a lower-class school board member may view his appointment as
an indicator of his "assimilation" into a higher social category and accordingly he may refuse to vote as the members of his subgroup might
expect him to do. The sense of his own individual liberty will thus
override the sense of his responsibility toward his own social or ethnic
group. This pattern is not unlikely when school administrators are
coming from social and cultural circumstances deemed to be higher
than those of the board members themselves.

In addition, the multiplicity of mechanisms of control characterizing the educational scene may introduce a number of loopholes such that a number of significant educational decisions are not directly acted upon at the local level by school board members, but rather indirectly through negotiations between school administrators and the personnel of relevant state or federal agencies. This increasing complexity of educational bureaucracies may limit the control functions of school boards which are ultimately expected to legitimize the decisions already taken by school administrators.

Regardless of these caveats, it is still possible to contrast school board members and more generally educational elites in terms of the cosmopolitan or local nature of the views they hold toward educational processes.[39] *Cosmopolitan* leaders more frequently tend to be born and raised in large cities. Enjoying a relatively high educational level, they are highly mobile and are more likely to work in large-scale organizations. Hence their dependence upon the immediate environment is minimal and their networks of interaction tend to develop along occupational rather than geographical lines. They are most likely to view formal education as a means of achieving occupational and geographical mobility and of reinforcing the development of the occupational group to which they belong. In the United States cosmopolitan leaders tend to stress the value of college preparatory programs; they insist also upon the necessity of enlarging both the scope of the academic curriculum and the network of interactions between the school and the outside world.

Local leaders are more likely to be born in small and middle-sized communities. Their educational background is more limited and they are engaged in small-scale economic activities. They have a more restricted educational philosophy; in fact their views on education are highly ambivalent. They favor schooling insofar as they recognize that formal education offers a crucial key for the most rewarding slots of the labor market. But at the same time they fear that schools contribute to enlarge generational gaps. Their fear is reinforced by the mistrust that they hold vis a vis the teaching force that they consider to be morally unreliable. To use the terminology of Gans in *The Urban Villagers,* they tend to be torn apart between *object-oriented aspirations* which stress the learning of the skills necessary for individual occupational achievement, and *persons-oriented aspirations* which emphasize the teaching of rules of behavior appropriate to the adult peer group society and give preeminence to the internalization of discipline over the growth of individual skills and aspirations. While cosmopolitan leaders recognize the value of exploration and innovation in the field of education, local leaders want to perpetuate tradition.

The relative power of these two types of leaders varies with the characteristics of their community. The smaller the community, the greater its homogeneity, the more limited the autonomy of school boards toward other local political institutions, and the more likely it is that "local" leadership will prevail.

Organizational Complexity of Educational Bureaucracies. The effectiveness of school boards as mechanisms of control requires a low differentiation in the definition of educational roles, processes, and structures. As this differentiation becomes more salient, their grasp of the issues presented becomes necessarily weaker. In fact the effectiveness of boards presupposes that the job can be performed by "enlightened amateurs."

As educational differentiation takes place, participation in decision-making processes requires prior access to informations which are often controlled by educational administrators themselves. As a result school boards are increasingly dependent upon the goodwill of school personnel. Two factors contribute to accentuate their dependence. Insofar as school board members represent highly heterogeneous interest groups and have no clear-cut constituencies, they have no alternative access to the sources of information concerning the relevant issues. Further, their own turnover—combined to disparities between the length of their tenure in office and that of superintendent's—also reduces the leeway they would need along these lines.[40] As noted by Litwak and Meyer, educational administrators enjoy a greater number of strategies to communicate with the board as well as with the public at large.[41]

Correspondingly the nature, form, and intensity of pressures exerted by school board members are shaped by specific patterns of socialization. Newcomers tend to learn their trade both from members with more seniority and from the superintendent himself. This limits the arenas in which members are willing to intervene and they are reluctant to invade the field of educational policies per se. This reluctance is particularly manifest in small districts where members prefer to devote their attention to financial and personnel questions.

Under such conditions, the superintendent seems to be placed in a strong power position. Vidich and Bensman show that the superintendent of Springdale could manipulate teachers and PTA leaders to exert pressures on school board members. They also show how this superintendent makes allies among certain board members by providing them with technical information that would not be available to them through alternative channels.

Placed at the hub of a complex system whose elements are increasingly distant from one another, superintendents derive their power from their positions as experts. Yet this power remains fragile, as Gans reminds us in the *Levittowners*. [42] Expertise is often perceived as a "trick" favoring certain groups at the expense of others, and it is difficult for the expert to avoid being identified as a member of a particular social class. His success does not depend so much on his technical skills as on the consensus within the community on the desirability of the changes for which he suggests concrete solutions. In brief, the ever-increasing inability of school boards to meet the demands resulting from changes in the size and the functions of educational systems as well as the fragile omnipotence of school administrators help teachers to redefine their roles in the community and to obtain advantages previously forbidden to them.

Conclusions. In identifying the limits of the liberty that the school personnel enjoys vis a vis outside agencies and various segments of the community, I have suggested that—far from being static—this liberty depends upon the pressures exerted on school administrators by the outside world. The object of these pressures is twofold. They pertain not only to the functions assigned to educational processes and hence to definitions of what schools should be doing, but also to the resources allocated to educational institutions.

There are variations in the object, the form and the intensity of these pressures. These pressures may be direct or indirect since they involve both the formulation of clear-cut instructions as well as the formulation of vetos to decisions already taken by school personnel. Similarly these pressures may involve the allocation of resources or the refusal to grant funds to specific projects or activities. [43]

By moving from a macro- to a microanalysis, I have tried to make effective use of the method of "successive approximations" to identify the determinants of variations in the object, the form, and the intensity of pressures. The range of variations in pressures depends mainly upon the degree of centralization of political and educational institutions. When both types of institutions are highly centralized, the pressures that voluntary associations may exert to alter the financing and the curriculum of schools or the recruitment patterns of teachers tend to be indirect and limited in scope and intensity. Conversely these pressures tend to be not only more intense (although more variable) but also more direct and more diversified among societies where both types of institutions are decentralized. Finally, disparities in the relative centralization of educational and political institutions, as in Great Britain, seem to protect schools from immediate local pressures. Insofar as schools remain private, certainly they are influenced by the aspirations and orientations of their clientele but the pressures they experience tend to be effectively channeled through national mechanisms. Both national political parties and churches influence the curricula offered by British schools; both are instrumental also in the actual allocation of funds among existing institutions.

Regardless of variations in organizational set-ups, pressures also are affected by the local community characteristics. With an increase in the complexity of local economic organizations, the pressures exerted on schools become more specific. In addition the community's social differentiation maximizes the inconsistency of its educational expectations. This probably gives more power to school administrators and enables them eventually to pit social groups against one another.

Finally, the pressures exerted on educational institutions vary with the personal characteristics of the elites interested in educational problems. Yet the influence these leaders exert on the economic and personnel resources of the school and on its curriculum depends also upon the characteristics of both the communities and the societies in which they participate. It also depends upon the institutionalized linkage among the various mechanisms of control exerted on schools. For example, the outcome of pressures exerted on school systems is affected by contrasts between the composition of PTAs (acting as educational pressure groups) and that of boards (supposedly representing the variety of interests and preoccupations prevailing in the community). Indeed the real power of cosmopolitan or local leaders is certainly not alike when they choose to channel their aspirations through PTAs or boards. Nor is this power alike when there are marked contrasts in the goals pursued by these two types of organizations, as was the case in Springdale or in Levittown.

All these forces contribute to influence the direction, the form, the scope and the intensity of the pressures that a community exerts on the communication functions of schools. They help determine the content of the cultural heritage to be transmitted. They also contribute to influence the relative salience of the role to be played by schools with regard to the transmission of this heritage as compared to the functions they perform as far as vocational training and social placement are concerned.

NOTES AND REFERENCES

1. See P. Bourdieu "Le systeme des fonctions du systeme d'enseignement," in M. A. Mathijsen and C. W. Vervoort, eds., *Education in Europe,* (Paris: Mouton, 1969), pp. 181–190.

2. For a further discussion of the models accounting for educational struggle, see R. Collins, "Functional and Conflict Theories of Educational Stratification," *American Sociological Review,* Vol. 36, 1971, pp. 1002–1018.

3. For a full discussion, see A. Stinchcombe, "Social Structure and Organization," in J. March, ed., *Handbook of Organizations* (Chicago: Rand McNally, 1965), pp. 142–193.

4. For an elaboration of the distinction between intra- and interrole conflicts, see R. Brown, *Social Psychology* (New York: Free Press, 1965), pp. 156–170. The historical account by M. Katz of the votes cast in 1860 concerning the public school of Beverly, Massachusetts constitutes a good illustration of the forms taken by inter- and intraroles in the educational field. "Wealthy and prominent citizens supported the school as a harbinger of urban growth," while the opponents comprized both wealthy childless citizens and the least affluent segment of the community who "felt that the high school would not benefit their children." For a summary of this example, see S. Michelson, "The Political Economy of Public School Finance," in M. Carnoy, ed., *Schooling in a Corporate Society* (New York: McKay, 1972), p. 145.

5. See D. Armor, "School and Family Effects in Black and White Achievement," in F. Mosteller and D. Moynihan, eds., *On Equality of Educational Opportunity* (New York: Random House, 1972), p. 186.

6. *Ibid.* Yet "performance" remains only one criteria among others to compare schools. Radical reformers would argue that happiness is at least as important a criteria.

7. A. Vidich and J. Bensman, *Small Town in a Mass Society* (Princeton: Princeton University Press, 1958), Chapter 7.

8. Similarly, in the academic year 1969–1970, a female teacher employed by a public school in Catholic-dominated western France was dismissed by the principal because she refused to marry the man with whom she was living. The principal was afraid that this would undermine her own efforts to compete successfully with the local private school. See Y. Le Vaillant, "Mon Village à l'heure de sa fille mère," *Le nouvel observateur,* No. 321, January 1971, pp. 33–39.

9. For a more complete discussion of this theoretical model, see M. Spector and J. Kitsuse, "Social Problems: A Reformulation," *Social Problems,* Vol. 21, 1973, pp. 145–159.

10. See M. Kirst and D. Walker, "An Analysis of Curriculum Policy Making," *Review of Educational Research,* Vol. 41, 1971, pp. 492ff.

11. See M. Katz, "From Voluntarism to Bureaucracy in American Education," *Sociology of Education*, Vol. 44, 1971, pp. 297–332; see also L. Fein, *The Ecology of Public Schools* (New York: Pegasus, 1973).

12. For concrete examples of the negative consequences attached to the centralization of French Universities, see A. Touraine, *Le mouvement de Mai ou le Communisme Utopique* (Paris: Le Seuil 1968); see also M. Crozier, *La societe bloquée* (Paris: Le Seuil, 1970).

13. See N. Gross, *Who Runs Our Schools* (New York: Wiley, 1958), p. 50.

14. See L. Wylie, *Village in the Vaucluse* (Cambridge: Harvard University Press, 1957), pp. 62–64.

15. See R. T. and B. G. Anderson, *Bus Stop for Paris* (New York: Doubleday, 1965), pp. 58–59.

16. For a description of the role initially played by primary school teachers in the local society, see G. Bonheur, *La Republique nous appelle* (Paris: Laffont, 1965).

17. Their aspirations in this respect might be reinforced by their dependence upon local authorities—which might make their daily routines rather unpleasant. Depending on the goodwill of the city council for some of the basic expenditures of the school, the teacher can be blamed by the bureaucracy when he or she fails to get the appropriate pedagogical materials which should have been provided by municipal authorities. See H. Bastide, *Institutrice de village* (Paris: Mercure de France, 1969).

18. For a discussion of historical differences in the roles assigned to university professors in France and Germany, see A. Mitchell, "Higher Education in France: 1848–1900," *Journal of Contemporary History*, Vol. 2, 1967, pp. 81–100; F. Ringer, "Higher Education in Germany in the XIXth Century," *ibid.*, pp. 123–138. See also P. Bourdieu and J. C. Passeron, "La Comparabilité des systemes d'enseignement," in R. Castel and J. C. Passeron, eds., *Education democratie et developpement* (Paris, Mouton, 1967), p. 30.

19. See J. Armstrong, *The European Administrative Elite* (Princeton: Princeton University Press, 1973), pp. 105–106.

20. For a full discussion, see O. Banks, *Sociology of Education*, (London, Batsford, 1969), Chapter 6, 8. See also D. Peschek and J. Brand, "Polities and Politics in Secondary Education, Case Studies in West Ham and Reading," *Greater London Papers*, Vol. 11 (London: School of Economics, 1966). See also Edmonds, *The School Inspector* (London: Routledge and Kegan Paul, 1962).

21. See O. Banks, *Sociology of Education, ibid.*, pp. 113–114.

22. For a discussion of the perceptions of the advantages and shortcomings attached to centralization, see A. Etzioni, *The Active Society* (New York: Free Press, 1968), Chapter 15.

23. For a review of the changes in the attitudes held toward decentralization, see L. Fein, "The Limits of Universalism: Community School and Social

Theory," in H. Levin, eds., *Community Control of Schools* (Washington: Brookings Institute, 1970), pp. 76–99. The author contrasts his views of the black urban communities of 1970 with those held by M. Lieberman with regard to the educational climate of decentralized white-dominated institutions. In one case community control is defined as the positive manifestation of a "primary group." In the second case it is viewed as leading to a dull parochialism and attenuated forms of totalitarianism.

24. See R. Corwin, *Militant Professionalism* (New York: Appleton-Century-Croft, 1970), p. 45.

25. This resistance was in fact effective until the end of the West African Federation. Both African and European representatives at the Grand Conseil were hostile to the diffusion of vocational training programs, the former because such programs were managed by the Federation and would induce higher taxes for the Ivory Coast, the latter because such expenses would raise local labor costs. See R. Clignet, "Ivory Coast," in *Encyclopedia for Education* (New York: Wiley, 1970).

26. A. Vidich and Bensman, *op. cit.*

27. See R. Corwin, *A Sociology of Education* (New York: Appleton-Century-Croft, 1965), p. 375.

28. For a full treatment of this point, see R. Corwin, *ibid.*, Part IV. For a more detailed treatment of the distinction between pyramidal and factional power structures, see J. Walton, "Discipline, Method and Community Power, A Note on the Sociology of Knowledge," *American Sociological Review*, Vol. 31, 1966, pp. 684–689.

29. See H. Gans, *The Levittowners* (New York: Pantheon, 1967), notably Chapter 5.

30. For a discussion of the interrelations between commitment and length of urban experience, see E. Litwak, "Voluntary Associations and Neighborhood Cohesion," *American Sociological Review*, Vol. 26, 1961, pp. 258–271.

31. For an account of these events, see the entire collection of *The Evanston Review* for the year 1969. For a discussion of the conditions under which a caucus system might be efficient, see D. Minar, "The Community Basis of Conflict in School System Politics," *American Sociological Review*, Vol. 31, 1966, pp. 822–834.

32. See D. Minar, *op. cit.*

33. For a general discussion of the effects of aggregate community characteristics, see S. Greer, "The Social Structure and Political Process of Suburbia," *American Sociological Review*, Vol. 25, August 1960, pp. 514–526. The effects of the particular demographic composition of American suburbs on the pressures exerted on schools should be noted here. The social networks of female suburbanites are close-knit, while those of their husbands tend to be loose-knit. The assymetry characteristic of such networks cannot but affect the consistency of the demands formulated by parents.

34. For a discussion of the effects of ethnic isolation on participation in this country, see C. Nohara, "Social Context and Neighborliness: The Negro in Saint Louis," in S. Greer et al., eds., *The New Urbanization* (New York: St. Martin's Press, 1968), pp. 179–188.

35. This can explain why the relationship between chances of getting ahead in the school system and the size of the place of birth or of residence of individuals is not linear. Schools in the main cities of French-speaking Africa, for example, are not necessarily as good as the institutions located in the hinterland. For a discussion of this observation, see R. Clignet and P. Foster, *The Fortunate Few* (Evanston: Northwestern University Press, 1966), Chapters 3, 4.

36. For a review of such studies, see R. Havighurst and B. Neugarten, *Society and Education* (Boston: Allyn and Bacon, 1962), pp. 27–28; see also R. Corwin, *op. cit.*, pp. 153, 378–379.

37. See R. Caughran, "The School Board Member Today," *American School Board Journal*, Vol. 133, November–December 1956.

38. See S. Michelson, "The Political Economy of Public School Finance," *op. cit.*

39. For a general discussion, see H. Gans, *The Urban Villagers* (New York: Free Press, 1963), pp. 129–136.

40. See N. Kerr, "The Schoolboard as an Agency of Limitation," *Sociology of Education*, Vol. 38, 1964, pp. 34–60. For another example of a discussion concerned with variations in modes of participation in decision making structures, their determinants, and implications, see M. Gittell, "Decision Making in the School: New York City, A Case Study," in M. Gittell, ed., *Educating an Urban Population* (Beverly Hills; Sage, 1967), pp. 205–239. The author shows how educational administrators have succeeded in convincing the various institutional groups who control their work that such a control can be exerted only by professional experts. Consequently public education policy has become the province of the professional bureaucrat with the tragic result that policy alternatives are neither weighted nor even offered.

41. "A Balance Theory of Coordination Between Bureaucratic Organizations and Community Primary Groups," *Administrative Science Quarterly*, Vol. 11, 1958, pp. 31–59.

42. For a full discussion see H. Gans, *The Levittowners, op. cit.*, pp. 351–353.

43. An example of this is President Nixon's proposal to limit the scholarship program and replace it by programs of grants-in-aid to be reimbursed. The cuts in federal programs of assistance to higher education resulted both from the financial pressures associated with the war in Vietnam and the negative stance taken by students toward it.

4

THE VULNERABILITY OF
SCHOOL PERSONNEL TO
EXTERNAL INFLUENCES

The effectiveness of the pressures exerted on the personnel of educational institutions depends upon the vulnerability of teachers and administrators and hence upon the degree to which they are able to form privileged, independent, and homogeneous subcultures. The formation of such subcultures enhances the immediate resistance teachers and administrators can mount against encroachments on their autonomy, and enables individuals to enjoy a maximal amount of liberty. In this chapter I examine the conditions under which teachers are granted the status of professionals. I identify the mechanisms by which an occupational group perpetuates its professional status and assess the degree to which teachers and educational administrators can make an effective use of such mechanisms. These mechanisms pertain to:

1. Patterns of access into the occupational group. Selectivity and standardization in modes of access enhance resistance against external pressures. As individual practitioners are recruited from socially and culturally privileged groups, they enjoy an additional amount of power which enables them to successfully bargain with political authorities. Further, the absence of variations both in the background of these individuals and in the legal rules underlying access to the occupational group maximizes its members' solidarity.

2. Patterns of socialization into the occupational group. Insofar as the effectiveness of the resistance that an occupational group can mount against external influences depends upon its cohesiveness, this effec-

tiveness should be increased by both the severity and the standardization of socialization processes. The more severe the *rites of passage*
necessary for gaining access to the activity, the more individual practitioners will value their affiliation to the group and the more occupational loyalty they will display. Similarly this loyalty is likely to be enhanced whenever successive groups of new members are everywhere
subjected to the same socialization processes.

3. The work organization of the occupational group. As the members
of an occupational group develop similar patterns of interaction with
their clients, their interpretations of what their tasks consist of will be
increasingly alike. So will be their relations with other segments of society.

The degree to which teachers and administrators can claim the status
of professionals also varies with (*a*) the modes of organization of the
school systems in which they are exerting their activities and whether
such systems are centralized or decentralized, (*b*) the differentiation of
schools into primary, secondary, and postsecondary institutions, and (*c*)
the differentiation of individual roles and activities within each type of
institution. Accordingly I examine how these three variables influence
the modes of recruitment of school personnel, their socialization processes to the demands and norms of their activities, and the autonomy
they enjoy in their occupational roles.

**Prerequisites to the Professionalization of Teachers and Administra-
tors.** School administrators and teachers justify their aspiration to
enjoy a maximal amount of liberty in their occupation, by the notion
that schools are primarily a locus of "professional" activities. What are
the conditions under which a particular occupational category is
granted the status of a profession and what are the consequences that
this status entails on its organization? [1]

The main criteria underlying the allocation of a professional status to
a particular occupation is the scarcity of the services it renders. Not
only must there be a universal demand for the occupation's services but
there must also be the belief that the practices mediating such services
are integrated in a full body of knowledge accessible to only a small
elite. Medical doctors, priests, architects, and lawyers are thus treated
as professionals because of the importance attached to the physical,
spiritual, material, and political survival of individuals and groups and
also because of the restricted access to the knowledge required to
render such services. For a long time, "professions" were deemed to

maintain privileged relationships with the "sacred," and law as well as medicine and architecture were dominated by religious prescriptions and subjected to the control of priests.

Initially, teaching activities in European countries were exclusively performed by groups who had already acquired the status of professionals (priests, lawyers, medical doctors). It is not difficult to understand how this status progressively spread to the entire teaching force. Yet the extent of this transfer varies with specific patterns of educational development. It has been more evident in the case of European secondary school teachers than in the case of their American counterparts because the early functions of formal schooling were more "elitist" in the first context. While the political and cultural history of many European countries raises the question of whether teachers are able to *maintain* their status as professionals, the decentralized nature of American institutions and the persistence of antiintellectual trends in the history of the country raise the question of whether American teachers are able to *achieve* such a status.

By modern times, two forces at least have enabled teachers to justify their claims to be treated as professionals. First, although the linkage between education and occupation becomes more formalized and bureaucratic, social views concerning the status of children have changed and tend to stress the variety of individual students' interests and aspirations.[2] In turn the emergence of this view calls for the development of personalized relationships between the teacher and his clients, and this personalization enhances the value—and hence the scarcity—of the services he renders. Division of labor has been conducive to specialization of knowledge and hence to an increased limitation in the controls that laymen are able to exert on the techniques and knowledges of teachers. In a way, the "expert" of today is the heir of the "professional of yesterday." Both invoke their competence as a basis for their claim to autonomy and to the control of their own activities.

Yet the claims of teachers to be treated as professionals are negatively affected by the enhanced diffusion of formal schooling. This diffusion has been associated with a decline in the significance of the rewards attached to academic achievement. Because of compulsory school attendance, the knowledge acquired in school has ceased to be treated as a scarce valuable. Compulsory attendance has also led to a sharp increase in the number of individuals engaged in teaching activities, hence to a sharp accentuation of differences in the social origin and teaching styles of teachers. Correspondingly pedagogy is not regarded as one single unified body of knowledge.

Further, industrialization and technological development are perhaps accompanied by an increase in the number of occupational groups demanding the title of professionals, but also by a rise in the social pressures exerted to maintain the number of occupational groups recognized as professionals as limited as possible. Since the privileges attached to this title vary as a reverse function of the number of the individuals who can claim it, lawyers and medical doctors, for example, have a vested interest in preventing other occupations from enjoying such a status. With the relative decline in the value of the services they render, teachers often have been unable to maintain or enhance the social position they had initially acquired.

Finally, the decline in the relative status allocated to teachers has been accelerated by the secularization both of the entire society, and of the teaching force itself. To the society at large, secularization implies the emergence of a variety of ideological or religious denominations and a subsequent decline in the belief that Truth is one and indivisible, and to schools, secularization implies a growing differentiation of educational objectives and techniques. This in turn has induced growing disparities in the organization of individual school systems and in their recruitment patterns. Correspondingly teachers have ceased to be regarded as an homogeneous occupational group and this has been particularly so in countries where school systems are decentralized and where teachers cannot protect their vested interests by the methods usually utilized by professionals.

The members of a profession are entitled to exert an exclusive control on the recruitment, socialization, and occupational activities of new members. An examination of these prerogatives should enable us to determine not only whether teachers are in fact professionals but also whether distinctions should be entered in this respect among various categories of the teaching force.

Recruitment of Teachers and School Administrators. An occupational group may be considered as a profession to the extent that its members' recruitment approximates the three following conditions:

1.   The practitioners of that occupation must legitimately control the definition and the administration of the prerequisites underlying access to the occupation itself. Political institutions should sanction as illegal the unlicensed practice of the activity defined as professional. For instance, the unlicensed practice of medicine is a punishable form of deviance but illicit access to "nonprofessional"—albeit strongly "union-

ized"—occupations is not. Printers, for example, might be inclined to punish intruders but the rest of society will not give its full approval. The extent to which an occupational group is legitimately expected to define its own standards for admission reflects the relative power that this particular group holds over other segments of the society at large. Further it necessarily enhances the solidarity which binds together the practitioners themselves and it increases the resistance they can mount against the claims and demands of outsiders.

2.   The control that the occupational group exerts on the recruitment of new members should be standardized across the entire system. Spatial or temporal variations in rules of recruitment lower the homogeneity of the practitioners and hence their cohesiveness.

3.   New members must be predominantly recruited from the upper segments of society. The positive selectivity underlying new member recruitment symbolizes the scarcity of the services rendered by the occupation and shapes the resistance that practitioners are able to display toward the pressures of their clients and of the public in general.

Autonomy and Standardization in the Recruitment Procedures of Teachers.   In general, access to teaching presupposes admission to an examination defined and administered by educational authorities themselves, and in this sense teachers can be considered as professionals. There are however significant crosscultural variations in this respect. Among centralized countries (for example, France) success in the examination guarantees automatic access into the national school system and the assignment of a new teacher to a teaching slot usually reflects compromises between the needs of the organization, the expectations of individuals with higher seniority than the candidate, and his own achievement, orientations and aspirations. The tight monopoly exerted by educators on certifying examinations enables them furthermore to control the volume of inputs in the profession. In France, the number of candidates admitted to the *Aggrégation* (the certifying competitive examination allowing individuals to teach in *Lycées*) is often markedly less than the number of persons officially defined as needed by the school system itself. This allegedly enables *Aggrégés* to claim that they maintain the quality of entrants in the system at an optimal level.

In a country with a decentralized system, (for example, the United States) the situation is somewhat different. The existence of an accrediting process symbolizes the value—and hence the scarcity—of the services rendered by teachers; yet in many states, teachers do not control the process, and in 10 states professional educators are specifically excluded from licensing bureaus.[3] Often enough, a teaching certificate is a necessary but insufficient condition for teaching, for the actual hiring of a candidate is left to the discretion of the superintendent or of the board. Further, the decentralized nature of American institutions introduces marked variations in the nature of the certifying examination itself, and there are significant disparities in the educational level attained by teachers occupying similar positions in parallel school systems.

In the United States the same disparities characterize the educational prerequisites underlying access to the position of principals or superintendents. In 1961, 32 states required primary school principals to have a master of arts degree, and in three other states principals were expected to go beyond the M.A. For their counterparts in secondary schools, 35 states demanded an M.A. and six states expected candidates to have more than that degree. Finally, while 12 states required more than an M.A. from their superintendents, this degree was sufficient in 34 states.[4]

Decentralization limits the control that educators can exert on the entry of new individuals into the teaching force. The corresponding lack of homogeneity in the characteristics of American teachers induces significant variations in the orientations and expectations they entertain toward their colleagues, their superordinates in the system, and their students. In fact decentralization prevents the socialization of prior generations and of colleagues from being complementary and mutually reinforcing.[5]

Selectivity of Recruitment.   An occupational group can be considered a profession when its new members are selected from narrow and highly valued segments of society. The corresponding forms of selectivity may be social, academic, or motivational—that is, candidates to the profession must present certain social, academic, and personality traits which distinguish them markedly from the society at large.

Early British educational history offers a case in point. During the nineteenth century teachers were often selected by headmasters among their "most intelligent and moral" pupils. During a five-year apprenticeship, those chosen individuals continued to receive daily 90 minutes of teaching from the headmaster who had selected them and for the rest of the time they acted as a teacher in the school.[6] After this trial period, those "fortunate few" were entitled to enter an examination of admission into a teachers training college. Thus future teachers had to satisfy both the particularistic demands of their own headmasters as well as the more universalistic requirements of the profession as a whole.

The control exerted on the recruitment of new secondary school teachers was analogous. Each school recruited predominantly the personnel it needed from among its own alumni (for example, three-quarters of the teachers appointed to Eton between 1801 and 1862 were themselves graduates of that institution).[7] This pattern served two functions: Candidates to the job had a most "proper" background, and they were "presocialized" to the demands of the occupation.

Social selectivity. Many European secondary schools early exerted a tight control on the recruitment of new teachers, but primary institutions generally did not. Variations in the initial degree of hostility or of indifference of European elites to the diffusion of literacy have been associated with parallel contrasts in the status ascribed to primary school teachers and hence in the relative position they occupied in the general social structure. At the end of the Ancien Regime in France, the teachers paid by the king were still very few in number. In fact teaching remained often enough a semiclandestine activity carried out by retired or crippled war veterans or by former convicts. In England the majority of the primary schools catering to the needs of the working classes were staffed by persons whose only qualification for that role was their unfitness for every other, while in Germany or Netherland the relative status of teachers was much higher.[8] The professionalization of primary school teachers and the consequent rise in their status did not take place before the middle of the nineteenth century, when both political and economic development required an accentuated diffusion of literacy and hence an institutionalization of primary schooling.

Thus, the professionalization of teachers depends upon the perceptions that the majority of the population holds toward the scarcity of the services rendered by this occupational group. As long as the formal schooling of the masses is of little value for the established elites, primary school teachers necessarily occupy a marginal position in the society at large.

Yet a further accentuation of the prevailing patterns of economic and social development leads to a decline in the control that primary and secondary school teachers may exert upon the modes of access into their own occupational group. As the number of opportunities offered in the white-collar labor market begins to increase, the relative attraction exerted by teaching careers declines and the recruitment into that occupational group becomes more open. This can be demonstrated both through a comparative analysis of the educational and occupational choices of a particular age group of students, and through a comparative examination of the recruitment patterns of teachers with differing ages. In the Ivory Coast, for example, although the number of white-collar jobs is still limited, teachers' colleges tend already to attract fewer students. Further, candidates to teaching come from families with a lower level of participation in modern structures than the families of pupils enrolled in institutions which offer a larger number of occupational outlets. Thus about one-third of the students attending *Cours Normaux* (the local equivalents of teachers' colleges) are children of farmers who are not engaged in a market economy, but the corresponding proportion declines to less than 27 percent among the students of *Lycees*. Regardless of the type of school attended, it is also the students coming from the least modernized background who are the most frequently attracted by teaching jobs.[9]

An analysis of the educational level of the male teaching force and the male adult population of Douala and Yaounde, the two major urban centers of Cameroun, confirms the declining attraction of teaching as an occupation [10] (Table 6). Thus the proportion of individuals with a postprimary education increases with age among teachers but the pattern is reversed among other adult male urban residents. Younger individuals with a postprimary training are less than seven times more numerous in the teaching force than in the remaining part of the adult population, but among older populations the percentage of individuals with this high educational background is 20 times larger among teachers than among other city dwellers. The significance of this difference is even greater when one realizes that opportunities for gaining access to postprimary institutions were few in number for the group over 45 years of age, and that access to such schools was limited to quite narrow segments of society. The corresponding opening of teaching jobs to relatively less educated and much more socially diverse segments of the younger populations reflects the intervention of two forces. The educational development of the Cameroun has been associated with an expansion of the white-collar labor market and with an increase in the number of jobs deemed to be more rewarding than teaching and hence preempted by younger elites. In addition, the diffusion of formal schooling has also required a lowering of the prerequisites governing access into the teaching force. The relationship between the decline in selectivity and the expansion of the educational system itself is suggested by the fact that individuals less than 35 years

Table 6. *Educational Level of Male Teachers and All Other Adult Males Residing in Douala and Yaounde, by Age (Percentage Distributions)* [a]

	Age					
	Less than 35		35–45		Over 45	
Educational Level	Teachers	Adult Population	Teachers	Adult Population	Teachers	Adult Population
Less than primary education	5.7	74.9	12.4	89.0	20.1	93.7
Primary education completed	61.0	19.4	53.4	7.4	37.1	4.0
Above primary	33.3	5.7	34.2	3.6	42.8	2.3
Total	100.0	100.0	100.0	100.0	100.0	100.0
N	(748)	(37048)	(105)	(15143)	(35)	(9622)

[a] Douala census (1964) and Yaounde Census (1962). Analysis conducted by R. Clignet and J. Sween.

of age are more numerous among teachers than in the remainder of
the population at large. Younger individuals represent almost 85 percent of the entire teaching population but only about 71 percent of all
the other residents of Douala and Yaounde. The recent expansion of
formal schooling in the urban environment leads schools to recruit a
larger number of younger teachers, but these teachers are proportionately less educated than their elders and their familial background is less
modern.

The decline in social selectivity is even more apparent in the case of
industrialized nations. In Great Britain, for example, among the educators who have the proper credentials for teaching in secondary institutions, no less than 54 percent of those 45 years and older have at least a
middle-upper-class origin as against only 41 percent of those under 35
years of age.[11] Decentralization also leads selectivity to vary markedly
with the type of secondary institution in which teachers serve. These institutions differ from one another in terms of their academic functions.
Modern schools provide their students with a terminal type of postprimary training, but grammar schools prepare their own pupils to enter
universities. These differences are associated with parallel disparities
not only in the academic abilities and the social background of their
student populations but also in the characteristics of their teaching
forces. The social origin of modern secondary school teachers is more
modest than that of their counterparts employed by grammar schools.
Further, changes over time in the respective profiles of these two types
of teachers have not followed similar patterns. In modern schools the
proportion of individuals with a modest origin (lower-middle-class and
below) hardly varies between 67 percent for teachers over 45 years of
age and 65 percent for their younger counterparts. Conversely the
prestige of grammar schools seems to have declined, since the corresponding figures are 49 and 58 percent respectively.[12]

British secondary schools differ also from one another in their specific historical development, their modes of financing, and their clientele. Usually older than maintained grammar schools, direct grant institutions more often have private endowments and they receive their
subsidies directly from the central Department of Education rather
than from local educational authorities. Because of their prestige and
their independence, direct grant institutions usually cater to more privileged segments of the British society than maintained grammar
schools. Correspondingly the status of direct grant grammar school
teachers is higher than that of their counterparts in maintained grammar schools (Table 7). Yet, the relative preeminence of the former

Table 7.   Social Origin of Teachers in Various Types of British Secondary Institutions, England and Wales, 1955 (Percentage Distribution) a

	Type of Institution					
	Modern		Maintained Grammar		Direct Grant Grammar	
Paternal Occupation	Men	Women	Men	Women	Men	Women
Professionals and managerials	7	11	13	18	20	30
Intermediate	46	55	55	63	62	57
Skilled manuals	37	28	25	16	14	10
Semi and unskilled manuals	10	6	7	3	4	3
Total	100	100	100	100	100	100
N	1128	1083	1209	1100	544	733

a Derived from J. Floud and R. Scott, "Recruitment to teaching in England and Wales" in J. Halsey, J. Floud and C. A. Anderson, eds., *Education, Economy and Society* (New York: The Free Press, 1961) Table 11, p. 540.

should decline with the growing centralization of the British educational system and the declining differentiation of secondary institutions.

However the decline in social selectivity is not necessarily the same in various industrialized countries. For instance, although in France and Great Britain the functions of secondary schooling were historically analogous and although in both countries the notion of elite implied the necessity of learning the humanities, there are significant contrasts in the developmental patterns of the two secondary teaching forces. In England from early times, to enter educational professions represented a slight lateral advance from the clergy and related occupations. But in France secondary school teaching remained a major upward mobility channel for a longer period of time. Between 1900 and 1914 only 5 percent of French secondary school teachers were the sons of individuals teaching at the same level and 14 percent had fathers who were themselves primary school teachers. At least three-fifths of the secon-

dary school teaching force of the time were from other lower-middle-
class working class and peasant families.[13] Contrasts in the early social
composition of teaching forces and in the periods at which they have
reached their highest social status have certainly a number of implications on the current ability of the British and French school systems to
attract candidates from desirable backgrounds.

If two industrialized countries whose educational institutions perform similar functions do not necessarily have teaching forces with similar social characteristics, one may expect that the relevant contrasts will
be even more striking when one compares countries whose schools
have different organizational profiles and serve distinctive purposes.
Indeed it is difficult to determine whether there has been a decline in
the selectivity of American teachers. To be sure, there has been a considerable increase in the size of the United States teaching force and
this increase should be associated with a corresponding decline in the
restrictions governing access into teaching.[14] There were 200,000 public school teachers in 1870, twice as many in 1900, and by 1960 the
number had risen to 2,060,000. This high growth rate of the American
teaching force has not been accompanied by a decline of its educational
qualification. Thus in 1908 Thorndike estimated that 55 percent of
American secondary school male teachers had less than a college degree and that the same was true of almost one-half of their female colleagues. But a study undertaken in 1930 indicated that the overall percentage of secondary teachers with less than a college degree had
dropped to 13 percent. Current data indicate a substantial continuing
increase in the educational quality of both primary and secondary
school teachers.

However increase in quality does not necessarily mean that access
into that occupation is still socially selective. In fact economic and educational developments in the United States have been associated with a
marked increase in the number of openings in the professional sector
of activity, as this term is defined by the Census Bureau, and hence
with a decline in the visibility of teaching within that sector.[15] While
teachers constituted 40 percent of all professional workers in 1900,
they made up only 28 percent of that particular population in 1950
despite a threefold increase in their own numbers. The decline is
largely due to the openings of new professional fields to educated females. With an erosion in the relative salience of teaching among other
"professions," is there a corresponding decrease in the social selectivity
of teachers? There are in fact two ways of testing this hypothesis. The
first one consists in examining whether students choosing teaching as a

career during their freshman year, and whether individuals defecting from that field or attracted into it during the course of their college experiences, share the same profile as the entire college population. The second one consists of examining current contrasts in the profiles of teachers and of the "common man."

In his study of the occupational choices of the American college population, Davis shows first that the education field is underchosen by males and by individuals coming from a high socioeconomic background and a large urban environment, but overchosen by blacks. Thus the field offers a sharp contrast with law or medicine which tend to attract a disproportionate number of males and individuals coming from an urban environment or from a high socioeconomic status. Davis also shows that females and black college students from smaller communities who had initially expected to enter a career other than teaching tend to move into that field. Thus he suggests that the segments of the college population who because of their ascriptive traits have a limited range of occupational choices, will ultimately enter teaching. Hence there is a negative social selectivity in the recruitment of teachers among college graduates.[16]

Similarly data on the educational background of the entire teaching force suggest that educated teachers are "closer" to the common man today than they were by 1940, since differences in the educational background of teachers and other segments of the adult population have declined (Table 8). Teachers are necessarily closer to the common man in social and cultural terms as well because access into college has become more open. Yet the decline in the attraction exerted by teaching is not necessarily consistent. Thus Table 9 shows that teachers of both sexes between 35 and 44 years of age in 1960 are better educated than their younger and older colleagues. The higher educational attainment of the intermediary group is related to variations in the overall opportunities offered by the labor market. The aftermaths of postwar depressions are probably responsible for these variations, and the most educated younger adults are likely to be attracted by new and more rewarding types of jobs, whereas such opportunities were not necessarily available to the age group which preceded them in college.

As teaching ceases to attract the most privileged segments of the male population, women tend uniformly more often to enter the field. Since these women tend still to originate from socially selected groups, there are increased contrasts between their own backgrounds and that of their male colleagues. In England, for example, the social origin of female teachers is not only uniformly higher than that of males but sex

Table 8. Educational Selectivity of the Primary and Secondary Teaching Force in the United States (% with More Than Four Years of College) [a]

	Males			Females		
Date	Primary and Secondary Teaching Force	Adult Population	Selectivity Ratio	Primary and Secondary Teaching Force	Adult Population	Selectivity Ratio
1940	73.7	5.7	12.9	51.7	3.8	13.6
1960	86.7	9.7	8.9	71.2	5.8	12.2

[a] Derived from J. Folger and C. Nam, *Education of the American Population*, Washington, U.S. Department of Commerce, Tables V-5, p. 143, and III-2, p. 85.

Table 9. Educational Characteristics of Male and Female Teachers in the United States (Percentage Distribution) [a]

	Males			Females		
	16–34	35–44	45 and over	16–34	35–44	45 and over
Less than four years of college	15	9	15	28	23	33
Four years of college	43	22	22	57	48	39
More than four years of college	42	69	63	15	29	28

[a] Derived from J. Folger and C. Nam *op. cit.*, p. 82, Figure III-5.

differences along these lines tend to be most marked in the highly prestigious direct grant grammar schools. Similarly in the United States, while the gap between the educational attainment of male and female teachers seems to shrink, the social selectivity of highly educated female teachers remains higher than that of their male counterparts. A study undertaken in 1960 shows that about 23 percent of male teachers held an additional job against only less than 3 percent of their female colleagues; this indirectly suggests that the latter's husband occupied a higher position in the occupational ladder.[17]

Data from France and Belgium confirm these trends. In the first country, female teachers are more frequently from an urban origin than their male colleagues.[18] No less than 45 percent of the former come from a middle-class background as against only 35 percent of the males. Most significant, about 27 percent of the husbands of French female primary school teachers can be considered middle class, whereas this is true of only 3 percent of the wives of their male colleagues. In Belgium, an analysis of the social origin of the students enrolled in *Ecoles Normales Moyennes* (the teachers' colleges that train individuals for positions in terminal postprimary institutions) showed that 37 percent of the male students had a lower class background as against only 29 percent of their female peers.[19]

However differentials in the recruitment patterns of male and female teachers do not imply that the latter are uniformly derived from privileged strata of society. A study of Brazilian teachers' colleges conducted by A. Gouveia in 1960 shows that the relative number of girls enrolled in teachers' colleges who intend to enter the teaching profession drops from 58 percent for the students with a lower-class origin to 33 percent among their classmates with a middle- or upper-class background.[20] As the labor market widens and offers new opportunities to educated women, the first to take advantage of the new situation are those who have appropriate channels of information to hear about such opportunities, who have adequate social networks to make use of the relevant information, and who run a minimal risk in indulging in such innovative behaviors. Upper- and middle-class educated women are evidently in a much better position in this respect than their counterparts from lower strata of society, especially in a country like Brazil where access to professional employment is still conditioned by particularistic and ascriptive forces.

Changes in patterns of access to teaching are alike for both men and women. These changes however occur later in the second case.

Academic selectivity. Despite the differing levels of occupational differentiation prevailing in countries such as Belgium, Brazil, and the Ivory Coast, the choice of teaching as a career appears to be negatively related to academic achievement. In Belgium the regents (the teachers graduating from *Ecoles Normales Moyennes* and trained to teach in the lower grades of postprimary institutions) are more likely to have followed the easy route of a modern curriculum than to have engaged in the academically demanding classical studies.[21] Further, those who have undergone modern training usually have specialized in economics, which is deemed to be the least demanding of all the branches offered in this particular curriculum.

Regardless of the institutions attended, secondary school students attracted by a teaching career are also more likely to have previously attained lower levels of academic performance. In Belgium one-third of the regents have repeated classes in the process of their secondary studies, and many of them were motivated to enter this career because of the low level of their prior academic performances. Similarly in the Ivory Coast, students currently enrolled in teachers' college are more likely to have repeated classes than their peers enrolled in classical or modern lycees.[22] Finally, Gouveia shows that in Brazil among female students enrolled in teachers' colleges, inclination to teach varies both with social class and academic achievement. Among students derived from fortunate circumstances, variations in level of academic achievement hardly affect degree of commitment to teaching—which remains uniformly low. Among their lower-class counterparts conversely, the percentage of students inclined to teach increases from 19 percent among those with top academic ranking to 40 percent among their underachieving counterparts in the state of Sao Paulo and from 21 to 56 percent for the two similar types of subpopulations in the state of Minas Gerais.[23]

Data available in the United States confirm these trends. Although the overall academic achievement of the college seniors choosing to enter an educational career is not lower than that of their total graduating class, their academic performance is still about 10 percent lower than that of their counterparts choosing medicine, physical and social sciences, or the humanities. Further, a lower educational attainment during college is likely to favor both the retention of teaching as an occupational choice and the drift away from other aspirations toward education. This is particularly true of men, whose occupational aspirations are more closely determined by objective and universalistic factors than those of women.[24]

To conclude, decline in the attraction of teaching as a career is uniformly associated with a decrease in the academic selectivity underlying the recruitment of future teachers.

Motivational selectivity. Changes in the composition of teaching forces should be associated with parallel variations in the value systems and orientations underlying their occupational choices. Gouveia argues that in view of the feminine character attributed to the teachers role and to the sheltered atmosphere of the school, Brazilian candidates to teaching should be characterized by a strong attachment to traditional norms and principles. Accordingly she constructed a scale comprised of 16 items designed to measure the degree to which the students entertained modern or traditional values with regard to the functions of formal schooling, participation in the labor force, and familial relations.[25] Although a majority of students obtained scores which placed them at the traditional end of the continuum, traditional attitudes were most frequent among students whose parents had a low educational attainment. Most important however, only 39 percent of the individuals with modern orientations were inclined to teach as against 48 percent of those with a traditional outlook.

The relationship between the nature of the attitudes held by students and their commitment to teaching as a career varied however along social class lines. Whereas differences in the percentage of upper-class girls attracted to teaching did not vary with the traditional or modern nature of their attitudes, there were sharp contrasts between students with a lower class origin, and almost two-thirds of the latter were willing to teach when they held traditional attitudes as against only 44 percent of those with modern orientations. Traditional orientations seem to exert a particularly strong impact on the projected career of individuals whose horizon is already limited by their social origin.

This is also so when that horizon is blocked by a lack of academic abilities. Whereas the less able students were uniformly the most likely to teach, traditional orientations enhanced their commitment toward teaching. In Sao Paulo the percentage of tradition-oriented students rose from 33 percent among individuals with a high academic status, to 53 percent among those with poor grade records. These differentials were less marked among the students with modern orientations, and the corresponding percentages were 25 and 38 percent respectively. The combined influence of traditionalism and of social as well as academic marginality on their occupational choices should lower their professionalization as teachers.

In the United States Davis shows clearly that the choice of teaching as a career is closely positively related to the desire of working with people and hence with service orientations but negatively associated with the desire to make a lot of money.[26] Such associations however are different for the two sexes. Because the occupational opportunities available to men are more numerous, the influence of positive orientations toward service activities and of negative orientations toward earning a lot of money is proportionately more visible among male than female students. Among male freshmen, no less than 21 percent of the individuals favorably oriented toward working with people but hostile toward earning a lot of money choose teaching as their future occupation as against only 4 percent of those with negative orientations toward service activities and positive attitudes toward money. In contrast, while 53 percent of the female freshmen with the first set of attitudinal characteristics decide to enter teaching, this occupational choice characterizes only 33 percent of their counterparts with negative attitudes toward working with people but positive orientations toward making money. Similarly 14 percent of the individual males with the first set of attitudes are ultimately attracted toward teaching despite an initially different occupational choice, against only 3 percent of those with negative orientations toward people but positive attitudes toward money. The relevant figures for women are 37 and 16 percent respectively. While in *absolute* terms certain sets of orientations predispose female students toward teaching, the *relative* effects of variations in such attitudes on occupational choices are more powerful among their male classmates.

Depending upon the sex of students, the influence of attitudes on the choice of teaching is also affected by their background as well as by their academic performances during college. Among white women, the proportion of seniors choosing to enter teaching varies from a maximal of 75 percent for those who come from a low socioeconomic background in a small town, have a poor overall level of academic performance, and have a favorable attitude toward working with people but hold a negative stance toward earning a lot of money, to a minimal of 24 percent for those who have an urban upper-class environment, had a high level of attainment during their college years, and are interested in earning a lot of money but are hostile to the idea of working with people. Among their male counterparts, the corresponding range is proportionately larger and the relevant figures are 42 and 1 percent respectively.

In brief, the choice of teaching as a career seems to decline as the number of perceived alternative channels for upward mobility increases. This number is itself determined by:

1. The general development of the social system in which students participate. In colonial countries, the relative attraction exerted by teaching jobs has constantly declined with political development. While the early graduates of the *Ecole William Ponty* in French West Africa were more favorably inclined toward this occupation than nursing or clerical work (for which they were also prepared), there was a progressive reversal in their choice toward the end of the colonial regime.[27] These graduates became aware of the new opportunities offered by the emerging economic and political development of their countries. Similarly in Brazil attraction toward teaching seems to be greater and more stable for the population of schools located in regions with low levels of urbanization and industrialization, hence for the students the least likely to perceive alternative occupational opportunities.

2. The social circumstances of the student population analyzed. As changes take place in the labor market, the knowledge of newer and more rewarding occupational opportunities is more widespread among high than among low social classes.

3. The orientation and value system of that population. Knowledge of new opportunities is insufficient to determine occupational choices, because of the differential characteristics of the populations willing to innovate and to enter careers within which patterns of mobility are still poorly defined. Despite the marginal economic role allocated to women, female students coming from favorable socioeconomic circum-

stances are more frequently willing to take risks and to act as pioneers in fields or disciplines previously forbidden to them.

4.   The academic skills of this population. Adjustment to the demands of the school system affects the width of occupational aspirations and the importance of the risks students are willing to take. Academic success probably enhances both individual self-esteem and innovativeness.

Although school systems tend to be increasingly unable to retain the most "attractive" students and hence to maintain a high status, the corresponding decline in the professionalization of teachers is not similarly experienced at the various levels of the academic hierarchy. In Belgium, for example, the social origin of the future agrégés who will teach in the upper strata of postprimary institutions is higher than that of future regents who teach in lower grades. Only 13 percent of the former are the sons of unskilled and semi-skilled manual workers, against 26 percent of the future regents.[28] In France access to the Ecole Normale Superieure, the school of university professors, continues to be characterized by a maximal level of social selectivity. Thus 51 percent of the candidates admitted to that school are the offspring of managerial and other upper classes. But more important, one-third of these candidates are the children of university professors, which tends to maximize the level of cohesiveness of that particular occupational group. Access to Ecole Normale Superieure also is characterized by a high level of academic selectivity. In 1963 15 of 18 French *Lycees* students crowned as the best for a particular discipline (after having sat for the *Concours General*) indicated their desire to teach in French universities and hence to join the prestigious Ecole Normale Superieure.[29]

Similarly, although in the United States, the substantial rise in the educational attainment of the secondary school teaching force which still remains dominated by men, does not seem to prevent a decline in the selectivity underlying patterns of recruitment, it continues to characterize the recruitment of university or college teachers. However this selectivity is probably differential and teachers of the most prestigious universities are not only recruited from among the privileged classes but also from among the most gifted students of the best institutions.[30]

Thus the personnel of various educational institutions are not uniformly unable to maintain a high status. The extent to which teachers lose the status of professionals varies however across cultures and is probably more marked among decentralized than centralized countries. The significance of this loss varies with the rung of the educational ladder taken into consideration; it is more marked among primary than secondary school teachers or university professors. Finally, it is certainly not experienced in the same way by teachers and by administrators. Although the latter share the fate of teachers insofar as they have the same social and cultural background, yet their status also depends upon their own origin.[31] In this regard Carlson shows that a distinction should be made between local school superintendents (who come from inside the system) and those labeled "cosmopolitans" (who come from the outside). The latter do not have as particularistic loyalties toward the system as their "place-bound" counterparts; they are more likely to orient themselves in the performance of their activities toward their peers engaged in similar functions rather than toward the board, and their search for new jobs is affected by their career needs. Cosmopolitan superintendents and administrators are more "professional" than the local-bound ones.[32] This is at least in part because of differences both in their socioeconomic or cultural origin and in their academic experiences.

Socialization. Although educational authorities enjoy perhaps a large amount of autonomy as to the definition of the curriculum most appropriate for teaching, often they have been unable to standardize that curriculum. In the United States, for example, there has always been a variety of routes allowing access to primary school teaching. In certain cases teachers' colleges are completely separated from other academic institutions; in other cases programs designed to train teachers are only specialized institutes attached to departments of education. As shown in *Equality of Educational Opportunities,* there are variations both in the training offered by these institutions and in the characteristics of their respective populations, and these variations do not facilitate the emergence of a homeogeneous teaching subculture.

In Brazil there are similarly three types of teachers' colleges. The first offers a terminal type of training in teaching; the second offers other vocational or academic courses also of a terminal nature. In contrast the third type offers one or two years of advanced courses in education and eventually facilitates the transfer of students toward other schools of higher learning. In France, where teachers have been anxious to maintain their high status, the number of routes allowing access to teaching positions at all levels of the educational hierarchy has kept increasing. Even at the top, access to the Ecole Normale Superieure is no longer both a necessary and sufficient condition for obtaining a position with a university.[33]

In view of the variety of the socialization procedures underlying access to the field of education, the decline in prestige attached to teaching positions in Schools or Departments of Education is not surprising. In American universities, departments of education rank relatively low in prestige, comparatively to other departments. They do not attract the best students and their faculties do not have a power comparable to those acquired by colleagues attached to more "successful" schools or institutes.[34] Although teaching graduate students is often considered more attractive than teaching undergraduates, professors consider their graduates as future specialists of their substantive fields rather than as future teachers. In the same way, the relative preeminence attached to research over teaching leads professors to think of themselves as professionals in their own field rather than in the field of education.[35] The situation is the same among superintendents who consider themselves professionals because they have been trained by teachers who view themselves as generalists in the field of administration rather than as specialists in the field of education.[36]

The decline in the prestige attached to teaching positions in teachers' colleges or similar institutions is not specific to the United States. While Durkheim considered this type of assignment the most rewarding of all the positions he could claim in the French university system, the number of "stars" in that particular field has declined constantly over the years. Further, the great names in French philosophy or literature (Sartre, for example) have been anxious either to leave teaching altogether or to satisfy themselves with positions outside the Sorbonne or the Ecole Normale Superieure (Merleau-Ponty moved to the prestigeful but "useless" College de France as soon as he could). This situation differs from that observed among the more classical professions, and teaching in law or medical schools is a privilege reserved to the most skilled practitioners.

While the effectiveness of the occupational socialization undergone by future teachers requires the institutions specialized in the training of teachers to offer demanding and standardized programs taught by well-known instructors, the problem remains to evaluate this effectiveness. It might be measured in terms of the degree to which commitment to teaching increases as the students get closer to graduation. Considering the changes occurring in the occupational choices made by Brazilian teachers' college students at the time of their entry at school and during their final year, Gouveia notes the extreme stability of the decisions taken in this respect by her interviewees. Only one-fifth of these students are anxious to reconsider the plans that they had initially drawn, and over 80 percent of those who had initially planned to enter the teaching force persist in their ideas. By contrast, less than half of those who entertained other occupational choices persist in their plans during their last year of college, eventhough the relative number of individuals moving away from and toward teaching are roughly identical. Individuals moving away from teaching tend to be relatively more frequently from a middle- and upper-class origin. Yet changes of choices toward teaching are also higher among upper- and middle-class than among working-class girls and the contrasts between these subgroups are particularly high for those individuals having traditional orientations. Thus 38 percent of the students with both traditional values and a privileged background have reconsidered their occupational aspirations as against only 22 percent of their peers who share the same values but come from a modest origin. Among the subgroups with modern orientations, the corresponding percentages were 23 and 20 percent respectively.

In the United States Davis indicates that 4 percent of the freshmen who chose teaching as a career shy away from that particular field while almost 12 percent of the freshmen who had other initial occupational orientations, later shift into it. In this sense the socialization of future teachers is effective because the departments of education seem to have better abilities than other departments both to retain their initial clientele and to attract new members. Yet these abilities must also be assessed in terms of the social, educational, and attitudinal characteristics of the population defecting from and attracted toward teaching. In effect, choosing teaching after four years of college experience tends to be most characteristic of individuals who because of their ascribed or achieved qualities, enjoy a limited number of occupational alternatives.[37] In this sense, the effectiveness of the procedures used to train teachers remains limited.

Changes in occupational choices must be analyzed also in terms of the structural characteristics of the schools attended. Differentiating the teachers' colleges in terms of the composition and the overall orientations of their respective student body, Gouveia shows that among institutions dominated by girls with a high social background, the predominance of modern orientations tends to lower the teaching inclination of individual students with traditional orientations. But the predominance of traditional orientations has a positive—albeit slight—influence on the teaching inclinations of "modern" individuals. However these patterns do not hold true among institutions where the majority of students come from lower classes. Further, while the aggregate characteristics of schools affect commitment toward teaching, they have little influence on changes in individual choices away from or toward teaching. The overall impact of their socialization processes on the final destination of their individual students is limited.

This low impact is also suggested by the fact that commitment toward teaching is more evident among the populations of teachers' colleges which are isolated from other academic schools, than among those which are located at proximity of such schools. When confronted with alternative academic courses and placed in a climate open to a variety of occupational opportunities, students cease to feel obligated toward the career to which they were initially destined.

Finally, the socialization of private Brazilian schools seems to be more effective than that of their public counterparts. This reflects the differential forms of selectivity underlying access to these two types of institutions. Enrollment in a private school often presupposes a certain type of religious commitment which is likely to diffuse into the occupational sphere; to teach becomes a by-product of religious faith and the students trained in religious teachers college have more uniform loyalties than their peers studying in public schools. The latter indeed are characterized by the variety of their occupational aspirations and orientations.[38]

Participation in teachers' colleges or similar institutions does not uniformly stimulate the commitment of students toward the educational field. Thus we can propose that teachers are not professional in view of (*a*) the low control that they exert on the proper socialization of newcomers into the educational scene, (*b*) variations in the training procedures used by the relevant institutions, (*c*) the low prestige attached to teaching positions in such schools, and (*d*) variations in the effectiveness of socializing procedures.

It is not sure that other occupational groups usually considered as professionals are more effective along these lines.[39] It may very well be that an effective socialization does not consist in enhancing the professional commitment of newcomers but rather in selecting the individuals already the most committed and in helping them internalize certain "rules of the game" concerning the occupation's most significant rewards.

Organization of the Occupational Activities of Teachers.   An occupational group may be considered as professional when (*a*) it is able to determine without external interventions the success and failures of its individual members, (*b*) it imposes upon these members a particular autonomous and uniform code of occupational ethics, and (*c*) its members are able to develop a highly personalized relationship with their clients. The obligations that a professional owes to his clients are not the result of prescriptions or proscriptions transmitted along hierarchical lines but rather of the competition developed among practitioners in the equalitarian context of their particular code of ethics.

University professors are able to organize their work according to the preceding criteria of professionalization. As soon as they are granted tenure, they become more seriously bound by the particular codes of ethics of the teaching profession than by the particular rules worked out by the organization within which they participate. Further, their relationship with their clientele is markedly personalized, and the only threat to professors is to lose their students. This situation characterizes a variety of countries. An excessive personalization of the relationships between Italian or German students and their professors seems to be at the origin of the agitation that recently plagued these two countries.[40] The autonomy of university professors vis a vis the organization which employs them is facilitated by their increasing mobility. In the United States this mobility is further facilitated by the mobility of the students themselves.

The situation is more complex at the lowest rungs of the educational hierarchy. The definition of the work to be done varies with a number of factors:

1. The characteristics of each school system and of their "managers." Even in the case of centralized educational structures and despite frequent tenure rules adopted in such structures, the fate of individual teachers remains conditioned by the degree to which they comply with the orientations of their superiors. In contrast to other professions, these orientations are particularistic and place-bound. While legal, architectural, and medical cultures contain a number of universal elements which are transmitted from one generation to the next, the experiences of teachers are not cumulative or transferable. Under such conditions geographic mobility lowers the potential solidarity of practitioners.[41]

2. The characteristics of the population to be taught. Teachers have difficulties in establishing personalized relations with their students, mainly because of the compulsory nature of the services they render and of the corresponding increase in the number of their pupils. Although the ratio of pupils to elementary and secondary teachers in the United States remain around 24 and is therefore relatively low, there

are significant contrasts between white and nonwhite educators in this respect. Among the latter the ratio varies from 30 in the South to 58.3 in the Northeast, and there are accordingly significant contrasts in the personalization of their relations with students. Variations in the treatment accorded to teachers with various ethnic backgrounds prevent a further professionalization of this group.[42]

Compulsory education also lowers this professionalization in that it fosters an equivocal definition of who is really the clientele of schools. Teachers' educational objectives do not always coincide with those of their students or the latters' parents. In the United States Suber and Wilder report that 69 percent of the mothers they interviewed have children in schools where teachers practice a teaching style at variance with their own orientations. A study in England suggests similar results and indicates that teachers underestimate the extent to which parents expect schools to provide children with moral training while overestimating the weight parents place on instruction and social advancement.[43] These disagreements in the expectations that various groups entertain toward the activities of a particular type of practitioner are likely to lower the latter's professional status.

3.   The changes in patterns of division of labor prevailing among educational institutions themselves. As the activities of the teaching force become specialized, communication difficulties among teachers become more frequent because of growing differences in their patterns of recruitment and socialization. Educational specialization results first from the differentiation of the programs and curricula offered to pupils of differing ages. Earlier I noted that, originally taught independently of their ages, European pupils have been increasingly regrouped in homogeneous age grades.[44] This regrouping has been associated with parallel changes in the nature of the teaching activities themselves. Since primary school teachers are not expected to use the same tools and techniques as their counterparts teaching in high schools, they also are neither recruited nor socialized according to the same rules.

There is a further specialization of high school teachers in terms of the particular disciplines they teach. This specialization induces marked constrasts not only in terms of the recruitment and socialization of the various categories of teachers but also in terms of their respective work load. For example, the marginal status frequently assigned to music or arts in American schools leads music or art teachers to work in several schools to fulfill their work load. It also makes them subjected to particular types of pressures from their colleagues and their students.[45]

Often these teachers complain that their role is only to fill gaps in the time schedule or to act as dumping grounds for students viewed as undesirable by teachers of more noble disciplines.

Viviane Isambert-Jamati has recently shown the implications of the specialization of teaching roles on the style of interaction prevailing among teachers.[46] To promote a greater equality of educational opportunities, French authorities have recently decided to abandon the perennial distinction between *Lycées* (which were the natural feeders of postsecondary institutions) and terminal types of secondary institutions (*cours complémentaires and others*). These authorities have decided to expose all pupils between the ages of 11 and 16 to the same pedagogical treatment and to enroll all of them in institutions called *Collèges d'Enseignement Secondaire*. The same authorities assumed further that equalization of the academic chances offered to this particular age group required pupils to be exposed not only to a uniform pedagogical material but also to the various types of teachers attached to the various types of secondary institutions that existed previously. As a consequence the personnel of these colleges is comprised of Professeurs Agrégés who formerly taught in the *Lycees,* and of instituteurs or other categories of teachers who used to teach either in the highest rungs of the primary school system or in terminal postprimary institutions.

The teaching force of such colleges is highly heterogeneous because its distinctive elements were not previously expected to perform the same roles, were not recruited and socialized according to the same rules and the same principles, and did not initially cater to the needs of the same clientele. Although these two groups of teachers now perform the same activities, initial contrasts in their modes of recruitment and socialization as well as in their prior occupational experiences are sufficient to limit the extent and the form of their interactions with regard to pedagogical issues, occupational aspirations, or extracurricular activities. Analyzing formal and informal meetings pertaining to teaching methods, V. Isambert Jamati has established that two-thirds of such meetings regroup individual teachers with a similar status and origin. When these meetings pertain to occupational aspirations the corresponding percentage rises to 70 percent, and to 75 percent when the topics discussed do not concern the educational universe. While the differential past of these various categories of teachers is strong enough to maintain segregation in their current daily routines, this segregation impedes the development of strong professional solidarities.

To sum up, the standardization of educational markets, the growth of educational facilities, and the segmentation of teaching activities are associated with a growing bureaucratization of school systems that lowers the control teachers exert on their occupational activities. Further, it is associated with accentuated contrasts in the definitions that various groups give of teaching activities.

Thus far however our analysis has been devoted to teachers. Should an examination of school administrators yield the same results? Insofar as superintendents and school principals are recruited among the ranks of teachers, one can expect them to be similarly socialized to the demands of teaching activities and to consider their role as that of professionals. Further, their training in educational administration programs exposes them to a "professional" ideology that stresses their affiliation to a class of generalists in the administrative processes. Finally, available evidence suggests a high consensus among these administrators as to the definition of their role and this seems also to indicate that they form an independent and homogeneous subculture—an achievement most frequent among professionals.[47]

Yet there are sharp variations in the educational and occupational background of this group. Such variations in turn induce disparities in both the level of commitment of individuals toward their job and in the behavior they actually adopt toward other educational subgroups. But these disparities are also produced by the equivocations surrounding administrative roles since, after all, both superintendents and principals are expected to act as middlemen between the public and the teaching force. In fact the actual leadership style adopted by administrators is dependent not only upon their background (we noted the relevant contrasts between place- and career-bound superintendents) but also upon the organizational characteristics of their environment. Both the degree of subservience of superintendents toward their boards, for example (and hence their lack of professionalization) and their solidarity with the teaching force seem to be influenced by the size of the system. The administrators of large systems appear to be both more independent of the board and more protective of their personnel. The professionalization of these administrators appears also to be affected by the relative status they enjoy in the community. The higher this status, the more likely an educational administrator seems to act as a *primus inter pares* and to be perceived as such by his teaching force; the more therefore he views himself and is defined by others as a professional.[48]

Finally, the relative professionalization of educational administrators depends upon the differentiation of the tasks which incumb upon them. In France, for example, administrative educational tasks are divided into two categories. A first group of administrators (*censeurs, proviseurs, intendants*) are involved in ensuring the proper academic and financial functioning of high schools, whereas *inspecteurs* are expected to evaluate the performance of individual teachers and to design the various curricula offered to the students enrolled in various classes and types of schools. Insofar as this differentiation is likely to induce invidious comparisons among categories of administrative personnel, it is unlikely to facilitate the formation of an independent and homogeneous occupational subculture.

Conclusions. My assessment of the relative professionalization of teachers and administrators suggests three conclusions. First, this professionalization tends to be lower than that of other groups such as physicians or lawyers. Physicians, for example, are in a better position to exert a tight and rewarding control over the recruitment and the socialization of medical students. Further, they have a more powerful influence on the definition and the handling of occupational deviances.

Second, although economic development lowers *uniformly* the importance attached to teaching, the relative professionalization achieved by teachers and administrators varies with the particular patterns of educational development prevailing in the countries under study. Teachers should be more frequently able to claim the status of professional whenever their role has been historically closely related to that of priests. Similarly teachers should be more successful along these lines whenever they operate within a centralized system with a low rate of physical or geographic mobility.[49] Correspondingly, while the main task of many European teachers is to identify the strategies most likely to enable them to maintain the professional status acquired earlier, the main problem confronting their American counterparts is to assess the strategies most likely to enable them to move toward such a status.

Finally, their relative professionalization varies with the characteristics of the population they teach. University professors often seem to be more professional than primary school teachers because of the higher value attached to their services. University audiences are both less captive and more selective than the clients of primary school teachers. In addition the activities of university professors are more closely linked with those at the top of the occupational structure; as a result their audience is more salient and visible than that of primary or secondary school teachers.

NOTES AND REFERENCES

1. For a review of the discussions pertaining to the problems raised by a
    sociological analysis of the concept of profession, see W. Goode, "En-
    croachment, Charlatanism, and the Emerging Profession," *American Socio-
    logical Review,* Vol. 25, 1960, pp. 302–314. See also T. Parsons, *Essays in
    Sociological Theory* (Glencoe: Free Press, 1954), Chapter 11, L. Cogan,
    "The Problems of Designing a Profession," *Annals of the American Academy
    of Political and Social Sciences,* January 1955, pp. 105–111. For a discussion
    of these themes with specific references to teachers, see H. Stub, "The
    Professional Prestige of Classroom Teachers: A Consequence of
    Organizational and Community Status," in Bell and Stub, eds., *The Sociology
    of Education, A Sourcebook* (Homewood: Dorsey Press, 1968). The ar-
    ticle includes a particularly rich bibliography on these issues.

2. For a review of the changes concerning the status of children in European
    societies, see P. Aries, *Centuries of Childhood* (New York: Knopf, 1962),
    Part I, Chapter 2; Part III, Chapter 2.

3. See M. Moskow, *Teachers and Unions* (Philadelphia: University of Pennsyl-
    vania, Wharton School of Finance and Commerce, Industrial Research
    Unit, 1966), p. 76. See also M. Lieberman, *Education as a Profession* (Engle-
    wood Cliffs, N.Y.: Prentice-Hall, 1956), pp. 91–92; J. Conant, *The Educa-
    tion of American Teachers* (New York: McGraw Hill, 1963), pp. 242–246.

4. R. Corwin, *A Sociology of Education* (New York: Appleton, Century Crofts,
    1965) p. 249.

5. D. Lortie, "The Partial Professionalization of Elementary Teaching" in S.
    Sieber and D. Wilder, eds., *The School in Society* (New York: Free Press,
    1923), pp. 315–323.

6. See A. Tropp, *The Schoolteachers* (London: Heinemann, 1957), pp. 24–24.

7. See T. W. Banford, *The Rise of the Public Schools* (London: Nelson, 1967).
    In addition, many of these teachers owed their professional status to the
    fact that they were clergymen.

8. See A. Merland, *J. M. de Lamennais, La Renaissance d'une Chrétiente* (Paris:
    Edition Bonne Presse, 1960), p. 96. For a description of variations in the
    status of primary school teachers among European countries, see C. Ci-
    polla, *Literacy and Development in the West* (London: Penguin, 1969), pp.
    29–32.

9. See R. Clignet and P. Foster, *The Fortunate Few* (Evanston: Northwestern
    University Press, 1955), Chapter 4, 6.

10. Table 7 is derived from analysis of the Yaounde census (1962) and of the
    Douala census (1964). The full results of a study of Camerounian teachers
    will be reported by R. Clignet and P. Foster, "Teachers as Agents of Mod-
    ernization in the Cameroon" (in press).

11. See D. Bachelor, "British Secondary Modern and Secondary Grammar

School Teachers: Contrasts and Similarities" (University of Chicago, Ph.D. dissertation, September 1970), p. 90.

12. *Ibid.,* p. 94.

13. See A. Prost, *Histoire de l'enseignement en France: 1900–1957* (Paris: Armand Colin, 1965), p. 363.

14. See J. Folger and C. Nam, *Education of the American Population* (Washington: U.S. Department of Commerce, 1960, 1967), Chapter 3.

15. This group includes all the occupations with codes from 000 to 195 in the occupational classification issued by the U.S. Census Bureau. See 1960 Census of Population, *Alphabetical Index of Occupations and Industries,* (Washington: U.S. Department of Commerce, 1960), pp. xix, xx.

16. J. Davis, *Undergraduate Career Decisions* (Chicago: Alidine, 1965), Chapter 2, 3.

17. See J. Folger and C. Nam, *Education of the American Population, op. cit.,* p. 100.

18. See Ida Berger, "Instituteurs èt institutrices," *Revue Francaise de sociologie,* Vol. 1, 1960, pp. 173–185.

19. See J. Delcourt, "L'evolution qualitative du corps enseignant dans l'enseignement secondaire," in M. Matthijsen and C. Vervoort, eds., *Education in Europe,* (Paris: Mouton, 1969), pp. 214–227.

20. See A. Gouveia, "Student Teachers in Brazil: A Study of Young Womens Career Choices" (University of Chicago, Ph.D. dissertation, March 1962), p. 37.

21. See J. Delcourt, *op. cit.*

22. R. Clignet and P. Foster, *The Fortunate Few, op. cit.,* Chapter 4.

23. See A. Gouveia, *op. cit.,* p. 84.

24. J. Davis, *Undergraduate Career Decisions,* p. 95.

25. For a definition of the items constitutive of the scale, see A. Gouveia, *op. cit.,* p. 167. Items were of the following type: Boys should receive more education than girls; women become less feminine when they work outside the home; it is not proper for a married woman to work outside her home.

26. J. Davis, *op. cit.,* p. 80.

27. The main reason for the preference given to teaching in that context was that teaching gave individuals a status close to that achieved by Europeans without obliging the individual to maintain close contacts with colonial authorities.

28. See J. Delcourt, l'enseignement secondaire," *op. cit.*

29. See P. Bourdieu et J. C. Passeron, *Les Héritiers* (Paris: Les Editions de Minuit), Chapter 1.

30. For a discussion of the influence that the social characterisitic of American professors exert on their career, see T. Caplow and R. McGee, *The Amer-*

can Market Place (New York: Science Editions, 1961), pp. 226–227. See also B. Berelson, *Graduate Education in the United States* (New York: Mc-Graw Hill, 1960). The latter author indicates that only 6 percent of doctoral students have a father who is himself a college or university professor while 15 percent of law or medicine students have a father who is engaged in the same field. The recruitment of professors appears to be more open, yet Berelson notes that the graduates from the top universities cluster more at the top of the social ladder (pp. 133–134). For an examination of the influence that the academic background of American professors exerts on their mobility, see D. Crane, "The American Market Place Revisited: A Study of Faculty Mobility Using the Cartter Ratings," *American Journal of Sociology,* Vol. 75, 1970, pp. 953–964.

31. For a review of this question, see C. Bidwell, "The School as a Formal Organization," in J. March, ed., *Handbook of Organizations* (Chicago: Rand McNally, 1965), pp. 972–1022. See also R. Corwin, *Sociology of Education, op. cit.,* p. 247 ff.

32. See R. Carlson, *Executive Succession and Organization Change* (Chicago: University of Chicago, Midwest Administrative Center, 1962).

33. This is especially so since 1968 when universities became allowed to recruit associate professors not having proper academic credentials. Even before the crisis, however, the monopoly exerted by the graduates of Ecole Normale Superieure had declined.

34. For example, see D. Wolfe, *American Resources of Specialized Talents* (New York: Harper and Brothers, 1954).

35. For a discussion of the definition of the future sociologists work see B. Beck and H. Becker, "Modest Proposals for Graduate Programs in Sociology," *American Sociologist,* Vol. 4, 1969, pp. 227–234.

36. See C. Bidwell, *op. cit.*

37. J. Davis, *op. cit.,* Chapter 1.

38. See Gouveia, *op. cit.,* pp. 128–129.

39. For example, H. Becker et al. in *Boy in White* (Chicago: University of Chicago Press, 1961) suggests that medical students are more socialized into the role of student than in that of future professionals, (Chapters X, XIV). For a further discussion of this theme, see C. Kadinshine, "The Professional Self Concepts of Music Students," *American Journal of Sociology,* Vol. 75, 1969, pp. 385–404.

40. For a discussion of the treament meted to Italian and German students, see E. Gelgi, "Structures and Function of Italian Universities." See also K. Winter, "Instruction and Education at the Medical Faculty of the Humboldt University," in M. Matthijsen and C. Vervoort, eds., *op. cit.,* pp. 241–246, 247–253.

41. See D. Lortie, *op. cit.,* and B. Geer, "Occupational Commitment and the Teaching Profession," in S. Sieber and D. Wilder, *op. cit.,* pp. 326–334.

42. See J. Folger and C. Nam, *op. cit.*, p. 94.

43. See S. Sieber and D. Wilder, "Parental Preferences and Professional Roles Definition," *Sociology of Education*, Vol. 40, 1967, pp. 302–315. See also F. Musgrove and P. Taylor, "Teachers and Parents Conceptions of the Teachers," *British Journal of Educational Psychology*, Vol. 35, 1965, pp. 171–178.

44. See P. Aries, *op. cit.*, notably Part 2, Chapter IV.

45. For a description of the conflicts among teachers with differing skills, see R. Corwin, *Militant Professionalism* (New York: Appleton-Century-Crofts, 1970). For a description of variations in the stereotypes attached to the teachers of different disciplines, see W. W. Charters, "The Social Background of Teaching," in N. Gage, ed., *Handbook of Research in Teaching* (Chicago: Rand McNally, 1963), pp. 715–805.

46. See V. Isambert-Jamati, "Un nouveau type d'établissement du second degré en France. Obstacles à la coopération entre les professeurs," in M. Matthijsen and C. W. Vervoort, eds., *op. cit.*, pp. 205–213.

47. See C. Bidwell, *op. cit.*

48. See M. Seeman, *Social Status and Leadership: The Case Study of the School Executive* (Columbus: Ohio State University, Bureau of Educational Research, 1960).

49. French educational history shows that despite the centralized nature of the system, secondary school teachers experienced many difficulties in their quest for a professional status because of the frequent transfers to which they were subjected. Due to political factors, their forced mobility prevented them from taking root in a particular community. For a discussion of this point, see J. Armstrong, *The European Administrative Elite* (Princeton: Princeton University Press, 1973), Chapter 6.

5

PROFESSIONALIZATION AND BUREAUCRATIZATION OF SCHOOL PERSONNEL:

THE ENSUING CONFLICTS

To the extent that the goals of school personnel and external pressure groups are divergent, these two distinct groups of actors will oppose one another. The outcome of the ensuing conflicts is of high significance because the particular actors able to gain control over the definition of formal schooling and the implementation of relevant policies will use their additional power to heighten their own educational liberty and to modify or perpetuate existing inequities.

In this chapter I analyze the forms, the objects, and the intensity of the conflicts between school personnel and outside pressure groups, as well as the tensions occurring among administrators or between them and teaching forces. Since I have indicated in the previous chapter, the limits within which teachers and administrators act as professionals, I identify in an initial section of this chapter, the potential influence of the professionalization and the bureaucratization of teachers and administrators on the form taken by their occupational demands. In the following section, I examine more specifically the extent and the determinants of variations in the form and the intensity of tensions (a) between boards and superintendents, (b) between boards and educational administrators on the one hand and school personnel on the other, and

180

(*c*) among various types of teachers or between them and their principals.

Educational Conflicts: An Overview. Clearly, the extent to which a group controls the recruitment, the socialization, and the daily routine of individual practitioners—and therefore entitles it to claim a professional status—shapes the strategies that a group as a whole uses to cope with internal and external tensions.

Since professionals stress loyalty to their clients and define the services they render as based on scarcity and on sacred values, one cannot expect an occupational group that has fully acquired the status of a profession to use strikes as a strategy designed to improve its bargaining position in the society at large. The images and stereotypes that underlie striking are incompatible with the aura of prestige that members of the occupational group under consideration claim to be attached to the exercise of their activities. Traditionally, "professionals" prefer to work out individual strategies to improve their relative position. In extreme cases they can also take advantage of the selectivity of their recruitment and hence of the implicit ties that bind them to other "elites" in order to lobby in political assemblies.

The professional organization of British teachers offers a case in point. Founded in 1870 in response to the Educational Act of that year, this organization worked toward the election of Parlamentarians amenable to their own goals and values, and by the 1950s there were 23 members of the National Union of Teachers in the House of Commons.[1] Although often the union has used strikes, it has also looked for the implementation of its goals through staffing local education authorities with both elected and co-opted members.

A history of the organization of French teachers tends to reveal somewhat similar trends. Many high officials began their careers as university or secondary school teachers (Tardieu, Giraudoux, Pompidou) and many of them have attempted to take advantage of their political responsibilities to achieve a higher professionalization of the teaching force. The direct participation of individual practitioners in the political process is often believed to enhance the prestige and the power of the profession as a whole.

In the United States the liberal and individualist ideologies of the early teachers still persist among those of small-sized systems, among the personnel of upper levels of the educational hierarchy, and among professors who still consider themselves to be part of the Establishment. After the first waves of strikes that paralyzed the New York system in 1967, an old teacher reported, "This is the blackest day of my entire career . . . teachers are supposed to be as dedicated as are the clergy." [2]

While professionals are unlikely to use strikes to enhance or maintain the privileged positions they enjoy, they also must find appropriate mechanisms to cope with the tensions likely to develop among themselves. In this respect, the main goal of a profession is to maximize both the occupational autonomy of each practitioner and the solidarity which binds him to his peers. The attainment of this goal requires the profession to be able to define *independently* what constitutes an occupational deviance, to maintain the number of such deviances at a minimal level, and to specify the mechanisms most appropriate to deal with these deviances. Hence there emerges a group of professional practitioners entitled to act as *primus inter pares* and expected as such to exert over their peers a limited-because egalitarian-authority over a restricted number of issues. The novels of C.P. Snow, for example, illustrate how English teachers use elections to certain key positions to make sure that the elected *master* will protect the occupational autonomy of individual teachers and prevent serious cleavages from developing among members of the teaching force. Similarly in the United States, the number of offenses for which a tenured university professor is accountable is quite limited and such offenses have to be evaluated and acted upon by committees where his peers are represented. Even at the level of primary and secondary schools, where the principle of *primus inter pares* is not institutionalized and where there is a marked hierarchical differentiation between the position of teachers and principals, the fact remains that teachers expect the latter to act according to the ideals of a professional morality and to protect them from parental interference, independently of the legitimacy of the issues involved.[3] The same professional morality accounts for the fact that an individual teacher should not publicly challenge the actions of a colleague.

Although claims to professional status influence the choice of strategies that teachers use to cope with conflicts, the use of these strategies is neither a necessary nor a sufficient condition to claim the status of professional. In fact the strategies used by teachers are also influenced by the growing bureaucratization of educational institutions. I therefore examine both the origin and the consequences of this on-going process.

Because bureaucratization is pervasive and affects all arenas of social participation, the emergence of a mass society is associated with a standardization of work procedures. Correspondingly there are growing uniformities in the definition of both occupational roles and of the prerequisites underlying access to them. As a result the influence of educational experiences on occupational attainment is increasingly depersonalized. Indeed the number of years spent at school becomes a more important determinant of occupational placement than the specific nature of the educational experiences acquired by an individual.[4] Under such conditions there are few variations in the definition that employers give of their needs in human resources, and teachers as well as administrators have correspondingly few incentives to "tailor" the curricula offered.

Bureaucratization of schools also results from the development of strong pressures toward educational equality. In most countries there has been a rise in the age to which school attendance is compulsory, and the enhanced demand for education often is associated with a concentration of educational facilities. Educational equality however implies not only an increase in enrollments but also the development of uniform educational curricula and programs. Equality is often believed to exist only insofar as all the individuals of a particular age group are uniformly exposed to a same pedagogical material and enjoy the same chances of moving ahead in the system. Standardization of educational curricula and books and concentration of educational facilities cannot take place without the formation of an educational bureaucracy whose function is to coordinate the activities of principals, teachers, and students and to regulate the flow of educational input and output.

The trend toward bureaucratization is also reinforced by the growing specialization of educational roles. Since the activities of teachers are increasingly different both from one another and from those assigned to principals, superintendents, and their associates, the patterns of access and of socialization into these various positions are increasingly distinct. This in turn cannot but accentuate the difficulties that school personnel experience in their communication within schools and with external agencies. Bureaucratization aims at enhancing the *predictability* of such communications and is correspondingly viewed as a mode of organization likely to facilitate the functioning of schools.

Yet the notion of bureaucracy is equivocal and involves a variety of dimensions which are not necessarily complementary to one another. Thus while bureaucracy is supposed to enhance the rationality indispensable for making human interaction smoother and less unpredictable, it also evokes images of useless rituals, red tapes, and a Kafka-like universe of frustration and oppressions. The latter image is often the one that prevails. "Like workers, teachers who line up in front of time clocks waiting to punch out in the afternoon create a crowded condition in the doorway." [5]

In addition it is not certain that all the dimensions that apparently constitute bureaucratic patterns of organization are really highly interrelated. What are these dimensions? First, they pertain to organizational complexity. Yet a review of the appropriate sociological literature suggests clearly that modes of associations among size (measured by the number of teachers), physical dispersion of the activity (measured by the number of spatially distinct institutions where teaching activities are carried out), functional dispersion (measured by the number of schools engaged in different training programs), and coordination (measured by the proportion of individuals performing staff functions) are not really univocal. [6] For example, the extent and the nature of similarities remain uncertain between districts which employ the same number of individuals, have the same number of schools differentially located on their respective territories, have the same number of institutions with distinctive curricula and tracts, and have the same proportion of employees engaged in staff functions.

Second, bureaucratic dimensions pertain to modes of communication taking place within the organization. Corwin indicates that this includes standardization of the behavior expected from teachers, strong emphasis on rules, centralization of the decision-making mechanisms, systems of close supervision, and marked differentiation of levels of authority. [7] Yet Corwin also shows that these dimensions might be concretely interrelated in three distinctive ways: They could be mutually reinforcing—in which case all these dimensions will be brought into play in support of one another. Alternatively they could be more functionally specific—and some of the mechanisms of bureaucratic control are more effective than others for controlling the performance of particular activities. Close supervision, for example, is perhaps the most adequate mechanism control in the case of assembly lines but not in the case of organization where units of work are more loosely defined. Third, it could be argued that these distinct mechanisms compensate for one another. Organizations are likely to use control mechanisms interchangeably, compensating for the relative neglect or emphasis of some by stressing or relaxing others.

Although close supervision is not significantly associated with school size and levels of authority, it frequently appears in conjunction with emphasis placed upon rules. In turn such emphasis is positively associated with organizational complexity and numbers of authority levels—and so is standardization. These findings suggest that bureaucratic forms of organization do not necessarily cluster around a single axis.

Finally, bureaucratization refers to the emergence of certain psychological traits. Merton, for example, defines a bureaucratic behavior as highly ritualistic.[8] This behavior characterizes all individuals who tend to overconform to the prescriptions and proscriptions of the organization and who are intolerant of ambiguities and therefore tend to develop rigid patterns of attitudes and behavior in their dealings with others, both inside and outside of the organization. In Corwin's terminology, teachers or administrators with "employee orientations" are those who believe that the overt goals of schools should prevail over the specific needs of students or teachers.

Regardless of these potentially conflicting aspects of bureaucracy, the development of large-scale organizations limits the use of the mechanisms by which professionals usually solve the conflicts which oppose them to one another or to outside agencies. This is because of corresponding changes both in the frequency of face-to-face contacts between teachers and in the definition of the school clientele. Thus teachers must share their loyalties among students, the students' parents, their own peers, and their superordinates within the school system.[9]

As the social distance between educational bureaucracies and teachers, parents, or educational voluntary associations increases, there is a decrease in the use of informal channels of communication but accentuation of more formal mechanisms of coordination.[10] For instance, there is a decline of the *common messenger* approach—that is, of the use of the dual membership of certain actors. Indeed parents and administrators rarely communicate with one another through children. Similarly there is a decline in the frequency of the *opinion leader approach,* for educational bureaucracies are unable or unwilling to identify such leaders.[11] Alternatively there is a marked increase in the use of mass media and of mechanisms of formal authority. Thus educational authorities are likely to rely upon the formal authority of truancy officers and to demand compliance with compulsory attendance. These changes often are selective, however. In communities where primary groups remain salient among teachers or among parents, educational administrators continue to rely upon voluntary associations to alleviate organizational and informal tensions. Further, as the resistance of primary groups to administrative decisions becomes both more salient and more socially costly, administrators are likely to use the *settlement house approach* and to enhance the visibility of the educational services rendered to each local community or of the fringe benefits extended to the personnel of local schools. As this resistance becomes even more salient, another strategy frequently used is to prevent a further mobilization of potential opposition groups and to use *detached workers* to informally convert individual teachers and parents to the goals of the educational bureaucracy.[12]

Yet as the distance between bureaucratic organizations and individual educational actors keeps increasing, the latter are likely to challenge the very legitimacy of educational institutions. Such challenges take a variety of forms. In a first phase, individual actors adopt patterns of behavior symbolic of alienation. Absenteeism, turnover, and resignation increase among teachers. Individual parents withdraw their children from school and students engage in truancy or in acts of diffuse violence against their peers or teachers.

In turn this modifies the forms of the challenges to the legitimacy of educational institutions. Thus there is a growing intervention of courts in the educational process. Indeed courts are expected to redefine the concept of educational equality by delineating new boundaries between districts and by forbidding ethnic segregation or, more recently, by identifying the characterisitics of teachers to be used by the schools of certain ethnic communities. In this quest for equality they are also expected to define the appropriate modes of financing schools and to minimize disparities in the resources that various communities allocate to education. But the decisions of courts are also expected to reaffirm the concept of educational liberty. Thus their intervention pertains to issues related to teachers' strikes, teachers behavior and dress, to parent boycotts, to the behavior of students; and in all cases the underlying issue is to identify the limits within which these groups of actors are entitled to exert their freedom.

Relations between Superintendents and School Boards.   The very definition of the tasks incumbing upon a school superintendent makes his status problematic. As a middleman he may assume that his prime loyalties are owed to the board or alternatively to his peers as well as to teachers themselves. Because of variations in the patterns of access to this particular job and because career-bound administrators do not have the same social profile or background as their place-bound counterparts who come from within the school system itself, there are parallel contrasts in the way these groups define and perform their responsibilities. Thus a place-bound administrator tends to emphasize the significance of preestablished rules in his dealings both with school board members and with the personnel of the district. But his career-bound contemporary is more likely to develop close informal contacts with his subordinates, these contacts being instrumental in facilitating the administrative innovations he wishes to introduce in the system.[13]

These disparities in goals should be associated with divergences in the strategies these two groups of superintendents use in the conflicts which eventually oppose them to the boards. Place-bound administrators should be more inclined to avoid open confrontations and to maintain a low profile, since they view themselves as "subordinates." By contrast, career-bound superintendents should be more inclined to take advantage of the cleavages existing within the board itself or between the board and particular segments of the public. In Springdale, for example, the superintendent was anxious to obtain more power by opposing the desires of the PTA to those of the board and by controlling the diffusion of informations corresponding to his own goals among various social groups in the community. During the last years of the 1960s the Evanston superintendent used a similar strategy against certain segments of the school board and he emphasized the potentially divergent views held by members of the board or by voluntary associations on the desirability of racial integration in the schools.

Finally, while the strategies used by superintendents reflect their own background and previous experiences, they also correspond to the composition of the board. Since variations in "cosmopolitanism" apply both to superintendents and to board members, their respective strategies are probably dictated by their perceptions of the relevant characteristics of their interlocutors. One can suspect that a place-bound superintendent working with a cosmopolitan school board will tend to slow down or to minimize the impact of the instructions he is given, whereas a cosmopolitan administrator employed by a local-oriented board will be more tempted to use the strategies evoked in the previous paragraph and to exacerbate tensions existing in the community or within the board itself.

Variations in the strategies used by administrators with distinct backgrounds are indicative of the equivocations surrounding the professionalization of their status. Although the particular strategies most often used by career-bound administrators are those of *professionals,* their *cosmopolitanism* also makes them prone to use judicial processes to achieve their goals. Yet reliance upon such processes has a variety of meanings. Insofar as going to court aims at enhancing the legitimacy of their individual roles, the strategies of superintendents or principals are professional in orientation. Conversely, insofar as their dependence upon courts concerns the fate of the occupation as a whole, these strategies are also bureaucratic.

Conflicts between Boards, Superintendents, and Teachers. Most professional groups tend directly to influence political institutions. Yet American teachers, for instance, often tend to be afraid of a direct intervention of federal or state government in their dealings with school boards; correspondingly they tend to maintain a political neutrality. In the 1965 mayoral election of New York no less than 80 percent of the teachers affiliated to the American Federation of Teachers (AFT) thought that their organization should not take an official stance and should not officially campaign for any one of the candidates. Yet many American teachers belong to professional organizations whose overt functions are to safeguard their occupational interests. Until recently the most important of these organizations was the National Education Association (NEA) which—although active in the diffusion of educational materials among its members—has for a long time failed either to intervene actively in politics or to protect the rights of individual teachers. For example, this association has not challenged the differential salary scales used for white and black teachers and has not initially taken any firm stand on the issues concerning racial integration. This results from the characteristics of its membership which was initially predominantly concentrated in rural or small school districts. By contrast, the AFT controlled the teaching force of larger cities and has been more involved in political as well as economic issues.[14]

Whereas the duality of such organizations is in itself an indication of the relative powerlessness of teachers in their dealings with their employers, merging negotiations are under way. Yet this merging raises significant questions as to the models underlying the strategies that teachers and low-rank administrators are likely to use in their conflicts with boards and superintendents. Does the growing unionization of the American teaching force reflect primarily the variety of economic and social threats facing individual teachers in the exercise of their activities? Insofar as unionism is associated with striking, does it symbolize the lack of professionalization of this teaching force?

The development of striking depends upon certain structural factors including the rigidity of the market and hence the number of alternative solutions that practitioners may use in order to see their demands satisfied. It also depends upon the characteristics of their clientele and hence upon the perceived scarcity of the services they render. The growing unionization of teachers and their propensity to strike have different meanings when the clientele of the school system is primarily made up of lower classes and when this clientele comprises a significant number of middle-class children who cannot be absorbed into alternative private institutions. Since boards are certainly more inclined to satisfy the demands of the teachers in the second context, the relationship between striking and increased professionalization should be more positive in that second instance.

Although the implications of unionization and of striking on professionalization are obviously contingent upon certain contextual factors, these implications also vary with the object of the demands formulated by the militant groups in the teaching force. Teachers strike not only to obtain economic advantages but also for political purposes and, for example, for enhancing their control upon the educational process.[15] Such was the purpose of the strike that plagued the New York school system in 1967. Cole suggests that strikes are increasingly concerned with the improvement of the status attached to teaching activities rather than with mere bread-and-butter issues.[16] Over two-thirds of the individual teachers interviewed wanted to improve the standards of teaching as an occupation and recognized the legitimacy of strikes as against only 43 percent who were not in favor of raising such standards. In the bureaucratic context, professional aspirations may lead teachers to be militant and to challenge the existing order.

But militant professionalism is not likely to evenly characterize all segments of the teaching force. The militancy and the professionalism of female teachers tend to be lower than that of their male counterparts. The social origin of women engaged in teaching is relatively high and this does not predispose them to consider conflicts and strikes favorably. In addition, they often belong to a household with two sources of income. This leads them to view teaching as a temporary occupation and lowers their occupational commitment. Finally, access to teaching still remains highly valued by the American female population, and the ensuing impression of having succeeded at least as well as their age peers does not induce female teachers to adopt patterns of action strongly oriented toward change.

In contrast, the greater stress placed upon the value of male occupational achievement leads male teachers to compare—unfavorably— their fate with that of their age cohort. Both their training and their social background often prevents them from transfering their skills into other activities when they are dissatisfied with their current job. The only solution available to them is to use "bureaucratic" strategies including unionization and striking. Their use of these strategies will be maximal where they are young and when their familial and cultural background predisposes them to hold favorable attitudes toward the labor movement.

However differences in patterns of recruitment and of socialization into occupational roles as well as in the definition of the tasks expected from specific groups of teachers are associated with contrasts in their motivations to strike. While dissatisfaction with their low prestige seems to have little effect on the striking behavior of the elementary school personnel of New York, this particular type of dissatisfaction has had a more powerful effect on the relevant behavior patterns of their colleagues attached to secondary schools. Alternatively, dissatisfaction with working conditions was a crucial determinant of the striking behavior adopted by the former but not of the latter. Finally, the proportion of elementary school teachers who did effectively walk out was higher in institutions where the majority of the student body was nonwhite, but there was hardly any variation in this regard among the secondary school teachers who struck.

These observations suggest that the meaning to be attached to militantism is probably not alike for all categories of personnel attached to elementary and secondary schools. In the first environment, striking and unionization seem primarily to serve defensive functions and appear to be a strategy designed to protect threatened specific privileges. In secondary schools these forms of militantism are more offensive and they aim at obtaining advantages which cannot be achieved by other means.

Similar trends are observable at the college level. Militant professionalism is likely to prevail among institutions or among disciplines where individuals cannot easily negotiate their skills. This militantism is likely to characterize rigid educational markets from which individuals cannot easily move in order to obtain a more rewarding economic, social, or political treatment. Alternatively it is likely to be low in the case of institutions and of disciplines characterized by a high degree of competition. Hence professors of engineering are more conservative than their counterparts in the social sciences because of their higher social origin and their greater ability to return to the "real" worlds of business or of government.[17]

Thus, the negative association between striking or unionism and professional status has ceased uniformly to hold true. Depending on the perceptions that practitioners have of both their commitment to their occupation and of their relative position in the social hierarchy, they may perceive striking and unionism as the most appropriate strategies for obtaining an additional amount of power and hence of liberty. It is not certain that these perceptions are always correct. After all, unionization requires teaching forces to participate in the labor movement as a whole, and the dynamics of the labor movement are not necessarily compatible with teachers' specific occupational aims.

School Conflicts: Forms and Actors.   Insofar as schools are subjected to the conflicting demands of bureaucratization and professionalization, they should be plagued by a significant number of intrarole conflicts.[18] The views that teachers have of their functions vary with the subject matters they teach, with their background, and with their experiences within the school system. Further, their views are also likely to differ from those held by administrators. Correspondingly it is possible to distinguish between bureaucratic and professional intrarole conflicts. Bureaucratic conflicts reflect the subordinate position that teachers believe to occupy in the hierarchical structure of the school and pit particular types of teachers against the administrators of the system. By contrast profession-oriented conflicts reflect the competition that opposes teachers to one another over control and the allocation of students. In universities and high schools the number and the quality of students assigned to a teacher reflect his relative status. To teach freshmen or upperclassmen does not confer the same amount of power as to teach "gifted" or intellectually deprived students.

What is the relative frequency and intensity of the professional and bureaucratic conflicts occurring in high schools? Five of the ten highest ranking specific type of conflicts involve authority issues and pit teachers against administrators. Teachers are likely to complain about the lack of their own authority. "I think that teachers feel they are being treated as underlings" is a comment frequently heard in American institutions. Other teachers add, "We don't have a great deal of weight as far as being considered is concerned." [19] Teachers react to their perceived powerlessness by engaging in acts of insubordination that constitute nearly 4 percent of all the incidents reported by Corwin. "There are some matters in which teachers will not cooperate." Sometimes these acts of insubordination pit teachers directly against administrators; sometimes they result from tensions initially opposing teachers to the nonprofessional school staff (janitors, for example). Finally, the lack of authority experienced by teachers may be relative, in which case they mostly complain about the arbitrary power granted to the teachers of particular disciplines. In short, their frustrations come from a feeling of relative deprivation: "In this school, sports are what makes the system go." [20]

Frictions also result from the apparent or real failure of administrators to protect their teachers from parents and students. Many teachers accuse school authorities, principals, and superintendents alike of being more concerned with the demands of the public than with those of their staff. "In this community, parents want to run the thing directly and that's about what they do." [21]

A third category of conflicts pertains to the distribution of functions and scheduling of facilities, as well as of students. These problems constitute about one-fifth of the difficulties reported to Corwin by his respondents. Teachers are likely to feel unhappy when their students are taken away from them—and this happens frequently because of the large number of extracurricular activities in which schools are usually engaged (musical events and sport activities, for example). Also in this category are a variety of tensions associated with the distribution of work loads. "Now, the big question is the prize plum called senior English." [22] Yet teachers complain not only about their respective individual work loads but also about the absolute or relative lack of facilities available to them. Some classrooms are deemed to be more desirable than others and conflicts pertain to who will use them and when.

A fourth category of conflicts (six and one-half percent of all the tensions reported) result from disparities in the expectations that various categories of educators entertain concerning the academic and extracurricular behavior of students. Because of differences in their background, their experiences, and their philosophies, teachers do not necessarily share similar views about the acceptable length of hair or of dress among students. Nor do they maintain comparable beliefs as to what constitute the curricula and the materials most fit to the needs of their clientele. Teachers are thus likely to criticize one another for excessive leniency or alternatively for excessive hardness. They are similarly likely to feel that principals are too repressive or, conversely, are prone to "pass the buck" to the staff placed under their authority. Finally, teachers are inclined to dispute the stand that counselors take in this respect and accuse them of being less acceptable judges of the appropriateness of student behavior than they are themselves. "If they put those counselors back to work, it certainly would solve a lot of the shortage of the teachers problem." [23]

A fifth category of tensions result from the bureaucratic nature of the school system. Teachers complain about the red tape which impedes their academic activities. They complain about the pass system, about the pressures exerted on them to meet arbitrary deadlines (getting grades to the front office, for example), and about the excess of regulations (for example, students frequently are not allowed to drop a course past a certain date).

A last category of conflicts results from competition over status. Teachers are likely to complain that their discipline is considered the dumping ground for students deemed to be undesirable by the other academic personnel. Thus they often complain that counselors steer the better students away from their courses. They are also prone to criticize their respective competence. "Well, she feels inferior to me and there is nothing I can do about it." [24] One way teachers challenge their respective competence is to evaluate the performance of their own students on standardized tests. Another way is to assess the standards of the universities or colleges from which they themselves graduated. Such comparisons lead educators to be particularly sensitive to the problems resulting from status inconsistencies: "She should not be teaching just because she is a board member's wife. She is that first, and secondly she is possibly a member of this faculty." [25]

Yet this review of the conflicts that oppose teachers, coaches, guidance counselors, and principals to one another is insufficient to determine how these various actors experience the dilemma between professionalization and bureaucratization. Is the number and the nature of these tensions the mere by-product of particular administrative arrangements, or is it the result of a complex network of interaction between such arrangements and the social psychological profile of the personnel manning these institutions?

Influence of Bureaucratic Control Mechanisms on School Tensions. Corwin shows that increases in the number of teachers present in a school, in the number of its level of authority, in its organizational complexity, and in the standardization of its activities multiply the number of incidents involving authority problems. Other bureaucratic control mechanisms have more diffuse effects and both emphasis on rules and close supervision, for example, apparently affect positively the *overall* number of disputes taking place in the institution.

Bureaucratic organizations are also characterized by the relative specialization of their personnel. In bureaucratic schools teachers specialize in the teaching of only one subject matter and are not expected to teach in other disciplines. This specialization limits communications among colleagues and lowers the cohesiveness of the entire teaching force. As a result the number of major incidents occurring in a school tends to increase with the proportion of teachers exclusively assigned to teach courses within their own fields of interest. This specialization of teachers is also associated with significant variations in their background. Teachers of mathematics and teachers of social and physical sciences do not necessarily have similar ages and similar ethnic backgrounds, and they have not necessarily followed the same training. As the heterogeneity of the teaching force increases in this regard, there seems to be a corresponding increase in the number of incidents opposing teachers to one another.

Yet teachers also differ from one another in the relative amount of time they have spent in the school system, and the heterogeneity of their experiences along these lines influences not only the number of conflicts involving teachers and administrators or the number of incidents pertaining to authority problems but also the overall number of incidents.

In brief, "discordant" schools are larger, and more heterogeneous than the tranquil ones. They are also characterized by a greater specialization in the tasks assigned to teachers and by higher rates of staff turnover and expansion. Yet, while friction and strains depend upon the control mechanisms at work, they are also influenced by the modes of interaction prevailing among teachers or between them and their principals.

Influence of the Dynamics of School Systems.   In general terms the number and nature of conflicts should vary with the differences in the views that principals and their school staff hold about their respective roles. Such differences could be expected to occur whenever teachers and administrators have not spent the same amount of time within the district or the school. One could, for example, anticipate that the appointment of a principal coming from outside the organization is likely to foster strains and tensions, particularly in the early phases of his leadership. But this is not the case. The number of incidents between teachers and administrators involving authority problems is at least one and one-half times larger in institutions where a principal has been recently appointed from within than in those institutions where the newly appointed principal comes from the outside. Thus lack of communication between hierarchical levels rather than perceived differences between the expected and the observed forms of such communication are often at the origin of discords. Faculties entertain fewer expectations toward principals from the outside than toward their former colleagues who have been promoted. Indeed expectations are conditioned by prior interaction.[26]

While modes of interaction between teachers and administrators are significant determinants of the form and the intensity of school conflicts, modes of interaction among colleagues play a similar role. As informal channels of communication among teachers become more numerous and as their contacts increase in frequency, their expectations concerning the responsibilities and the function of each category of the school personnel become more focused and teachers are accordingly more prone to experience conflicts over specific issues or individuals. Thus Corwin observes that both the incidence and the severity of conflicts increase with the frequency of contacts that teachers have with one another outside of the school and with the degree to which they eat lunch together. The effect of these informal contacts are however selective and they primarily affect teachers who are older than average and have more seniority than the bulk of the personnel. Again this suggests that conflict depends upon the relative crystallization of the sets of expectations that individuals experience toward the school system.

If informal contacts facilitate conflicts, what about participation in professional organizations? While participation in unions reflects feelings of horizontal solidarity which enable teachers to overtly oppose the demands and pressures of their administrators, unions also may channel latent forms of discontent into specific patterns of action and to lower the overall level of incidents taking place in the school scene. The second hypothesis proves to be correct. The number of open conflicts with the administration decreases with the proportion of teachers participating in unions or in professional associations. Thus the existence of formal channels to air grievances is a conflict-reducing mechanism in the educational context. The greater militancy of teachers opposed to unions and professional associations probably reflects the marginality of the status that they occupy in the society at large. But it results also from their need for achievement and from the strategies they believe most appropriate to achieve this particular goal.

Finally, conflicts vary with the discrepancies between the organizational profile of the schools examined and the social psychological profile of their respective teaching force. Because individual teachers differ in terms of their "employee" and "professional" orientations, their corresponding differences may be summed up and schools can therefore be compared with one another in terms of the aggregate scores obtained by their entire teaching force on the employee and professional scales constructed by Corwin.[27] More important, these institutions also can be compared in terms of the extent to which their organizational set-up does correspond to the general orientations of their personnel. Although bureaucratic patterns of organization could be expected to increase predictability in social interactions and hence to reduce conflict, their success is likely to vary with the overall orientations and expectations that teachers entertain along these lines. For instance, Corwin found that among schools where the majority of teachers have "professional" orientations, incidents between the teaching force and the administration increase with the extent to which the principal or the superintendent use bureaucratic types of control mechanisms. In brief, conflicts prevail among schools where the professional orientations of the personnel contrasts with the bureaucratic nature of the organization itself.

Influence of Individual Variables. Yet conflicts between bureaucratization and professionalization also vary with the individual characteristics of administrators and teachers. Career-bound superintendents tend to favor the conception and implementation of educational innovations; place-bound superintendents intend primarily to maintain the status quo and to prevent the overt expression of the tensions likely to oppose the various categories of actors to one another. As a result the expectations they hold toward their personnel are different and such disparities are likely to affect the form, the frequency, and the intensity of the conflicts occurring in the schools placed under their control. Indeed issues over authority should be more frequent in districts where the superintendent is place-bound and where the majority of teachers have professional orientations.

There are similar variations in the orientations and leadership styles of school principals. A professional leadership style—that is, a style that stresses the significance of the attention to be paid to the needs of individual students and to their academic success—is most characteristic of individuals with a relatively high educational attainment and a middle-class origin. It tends furthermore to prevail among principals who have been appointed late in their career although it is not directly related to their seniority as teachers.[28] Again we can expect that disparities in the administrative style of principals affect the climate of the schools and more specifically the seriousness of the tensions among various categories of personnel.

Most important, this climate also depends upon the characteristics of individual teachers. Teachers having "employee" orientations are likely to stress the importance of the loyalty due to the administration and to the school system itself. They similarly emphasize the significance of standardization in the performance of their work, the positive effects of conforming with strictly defined rules in their teaching, and the necessity of considering the satisfaction of the public as the ultimate goal of the educational enterprise. By contrast, individuals with professional orientations emphasize the obligations that they owe to their individual clients, and they similarly stress their rights to participate in the decision-making processes of the school and in all the institutions serving to the advancement of pedagogical knowledge.[29]

While these two orientations are not necessarily mutually exclusive, employee orientations tend to prevail more frequently among older women but professional attitudes tend to be more characteristic of middle-aged men with seniority. Whether at the individual or at the aggregate level, employee orientations are not significantly related to the incidence and the nature of conflicts. By contrast the total number of incidents, the number of incidents between teachers and administrators, and the number of issues pertaining to authority problems increases markedly with the *intensity* of professional orientation.

Since there is a marked correlation between professionalism and participation in conflict, Corwin examines in greater detail the traits of individuals simultaneously characterized by a maximal level of participation in school conflicts and a maximal amount of professional orientations. Generally they are middle-aged men with enough seniority to have both a sense of security and of commitment toward their job. They also have a higher educational attainment than the teaching population at large and they are heavily concentrated in the social sciences. They occupy a particular position in their schools in the sense that they have gained the respect and the esteem of their peers and have a particularly high commitment toward their students. Finally, ultramilitant professionals become particularly involved in conflicts pertaining to authority issues.

The conclusions that can be derived from Corwin are convergent with those of Cole. Whether conflicts take an institutionalized or a noninstitutionalized form and whether they lead to strikes or to mere disputes, they primarily involve teachers who have the strongest aspirations to be treated as professionals. In fact their militancy seems to be the very sign of their commitment to teaching activities. The evidences of this commitment are manifold. Schools with a high concentration of militant professional teachers tend to attach more importance to the critical thinking of their student populations. They also tend to have lower drop-out rates and to be able to send a larger number of students to colleges.

This array of observations is particularly significant because it suggests that conflicts might have a positive effect on the functioning of an institution and that—far from resulting from social disorganization—they may symbolize the emergence of new forms of organization.[30]

These observations apply only to the American scene. The conflicts which oppose teachers to administrators or these two groups to external agencies do not necessarily have the same meaning in other contexts. For example, while American teachers engage in a variety of forms of conflicts to obtain the status of professionals, many of their European counterparts struggle to avoid the loss of such a status. Accordingly they do not use similar strategies. Their choice along these lines is often made more complex by the centralization of educational structures and by the fact that changes in their activities and roles are acted upon at the very center of the political system. While this makes teachers prone to use political pressures, their efforts frequently are thwarted by the diversity of the organizations to which they belong. In France, for example, the erosion of professional status experienced by teachers is reinforced by the multiplication of their unions which weakens the cohesiveness of the entire teaching force. Declines in this cohesiveness are usually associated with corresponding decreases in commitment and hence with increase in rates of designation. Thus while in the United States the average length of teaching careers has doubled and is now about 14 years, there has been a decrease in the length of such careers in many European countries.[31] In Belgium, for instance, a particular group of teachers tends now to be entirely replaced every twenty years.[32] As this occupation becomes more bureaucratic, individual teachers are more likely to feel alienated and to resign in order to change occupation.

Conclusions. A tridimensional model accounts for variations in the relations between the teachers and the administrators of various educational institutions. The first dimension concerns the intensity, the form, and the object of the pressures exerted on schools by the public. These pressures vary with the prevailing organizational profiles of the countries under study but they also depend upon the age, the economic profile and the stability of the community, upon its internal and socioeconomic composition, and upon the general orientations of its leaders. The second of these dimensions concerns the relative vulnerability of school personnel to external influences. This vulnerability is influenced by the relative strength of the professionalization processes operating within school systems. The degree to which teachers can claim the status of professional does not remain the same across cultures but is affected by the specific historical patterns of educational development prevailing in the countries under study. This claim also varies with the nature of the educational services rendered by the schools examined, and it is not alike in the context of primary, secondary and postsecondary institutions.

The third dimension concerns the way in which various categories of teachers and administrators internalize the dilemma between professionalization and bureaucratization. While such a dilemma is necessarily conducive to conflicts, the responses it elicits depend not only upon the psychological characteristics of teachers but also upon the profile of their working enviroment. The outcome of the dilemma does not depend only upon the organizational profile of a school system but also upon the degree to which this profile corresponds to the orientations of the personnel. In effect, bureaucratic patterns of organization reduce overt conflicts *only* in those schools where teachers have employee orientations that predispose them to accept the particular style of interaction demanded of them.

Yet because of the dilemma, the most "professional" teachers who aspire to be more autonomous and to have a more direct control over the fate of their clients are induced to use militant strategies which are more characteristic of a bureaucratic setting. The use of "bureaucratic" means (unionization, strikes) reflects the particular background of the vast bulk of the teaching force, its particular socialization into teaching activities, and its relative inability to move into other sectors of employment.

These observations underline three major themes of this book. First, the desire that teachers have to achieve a professional status and hence an additional amount of liberty in the exercise of their occupational activities is incompatible with the authority that administrators or external agencies want to exert upon educational processes. The respective educational liberties of these two groups are mutually exclusive.

Second, while the liberty that teachers enjoy reflects their differential status in the society at large and is therefore the result of inequalities in the modes of access of various social categories into that group, the exercise of this liberty requires individual practitioners to be equal to one another. Yet the growing differentiation of tasks expected from primary, secondary, and postsecondary teachers is incompatible with the development of intense face-to-face contacts and hence with the development of professional strategies.

Third, the liberty of teachers along these lines is not an individual attribute. The merit of the study of Corwin is to stress that such a liberty is shaped both by the internal organizational patterns of schools and by the composition and hence by the prevailing orientations of their teaching and administrative force. The significance of individual educational liberties always depends upon contextual and environmental factors.

NOTES AND REFERENCES

1. See O. Banks, *Sociology of Education,* (London: Batsford, 1969) pp. 152ff.

2. As quoted by S. Cole, "The Unionization of Teachers," *Sociology of Education,* Vol. 41, 1968, pp. 66–78.

3. See H. Becker, "The Teacher in the Authority System of the Public School," *Journal of Educational Sociology,* Vol. 27, 1953, pp. 128–141.

4. For a development of the negative implications attached to this bureaucrazation of formal schooling, see I. Illich, "Schools Must be Abolished," *New York Review of Books,* Vol. 15, No. 1, July 2, 1970.

5. See B. Kaufman, *Up the Down Staircase* (New York: Avon, 1966), p. 198.

6. For a review of the literature, see G. Ingham, *Size of Industrial Organizations and Worker's Behavior* Cambridge Papers in Sociology, 1 (Cambridge: Cambridge University Press, 1970).

7. R. Corwin, *Militant Professionalism* (New York: Appleton-Century-Crofts, 1970), p. 207.

8. R. Merton, *Social Theory and Social Structure* (Glencoe: Free Press, 1964), Chapter 6.

9. This split of loyalties is not specific to the school scene. Even the most established professionals face increasingly serious difficulties along these lines. Thus medical doctors operating in the context of large institutions must divide their loyalties among their patients, their peers, and the administrative personnel of the hospitals. Similarly lawyers must also define their duties not only in terms of their obligations to their clients but also in terms of their obligations to the firms that employ them. The same is true of architects working on large-scale developments since their clients are *perhaps* the future tenants or owners of the dwelling units they build but more *certainly* and *immediately* the public or private developers who sponsor the operation.

10. See E. Litwak and H. Meyer, "The School and Family: Linking Organizations and External Primary Groups," in S. Sieber and D. Wilder, eds., *The School in Society,* (New York: The Free Press, 1973).

11. Bureaucratization of schools is associated with a decline in the salience of "opinion leaders." Further highly bureaucratized administrators view such leaders as threatening.

12. The circumstances underlying the adoption of this "human relation" approach remains problematic. Whether it may be attributed to particular traits of educational administration or whether it reflects specific organizational strains is not clear.

13. See R. Carlson, "Executive Succession Organization Change, and Performance Among School Superintendents," *Administrative Science Quarterly,* Vol. 6, 1961, pp. 210–227. For a discussion of the same theme, see M. Seeman, "Social Mobility and Administrative Behavior," *American Sociological Review,* Vol. 23, 1958, pp. 633–642.

14. For a review of the growth of unions among teachers, see R. Corwin, *A Sociology of Education* (New York, Appleton-Century-Crofts, 1965) pp. 244–471. See also I. Berg, "Unionized Educators: Some Comparisons with the Private Sector" in P. Sexton, ed., *School Policy and Issues in a Changing Society* (Boston: Allyn and Bacon, 1971), pp. 264–271. For another and more limited study, see A. Rosenthal, "The Strength of Teachers Organizations: Factors Influencing Membership in Large Cities," *Sociology of Education,* Vol. 39, 1966, pp. 359–380. For a further elaboration of the views held on teachers strikes, see C. Wimere, "When Teachers Strike," *Teachers College Record,* Vol. 64, 1963, pp. 533–604.

15. See M. Lieberman and M. Moskow, "Collective Negotiations for Teachers," in P. Sexton *op. cit.* pp. 280–288.

16. See S. Cole, "A Teachers Strike: A Study of the Conversion of Predisposition into Action," *American Journal of Sociology,* Vol. 74, 1969, pp. 506–520. See also S. Cole, *The Unionization of Teachers* (New York: Praeger, 1965).

17. See C. Spaulding and M. Turner, "Political Orientations and Fields of Specialization Among College Professors," *Sociology of Education,* Vol. 41, 1968, pp. 245–252.

18. Conflicts discussed here are intra roles in this sense that there is no consensus among individuals holding similar or complementary positions within the educational structure. Thus teachers are not likely to agree among themselves as to their functions. Nor are they likely to agree with administrators on this very point. For an elaboration of the definition and the implications of inter and intrarole conflicts, see R. Brown, *Social Psychology,* (New York: Free Press, 1965), p. 154ff.

19. R. Corwin, *op. cit,* p. 109.

20. *Ibid.*, p. 115.

21. *Ibid.*, p. 117.

22. *Ibid.*, p. 156.

23. *Ibid.*, p. 133.

24. *Ibid.*, p. 131.

25. *Ibid.*, p. 165.

26. For a further elaboration of this point and for a socio-psychological description of the history of interindividual relations, see G. Homans, *Social Behavior, Its Elementary Forms* (New York: Harcourt Brace, 1961).

27. For a description of these scales, see R. Corwin, *op. cit.*, pp. 363–374.

28. For a summary of the findings and their implications, see N. Gross and F. Herriott, *Staff Leadership in Public Schools: A Sociological Enquiry* (New York: Wiley, 1965), Conclusions.

29. It should be stressed however that the two scales are independent of one another. Individuals might be oriented toward both professionalism and bureaucratization. For a further discussion, see R. Corwin, "Militant Professionalism, Initiative and Compliance in Public Education," *Sociology of Education*, Vol. 38, 1965, pp. 310–331.

30. L. Coser, *The Functions of Social Conflict* (New York: Free Press, 1956).

31. J. Folger and C. Nam, *Education of the American Population* (Washington: U.S. Department of Commerce, 1960) p. 91.

32. See J. Delcourt, "L'évolution qualitative du corps enseignant dans l'enseignement secondaire," in M. Mathijsen and C. Verwort edts *Education in Europe* (Paris, Mouton: 1969) pp. 214–227.

6

PATTERNS OF ACCESS
TO SCHOOLS:

AN OVERVIEW

As educational experiences affect the attitudes and behaviors individuals adopt toward familial, economic, political, and religious organizations, they increase liberty in these areas of social participation. In this sense formal schooling is a privilege that enhances the range of choices open to individuals.

The relative occupational liberty of teachers and administrators varies with their schools and the profile of their student population. Although the age of students prevents them from being entitled to exert direct control on their learning activities, their backgrounds have some effect both on the power granted to the personnel of their schools and on the overall status of that personnel. As a result, it is pertinent to determine whether the various social groups that constitute a particular society (social classes, age groups, cultural and ethnic minorities) enjoy similar chances of gaining access to educational institutions. It is important to identify the forms and the mechanisms of selectivity operating in a variety of educational institutions. Are contrasts in the relative proportion of students with differing age, sex, socioeconomic, and cultural characteristics the same for the educational system as a *whole* and for its differing *subparts* (e.g., for primary and secondary schools and for universities)?

The examination of social and cultural inequalities in patterns of access into schools necessitates the use of differing strategies in countries characterized by differing levels of educational development. In this chapter I stress the consequences of variations in educational development on the meaning and significance of educational inequalities, and more specifically I show that as educational development proceeds, there is a corresponding differentiation of educational institutions and hence a corresponding differentiation of educational inequalities. This will enable us in the next chapter to undertake a detailed analysis of the extent, the determinants and the implications of these inequalities in the patterns of access into educational institutions.

As long as an education system remains limited in size and serves only one single set of functions, the socioeconomic and cultural backgrounds and the value orientations of those individuals of a particular age group who do attend educational institutions can be compared to their counterparts who do not. In short, the underlying model of analysis is *anthropological* since the main question pertains to who does and who does not attain any type of education. As an educational system develops and becomes more complex, there is an increased differentiation in the nature and the relative importance of the hurdles candidates to formal schooling must overcome. Schools differ in their curriculum, the length of the studies offered and the composition of their student population. Because these differences are associated with differential rewards, educational institutions do not recruit their populations evenly from all social strata. In short, the underlying model of analysis is *sociological,* for the main question is to assess variations in the characteristics of individuals who obtain access to the most rewarding kind of educational experiences.

Educational Development and Selectivity.   As a society increases in scale and becomes more complex, an increased division of labor results. As jobs become increasingly distinct from each other, there are parallel contrasts in the educational prerequisites underlying their respective patterns of recruitment. To gain access to the top of the occupational hierarchy, individuals must show not only that they have completed so many years of formal schooling but also that they have taken certain selected types of courses at institutions deemed best in the relevant academic disciplines. Increase in societal scale and its correlate, social differentiation, are associated with greater variations in the types and length of curricula offered by educational institutions, in their organization, and in the profile of their populations. Social differentiation also implies increased contrasts in the resources or means of various social and cultural segments of a particular country and in their respective ends, orientations, and life styles. Hence the purpose of this chapter is to identify the processes by which the combination of these two aspects of social differentiation influences educational selectivity.

In the first section I examine early forms of educational differentiation, and thereafter I analyze the variety of forms taken by educational selectivity as they appear in later stages of educational development. The second section is devoted to an examination of the extent and the determinants of variations in the composition of the populations attending primary schools, secondary schools, and universities. Within these three categories I also examine the significance of the contrasts among institutions characterized by differing proprietorship status, differing organizations, or differing student populations.

Early Forms of Educational Differentiation. Early stages of economic changes obviously are associated only with a gross differentiation of the population in two subcategories—literates and illiterates—and this dichotomy tends to supersede an equally gross distinction between manual and nonmanual occupations. The relationship between literacy and division of labor is as yet uncertain, and variations in the literacy levels of European preindustrial countries are significant. In the seventeenth century Scotland enjoyed a higher rate of literacy than England despite a lower level of economic development, and although poor, the populations of Switzerland were characterized by a high level of literacy.[1]

Relationships between basic economic and educational changes are often linear. In countries as different as France, the United States, and Russia, literacy rates increased regularly as they approached the Industrial Revolution. In France the proportion of bridegrooms able to sign their names on civil registers increased from 29 percent at the end of the seventeenth century to 81 percent in 1876–1877.[2] In Flatbush, New York, the incidence of literacy (as measured by the ability to sign one's name) increased from 63 percent in 1675 to 95 percent in 1738.[3] In the European parts of Russia the corresponding figures were 23 percent for the year 1897 and 33 percent in 1920.[4] Although the relationship between economic development and growth of literacy rates seems to be uniformly linear, gradient or slope varies across cultures.

My purpose, however, is not so much to evaluate the extent of variations in overall levels of participation in educational structures as to determine whether an increase in educational facilities is necessarily conducive to a decrease in the relative magnitude of educational inequalities. The association between overall enrollments and contrasts in the relative educational "share" of distinct social and cultural groups takes a variety of forms. It is sometimes linear (in which case an increase in enrollments is accompanied by a systematic decline of educational inequalities), but it is also sometimes curvilinear (in which case an increase in enrollments is initially conducive to an accentuation of these inequalities, which tend to decline later on).

Table 10 illustrates curvilinear patterns in this regard and shows quite clearly that *initially* a rise in the overall level of literacy of the French population as a whole has been associated with an accentuation of the differences in the aggregate educational attainment of the male and female populations of the basic French political units called *departements*. The relative growth of educational facilities does not necessarily

Table 10. Mean and Range in the Levels of Literacy among French Departments [a]

Dates	Male Population		Female Population	
	Mean	Range	Mean	Range
1686–1690	29	50	4	40
1786–1790	47	85	27	65
1816–1820	54	85	35	75
1854–1855	68	70	53	80
1876–1877	81	50	71	65

[a] Derived from C. A. Anderson, "Patterns and Variability in Distribution of Schooling," in C. A. Anderson and M. J. Bowman, eds., *Education and Economic Development*, p. 333. Published in Great Britain by Frank Cass and Co. Ltd., London, 1966.

enhance the *equalizing* functions of schools. Initially at least, the *demand* for education varies along geographic social and cultural lines: Only after the educational development of the French society as a whole passed a critical threshold, did inequalities in the literacy levels of these basic political units begin to decline in size.

Table 10 also shows that with an increase in the overall level of literacy of the French population, there is a systematic decline in sex differences in this respect. However, changes in educational competition between the sexes are culture-bound. In contrast to France where educational development has been associated with a systematic and linear decline in the sex ratio of literate subpopulations—that is, with a decline in the difference between the relative numbers of educated males and females, the corresponding relationship is curvilinear in urban Russia (Table 11). In 1897 literacy was more frequent among young

Table 11. Distribution of Literacy among Urban and Rural Populations in Russia (1897) [a]

	Age Groups					
	10–19	20–29	30–39	40–49	50–59	60 and over
Level of Literacy of the Urban Population	64	59	52	47	42	35
Differences Males/ Females	15	20	24	27	22	21
Level of Literacy of the Rural Population	29	26	23	19	15	12
Differences Males/ Females	24	24	23	19	15	10

[a] Derived from A. Kahan, "The Development of Education and the Economy in Czarist Russia," in C. A. Anderson and M. J. Bowman, eds., *Education and Economic Development,* p. 357. Published in Great Britain by Frank Cass and Co. Ltd., London, 1966.

urban individuals than among their elders, and the differential distribution of literacy by sex among urban populations varied between distinct age groups. Women between 40 and 49 years of age had proportionately less chances to acquire basic skills in reading and writing than those under 40 and over 49. Since educational development in the hinterland was accompanied by an accentuation of differences between the relative numbers of educated rural males and females, the impact of change in the differentiation of sex roles on male and female literacy rates is curvilinear in Russian cities, but linear in rural areas. The influence of educational development on the distribution of literacy among urban and rural populations suggests that the most severe educational competition during that period was between urban females and rural males who have probably obtained more than their "fair share" in the educational enterprises of the time.

As formal schooling becomes institutionalized, so do the forms of educational selectivity. In early days basic skills in reading and writing were acquired through a variety of sources, which ceases to be true with the institutionalization of schools. In the province of Moscow in 1883, only 36 percent of individuals included in a sample of literate factory workers had learned how to read and write in village, town, and district schools; the majority of them had become literate as a result of their contacts with the clergy (9 percent), of their experiences in the army (7 percent), in industrial organizations (10 percent), or elsewhere (38 percent). Clearly this distribution would have to change at the turn of the century after schools became a primary mechanism in the diffusion of literacy.[5]

Correspondingly, as educational development proceeds, the magnitude of differential literacy rates may decline, but sharp contrasts in the overall enrollment rates of various segments of the population at large persist. For example, as early as 1877, only three of the 87 French departments still had a majority of bridegrooms unable to sign their names, and this proportion was already below 10 percent in 29 of these departments. From that time on, French departments could therefore no longer be significantly differentiated in terms of their literacy rates. Educational development was already sufficiently institutionalized, and whether persons were able to read or write was no longer what made a difference on their station in life but rather whether they had attended primary schools. At the same time, however, the distribution of primary school enrollments among French departments in the nineteenth century remained differentiated, and those departments with the highest primary school enrollments were those with the highest literacy rates two centuries earlier. Although specific forms change over time, educational differences among regions are a long-lasting feature of a country's history.[6]

During the early stages of educational development, social differentiation only operates in terms of *who* is literate and *who* is illiterate. In the subsequent stage, the determinants of the selectivity of access into basic educational facilities remain simple enough. To the division of the school aged population into those who do and who do not attend any educational institution, corresponds a dichotomy of the adult population by sex, urban or rural residence, or occupation (non agricultural versus agricultural, manual versus non manual). In short, the paradigm summarizing early educational selectivity is simple and takes the form of a four cells table, the two opposite quadrants of which should only be filled out (Figure 2).

	Educational Differentiation	
Residential Differentiation	Attend School	Do Not Attend School
Urban	+	−
Rural	−	+

Figure 2. Early forms of selection in access to schooling.

Rapidly enough, however, the diffusion of literacy becomes so widespread that it ceases to yield significant social rewards. Educational competition begins to move toward the higher rungs of the educational hierarchy. Competition among individuals and groups begins to be defined in terms of who graduates from primary or secondary schools and who reaches the top of the academic ladder.

Further, this competition takes more complex forms that are associated with the differential changes affecting the definition of the economic and social roles allocated to the various subgroups (men and women, urban and rural, regions, etc.) that constitute the society at large. Since none of these groups remains excluded from educational enterprises, inequalities cease to be absolute, and distinctions between the educational "have" and the "have not" become more complex.

Forms of Selectivity in the Modern World. Later stages of educational development are accompanied by the emergence of three distinctive forms of selectivity in the access of school-aged populations to educational institutions. The demands and the rewards associated with formal schooling vary with the length of time in school, nature of the studies undertaken, and types of institutions.

Length of Time in School. As an educational system grows and becomes more complex, the rewards attached to formal schooling increase with the intensity of individual exposure to the norms and values of the educational milieu, and school-aged populations are differentiated in terms of the amount of time they attend school.

The significance of time varies of course with the general level of educational development in the countries under study. Among African countries, this form of selectivity operates most forcefully within the primary school system, and the highest drop-out rates are observed at this stage. The passage from primary to postprimary schools constitutes another significant point. Enrollments in postprimary institutions tend to be much less than half as large as those observed in primary schools, and except in Ghana, they do not exceed 6 percent of a particular age group.[7]

Until 1920, primary enrollments represented only 40 percent of the Sao Paulo, Brazil, school-aged population; up to that point Brazilian children, like their African counterparts of today, were differentiated primarily in terms of their abilities both to enter and to finish primary school. This criterion is no longer useful because primary enrollments currently approximate 99 percent of a particular age group.[8] Accordingly, selectivity probably operates most significantly at the entry into the postprimary system, in which only 18 percent of the 12- to 18-year-old group participate.

As educational development proceeds, contrasts in the participation of various social categories in primary educational structures cease to be significant, but these categories differ increasingly in their ability to enter postprimary institutions and in their relative enrollments in the corresponding structures. In France, although postprimary enrollments doubled from 28 to 56 percent between 1949 and 1963, they still vary between 30 and 78 percent among *departments*.[9] Despite a marked increase in the proportion of children originating from deprived social, cultural, or geographic groups who enter postprimary schools, a large number are unable to complete their studies. Only 2 percent of the cohort of French students graduating from primary schools in 1962 were obliged to enter the labor force immediately. Yet two years after, they were joined by 19 percent of their initially more fortunate peers, and by 1966 one third of the students from this particular graduating class had effectively joined the labor force.[10]

This attrition, however, is not necessarily socially selective. While the relative proportions of social groups entering the most prestigious secondary schools, *lycées*, vary from one to seven, disparities tend to decline at later stages of the postprimary system; and the proportions of social classes still present in *lycées* four years after the completion of their primary studies vary only from one to five.[11] Selectivity operates again at the level of universities. Whereas the children of managerial classes have one chance out of two to join an institution of higher learning, the offspring of hired agricultural laborers have less than one chance out of 100 to follow a similar path.[12]

A diachronic analysis confirms the fact that different rates of educational development are associated with variations in the points of the academic hierarchy at which selectivity operates most forcefully. The history of the United States offers a case in point. During the second half of the nineteenth century the enrollment rates of the school-aged population only increased from 47 percent in 1850 to 55 percent in 1900—and this in spite of a sixfold increase in the absolute number of children attending schools. Despite this growth, there were still marked differentials among individual states. Thus, in 1890, the percentage of between five and nine years old children attending school was much higher in industrial than in agricultural states. Enrollments in Massachusetts averaged 72 percent compared to only 40 percent in Kentucky. Children of agricultural states were perhaps late in entering educational institutions, but they were also likely to stay longer than their counterparts living in industrial regions. For the age group 15 to 19, enrollments were 36 percent in Kentucky but only 25 percent in Massachusetts. The need of emerging industries on the Eastern seaboard for an ever-increasing labor force explains the sharp decline in the enrollment rates of elder children in that particular region.[13]

However, enrollment rates have markedly increased for the eldest segments of the school-aged population. By 1940, 79 percent of the individuals between 14 and 17 years of age were still at school, and the corresponding percentage increased to 88 percent by 1960. With the increase, inequalities in primary and high school enrollments have declined. For the cohort 16 and 17 years of age, for example, enrollment rates vary currently between a high of 85 percent for suburban populations and a low of 77 percent for nonfarm rural populations. Similarly the highest rates are obtained by white children born in second generation families (89 percent), while lowest rates characterize black and American Indian children (73 and 70 percent respectively).

The points at which selectivity now operates most forcefully are graduation from high school and entry into college. Thus, the number of high school dropouts is still remarkably high, estimated to be 2.3 millions in 1962.[14] As could be anticipated, they come predominantly from marginal socioeconomic and cultural groups and are characterized by a low level of educational abilities.

By 1960, college enrollments represented slightly over 36 percent of the population between 18 and 21 years of age, or slightly over 40 percent of high school graduates. Chances for these graduates to attend a college were slightly affected by their ethnic background or their sex. About 70 percent of white high school graduates who did plan to go to college realized that goal compared to only 50 percent of their nonwhite counterparts. However, college enrollments were more significantly affected by the socioeconomic origin or the academic record of high school graduates. The proportion of high school graduates enrolled in college exceeded 60 percent for those belonging to households whose heads were in nonmanual occupations but was only 30 percent for those attached to families whose heads were engaged in other activities. Similarly, over 50 percent of the graduates were in college when they ranked in the upper half of their high school class, but the corresponding figure went down to 20 percent among their peers whose rank was in the lower half. Finally, almost 70 percent of those who had planned to go to college did so compared to less than 10 percent of the individuals who had made other plans.

Despite a continuous increase in college enrollments, there are still marked contrasts in the attendance rates of various income groups. In 1971, for instance, such rates varied between a maximum of 66 percent for individuals between 18 and 24 years of age from families with a total annual income of over $15,000 and a minimum of 23 percent for their counterparts coming from families with an income under $3,000. Twenty-seven percent of the families of college students had an annual income of over $15,000, whereas families with children in the same age bracket and the same financial means represented only 16 percent of the total population. By contrast, families of only 5 percent of college students earned less than $3,000 per year, although families with children in this age group and with such low resources represented over 8 percent of the total population.

Patterns of access in various streams and cycles.   With the growth of educational systems, postprimary schools tend to offer their students differing curricula. Since access into adult social and economic structures increasingly depends upon the nature of postprimary academic experiences, the social composition of postprimary institutions begins to vary with the type of curriculum offered.

Havighurst and Neugarten show that college preparatory curriculum in the United States is chosen by boys and girls of all social classes of two midwestern high schools—with the possible exception of the lower segments of the population. In contrast, very few members of upper and upper-middle classes enroll in commercial and general curricula.[15] In Switzerland Girod observed in 1962 that within a cohort of pupils 12 years of age, only 7 percent of the offspring of unskilled workers are engaged in studies leading to higher education compared to 65 percent of those born to upper-class families. For their counter-

Table 12. *Social Origins of Students Graduating from French Primary Classes in 1962 by Their Academic Situation Four Years After (Percentage Distribution)* [a]

Social Class	Percentage in Relevant Age Group	Percentage Graduating from Primary School	Work Situations	Vocational Schools [b]	Third Year of Short Academic Institutions [c]	Fourth Year of Short Academic Institutions	Third Year of Lycées [d]	Fourth Year of Lycées	Fifth Year with Liberal Arts Curriculum	Fifth Year with Scientific Curriculum	Fifth Year with Technical Curriculum
Low	60.2	60.2	78.4	67.8	53.5	54.4	34.7	33.3	41.8	35.1	60.7
Middle	30.7	26.9	19.1	26.3	31.7	33.4	38.2	34.7	33.2	29.3	29.1
High	19.1	12.9	2.5	5.9	14.8	12.2	27.1	32.0	25.0	35.6	10.2

[a] Derived from A. Girard and H. Bastide, "Orientation et Selection scolaires sannées d'une promotion, *Population*, Vol. 24, 1969, p. 204.

[b] Short-cycle institutions to semi-skilled positions in industrial or commercial organizations.

[c] Short-cycle institutions leading to BEPC, a terminal kind of examination after four years of postprimary studies.

[d] Long-cycle institutions leading to universities after seven years of studies.

parts three years older, the corresponding percentages are 5 and 75 percent respectively.[16]

To understand this selectivity, we must ask not only whether postprimary studies lead directly to higher education, but also what rewards result from specific contents of the curriculum. In France postprimary institutions are also divided in terms of *streams*. At one end of the continuum one finds academic schools (within which a more refined distinction is made between the curricula that include Latin and those that do not). At the other end of the continuum are *technical* schools, *teachers colleges*, and *agricultural* institutions, each one of them divided into two cycles highly differentiated and with few bridges between them.

Table 12 shows that in France both overall drop-out rates and enrollments in institutions of various types vary along class lines. While upper class children are overrepresented in *lycées* and institutions with scientific curricula, lower classes tend to be proportionately more numerous in technical schools as well as in the liberal arts. Socioeconomic selectivity continues to operate at higher levels but its form is somewhat different. Sons of manual workers are most likely to study sciences. The few daughters of hired agricultural laborers able to enter institutions of higher education are most likely to study liberal arts. In contrast, as Table 13 shows, the children of middle and upper classes have more diversified and more prestigious careers. Indeed they represent over 50 percent of the student body of grandes écoles such as Polytechnique or Ecole Normale Supérieure, which are the true seedbeds of the French elite, but their enrollments in new technical, and hence low prestige, institutions like I.N.S.A. are significantly more modest.[17]

As long as postprimary school enrollments remain low, variations in the types of postprimary institutions attended are without effect on the future career of an individual. In the Ivory Coast, which follows closely the French pattern of postprimary studies, there are marked social inequalities in access into the entire postprimary system but there are no significant variations in the relative representation of the various socioeconomic, religious, or ethnic categories in the secondary, technical or agricultural institutions of the country.[18]

In a more educationally developed country like Brazil, inequalities are marked in the participation level of the three basic social classes in the distinctive streams of the postprimary system (Table 14). Higher classes are concentrated in the most prestigious secondary schools; middle classes have more diversified academic careers; but lower classes are more likely to cluster within commercial institutions. Even when these differing types of curricula have the same duration, social groups dif-

Table 13. Social Origins of Students Enrolled in French Grande Ecole (Percentage Distribution)[a]

Paternal Occupation[b]	Polytechnique[b]	Ecole Centrale[b]	INSA[b] Lyon	Ecole Normale Superieure[c]	Sciences Politiques[d]	Institute National Agronomique[e]	Universities	Percentage in Adult Population
Farmers	1	2	6	1	8	20	6	21
Agricultural workers	0	0	1	0	0	0	0	6
Businessmen	13	12	18	9	19	37	18	12
Managerials and professions	57	47	19	51	44	29	29	3
Supervisory and technicians	15	18	16	26	13	0	18	6
White-collar workers	8	9	16	5	8	7	8	11
Manual workers	2	2	14	3	2	0	6	34
Services	0	0	2	0	1	0	1	3
Others	3	4	5	1	2	0	8	3
Jobless	1	6	3	4	3	7	6	4

[a] Derived from La Documentation Française no. 45, 1966, as quoted by P. Bourdieu, Les Héritiers (Paris: Editions de Minuit, 1966), p. 21.
[b] These are engineering schools with varying prestige (Polytechnique opens a maximal number of doors, INSA & minimal).
[c] This is a high prestigious school for university teachers in science and literature.
[d] This school trains executives for public and private bureaucracies.
[e] This school trains agricultural engineers.

215

Table 14. Social Origins of Brazilian Secondary School Students by Cycle and Stream, State of Sao Paulo [a]

	Social Classes					
	High		Medium		Low	
	Cycles					
Stream	1	2	1	2	1	2
Secondary	30	30	77	20	51	15
Commercial	7	15	14	25	23	46
Industrial	1	27	7	22	24	16
Normal (teaching)	—	26	—	30	—	20
Agricultural	2	2	2	3	2	3
Total	100	100	100	100	100	100

[a] Derived from J. Dias, *Ensino Medio* (Ministerio da Educacao e Culture, 1967) , p. 45.

fer in terms of the choices they make. The lower a group in the social, ethnic, or religious structure, the more limited is the range of schools its children attend.

Initially, this particular form of selectivity should only differentiate among the broadest types of postprimary institutions. While there should be no differences in the relative enrollments of various groups in the sections of a given institution (e.g., in the "modern" and "classical" sections of a *lycée*), there should be contrasts in the social or ethnic composition of the populations attending *lycées* and those attending vocational training programs. Yet evidence available in the Ivory Coast does not validate this particular hypothesis. There are no marked differences in the social, ethnic, and religious background of the students attending the various streams of the postprimary system, but there are significant cleavages between classic and modern students of the lycées, the "classic" students being by far the most "modernized" of the entire postprimary population.[19] Thus, selectivity by type of postprimary institution does not necessarily evolve from the simplest to the most complex types of distinction. This is because of variations in the size of the subpopulations competing for access into a particular curriculum and because of discontinuities in the hierarchy of values that these subpopulations attach to the curricula offered to them. Although the ultimate educational and occupational destination of an individual is less influenced by the distinction between classical and modern than between academic and technical curricula, the choice of students continues to be affected by the past—and obsolete—preeminence attached to a classical curriculum. In short, there seems to be a time lag in the responses of students to changes in the hierarchy of courses and training programs.

Access into various types of institutions. The socialization that parents expect from educational institutions concerns not only the acquisition of appropriate knowledge or modes of learning but also the acquisition of adequate modes of adjustment to the norms and values of the immediate environment. They consider that schools should provide a sort of marketplace to find suitable friends, work associates, and conjugal partners. Schools should differ in terms of their sex, ethnic, religious, and social composition; quality of educational facilities (as measured by student–teacher ratio, number of books present in libraries, etc.); or the timetable within which they operate. Schools which operate during the academic calendar and summer schools, day schools and night schools do not serve the same populations. Nor do they offer similar opportunities.

As long as educational systems remain small in size, variations in the composition of public and private institutions are limited. Religious schools in the western European countries of the seventeenth and eighteenth centuries were quite open in their recruitment patterns as is true today in the Ivory Coast.[20] Of course, even at this low stage of development, this particular form of selectivity may still operate as a result of cultural factors.

The Camerounian educational system offers a case in point. In the French-speaking eastern part of the country, educational institutions follow the traditional French pattern, and the populations attending public secondary schools are more likely to originate from the most modernized ethnic groups and the most urbanized or educated families. In the English-speaking western region, schools follow the traditional British pattern. To attend a private, usually well established school is more prestigious than to attend the more recent institutions directly supported by the state. As a result, the social and economic background of private school populations often tends to be higher than that of their public school counterparts.

When a country stresses the merits of centralization and gives preeminence to public educational arrangements, public secondary schools or universities tends to attract primarily the offspring of established elites. When a country emphasizes the significance of decentralization, the status of private secondary institutions or universities is higher than that of public schools, and their population is derived from narrower segments of the society. Similarly, in a recent study on the patterns of selection prevailing in the public and private schools of La Paz (Bolivia), Santiago (Chile), and Buenos Aires (Argentina), private institutions in the first two countries recruit their students from significantly narrower segments of the population than those of Buenos Aires.[21] Since the functions of private academic schools in Buenos Aires seem to be more differentiated than those expected from their counterparts in the two other cities, the social origin of students varies within broader limits there than in the two other cities. In short, contrasts in the composition of schools depend upon historical legacies.

Of course the significance of the distinction between public and private sectors is not necessarily the same for the male and female segments of the school-aged population. When there is a sharp differentiation in the definition of educational functions along sex lines and when the formal schooling of girls is aimed at perpetuating traditional familial arrangements, variations in the social and academic background of students should be more marked in the case of females than of males. In Spain, for example, the daughters of middle and upper classes are overwhelmingly enrolled in private schools; males of these classes are relatively more evenly distributed between public and private institutions.

Finally, in countries with higher levels of educational development, the functions of private institutions, and hence their patterns of recruitment, are not necessarily alike at various points of the educational hierarchy. In France, for example, the overt function of private primary institutions is to act as a feeder toward the most prestigious secondary schools; the functions ascribed to public primary schools are more differentiated.[22] By 1954, for instance, only 14 percent of the French students enrolled in public primary schools were able to proceed directly to classical *lycées* compared to 28 percent of private school students.

The situation is the same in the United States, since the rewards derived from higher learning are not alike for all colleges. Neugarten and Havighurst have noted sharp differences in the composition of the student body of various types of colleges.[23] While upper and upper-middle classes are concentrated in prestigious institutions with long and respected traditions and highly selective admissions policies, lower-

middle classes generally attend opportunity colleges characterized by low
costs and easy admission standards. Middle classes are most likely to attend metropolitan and state colleges and small church-related arts colleges usually located in middle-sized communities. Similarly, a comparison between two- and four-year colleges shows that the population of
the first type of institution is less likely to have followed preparatory
programs, has lower academic abilities, and is derived from a lower-
class, urban background.[24] In 1970, only 15 percent of the freshman
enrolled in the C.U.N.Y. system two-year colleges had at least a B + as
a grade-point average in high school as against 47 percent of those attending four-year colleges. At the national level, 16 percent of those attending two-year colleges had such a high grade point average as
against 37 percent of those enrolled in four-year institutions. Similarly,
in the C.U.N.Y. system, 21 percent of the first type of freshmen had fathers with at least a college education as against 29 percent of their
counterparts in four year colleges. The trend was the same at the national level and the corresponding figures were 31 and 47 percent, respectively.

These figures suggest that there are regional variations in the selectivity of access into the two types of institution. In relative terms, academic standing seems to a better predictor of four-year college enrollments in the New York system than in the nation as a whole but the
pattern is reversed as far as the predictive power of paternal education
is concerned. In short, the meaning of the distinction between two- and
four-year college depends both upon the stress placed upon equality
and upon the institutional mechanisms used to implement the corresponding ideals.[25]

In the United States, however, selectivity operates not only in terms of
the proprietorship or of the legal status of schools, but also in terms of
the ethnic composition of their population as well as of the differential
facilities they offer to their respective students. The percentage of
black students attending schools whose populations are predominantly
black varies between a minimal of 21 percent for New York City, a high
of 77 percent in the case of a highly industrialized city like Buffalo, and
a maximal of 99 percent in the case of Tuscaloosa.[26] Whereas in the
metropolitan Midwest, for example, black students attend institutions
where there are 54 students per room, their white counterparts go to
schools where there are only 33 pupils per class. At the national level,
white students attend high schools where there is one teacher for every
22 students, but for their black counterparts, the corresponding ratio
goes up to one teacher for 26 pupils. Finally, black students tend to

have a more limited access to extracurricular activities such as drama club, debate teams, school newspapers, science and language laboratories, and accelerated curriculum programs.

Such differences are significant insofar as they may affect the ultimate educational and occupational destination of the individuals as well as the meaning and satisfaction they attach to their immediate learning experience. Although the influence of educational environment on achievement is limited for the student population as a whole, it still is higher for black than for white students.[27] In addition, black students enrolled in segregated schools are less likely to venture into new occupational fields because they have established fewer contacts during their school years. They also tend to earn less than their counterparts from desegregated institutions.[28]

Finally, selectivity operates in terms of the timetable within which various schools operate. In Brazil, where the system involves both day and night schools, the day-school populations have more chances than night-class students to negotiate successfully the various hurdles of the academic hierarchy. Students of day schools are younger and come from more fortunate circumstances. Only 25 percent of day students in the state of Sao Paulo come from lower classes compared to 41 percent attending night classes.[29]

Conclusions. Three facts emerge from this analysis. First, as educational development proceeds, the rewards and demands attached to various types of educational experiences become increasingly different from one another. As a result, there are corresponding changes in the level of studies at which social selectivity operates most drastically. At an early stage, the most significant contrasts are between the backgrounds and occupational destinations of literate versus illiterate persons. As educational development proceeds, this cleavage contrasts individuals who have attended primary schools to those who have not. In a final stage subpopulations are differentiated in terms of their dropout rates at various stages of the academic ladder, the type of studies undertaken, and the nature of the institutions they attend. Further, whereas the first forms of differentiation operating in the educational market are simply dichotomous, later forms are of "the more or less" variety.

The relationship between educational development and selectivity is not necessarily linear in nature. The growth of a particular branch of the school system does not necessarily lead to an immediately more even level of participation of all social groups in corresponding institutions. There may be time gaps in the extent to which the demands for further schooling of each one of these groups do increase or in the extent to which they are able to obtain an easier access to educational facilities. Correspondingly, the growth of certain educational amenities often induces greater disparities in the relative shares of the "pie" allocated to the various sex, age, social, or cultural categories of the society. Similarly, this growth is not necessarily conducive to a lowering of the selectivity underlying access to lower echelons of the academic hierarchy. Selectivity may act according to the principles of "progressive distillation" (the upper segments of the academic ladder being exclusively populated with the upper segments of the social hierarchy). Alternatively, selectivity may be also a "one shot affair" (the weeding out of the underprivileged groups of society taking place at *only* one crucial cutting point of the academic hierarchy).

It is not sufficient, however, to identify the overall limits within which schools act as equalizing factors in the allocation of societal values and assets; to understand changes in patterns of access to educational institutions necessitates an exploration of the independence of the determinants of social and cultural selectivity. As educational development proceeds, the number and the independence of the factors conditioning school experiences should increase.

NOTES AND REFERENCES

1. C. Cipolla, *Literacy and Development in the West* (London: Penguin, 1965), p. 18.
2. See C. A. Anderson, "Patterns and Variability of Distribution and Diffusion of Schooling," in C. A. Anderson and M. J. Bowman, eds., *Education and Economic Development* (Chicago: Aldine, 1965), pp. 314–333.
3. See C. A. Anderson, "Literacy and Schooling on the Development Threshold, Some Historical Cases," in C. A. Anderson and M. J. Bowman, *op. cit.*, pp. 347–362.
4. See A. Kahan, "Determinants of the Incidence of Literacy in Rural Nineteenth Century Russia," in C. A. Anderson and M. J. Bowman, *op. cit.*, pp. 258–302; and "Social Structure, Public Policy and the Development of Education and the Economy in Czarist Russia," *ibid.*, pp. 353–375.
5. C. Cipolla, *Literacy and Development in the West, op. cit.*, p. 25.
6. See C. A. Anderson, "Patterns and Variability in Distribution and Diffusion of Schooling," *op. cit.*, pp. 314–344. See also C. Cipolla, *op. cit.*, p. 18.

7. See, for example, "Première mission du groupe de planification de l'éducation en Côte d'Ivoire," (Paris: UNESCO, 1963).

8. See J. A. Dias, *Ensino Medio e estructure socio economica* (Sao Paulo: Ministero da educacao y Cultura, 1967), p. 17.

9. See A. Girard and H. Bastide, "Orientation et sélection scolaires: 5 années d'une promotion; de la fin du cycle élémentaire à l'entrée dans le 2 eme cycle du 2 eme degré," *Population,* Vol. 24, 1969, 195–261. See also M. Segre Brun and L. Tanguy, "Quelle unité d'analyse retenir pour étudier les variations geographiques de la scolarisation," *Revue Francaise de sociologie,* Vol. 8, 1967, 117–139.

10. See A. Girard and H. Bastide, *loc. cit.*

11. *Ibid.*

12. See P. Bourdieu, *Les Heritiers* (Paris: Les Editions de Minuit, 1968), Chapter 1.

13. R. Folger and C. Nam, *Education of the American Population* (Washington: Department of Commerce, 1960), Chapter 1, 2.

14. *Ibid.,* Chapter 2.

15. See R. Havighurst and B. Neugarten, *Society and Education* (Boston: Allyn and Bacon, 1962), p. 241.

16. See R. Girod, "Système scolaire et mobilité sociale," *Revue francaise de sociologie,* Vol. 3, 1962, pp. 3–19.

17. See P. Bourdieu, *op. cit.,* Chapter 1.

18. See R. Clignet and P. Foster, *The Fortunate Few* (Evanston: Northwestern University Press, 1966), chapter 4.

19. See R. Clignet and P. Foster, "Un exemple d'assimilationi la preeminence de l'enseignement classique en Côte d'Ivoire, *Revue francaise de sociologie,* Vol. 7, 1966, pp. 32–47.

20. See R. Clignet and P. Foster, (Evanston: Northwestern University Press, 1966) *loc. cit.,* chapter IV.

21. R. Myers et al., "Social Selectivity in the Secondary Schools of Buenos Aires, La Paz and Santiago de Chile," *Sociology of Education,* Vol. 45, 1973, pp. 355–360.

22. See A. Girard, "Selection for Secondary Education in France," in A. Halsey and J. Floud and C. A. Anderson, eds., *Education Economy and Society* (Glencoe: Free Press, 1961), pp. 183–194.

23. See T. Dye, "Urban Schools Segregation: A Comparative Analysis," *Urban Affairs Quarterly,* Vol. 4, 1968, pp. 141–166.

24. For an examination of the variations in the characteristics of educational institutions and of their teaching force, see J. S. Coleman et al., *Equality of Educational Opportunity,* (Washington, D.C.: Office of Education, 1966). The authors show that the percentage of total variance in individual ver-

bal achievement that lies between schools, is always lower for white than for black populations, although for the latter, it varies among regions (p. 236). They show similarly that whereas the part of this variance accounted for by characteristics of teachers increases as we could expect with age, gains are significantly greater for black than for white populations. Thus for the 12th grade the selected characteristics of the teaching force account for 9.35 percent of the overall variance in the distribution of the results obtained by black students on a verbal achievement test, compared to only 1.82 percent in the case of whites.

25. Material derived from L. Buder, "50 percent dropout under open admissions; but City U. sees progress," *The New York Times,* July 15, 1973, p. 42.

26. For a description of the differential occupational destination of Black students see R. Cain, "School Integration and Occupational Achievement of Negroes," *American Journal of Sociology,* Vol. 75, 1970, pp. 593–606.

27. See R. Havighurst and B. Neugarten, *Education and Society, op. cit.* p. 263.

28. *Ibid.,* pp. 63ff.

29. See J. Dias, *Ensino Medio e estructure socio economica,* p. 57.

7

FACTORS OF SELECTIVITY:

WHO CAN, SHOULD, AND DOES GO TO SCHOOL?

The "equalizing" functions of schools are limited. School markets are like other markets and follow the principles of a liberal economy; thus their functioning results from an interaction between demand and supply. Patterns of access into various schools reflect the relative scarcity and the relative value attached to differing types of academic experience. They also reflect the differential distribution of the attributes deemed necessary for academic success across varying segments of the school-aged population. This chapter is devoted to an examination of the extent, the type and the determinants of educational inequalities.

These inequalities result from

1. The ascriptive characteristics of the individual. Variations by age and sex in distinct types of enrollments do exist.
2. Differential profiles of the microenvironments from which individuals derive and thus of their familial worlds and prior academic experiences.
3. Contrasts in the dominant traits of the larger social groups to which individuals belong and thus the differential position occupied by these individuals in the geographical, social, and cultural space.
4. Political and overall social composition of the society at large.

224

Determinants of Educational Selectivity. Participation in rewarding educational structures results from an interplay between the abilities, aspirations, and information of the individual.

Abilities. As a society modernizes, it tends to use more universalistic criteria to regulate access to the various slots of the educational hierarchy. Individual educational and occupational trajectories cease to be overtly determined by ethnic social and religious backgrounds or by familial positions. They are more directly influenced by intelligence and intellectual abilities. Today, evidence reveals significant correlations between intelligence (as measured by IQ) and educational attainment or between intelligence and occupational achievement (i.e., access to the top of the occupational hierarchy and success in a particular career).[1]

Yet the concepts of intelligence and intellectual abilities remain problematic. Are these terms "real," and are such "realities" located in a particular part of the brain, or are they mere scientific or social and hence culturally relative constructs? In the first perspective these attributes are assumed to exist regardless of the conscience of the observer, and it is perfectly meaningful to study objectively the determinants and the consequences of the distribution of these attributes across the various segments of a particular society or across societies. In the second perspective these attributes are assumed to be primarily subjective labels, and the task of the sociologist is to ascertain the source of the corresponding labeling processes and to evaluate their implications on the fate of the relevant categories of individuals.

In addition, the problematic nature of these concepts results from the debate concerning their origin. Is intelligence the product of heredity or of environmental factors? Data suggest that heredity contributes at least partly to determine individual levels of intelligence. Thus while the correlation between the IQ scores of monozygotic twins reared together reaches .92, the corresponding correlation declines to .44 in the case of siblings reared apart, to reach $-.04$ in the case of unrelated children living in distinct familial environments.[2] Other data also show the significance of environmental factors along these lines. The study of Skeels on the IQ scores of children left in a cold and impersonal orphanage reveals that decreases in individual scores are markedly affected by the length of institutionalization and that the persistence of negative environmental conditions make their effects increasingly difficult to change. At the other end of the continuum, many studies have shown that marked improvements in environmental conditions are likely to be associated with significant rises in both individual IQ scores and academic performances.[3]

The educational implications of the answers to the dilemma between the hereditary and environmental origin of intelligence are obvious. Should we believe that intelligence is exclusively a genetic factor, we could be tempted to conclude that schools can be only "sorting out" agencies and that their function consists of identifying students with differing levels of intelligence and ability and providing them with the curricula most appropriate to their intellectual standing. Schools can only contribute to the *perpetuation* of the current social order. Should we believe conversely that intelligence is a by-product of environment, schools can perform equalizing functions and can act as substitutes to a faulty familial environment. Schools can contribute to individual mobility and hence *modify* existing social hierarchies.

However, the fact is that, far from being mutually exclusive, the concepts of heredity and of environment are complementary. Dobzhansky writes that "there is no organism without genes and any genotype can act only in some environment." [4] The interaction between heredity and the environment is dynamic, and their relative contributions to a particular function, trait, or characteristic are necessarily unstable. As individuals are immersed in a standardized and uniform environment, they still differ from one another in one or several particular traits or functions, and these differences are chiefly attributable to contrasts in their genetic make up. Conversely, as individuals participate in a heterogeneous milieu, their behavior is increasingly influenced by variations in the prevailing characteristics of their immediate surroundings.

Further, the complementary character of heredity and environment takes a particular meaning in human societies. Human societies practice various forms of homogamy or assortative mating, and individuals with analogous educational cultural and ethnic or religious characteristics tend to marry one another. Assortative mating is an environmental factor in that it reflects current systems of social stratification, but it also has genetic implications. To be sure, the mechanisms by which assortative mating affects intelligence remain unclear. Yet it is possible to suggest that social differentiation (and hence educational inequalities) is not a "timeless" phenomenon but a continuing and cumulative process, in which case heredity is in part the enduring manifestation of social stratification and hence of environment. This remark is of significance at a time when the debate about the relative contribution of heredity and environment to intelligence presents marked political overtones and is aimed at determining the functions that formal schooling should perform for the black minorities of the United States.

Underlying this debate is thus the question of the meaning to be attached to the concept of race. Clearly, races have differing genetic pools and hence differing physical traits. Insofar as interracial differences in physical traits can be attributed to genetic factors, can the argument be generalized to assume that interracial differences in IQ scores are also attributable to racial genetic determinants? This assumption does not seem tenable for two reasons. First, the effects of genes on a trait or function are highly specific, and some evidence suggests that as a psychological function increases in complexity, the role of heredity decreases while there is a marked instability in the interaction between genotypic and nongenotypic factors on its actualization.[5] Second and more important, interracial differences in IQ scores cannot be considered as immutable and permanent. Such differences can result from the particular history of various ethnic groups and from the implications of this history on breeding structures. Although differences between black and white IQ scores may reflect genetic factors, such factors are not independent of the enduring effects of the particular ethnic stratification operating in the United States. Under such conditions the differences cannot be used as rationales for justifying discrimination in educational or occupational structures.

To conclude, while intelligence affects both the academic career of an individual student and the functions assigned to formal schooling, the definition of this quality is "what is measured by intelligence tests". But the fact remains that decisions of teachers and administrators concerning both the definition of intelligence and its implications are *culturally relative*.

This cultural relativeness presents many facets. The evaluation of individual intelligence in the educational milieu involves the use of different tools characterized by differing degrees of reliance. Some schools use psychological tests; others rely upon the evaluations of teachers. Whatever the tools, the assessment of ability is not necessarily culture-free, and it advantages children derived from dominant positions in the current social hierarchy. Furthermore, it is often difficult not only to distinguish the relative influence of ability and of aspiration on individual performances but also to identify the effect of these test performances on later educational experiences. Results for the two variables are frequently computed not on a representative sample but on the subpopulations that have successfully negotiated a specific hurdle. Thus the distributions of intellectual and academic performances are skewed, which limits the validity of the appreciation of the impact exerted by abilities on selectivity. It is also difficult to determine whether the corresponding relationships are linear (the greater the abilities of an individual, the more chances he has to reach the highest rungs of the hierarchy) or follow a threshold model (the prediction of selectivity takes the simple form of a dichotomy). Finally, this relationship is not necessarily stable and varies, for example, with sex.[6]

Yet some evidence indicates that abilities affect chances of selection. In France, for example, ability (as negatively measured by repeating the last class of the primary system) markedly affects the chance to proceed to further schooling. Forty-three percent of children who have repeated the terminal primary class are no longer in an educational institution four years later compared to only 20 percent who have not repeated that class. The former are less likely to be in a *lycée* than the latter (22 percent compared to 35 percent), and they are more likely to follow a technical rather than a classical course (26 versus 13 percent).[7] Observations in Brazilian schools are similar. Only 20 percent of secondary school students have been delayed in their career compared to more than two thirds of their counterparts in agricultural studies.[8]

Evaluations by primary teachers show an analogous relationship between the current and future academic careers of French students. Ninety-three percent of the students judged to be excellent by their primary school teachers are still attending school four years after. Yet only 75 percent of these "excellent students" are enrolled in a *lycée,* and no more than 59 percent of them have followed a normal secondary academic career.[9] The predictive power of the ratings used by teachers declines with a narrowing of the definition of future academic performances. This decline suggests that differential abilities are probably not the exclusive determinants of access to the upper rungs of the educational system. The narrower the definition of future academic achievement, the more likely it is that this achievement is affected both by abilities and other motivational factors.

McPherson has established in England that those who drop out of five-year courses are lower in intelligence and less successful in the teachers' judgment than those who complete these courses.[10] In the United States there is a linear relationship between ability as measured by the Army General Classification Test and various schooling achievements. The average scores for the populations entering high school, graduating from high school, entering college, and graduating from college are 105, 110, 115, and 126 respectively. Further, the proportion of individuals entering college among those obtaining the highest ranks in high school exceeds 50 percent; the same percentage does not exceed 17 percent among those who are at the bottom of their class in high school.[11] A special study conducted by the U.S. Census Bureau in 1960 shows that less than 2 percent of the potential high school senior classes in the first quantiles of IQ tests were unable to reach their senior year compared to 39 percent of their counterparts ranked in the lower quantiles.[12] However, as in France, the predictive power of abilities on academic performance declines regularly as one moves up in the educational ladder. Correlations between these two variables go from .60 at the high school level down to less than .40 at the graduate school level.[13]

Aspirations. Educational attainment and educational fate are also believed to reflect the nature and level of individual aspirations. Data available for American colleges show significant variations in the frequency of students primarily oriented toward money, people, or individual creativity as well as marked correlations between such orientations and individual choices of graduate studies.[14] To a large extent educational attainment is deemed to require the specific moral and emotional qualities associated with the Protestant ethic. This should have been expected; patterns of emotional adjustment to educational, occupational, or social adult roles should be parallel insofar as the school situation aims at repeating the patterns of interaction associated with participation in adult social structures.

Yet insofar as there are crosscultural variations in the degree to which schools constitute mirrors of adult social organizations, such variations reflect disparities in the relative degree of autonomy enjoyed by the actors of educational institutions. The demands imposed by teachers on their students necessarily vary with the position they occupy in the society at large. Further, the influence of aspirations on the ultimate educational destination of individuals varies with social, cultural, and psychological characteristics. The possibility of building a relevant universalistic measurement of individual aspirations is therefore doubtful. Further one must also decide whether such measurements should be primarily used to identify the destination of individual students or, alternatively, to designate the differential pedagogical treatment to which they should be subjected. The need for achievement, far from being a stable and fixed attribute, can be enhanced by exposing individuals to sets of appropriate stimuli.[15]

Information. As the organization of the school system becomes more bureaucratic and more complex, there is an increased differentiation in the forms and mechanisms of educational selectivity, and individuals need additional amounts of information in order to obtain maximal

Table 15. Educational Attainment of French Students Graduating from Primary School in 1962, Five Years after Graduation [a]

Age at End of Primary Studies	%	Level of Academic Performance in Primary School	%	% Still in School	% in Second Cycle of Lycées (Five Years of Postprimary Education)
Over 13½	4.6	Excellent	0.6	50	0
		Good	3.5	11	6
		Average	20.7	6	1
		Poor	37.1	4	0
		Very poor	38.2	0.2	0.2
13	5.6	Excellent	1.0	18	—
		Good	12.7	47	17
		Average	32.8	21	3
		Poor	32.8	21	1
		Very poor	21.3	12	0.3
12½	7.6	Excellent	1.8	51	35
		Good	15.4	45	14
		Average	34.4	29	3
		Poor	32.5	25	0.3
		Very poor	15.9	15	0.3
12	19.6	Excellent	5.0	80	38
		Good	28.5	75	22
		Average	37.0	58	6
		Poor	20.8	43	1
		Very poor	8.7	37	0

"returns" from their educational investments. Increases in the number of, and changes in the nature of the rules pertaining to prerequisites for admission, financial aid, or challenging decisions of educational authorities increase the complexity of education. To give a concrete example, an individual student is not necessarily aware of the fact that, when they consider his file for admission, colleges and graduate schools do not attach a similar significance to the number of courses he audited or did not complete.

As knowledge of the ropes becomes more important, there are accentuated variations in the distribution of the relevant information

Table 15 (continued)

Age at End of Primary Studies	%	Level of Academic Performance in Primary School	%	% Still in School	% in Second Cycle of Lycées (Five Years of Postprimary Education)
11½	19.1	Excellent	4.8	89	53
		Good	27.8	81	23
		Average	39.6	65	9
		Poor	21.4	51	1
		Very poor	5.4	40	0.3
11	20.6	Excellent	15.8	93	60
		Good	40.5	92	32
		Average	32.2	78	10
		Poor	3.4	72	3
		Very poor	1.6	67	0
10	16.0	Excellent	15.9	97	66
		Good	43.3	93	37
		Average	30.3	87	10
		Poor	9.1	76	2
		Very poor	1.4	71	0
10	6.9	Excellent	30.8	100	67
		Good	48.2	99	35
		Average	18.8	98	15
		Poor	2.0	100	10
		Very poor	0.6	100	20

[a] Derived from H. Bastide and A. Girard "Orientation et Sélection scolaires: Cinq années d'une promotion; de la fin du cycle élémentaire à l'entrée dans le 2eme cycle du 2eme degrè *Population,* Vol. 24, 1969, pp. 225, 2101.

among the various subgroups of the population. Such variations reflect contrasts both in the nature and in the extent of the formal and informal networks in which individuals participate. Hence, these variations are a result of differential placement in the social structure. The perceptions of such differences have often led to the emergence of counselors, a category of educational personnel specializing in the collection and the diffusion of the appropriate information. However, access to such services is not itself evenly distributed among the various components of a particular social system.

Individual Factors of Selectivity

Age.   Variations in the age composition of a given cohort are indicators of a strong selectivity at earlier stages of the academic hierarchy. The age at which populations start sending children to school varies and it might be hypothesized that a late start in this regard, reflects a lack of parental motivations as well as the financial or technical difficulties they encounter to meet the standards of the school. For example, there is a frequent relationship between entry age and distance between school and home, which is probably the reason why, even in the United States, the incidence of scholastically retarded pupils is highest among rural populations. By 1960 this incidence was 15 percent among pupils 16 to 17 years of age living in rural areas, but it dropped to 10 percent among their counterparts living in the urban fringes.[16]

Variations in the age composition of a given class may also reflect contrasts in the proportions of individuals repeating a class. Table 15 indicates the relative impact of age and abilities on the selectivity of recruitment into French postprimary structures. Both factors are obviously significant determinants of the chances pupils have to attend postprimary schools four years later and to attend the highest level of the *lycée.* However, variations in ability most strongly condition the academic success of the younger age groups. While abilities are not good predictors of the chances that older individuals have to reach the first year of the second cycle of *lycées,* their predictive power is most marked for pupils under 11 years of age. Although the majority of youngsters are able to enter postprimary structures, students must be both *young* and *bright* to enjoy the most rewarding educational fate—specifically to join a *lycée.*

Sex.   In the Ivory Coast, as in many other African countries, there is an inverse relationship between the sex ratio of primary school students and overall enrollment rates (see Figure 3). As the overall number of pupils increase, so does the proportion of girls attending the primary institutions of the country. More generally, increases in overall literacy rates are associated with a corresponding rise in the relative number of educated women.[17] There are of course reversals in the differential access of the sexes into educational structures. In certain rural areas of France, for example, girls are more likely than boys to attend schools. The mechanization of agriculture has not modified

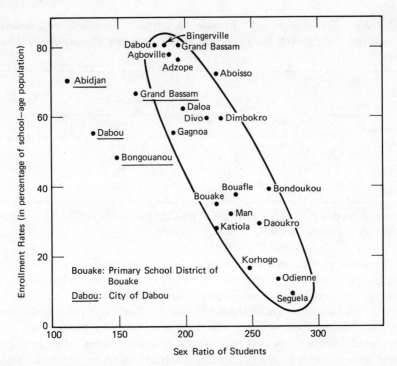

Figure 3. Enrollment rates and sex ratio of student populations in the Ivory Coast. Derived from *Côté d'Ivoire: Population, 1965* (Abidjan, 1967), p. 52.

the profile of male agricultural activities but has lowered the demand for a female labor force. Technological changes do not necessarily have uniform effects on the relative enrollments of men and women.

As the size of basic educational facilities increases, competition between the sexes shifts to access to institutions of higher education as well as access to their various branches. In countries with a low level of educational development, as the Ivory Coast, girls tend to be proportionately more numerous in short-cycle institutions and technical schools. With further educational development, however, the types of limitation imposed upon the educational choices of girls tend to change. In Brazil, for example, the first cycle of secondary schools has the lowest sex ratio of all institutions (89 males to 100 females), but in the second cycle girls are overwhelmingly concentrated in the teachers colleges (94 percent of all enrollments).[18] Trends are similar in countries with more developed educational systems where there are still marked differences in the type of university attended by male and female students (Table 16).

Table 16. Percentage of Female Students Enrolled in Selected Institutions of Higher Learning in Mediterranean Countries in 1960– 1961 [a]

	Total University	Liberal Arts	Medicine
France	41	63	26
Italy	30	71	8
Spain	19	6	59
Turkey	21	58	17
Yugoslavia	41	55	39

[a] Derived from UNESCO, L'Education dans le Monde (Paris 1966) Vol. III and from data collected by the I.N.S.E.E. in France.

Obviously the underrepresentation of girls in certain streams of certain cycles as well as in the totality of an educational system does not result from their lower abilities, since their performances in a variety of tests are in fact superior to those of males.[19] Rather, it reflects the inferior position ascribed to women in the labor market, a position which in turn results from the social stereotypes of female roles. Male academic underachievement is always socially defined as a form of deviance; female academic overachievement has often been similarly stigmatized, at least during the early stages of educational development. As a result, the first girls to attend school are often those who are allowed to innovate because of a fortunate social background.

Female participation in educational structures continues to remain sensitive to social and psychological factors in countries with more developed educational systems. Table 17 shows the educational aspirations of American female high school seniors to be more strongly affected by variations in paternal level of education or in level of intelligence than those of their male classmates. Controlling for intelligence, the percentage of girls planning to go to college declines more markedly than the corresponding proportion of boys with low paternal education.

Cultural variables. The relative size of female enrollments depends upon the degree to which cultural arrangements introduce a sharp differentiation of social and occupational roles along sex lines and define the intensity and the form of incompatibilities between female roles and formal schooling. Figure 3 shows female enrollments among the

Table 17. *Percentage of Wisconsin High School Seniors Planning to go to College by Sex, Paternal Education, and Level of Intelligence* [a]

| | Fathers Education [b] | | | | | |
| | High | | Medium | | Low | |
Intelligence [c]	Men	Women	Men	Women	Men	Women
High	85.2	80.5	64.7	49.3	49.2	35.2
Medium	55.0	63.5	37.9	28.3	28.8	20.3
Low	34.5	35.3	18.9	19.5	11.3	8.5
N	(642)	(595)	(1.164)	(1158)	(2.582)	(2.866)

[a] Derived from W. Sewell and V. Shah, "Parents' Education and Children's Educational Aspirations and Achievements," *American Sociological Review,* Vol. 33, 1968, pp. 191–205.
[b] Measured in terms of less than high school, high school, some college education.
[c] Measured in terms of scores obtained on the Henman-Melson Test of Mental Abilities.

matrilineal groups of the Ivory Coast (Dabou, Grand Bassam, and Bongouanou) to be higher than total enrollments would lead us to believe. The data reflect the traditional economic and social independence granted to the women of such peoples. Similarly, the type of institution attended by women varies with the stereotypes held toward female roles. Depending on the socially acceptable ways of defining fields of eligible mates, girls are raised in segregated or in coeducational institutions. The first pattern is likely to prevail among societies or social groups where the choice of a bride is determined by the group rather than by the individual and where girls must learn to conform to the immutable requirements of their future conjugal duties.

The significance of these requirements is evidenced in Spain by the remarkable decline in female enrollments as between secondary and university levels. Women represent 38 percent of the secondary school population, but only 18 percent of overall university enrollments. While secondary institutions are segregated along sex lines, most institutions of higher learning are coeducational and this type of arrangement obviously lowers the control that Spanish parents might exert on the interaction of their daughters. In fact, variations in female enrollments by level of studies should be far less apparent in countries where

coeducational institutions are found at all levels and where correspondingly, the choice of appropriate conjugal partners is more individualized.

The more modern the views of elites toward their daughters, the
more likely they are to send their daughters to institutions of higher
learning, to allow them to enjoy the attendant occupational rewards
and to choose their own mates.

Temporary changes in the labor market. During the World Wars
there was a temporary rise in the size of female enrollments at both secondary and postsecondary levels. In France female enrollments at the
university level went up from 10 percent of all enrollments for the year
1910–1911, to 26 percent for the academic year 1915–1916 and
dropped back to 15 percent after the war. Although more limited, the
same phenomenon was observed during World War II in France and
in the United States.

Long-term trends in economic development. As the occupational
hierarchy opens up and becomes diversified, there are variations in the
relative prestige held by various occupations. Accordingly, male populations tend to transfer their skills toward jobs that yield higher returns.
The jobs of secretary, nurse, or teacher—considered to be male occupations as long as division of labor remained simple—tend to become
female occupations as a result of the increased diversity of the occupational structure.[20]

Long-term trends in educational development. As the number of female graduates from various educational institutions increases, intergenerational relations change substantially. More specifically,
changes in the expectations mothers entertain toward the roles of their
daughters are associated with parallel changes in the general orientations of society toward women.

The relationship between educational development and the educational equality of the two sexes is not necessarily linear. The form of
this relationship depends on the severity of competition between the
sexes over access to education. Most often, this competition pits women
from upper segments of society against males from lower social and
cultural backgrounds. The outcome varies with the degree to which the
effects of class solidarity overcome those of sex solidarity. Reversals in
the direction of the association between overall enrollments and the sex
ratio of the educated population are thus affected both by variations in
the rigidity of the existing system of social stratification and by changes

in the stereotypes that social classes hold toward the definition of female roles. For example, urban and rural females in Russia did respond differently to educational development; in spite of the overall educational development of their country, Russian rural females have been initially unable to reach a higher level of participation in educational structures.

The influence of sex on selectivity reflects both the impact of motivations and information. The multiplicity of factors accounting for the relative ratio of female enrollments explains why Anderson, considering a sample of societies both synchronically and diachronically, observes that the relationship between societal differentiation (as measured by the proportion of active populations engaged in primary activities) and female enrollments in higher education is only moderate.[21]

Influence of the Microenvironment. Participation in a variety of educational structures is not only a function of individual psychological and demographic characteristics but is also affected by immediate surroundings—by familial arrangements and previous school experience.

Familial Arrangements. The negative relationship between family size and educational performances is emphasized by the finding that in France there is a correlation of .58 between enrollments in the first cycle of postprimary studies by department and the proportion of families with two children and less. Further examination shows, however, that departments characterized both by *high* enrollments and *low* fecundity are regions where small or middle-sized farms prevail. In contrast, departments with *low* enrollments and *high* fecundity are characterized by a system of absentee landownership. Relationship between family size and enrollments depends upon existing patterns of economic organization and stratification.[22] In fact, family size affects the enrollments of a department only insofar as there are marked variations in the distribution of fertility among the various social classes of a department and insofar as such variations reflect contrasts in the actual role that children perform in the field of economic activities.[23]

Social selectivity appears to be influenced by the presence of appropriate educational models (siblings, parents) and the availability of educational information in the immediate social environment of the populations investigated. In France, for example, 81 percent of the pupils attending *lycées* in 1964 had an older sibling in this type of institution.[24] In contrast, the presence of a sibling in a *lycée* characterized only two-thirds of the students in less rewarding short academic institutions and slightly over one-third of those in senior primary schools. In addition, Bourdieu shows that whereas the chances of going on to French universities vary from one for the sons of workers to 40 for those of managerial classes, the corresponding chances vary only from one to four when families rather than individuals are used as units of analysis.[25]

Of course, the effect of family on selectivity reflects its position in the social structure, and this position influences its resources (or means) and orientations (or ends). Obviously resources influence the course of curriculum followed by French students. The average income of the parents of students entering *lycées* exceeds $325 per month, while that of the families of individuals attending short academic institutions is only $260 dollars, and that of the families of postprimary students is $225. These variations, however, affect academic aspirations more than academic abilities.[26]

The cultural orientations (or ends) of the family exert a more significant influence on academic abilities. Holding income constant, the proportion of French students assessed as excellent by their teachers increases regularly with the level of schooling of their fathers; such an increase is not apparent when one controls for education and allows income to vary.

However, the role of parental variables on educational attainment is not always clear or uniform. For example, the influences that the economic and cultural or educational characteristics of black and white American parents exert on the verbal achievement test, and hence on the final academic destination of their offspring, are not comparable. The percentage of variance in the distribution of the results to this test explained by parental background is always greater for white than for black pupils. Eight factors that are deemed to reflect familial background (parental exposure to urbanization, parental educational level, structural integrity of the home, size of the family, educational items present in the home, reading material present in the home, parent interests, and educational desires) account for 15 percent of the variance in the verbal achievement distribution of black sixth graders and for almost 18 percent of the variance in the corresponding distribution of their white counterparts.

Further, the relative contribution of economic and cultural aspects of familial background is not the same for blacks and whites.[27] Considering eight variables related to school and familial environment, the educational level of the white student's home accounts *alone* for 1.74 percent of the variance in the results obtained at the sixth-grade level and

2.17 percent by twelfth graders. The corresponding figures are 0.37 percent and 0.11 percent for economic variables. In brief, whereas the impact of the familial cultural environment on the verbal achievement of white students becomes more marked as one moves up in the educational ladder, there is a symmetric decline in the role that economic resources play in this regard.

Alternatively, however, if we consider the black population, the percentage of variance accounted for by economic factors is always greater than that explained by cultural variables, and in addition, the relative explanatory power of these two sets of factors declines as one moves up in the educational ladder. Among black sixth graders familial economic resources alone account for 1.76 percent of the variance in the results obtained on verbal achievement tests compared to only 0.56 percent for educational variables. Among their twelfth-grade counterparts, the corresponding proportions are 0.57 percent and 0.15 percent respectively.

These data suggest that economic difficulties play a greater role on the academic fate of black than of white children, but more importantly, the culture of black parents tends to be irrelevant to the academic progresses of their children.

Although the prior observations make it difficult to pass any generalized proposition about the role that parental background exerts on academic achievement, this achievement seems also to depend upon the cultural homogeneity of the parents. In the United States, Sewel and Shah have recently demonstrated that both fathers' and mothers' educational achievements exert a joint and independent influence upon their children's college plans, attendance, and graduation. Moderate contrasts between fathers' and mothers' levels of educational attainment are more beneficial than sharp differences. Generally speaking, parental level of education is the most powerful predictor of the academic aspirations and behavior of individuals with a high intelligence. But mother's education is the chief determinant of the college plans and of the success of such plans for students with low level of ability. Similarly, maternal schooling is more important for the academic career of girls than of boys.[28]

To conclude, the impact of family background on selectivity results from the interplay of the three factors mentioned at the onset of this chapter: abilities, motivation, and information. Abilities are indeed affected both by the genetic and environmental profile of the familial group. Further, both motivations and informations reflect the *means* and *ends* of familial group.

Previous Educational Experiences.   The second component of the microenvironment affecting selectivity is the previous educational environment of the subpopulations examined. Primary schools vary in terms of their resources and hence in terms of the quality of their teaching force and their teacher–student ratio. Furthermore, they also vary in terms of the relative discrepancy between students' and teachers' orientations as well as between their respective life styles.

We could expect, therefore, that the populations of schools with lower resources or with high discrepancies between teachers and students in the terms described above will be characterized both by maximal drop-out rates and a marked inability to fill the higher rungs of the academic ladder proportionately. In the United States this point can be substantiated indirectly by an analysis of the distribution of the relevant variables among various social classes or ethnic groups. Chances of attending college are minimal for individuals who have attended overcrowded classrooms in the schools of ethnic slums. Yet such effects are not always conclusive, and the lower chances of black students to reach the top of the educational ladder do not necessarily result from the more limited number of cultural stimuli to which they are exposed. Although at the elementary level, white students attend elementary schools where 75 percent of the population enrolled report having an encyclopedia at their home as compared to 54 percent for black students, differences decline at the secondary level and the relevant figures are 82 percent and 69 percent respectively. Similarly, the more immediate cultural stimuli to which the two populations are exposed are not alike; 40 percent of the populations of the schools attended by black students have mothers who graduated from high school, as opposed to 58 percent in the case of their white counterparts. Although declining, these differences in cultural profile still suggest the difficulties confronting minority students during their academic career.

At the same time, however, black students attend institutions where the level of involvement of parents in educational matters is not necessarily lower than at schools where white children are enrolled. In the secondary schools attended by the average black student, 49 percent of parents discuss school matters compared to 47 percent of the institutions of his white counterparts. In the secondary institutions attended by black pupils, 51 percent of the parents attend PTA meetings, but only 37 percent of white parents do so. In brief, variations in the cultural profile of the institutions attended by black and white students do not seem to be consistent nor sufficient to account for their differential of level of attainment.

School characterizations do influence the educational fate of students in other parts of the world. In the Ivory Coast, for example, the location and type of primary schools attended by individuals affect their chances of entering *lycées,* and populations coming from the backward rural schools are at a disadvantage. Yet, as they move through the system, the chances of such populations to negotiate later hurdles successfully are relatively higher than those of individuals derived from better educational environments. Indeed, the negative forces operating against such individuals at earlier stages of their career induce a higher "fit" between their abilities and their aspirations than that existing between the corresponding attributes of their more fortunate classmates.[29] This confirms the proposition of Blau and Duncan: "Those men who have overcome initial handicaps are more likely than those never confronted by them to progress to further achievement." [30]

In the same way that primary school experiences affect chances to move up the educational ladder, the hierarchy of postprimary institutions shapes the paths that individuals can follow through the system. Wherever this hierarchy is both institutionalized and highly visible, access to the second cycle of regular academic studies is a privilege almost entirely reserved to students having followed the first cycle of the same branch. This is true in countries as different as Brazil, France, and the Ivory Coast. To enter the most prestigious institutions of this type of educational system does not necessarily enable individuals to complete the corresponding cycle of studies, and a substantial number of students from these top-notch schools are obliged to lower their goals and attend less prestigious commercial or agricultural institutions which yield narrower occupational choices.

The hierarchical arrangement of disciplines in American colleges has the same implications. Thus Davis suggests that the departments with relatively low academic standing attract a large number of usually unqualified defectors from other disciplines with a higher academic standing. While there is an overall increase of 31 percent in the percentages of individuals choosing education as an occupation between their freshman and senior year, there is a loss of 41 percent in the percentage of individuals choosing engineering during that period. Further, the "defectors" from certain highly valued fields such as medicine, tend to have lower levels of achievement than the remaining part of the population.

Influence of the Macroenvironment.

Urban–Rural Differentials. Chances of participating in the most rewarding types of educational structures are usually hypothesized to
vary with community size. The demand for jobs requiring most sophisticated skills is strongest in large communities where levels of occupational aspiration and information are correspondingly highest. Further,
large settlements often act as centers from which educational development is most likely to diffuse, and their populations are most likely to
keep their initial advantages along these lines.

Against this particular hypothesis, however, we could argue that in
such large communities there is greater division of labor and more accentuated patterns of social stratification with resulting discontinuities
in the information flows pertaining to educational matters. In addition,
we could also argue that the relationship between urbanization and
school enrollments is relative and varies both in direction and magnitude with the economic organization of the cities and their hinterlands.

In fact, data on French enrollments at the secondary level indicate
that these enrollments are only weakly correlated with city size. Correlation between the distribution of urbanization by French departments
(as measured by proportion of persons living in towns of 2000 inhabi-
tants or more) and of enrollments at the secondary level is minimal
(.16). Further, holding constant other variables such as family size and
educational level of the active population, the correlation between enrollments and urbanization tends to be negative (−.39). In fact, among
those departments with medium proportions of small-sized families
and high proportions of educated adults, those with a high urbanization level have low enrollments. Thus, the influence of urban-rural
contrast on the differing schooling rates of French departments varies
both with the functions performed by cities vis-a-vis their hinterland
and with the density of rural settlements, for these two factors affect
the diffusion of new ideas and norms.[31]

Similarly, educational contrasts between American cities and the
rural hinterlands depend on the dominant economic characteristics of
both the regions and communities studied. In addition, the positive effects of urbanism on academic performance do not hold true for major
American metropolitan areas, where the benefits of a cosmopolitan culture are probably reduced by the negative effects of the rigid mechanisms of social stratification.[32] The particular form of selectivity at work
in the segregation of black students also varies both with the age and
the size of cities in the northern regions of the United States, but such

patterns are not evident in the South. While the coefficient of correlation between segregation of black students and age and size of northern cities are .54 and .49 respectively, such coefficents are only .15 and .12 for southern cities.[33]

Among less developed nations, urban populations tend to be frequently overrepresented in the most rewarding types of schools, but this relative overrepresentation differs as between nations. For example, the relationship between size of birthplace and chances of admission into secondary schools is linear in Ghana but curvilinear in the Ivory Coast. In Ghana access to secondary schools increases as a direct function of the size of the place of residence of school-aged populations; in the Ivory Coast populations of Abidjan enjoy fewer such opportunities than their counterparts living in the middle-sized towns of the hinterland.

Clignet suggests that these differences reflect contrasted types of political organization. In the centralized Ivory Coast the distribution of cities by size is skewed, and Abidjan, the capital city of the country, shelters the majority of the urbanized populations as well as the majority of the secondary institutions of the country. In decentralized Ghana the distribution of urbanized populations is more geographically widespread among a large number of medium- and large-sized urban centers, and the distribution of educational facilities follows a similar pattern. Differences in the relationship between urbanization and secondary school enrollments in the two countries probably reflect contrasted geographic distributions of overurbanization (i.e., disparities between the size of adult urban populations and their unemployment rates). Indeed the negative effects of overurbanization on existing cultural organizations, and hence on schooling, should be maximal in the case of centralized nations where one city alone tends to attract the majority of urban migrants. Differences between Ghana and the Ivory Coast also reflect variations in the number of "educational markets." Because of centralization, there is one single educational market in the Ivory Coast, where the mass of rural primary school students compete with the relatively less numerous urban pupils. By contrast, urban—rural competition in Ghana concerns access to a larger number of institutions and it can be proposed that an increase in this number accentuates the magnitude of urban—rural educational contrasts.[34]

One can of course wonder whether this proposition may be generalized to the American scene, and whether the magnitude of urban–rural differentials in primary and secondary enrollments varies with the degree to which the distributions of urban centers and secondary institutions follow a statistically "normal" pattern. Should this generalization be possible, urban–rural differentials should be more marked in states where both urban populations and educational institutions are more physically dispersed.

Finally, the intensity of the influence exerted by urbanization on enrollments varies along social-class lines. Upper classes have a larger number of choices; but lower classes are more constrained by the additional expenses associated with formal schooling. They are also more sensitive to the additional economic opportunities that academic experiences may offer. In Norway Lindbekk shows that when one considers local elites (i.e., businessmen, civil servants, professionals, and other populations engaged in middle-class activities), rates of enrollment in higher secondary institutions do not vary with the size of place of residence nor with the distance between such places and schools. Among fishermen, farmers, and workers the proportion of children attending *realskols* drops from 42 percent when the school is located in the same village as the place of residence of these children to 0 percent when the distance between these two institutions exceeds 18 miles.[35] Further, the data lead to the conclusion that rural Norwegian children with lower-class origin are not tempted to attend the second cycle of secondary studies whenever the existing economic structure of their villages of residence offers both rewarding and stable economic opportunities. In other words, the marginal segments of rural populations are interested in formal schooling only when the school offers them attractive economic rewards not regularly guaranteed by current modes of economic exploitation.

Regional Variations.   Table 18 shows the impact of a variety of social and demographic factors on enrollments in the first cycle of postprimary studies by French departments. Of these factors, three alone (family size, educational level of the adult population, and level of urbanization) explain half of the variance of the national distribution of enrollments by department. Variations in enrollments, however, are not explained so much by patterns of diffusion, and hence by geographic factors, as by variations in the demographic and social profile of these territorial units. Further, enrollments also vary with the relative dependence of departments on Paris. As the dependence of already industrialized departments increases, enrollments decline correspondingly because this dependence lowers the needs of these units for "elites" with a secondary education.

A similar kind of study conducted in the United States shows that by 1960 public school expenditures per pupil (and hence level of economic development) was the best predictor of state enrollment rates for the population five to nine years old, with a zero-order correlation coefficient of .56, followed by the educational attainment of adult pop-

Table 18. Zero Order Correlations between Enrollments in the First Cycle of Postprimary Institutions of French Departments and Various Indicators of Educational and Social Development [a]

Variables	1	2	3	4	5	6
Family size	1.00	.37	.04	.31	.29	.58
Number of adult individuals with a postprimary diploma	—	1.00	.59	.73	.67	.47
Socioeconomic profile	—	—	1.00	.60	.49	.14
Level of urbanization	—	—	—	1.00	.49	.16
Composite indicator of economic development [b]	—	—	—	—	—	.30
Enrollments in first cycle of postprimary studies	—	—	—	—	—	—

[a] Derived from M. Segre Lebrun and L. Tanguy, "Quelles unités d'analyse retenir pour étudier les variations géographiques de la scolarisation," *Revue francaise de sociologie,* Vol. 8, 1967, pp. 128.
[b] Taking into account change in average salaries and in migrations, this indicator is called *indice madinier.*

ulations with a coefficient of .24.[36] Another study reveals sharp inequalities in the college enrollments of the various states (they vary from 30 percent for Utah to 10 percent for Virginia). [37] As in France, the distribution of these enrollments is not necessarily geographically patterned, and interstate contrasts are usually paralleled by variations in the number and the quality of educational institutions located in each state. Although correlated with indexes of economic development, such enrollments also depend upon the actual form of economic development, and hence upon the cultural orientations prevailing in a region. The relative importance of both professional and bureaucratic elites in a region affects the value attached to formal schooling by the entire population.

Social-Class Affiliation. Clearly, social classes are unevenly represented in various parts of educational systems both because of their differential resources (means) and because of differential orientations
(ends). To reach a certain educational level requires a certain amount
of resources. In 1960, individuals coming from families with a yearly
income of at least $10,000 represented 32 percent of the American
college students but only 19 percent of the overall population of the
relevant age group. To put it another way, over one-half of the high
school graduates coming from families with a yearly income of $10,000
and more were enrolled in college as opposed to only 30 percent of
their counterparts whose familial income did not exceed that sum.[38]
Not only does schooling entail additional expenses, it also requires
familial groups to forfeit income from the participation of children to
the labor force. This is why certain lower-class families withdraw their
offspring from school. The definition of social maturity—that is, the
age at which an individual either must become economically independent or at least contribute to familial resources—also varies along social
class lines. Among the groups where this maturity takes place early, individuals who desire to go on with their studies are often treated with
contempt and viewed as "sissies." This contempt characterizes lower
classes both crossculturally and over time.[39]

Lower classes also entertain serious doubts as to the mobility associated with formal schooling. They perceive both education and its
occupational correlates as *products* rather than *determinants* of the existing social structure. They believe (and not without reasons) that education explains only part of upward mobility and that the returns of individual educational "investments" are lower than is usually believed.

Finally, the underrepresentation of lower social strata in a given school
system reflects their childrearing practices and hence differences between their life style and that expected from pupils by most educational
agencies. Many researchers have suggested that individual adjustment
to academic requirements demands a strong sense of autonomy and a
proper internalization of competitive values. They often affirm that
nothing in the organization of the lower classes facilitates the acquisition of such qualities. Similarly, these researchers have indicated that
while academic success depends upon the acceptance of delayed gratifications, lower classes are oriented toward immediate gratification. Although contrasts in childrearing styles of various social classes are not
stable throughout time, this does not prevent lower classes from being
at a permanent disadvantage to meet the demands of the educational
milieu. Such demands tend to be most significantly influenced by the

values and the strategies of the dominant social groups both because of the composition of the teaching force and of parental pressures.[40]

Obviously, social-class origin affects ability, aspirations, and information. Yet, insofar as the distributions of these three attributes within a particular population are partly independent of social stratification, it becomes necessary to evaluate the effects of their interaction on the educational attainment of various social classes. In the United States *plans* to attend college (aspirations) are more significantly associated with level of paternal occupation than with IQ, and the influence of variations in abilities on plans to attend college is more marked among lower than upper classes (Table 19). However, a more recent study shows

Table 19. Percentage of Sophomores and Juniors in Selected Public High Schools of the Boston Area Planning to Go to College, by IQ and Father's Occupation [a]

	Fathers' Occupation				
IQ Quantile	5 (High)	4	3	2	1 (Low)
5	89	76	55	40	29
4	82	53	29	22	14
3	79	47	22	19	10
2	72	36	20	15	6
1	56	28	12	4	9

[a] Derived from J. Kahl, "Educational and Occupational Aspirations of Common Man's Boys," *Harvard Educational Review*, Vol. 23, 1953, p. 188.

that the probability of a student entering college is more significantly affected by ability than by social-class origin. For the white population, for example, ability alone explains 76 percent of the variance in the probability distribution of male college attendance, while socioeconomic status accounts for only 21 percent of this distribution. For females, the percentage of the corresponding variance accounted for by ability alone declines to 71 percent. Socioeconomic origin alone accounts for 22 percent of the same variance, while the relative role of the interaction between ability and socioeconomic status increases up to 7 percent.[41]

P. Clerc has demonstrated that among students considered to be excellent by their teachers in France, 75 percent of those coming from managerial and professional classes enter the most prestigious *lycées*

compared to only 28 percent of their counterparts with a working-class
origin. Among these pupils considered to be academically weak, however, the corresponding percentages drop to 35 and 1 percent, respectively. Variations in academic abilities more strongly affect the educational fate of working-class students than that of their classmates from
more fortunate circumstances.[42] For lower-class students, unlike their
more fortunate counterparts, abilities are necessary, but not sufficient
conditions for gaining access to the upper strata of the academic ladder.

Yet the specific modes of interaction between ability and aspirations
by social class usually lead to reversals in the direction of educational
selectivity. To get over the first academic hurdles and screenings, working-class students must have high abilities, high aspirations, and high
information. The conditions for the success of students with high-class
origins are less stringent. As a result, children from lower socioeconomic groups are less numerous at the bottom of academic hierarchies
than those from higher classes, but the extent of their underrepresentation becomes less apparent after these initial screenings. The severity
of initial academic requirements enables most lower-class students to
hold their initial positions. By contrast, a larger number of middle- and
upper-class pupils are obliged to lower their levels of ambitions and to
migrate from the most rewarding, most demanding streams or cycles of
studies toward less exacting types of institutions.

However, the advantages of upper classes for attending the most
rewarding educational institutions vary with the type of social stratification characteristic of the countries under analysis. In societies dominated by a rigid and ascriptive hierarchical organization, (Africa, for instance) the initial clients of schools are often recruited among the sons
of slaves, the marginal elements of a familial group, or the offspring of
inferior "castes". For the formal education of "inferior or marginal"
subgroups is regarded as having little or no effect on a proper functioning of the current social system. In contrast, members of the elite
deem the formal schooling of their children to be incompatible with
their socialization into their future roles; that is, they do not initially
perceive the potential contradictions between a system of social placement based upon ascription and the potential functions of mobility
through education.[43] Patterns of access into the educational systems of
traditional countries run against existing principles of social stratification and they become more restricted only after the rewards derived
from academic experiences become more visible.

Variations in social-class selectivity are also dependent upon the age and the size of educational systems. In countries with both recent and limited educational institutions, social selectivity remains moderate. In Africa, for example, the children of farmers who still constitute the largest occupational group are not markedly underrepresented in the postprimary hierarchy, although selectivity already operates against the children of urban manual workers. Participation in new modern urban structures increases the number of choices open to certain individuals and subgroups, but also increases the number of constraints imposed upon the less fortunate segments of the urban population.[44]

As an educational system grows and becomes older, the fact that various social groups should benefit *evenly* from the corresponding increase in educational services is often stressed by the official educational ideology. But these benefits are unevenly distributed. In Russia for instance, the increase of secondary school enrollments between 1826 and 1914 has been most advantageous to urban tax payers (the urban middle classes).[45] An examination of changes in the social composition of the American population attending institutions of higher learning would reveal the same trend. To be sure, the proportion of upper lower class children attending college is twelve times larger in 1960 than in 1920, while the corresponding percentage has only doubled as far as upper classes are concerned. However the fact remains that in 1960, 80 percent of the upper class population between 18 and 21 years of age were attending college as against only 24 percent of their upper lower class counterparts. In this sense, the gains of the former are more significant than those of the latter.[46]

As individual achievement becomes an important determinant of individual placement and as schooling is intended to enhance individual chances of upward mobility, the mobility experienced by the parents themselves becomes as important a determinant of academic trajectories as their social position *per se*. In Switzerland, paternal occupational mobility influences as much as paternal level of occupation academic success (measured both by propensity to repeat a grade and by participation in the most rewarding sections of the post-primary system).[47] The downward mobility of skilled manual workers and clerical employees is associated with a decline in the academic performances of their offspring and their reorientation toward streams of studies of leading to manual occupations. No less than 79 percent of the children of individuals who, initially skilled workers, are currently engaged in unskilled activities, have repeated one or several classes during their academic career. The corresponding figure declines to 55 percent among those children whose fathers have been and are still skilled workers and decrease even lower to 29 percent for the children of initially skilled manual workers who are currently performing supervisory or executive functions. If we consider the proportions of the children of these three subgroups currently engaged in the most rewarding modern or classical secondary institutions leading to universities, we obtain alternatively the following figures: 43 percent, 49 percent, and 75 percent. Thus, the occupational mobility of fathers commands the academic mobility of their sons.

Finally, the relationship between educational development and social selectivity is often curvilinear in nature. Up to a certain point, the growth of educational institutions is accompanied by accentuated disparities in the share of the educational "pie" allocated to the various components of the social structure. Only after the system reaches a certain maturity, do educational inequalities level off or decline. Crosscultural differences in the gradient of the association between these two variables explain why Anderson has been able to demonstrate that variations in the degree of societal differentiation are not necessarily associated with parallel contrasts in the relative share of educational amenities allocated to agricultural, manual, and nonmanual classes.[48]

Ethnic Differentiation.   In many countries ethnicity is an important determinant of the position occupied by an individual in the social structure and hence of his academic future. In new nations variations in ethnic origin mean variations in places of residence and hence variations in the relative degree of exposure to European norms and values. In Africa, for example, coastal groups have had more durable and more intense exposure to colonial experiences than those further inland.[49] These ethnic groups also vary in their receptivity to new values and techniques and in their ability to adjust successfully to educational demands. For instance, variations in traditional political and social arrangements are shown to be accompanied by parallel cleavages in personality orientations and hence in educational achievement.[50] The significance of ethnicity to student recruitment depends as well on the visibility of each ethnic group and, more specifically, on the perceived differences between its organization and orientations and those of the remainder of the population and the interpretations given of such differences.

These factors also account for the differential amount of education achieved by black and white American subpopulation aged 25 and over.[51] In 1966, the proportions of white Americans of this age group having attended college was more than twice as large as the corresponding percentage among black peoples (20 versus 9 percent).[52] The proportion of persons having attended less than five years of elementary school were only 5 percent among whites but 18 percent among blacks. Such contrasts primarily reflect strong stereotypes about the amount and the kind of formal schooling most appropriate to blacks. They reflect, in fact, limitations in the educational and occupational opportunities offered this particular segment of the American population, as well as the subsequent restrictions in the educational and occupational orientations of this subpopulation. Thus such contrasts reflect sharp divergences between the cognitive and normative orientations of black persons and those prevailing in many school systems. As a result, the percentage of nonwhite students who are one or more grades below others of the same age keeps increasing as one moves up the American educational ladder. In 1960, 8 percent of nonwhite male students between seven and nine years of age were at least one grade below the one they should have been in; but the percentage increased up to over 57 percent for those between 18 and 19 years of age.

The figures are significantly lower among female nonwhite students. At the lower end of the age continuum, only 6 percent of young nonwhite girls were below their expected grade, as opposed to 46 percent of the older girls.[53] There are other evidences of the higher educational attainment of nonwhite female students. For example, a large majority of black honor students in high schools are girls, and 62 percent of the black nominees for the National Achievement Scholarship program in 1964 were girls. In addition, although white male enrollments in college were twice as large as female attendance rates between 1953 and 1962, the reverse was true for the black population; the same trend tends to hold true at the graduate level.[54]

Thus, ethnicity has different meanings and implications for the educational attainment of black male and female students. Certain authors argue that there is less discrimination and prejudice against black women than against black men and that, to a certain degree, the negative influence of the stereotypes attached to ethnic and sex roles cancel one another.[55] Other authors, however, propose that the higher achievement level of black girls is more likely to reflect the particular domestic power structures of many black families in which men often play a marginal role.[56] Yet the origin of this marginality has still to be accounted for.[57] It may be viewed as the result of the prolonged negative impact of slavery and of the massive migrations that followed the Civil War on black familial structure. The effects of this disorganization have been more pronounced on male than on female roles. However, the preeminence of the domestic role assigned to black women is also attributed to cultural legacies and more specifically to the traditional power of women in traditional Africa. Regardless of its origin, the differential position occupied by black male and female individuals seems to affect their respective attitudes toward formal schooling and hence their level of educational attainment.

Ethnic and social selectivity are of course interrelated. As African data tend to show, the social background of students whose ethnic groups have already been highly involved in formal schooling is quite diverse. In contrast, among ethnic groups whose educational involvement remains limited, only the sons of the most modernized "happy few" go to secondary and postsecondary institutions.[58] Social and ethnic selectivity are not, however, necessarily distinguishable by the actors present in the educational scene. While many Africans who drop out often attribute their failure to ethnic discrimination, it is often the by-product of unfavorable economic circumstances. Under such conditions, ethnic selectivity may be a force slowing down the processes of nation building.

Interaction between ethnic and social selectivity is more complex in the United States. This interaction influences not only the level of studies a minority person achieves but also the type of institution that he attends. Thus, the isolation of students in segregated schools varies both with their social and economic characteristics and with the profile of the communities in which they live. More specifically, this segregation increases most markedly with the absolute size of minority enrollments.[59] In addition, this segregation varies as an inverse function of the general educational and occupational levels of the community at large, especially in the North. Further, in the North, this segregation is independent of, or positively affected by, the ethnic heterogeneity of the white population; but it is adversely affected by such a factor among southern cities, for this heterogeneity implies a decline in the ability of whites to resist changes. Finally, segregation is increased by the growth of enrollments in private schools in southern but not in northern cities.

In fact, these data throw some additional light on the conditions under which the concept of community control leads to inequalities in the amount and the form of education enjoyed by various social groups. The communities of white middle-class families are communities of limited liabilities and are hardly self-contained territorial entities. Such families have the ability of moving until they find a neighborhood with educational characteristics compatible with their own orientations and interests. They may also form a community that is independent of physical boundaries by sending their children to any private school. The communities in which black families participate are physically limited and the constraints to which they are correspondingly subjected are externally induced. In addition, the oppression confronting black families in the educational realm varies both throughout the American physical and social space.

Religious beliefs. In Chapter 11, I indicated that the effects of religion on educational attainment were contingent upon other social economic and cultural factors. Insofar as access to graduate school depends upon academic achievement during college, it is evident that this achievement varies along religious lines but that religious selectivity is not independent of the socio-economic and the geographic origin of the students sampled (Table 20). Regardless of sex, Jewish students have the most chances of entering graduate schools, and their chances in this respect are independent of their background. This reflects the concentration of Jewish people in the professions and the high value they attach to formal schooling. As we could expect, conversely, the influence of Protestantism on the academic attainment of undergraduate students varies markedly with their socio-economic origin and the size of their place of origin. Finally, the negative effects of Catholicism on attainment are most visible among the lower class male students derived from small towns. These effects conversely are not visible among their female counterparts.

Influence of Social Organization on Selectivity. Thus far we have seen how selectivity changes over time and we have also identified its various determinants. The extent and the form of social inequalities, however, are influenced by political structures and ideologies.

Influence of Educational Centralization. The extent and the forms of social inequalities depend upon the degree of centralization. In the French system centralization is viewed as the symbolic translation of the universalistic tendencies of French culture, which tends to be associated with a minimization of particularistic forms of selectivity such as ethnicity. Local autonomy as practiced by the decentralized Anglo-Saxon governments favors the intervention of ethnic differentiation. Despite relative similarities in the economic and political developments of Ghana and the Ivory Coast, ethnic selectivity is more powerful and more independent of other forms of social differentiation in the British-oriented former country than in the French-dominated latter one.[60]

Table 20. *Percentage of United States College Students with High Academic Performances (API)*[a]

Socioeconomic Status	Hometown	Sex					
		Male			Female		
		Religion					
		Catholic	Protestant	Jewish	Catholic	Protestant	Jewish
High	Large	51	61	67	73	70	78
	Small	43	53	61	66	66	71
Low	Large	47	51	56	55	63	66
	Small	40	42	x[b]	55	57	x[a]

[a] Derived from J. Davis, *Undergraduate Career Decisions*, (Aldine, 1965), p. 220. The table includes white students only.
[b] Too small numbers to be translated in percentages.

Degree of centralization also affects the extent to which forms and severity of selectivity vary by region or community. In a decentralized country like the United States, contrasts in forms of municipal government or of school boards are associated with significant disparities in ethnic selectivity and hence in the relative isolation of black students in segregated institutions.[61] Especially in the South communities characterized by an elected rather than an appointed body and by a high degree of political participation are less prone to segregation than townships administered by an appointed government which does not favor a high participation on the part of voters. In contrast, the uniformities that the French centralized system imposes upon local communities minimize variations in the composition of schools located in townships with differing political orientations and ideologies. The significance of selectivity varies more markedly among the local components of a decentralized than a centralized system.

Although social selectivity depends upon the keenness of the competition for access into scarce educational amenities, it is also shaped by the rules underlying this particular type of competition.

Influence of Elite Structures.   Rules pertaining to educational competition are usually underwritten by existing elites. Accordingly, the extent and the form of social inequalities vary with the relationships established between elites and the remainder of the population. R. Turner has proposed that forms of social selectivity are influenced by the number of socially acceptable modes of mobility and the differentiation of elites.[62] In countries dominated by a system of sponsored mobility, elites tend to be monolithic and to exert a tight control over the recruitment patterns of their new members. In countries characterized by contest mobility, there is a plurality of elites and a variety of acceptable routes of upward mobility.

In a sponsored-mobility system the control exerted by elites upon the recruitment of new members is tight, and a marked emphasis is placed upon the selectivity of access into educational institutions; schools function as sorting agencies, and they screen candidates to elite roles as early as possible. The perpetuation of the system requires that individuals be prevented from entertaining unrealistic aspirations and expectations about their occupational destinations. Sponsored-mobility systems also involve competition for access into institutions with increasing levels of academic difficulties rather than into institutions delivering similar types of education but differentially linked with adult occupational and social structures. The main problem of school candidates in such systems is to proceed from high schools to colleges or from colleges to doctoral programs rather than to gain access to a Harvard instead of a small obscure land grant college. Traditional British and French systems are examples.

In contrast, the rules operating in the context of contest-mobility systems stress the necessity of providing children with a maximum number of chances to find the channels of upward mobility most appropriate to their talents. Accordingly, selectivity occurs later. Such systems also have a relatively high rate of attrition and of part-time students because academic careers tend to be more closely affected by individual motivations than by institutional arrangements. Selectivity is more likely to be lateral than vertical, and the main problem faced by students is not so much to determine whether they will reach a higher rung in the educational ladder as to decide from which institution they will ultimately graduate. The mechanisms by which selectivity operates in contest-mobility systems differ from those in sponsored-mobility societies. Examinations do not have the same significance or the same forms in the American and the French contexts.

Influence of Legal Measures on Selectivity. Social inequalities may be the products of ascriptive forces rather than of differential abilities, aspirations, and orientations. In a variety of countries certain types of studies have been an exclusive male privilege. Women are still forbidden to enter careers such as the priesthood.[63] Certain social categories have also been barred from parts or the totality of certain educational systems. In the pre-Meiji Japan, only the Samurai could join the more rewarding types of educational institutions. In Russia, a decree passed in 1887 aimed at preventing the entry of children of coachmen, servants, cooks, laundry women, and small shopkeepers into the "elite" gymnasiums and pro-gymnasiums because such children would be enabled to escape from the environment to which they belonged and, therefore, to resent the existing inequality of property status.[64] The Russian government also attempted through the distinction between the technical-oriented *real* schools and the academic-oriented gymnasium, to provide the business community and the gentry with segregated types of formal schooling.

Influence of Ideologies. The severity and the nature of social inequalities may reflect the prevailing ideological orientations of a society. These ideologies affect the functions assigned to schools. French traditions view education as a right guaranteed by the central government to all children, while the Anglo-Saxon philosophy sees educational ventures as private investments to be exerted individually and to be controlled by local communities. In France selectivity may be accentuated or diminished through government interventions, which is less likely to occur where Anglo-Saxon orientations prevail. Correspondingly, French schools are more examination oriented than their Anglo-Saxon counterparts.

This influence of ideological factors may concern the position assigned to various social classes, and an analysis of the changes in various communist countries is pertinent. The Russian government has been eager to increase the share of education allocated to the children of workers. Whereas such individuals represented only one-third of the enrollments in the Engineers School of Sverdosk in 1940, they represented no less than 60 percent of such enrollments in 1963.[65] The government has also facilitated the access into such schools of individuals already engaged in the labor force. In 1940, only 3 percent of entrants to the Sverdosk school were manual workers. In 1963, the corresponding proportion was 62 percent, while the proportion of entrants coming from other schools dropped from 86 to 13 percent between these two dates.

Yet the political control that a government is able to exert on the educational destination of students should not be exaggerated. In Hungary, for example, chances of access to the university for the offspring of the most deprived social categories have increased from 1 out of 425 before World War II to 1 out of 62 currently. Even now, however, the children of Hungarian nonmanual workers are twice as numerous in secondary schools as they are in the population at large (39 percent compared to 18 percent).[66] The children of agricultural workers and farmers are significantly less numerous in such institutions than those of the urbanized occupations (17 percent compared to 25 percent).[67]

Similarly, in Yugoslavia, the proportion of university students with a working class origin has perhaps increased from 3 percent in 1938–39 up to 20 percent in 1960–61, but their gains have not necessarily been acquired at the expense of the segments of the population most likely to be hostile to the regime. Thus, during the same period, the representation of nonmanual workers has only declined from 50 to 41 percent. In effect, changes in the social origin of Yugoslavian students reflect overall changes in the occupational profile of the country, most notably increased industrialization, more than they reflect changes in patterns of selectivity.[68]

In a short term perspective, governmental measures designed to regulate patterns of selectivity have had only moderate effects and the differential abilities, aspirations and information of various social groups continue to entail educational inequalities. In Hungary, disparities in paternal levels of education or occupation are still associated with parallel contrasts in the academic performances of secondary students. The cultural practices most likely to stimulate academic performances (access to mass media and to books) vary as much with level of education or urbanization as with level of resources. The occupational choices of Hungarian students remain influenced by parental background, and 89 percent of the managerial classes want their children to enter a nonmanual occupation compared to 18 percent of the unskilled workers. Up to now, cultural inequalities continue to affect the educational trajectories followed by the students of communist countries.

In brief, political revolutions do not necessarily affect the profile of educational institutions immediately; government desires to change the social composition of the educational elites require a variety of strategies, and it is insufficient to bar certain categories of the population from certain schools or to impose certain "educational quotas" and manipulate the allocation of scholarships. All these measures must be combined and be associated with a marked effort to diffuse a variety of informations concerning both educational facilities and the rewards to be expected from formal schooling.

Regardless of these measures, however, the efforts of the State to change the social composition of the school population are liable to introduce some temporary confusion. In Africa, for example, certain governments have attempted to reduce ethnic inequalities by creating a disproportionate number of educational facilities in regions occupied by underprivileged ethnic groups. Such schools have been often populated mostly by students coming from already educated ethnic groups and unable to succeed in the schools of their regions of origin. Another strategy has been in the institutionalization of ethnic quotas among existing institutions. Yet the introduction of such quotas is probably conducive to the introduction of double-standard rules that in the short run will aggravate rather than alleviate existing ethnic tensions.[69]

Conclusions. As a society becomes more complex, a more thorough and more rational system of mobilizing individual energies and talents becomes necessary. Hence it is important to determine how societies with differing levels of economic and political development channel individual talents into educational institutions. Increasing societal complexity is obviously not automatically accompanied by a more equalitarian profile in the composition of schools. As a society becomes more complex, so do the resistances of the groups with initial cultural advantages.

Correspondingly, the mechanisms of educational selectivity are increasingly numerous and differentiated. Rewards attached to academic experiences differ markedly with the types of institution attended as well as the length and nature of the studies undertaken. However, a growing complexity of the determinants of educational selectivity corresponds to this growing complexity in the definition of educational rewards. While access to these rewards depends upon a proper interaction between abilities, aspirations, and information, the distributions of each one of the prerequisites across a variety of social groups cease to be highly interrelated. As a result, chances of entering the most rewarding kinds of schools are influenced by a growing number of factors operating both independently and in conjunction with one another.

Academic careers are influenced by individual ascriptive characteristics (age and sex). They are also conditioned by the time and the space within which the individual evolves, by his own educational history as well as that of his society, and by the nature of his spatial, social, cultural, and familial affiliations.

While older students or students who have been retarded in their studies are unlikely to reach the highest rungs of the academic ladder, their handicap varies with their social origin and is maximal for those coming from the lower classes. While rural students are at a disadvantage compared to their urban counterparts, the relative importance of such a disadvantage is minimal for the pupils coming from the "best families" of the rural environment. Thus, each determinant of educational selectivity operates only within certain limits which are defined by the intervention of other determinants. This interaction among factors also explains why few relationships between the variables indicative of an individual's background and his chances to move in the academic ladder are linear. The groups with the highest levels of participation in educational structures do not necessarily remain the same throughout history, and the elites of a number of countries do not necessarily share identical privileges.

Even in the most highly industrialized nations, formal schooling remains as much a *by-product* as a *producer* of current systems of stratification. Differential access to school reflects existing patterns of inequality, although it also contributes to engender other ones. Thus the impact of the socializing functions of school systems cannot be evaluated independently of the characteristics of the student population. The educational liberty of students in their learning activities depends indeed upon the liberty they enjoy in their family and in turn upon the liberty that their family enjoys in the society at large. Schools are supposed to create gentlemen in certain countries. In other countries they are supposed to form concerned, responsible, and skillful citizens. But how can we say that such goals have been achieved if we suspect at the start that their students were already gentlemen or already concerned, responsible, and skillful citizens?

NOTES AND REFERENCES

1. For a full discussion of these points, see "Environment, Heredity, and Intelligence," *Harvard Educational Review,* Reprint series No. 2, 1969.

2. See S. Vandenberg, "What Do We Know Today About the Inheritance of Intelligence and How Do We Know It?" in R. Carnero, ed., *Intelligence Genetic and Environmental Influences* (New York: Gross and Stratton, 1971), p. 187.

3. See J. McV. Hunt and G. Kirk, "Social Aspects of Intelligence: Evidence and Issues," R. Carnero, ed., *op. cit.,* pp. 262–299.

4. As quoted by S. Bijou, "Environment and Intelligence: A Behavioral Analysis," R. Carnero, ed., *op. cit.,* pp. 221–222.

5. See R. Zazzo, *Les jumeaux le couple et la personne* (Paris: Presses Universitaires de France, 1960).

6. For a full discussion of the relationship between sex and success to intelligence tests, see D. Lavine, *The Prediction of Academic Performances* (New York: Russell Sage, 1965), Chapter 3.

7. See A. Girard and H. Bastide, Orientation et sélection scolaires, *Population,* vol. 24, 1965, pp. 195–251. See also A. Girard, "Facteurs psychologiques et sociaux de l'orientation et de la sélection scolaire," *Population,* Vol. 21, 1966, pp. 691–750. See also A. Sauvy and A. Girard, "Les diverses classes sociales devant l'enseignement," *Population,* Vol. 20, 1965, pp. 205–232. A. Girard and P. Clerc, "Nouvelles données sur l'orientation scolaire au moment de l'entree en 6 eme," *Population,* Vol. 19, 1964, pp. 830–872.

8. See J. Dias, *Ensino medio, e estructure socio. economica* (São Paulo, Ministerio de educacion y cultura, (1907), p. 111.

9. See A. Girard and H. Bastide, *Orientation et selection scolaries, op. cit.*

10. See J. S. McPherson, "Selection of Secondary Scottish Schools," in A. Halsey, J. Floud, and C. A. Anderson, eds., *Education, Economy and Society,* (New York, The Free Press, 1963), pp. 195–208.

11. See D. Wolfe, "Educational Opportunity, Measured Intelligence and Social Background," in A. Halsey, J. Floud, and C. A. Anderson, eds., *op. cit.*, pp. 216–240.

12. See R. Folger and C. Nam, *Education of the American Population*, (Washington: Department of Commerce, 1950), p. 52.

13. See D. Lavine, *The Prediction of Academic Performances, op. cit.*, Chapters 3, 7.

14. See J. Davis, *Undergraduate Career Decisions* (Aldine, 1965).

15. See V. Pareek, "A Motivational Paradigm of Development," *Journal of Social Issues*, Vol. 24, 1968, pp. 115–120.

16. See R. Folger and C. Nam, *op. cit.*, p. 52.

17. For another example of diachronic study of the relationship between overall enrollments and the enrollments of women, see P. Bourdieu and J. C. Passeron, *Les heritiers* (Paris: Editions de Minuit, 1964), p. 124.

18. See J. Dias, *op. cit.*, p. 59.

19. See D. Lavine, *op. cit.*, notably Chapter 4.

20. For a full discussion of the history of the jobs initially deemed inacceptable for educated women, see C. Bird, *Born Female* (New York: C. McKay, 1968), Chapters 4, 5.

21. See C. A. Anderson, *The Social Status of University Students in Relation to Types of Economy: An International Comparison.* Transaction of the 3rd World Congress of Sociology (London: International Sociological Association, 1956), 1, pp. 51–63.

22. See M. Segree Lebrun and Monique Tanguy, "Quelle unité d'analyse retenir pour étudier les variations géographiques de la scolarisation en France," *Revue francaise de sociologie*, Vol. 8, 1967, pp. 117–139.

23. See A. Darbel, "Inégalités sociales ou inegalités régionales," *Revue francaise de sociologie*, Vol. 8, 1967, pp. 140–166. In that paper the author insists thus on the high significance of contextual variables.

24. See A. Girard and P. Clerc, *op. cit.*

25. See P. Bourdieu and J. C. Passeron, *op. cit.*, p. 42.

26. See A. Girard and P. Clerc, *loc. cit.*

27. See J. S. Coleman et al., *Equality of Educational Opportunities*, (Washington: Office of Education, 1966), p. 301.

28. See W. Sewel and V. Shah, "Parents' Education and Children's Educational Aspirations and Achievement," *American Sociological Review*, Vol. 33, 1968, pp. 191–209.

29. See R. Clignet, "Etude de la signification des tests en milieu Ivoirien" (Abidjan: 1959). Mimeographed. The average grades obtained by students enrolled in the fifth form (equivalent to the American seventh grade), went from 10.8 out of 20 for students having completed their primary studies in Abidjan up to 11.25 for those who had completed their

primary studies in the schools of the hinterland. This probably explains why attrition rates from the highest rungs of the Ivorian academic ladder were proportionately higher for children coming from the most modernized families than for their counterparts derived from a rural origin. See R. Clignet and P. Foster, *The Fortunate Few* (Evanston, Northwestern University Press), Chapters 4, 5.

30. P. Blau and O. Duncan, *The American Occupational Structure* (New York, Wiley, 1963), p. 412.

31. See M. Segree Lebrun and Monique Tanguy, "Quelle unité d'analyse retenir," *op. cit.,* and also A. Darbel, "Inégalites régionales et inegalites sociales," *op. cit.* Darbel shows in fact a curvilinear relationship in the association between urbanization and school enrollments. For a more detailed analysis of the geographic aspects of the diffusion of formal schooling, see T. Hagerstrand, "Quantitative Techniques for an Analysis of the Spread of Information and Technology," in C. A. Anderson and M. J. Bowman, eds., *Education and Economic Development* (Chicago: Aldine, 1966), pp. 244–280.

32. See N. Washburne, "Socio Economic Status, Urbanism and Academic Achievement," *Journal of Educational Research,* Vol. 53, 1959, pp. 130–137.

33. T. Dye, "Urban School Segregation: A Comparative Analysis," *Urban Affairs Quarterly,* Vol. 4, 1968, pp. 161–166.

34. See R. Clignet, "Inadequacies of the Notion of Assimilation in African Education," *Journal of Modern African Studies,* Vol. 8, 1970, pp. 625–666.

35. T. Lindbekk, "Ecological Factors and Educational Performance," in M. Matthijsen and C. E. Vervoort, eds., *Education in Europe,* pp. 25–29.

36. See E. Wolfle, "Educational Opportunity Measured Intelligence and Social Background," in A. Halsey, J. Floud, and C. A. Anderson, *op. cit.,* pp. 215–240.

37. See R. Folger and C. Nam, *op. cit.,* p. 29.

38. *Ibid.,* pp. 64, 67.

39. For an example, see H. Gans, *The Urban Villagers* (New York: Free Press, 1963), pp. 245–248. See also W. Green, "The Cult of Personality and Sexual Relations," in N. Bell and E. Vogel, *A Modern Introduction to the Family* (New York: Free Press, 1960), pp. 608–615.

40. For a full discussion of this theme, see J. C. Combassie, "Education et valeur de classe dans la sociologie américaine," *Revue francaise de sociologie,* Vol. 10, 1969, pp. 12–36.

41. J. C. Flanagan and W. W. Cooley, Project TALENT one year follow up studies, Cooperative Research Project Number 2333, School of Education, University of Pittsburgh, 1966.

42. See A. Girard and P. Clerc, *loc. cit.*

43. This situation was obtained in most West African colonial territories. For an illustration of such cases and of the strategies that French administra-

tors had to display for recruiting a minimal number of students; see D. Bouche, "Les écoles francaises au Soudan, 1886–1900," *Cahiers d'Etudes Africaines,* Vol. 6, 1966, pp. 225–267.

44. For an example of the differential recruitment of various social classes in West Africa see R. Clignet and P. Foster, "Potential Elites in Ghana and the Ivory Coast; a Preliminary Comparison," *American Journal of Sociology,* Vol. 70, 1964, pp. 345–362.

45. See A. Kahan, "Determinants of the Incidence of Literacy in Nineteenth Century Rural Russia," in C. A. Anderson and M. J. Bowman, eds., *op. cit.,* pp. 298–302.

46. See R. Havighurst and B. Neugarten, *Society and Education* (Boston, Allyn and Bacon, 1962), p. 252 and 4.

47. See C. L. Bartholdi, "Critique de l'utilisation de la Donnée Profession du Père dans les Recherches de Sociologie de l'Education," in M. Matthijsen and C. C. Vervoort, *op. cit.,* pp. 30–44.

48. See C. A. Anderson, "The Social Status of University Students," in *op. cit.*

49. For a full discussion of this particular point see R. Clignet and P. Foster, *op. cit.,* Chapter 4.

50. See R. Levine, *Dreams and Deeds* (Chicago: University of Chicago Press, 1966).

51. For an account of ethnic differentiation in Ghanaian secondary schools, see P. Foster, *Social Change and Education in Ghana* (Chicago: University of Chicago Press, 1965), Chapter VII. For the Ivory Coast, see R. Clignet and P. Foster, *op. cit.,* Chapters 3, 4. For an analysis of the ethnic distribution of Nigerian university students, see P. Van Der Berghe, *Power and Privilege at an African University.* (Mimeographed, no date), Chapters 6, 9.

52. See *Current Population Reports* (Washington, D.C.: U.S. Bureau of Census, 1966).

53. See *1960 Census* (Washington, D.C.: U.S. Bureau of Census, 1960), School Enrollment P.C. (2), 5A, Table 3, p. 24.

54. See A. Jensen, "The Race and Sex and Ability Interaction," in R. Carnero, ed., *op. cit.,* pp. 111, 121.

55. *Ibid.,* p. 111.

56. See L. Rainwater and W. Young, eds., *The Moynihan Report and the Politics of Controversy* (Cambridge: MIT Press, 1967), p. 72.

57. R. T. Smith, *The Negro Family in the British Guyana* (London: Routledge and Kegan Paul, 1956), pp. 221–228.

58. For an elaboration of this theme, see R. Clignet, "Secondary Schooling, Ethnic and Social Selectivity in West African Secondary School Systems," *Cahiers d'Etudes Africaines,* Vol. 7, 1967, pp. 360–378.

59. T. Dye, *op. cit.*

60. See R. Clignet and P. Foster, "Convergences and Divergences in the Edu-

cational Development of Ghana and the Ivory Coast," in P. Foster and A. Zollberg, eds., *Ghana and the Ivory Coast: Perspectives on Modernization,* (Chicago: University of Chicago Press, 1971), pp. 215–229.

61. T. Dye, *op. cit.*

62. R. Turner, "Sponsored and Contest Mobility Systems," *American Sociological Review,* Vol. 25, 1960, pp. 855–867.

63. Although many of the rules preventing women from gaining access to certain careers have been officially abolished, some of them are still enforced. The "major" of the class of 1969 of the French Ecole Nationale d'Administration, that is, the best student of her class, Miss Chandernagor, daughter of one important public official, was strongly advised not to choose the traditionally male-oriented Inspection des Finances.

64. See A. Kahan, "Social Structures, Public Policy and the Development of Education and the Economy in Czarist Russia," in C. A. Anderson and M. J. Bowman, *op. cit.,* p. 364. See also H. Passin, "Portent of Modernity and the Meiji Emergence," in C. A. Anderson and M. J. Bowman, *op. cit.,* pp. 394–421.

65. See J. Markewitz-Lagneau, "Ecole et changement social; Le role de l'enseignement secondaire en Russia," *Revue Francaise de sociologie,* Vol. 8, 1967, pp. 80–97.

66. S. Ferge, "La démocratisation de la culture et de l'enseignement en Hongrie," in R. Castel and J. C. Passeron, *op. cit.,* pp. 63–78.

67. *Ibid.*

68. See M. Martik and R. Supek, "Structures de l'enseignement et catégories sociales en Yougoslavie. R. Castel et J. C. Passeron, *op. cit.,* p. 97.

69. See P. Foster, *op. cit.,* pp. 209–212.

8

VARIATIONS IN CURRICULA AND TEACHING STYLES:

ASSIMILATION AND ACCOMMODATION AS MODES OF ADAPTATION OF TEACHERS TO STUDENTS

Educational liberty and equality also result from modes of *interaction* among the various categories of actors involved in the educational process. Insofar as formal schooling liberates students from the constraints imposed upon them within familial, economic, political, or religious institutions, are its effects the result of conscious strategies adopted by school teachers, and do they reflect both the nature and the effectiveness of the curricula to which students are exposed and of the teaching style of the personnel attached to the institutions they attend? Or do such effects take place independently of *what* is taught at school and independently of *how* it is taught?

The effectiveness of pedagogical communications is problematic. Recent studies on the verbal achievement of American students seem to suggest that school characteristics account for a limited amount of the variance of the distribution of individual verbal performances and thus that variations in the human or material resources of primary or secondary schools are inadequate predictors of the level of achievement attained by individual students in this particular skill.

Two other studies suggest that the effectiveness of the pedagogical communication in a particular discipline varies as a direct function of

265

the value assigned by schools to that discipline (measured in terms of the number of hours it is taught per week, the number of hours of homework demanded of students during the same time period, and the significance attached to performances in that particular field). An international study on the teaching of mathematics indicates that individual achievement is not independent of the level of the curriculum and of the organizational mechanisms schools use to translate the hierarchy of disciplines in the curriculum.[1] Similarly a study dealing with the effectiveness of the methods used in the teaching of French in European countries shows that the higher level of proficiency in that language attained by Dutch or Flemish pupils, compared to that of their English counterparts, seems to reflect the greater importance attached to competence in French by Dutch or Flemish educational authorities.[2]

Evaluating the effectiveness of pedagogical communications involves qualitative as well as quantitative assessments. Thus, the main purpose of the present and the following chapters is to underline the problematic aspects of the interaction between students and teachers. In this chapter, I examine the extent and the determinants of variations in curricula and in teaching styles; in Chapter 9, I analyze the extent and the determinants of variations in learning style before evaluating the interaction between these two perspectives and assessing the effectiveness of the pedagogical communication. In both chapters I demonstrate that both teaching and learning oscillate between two poles of adaptation labeled "assimilation" and "accommodation" by various psychologists.

Assimilation and Accommodation: The Two Poles of Adaptation to the Educational Scene.   Frequently used in sociology, the concept of assimilation refers to the integration of new or marginal subgroups into the mainstream of a particular social system. As assimilation corresponds to the eradication of cognitive, emotional, and normative differences among the various social strata of a country, it entails the decline of ethnic, religious, cultural, or sex identities. Assimilation requires both a variety of specific institutional mechanisms and, for example, the enforcement of laws forbidding discrimination in a number of arenas of social participation (familial, political, economic, educational and religious) as well as more diffuse processes such as intermarriage or formal schooling. While intermarriages erode initial contrasts in the cultural outlooks of distinct ethnic or religious or social classes, formal schooling remains the main arrangement designed to perform the "melting-pot" functions in which so many societies are interested.

For schools are expected to "melt" the values, norms, and practices of both the oncoming generation and, within the present generation, the marginal segments of a society. Within a particular discipline or across a number of disciplines, students are expected to learn how to conform to the prevailing and socially accepted theories and practices of their elders who hold positions of power.

Since in its current usage, the word *assimilation* is an ideological rather than a scientific concept, the first step of my analysis is to define this term in a sociopsychological perspective and compare it to the opposite concept, accommodation. Quite clearly the use of a term is ideological when it is based upon socio-, ethno-, or egocentric generalizations.[3] Such generalizations cause confusion not only between the means and the ends to which the term refers but also between the perspectives adopted by the variety of actors involved in the situation. All these traits characterize the current usage of the word *assimilation*. First, the word is not emotionally neutral. "They shall be made English and it is to *elevate* them from that inferiority that I desire to give them our English character," wrote the Earl of Durham to justify the measures of assimilation that he wanted to introduce in Canada.[4] Assimilation presupposes initial *valued* differences in the levels of adaptation of interacting subgroups or individuals. The colonizer is deemed superior to the colonized; the migrant is believed to be inferior to the native or an earlier settler; more relevant to my concern here, the position of teacher is perceived as superordinate to that occupied by the student.[5]

Second, the valued difference between teachers and students induces confusion between the ends to be achieved through assimilation and the means that such ends require. The "assimilation" of former French colonial subjects by the Metropole required these subjects to acquire the same rights and duties as their metropolitan counterparts and to be given the same treatment as that applied to French pupils themselves. Yet the consequences remained unknown as long as there was no attempt to evaluate the responses of colonial subjects to the new stimuli to which they were exposed. *Assimilation* in the United States implies a generalization to migrant or minority populations of the rights, duties, and educational programs initially applicable to white Anglo-Saxons. Yet, as in the former case, practitioners and ideologists do not distinguish between the goals of the assimilationist strategy and the means that such a strategy involves.

Third and most important, the current usage of the word *assimilation* does not overtly distinguish between the perspectives of the actors involved in the underlying type of relationships. Most frequently the perspective implicitly adopted is that of the preeminent subgroup. Thus, when Gordon chooses the title *Assimilation in American Life,* he examines the relevant categories of phenomena from the "American life" viewpoint, that is, from the perspective of the segments of the population who have already "made it." [6] Similarly, when Price writes "though a few [migrants] assimilate completely," his implicit perspective is also obviously that of the dominant group and he really means "though a few are completely assimilated." [7] In fact, the confusion of perspectives manifests itself when the concept of assimilation is used in an untransitive manner and when no distinctions are clearly established between active or passive forms of *assimilation.*

Insofar as the use of the word is ideological, the generalizations it involves are alienating because they superimpose implicitly the values and the practices of the superordinate poles of a communication over those of the subordinate ones and lead the latter to be treated as objects.

The term must be redefined. This redefinition involves two phases: first, distinguishing the way each actor uses *assimilation* from the way he uses *accommodation* as modes of adaptation to the situation in which he participates; second, assessing parallels and complementarities in the modes of adaptation used by individuals involved in a similar situation.

The Distinction between Assimilation and Accommodation.   Assimilation as a mode of adaptation results from the reinterpretation of external stimuli in terms of the preexisting cognitive or normative frame of reference of the individual or subgroup under study.[8] To give a very concrete biological example, the assimilation of foods implies their destruction and their transformation into elements that are compatible with the structures and processes of the intestinal tract. Thus, assimilation represents a particular type of "generalized" answer evolving around systematic properties. In cognitive terms, both deduction and memory are examples of assimilation-based modes of operation. The subject reduces the problem with which he is confronted to an already-established scheme of action or analysis: the external stimulus loses its originality and is integrated into a preexisting framework.

At the opposite end of the continuum, accommodation is associated with a readjustment of the individual or group's preexisting cognitive or moral framework so that it meets the challenges of the new stimulus. For example, the eye accommodates when its lens transforms itself in order to attain a proper perception of the external object. Thus, accommodation represents a particular type of differentiating answer that entails a modification of the preexisting systematic properties of the individual or the group. In cognitive terms, induction represents a particular illustration of an accommodation-based mode of operation. Indeed it involves a differentiation of the currently prevailing framework of analysis. Assimilation is an *inward* process of adaptation; accommodation is *outward* oriented. The first process entails a modification of external reality, and the individual stresses *similarities* between the outside world and his own conceptions. The second process fosters a modification of the individual or the group's perceptive or normative structures, and the individual emphasizes *differences* between these two realities and the originality of the outside world.

Of course this distinction is not absolute. An individual or a group who would rely exclusively upon assimilation as a mode of adaptation would have increasingly impoverished contacts with the outside world; one who would make exclusive use of accommodation would not be able to make sense of the universe in which he participates. In each case such absolute imbalances induce different neuroses. Assimilation-based neuroses consist of the systematic repetition of attitudinal or behavioral responses whose structures are arbitrarily generalized to all the types of relationships in which the individual is engaged.[9] Accommodation-based neuroses consist of the dissolution, or more specifically the excessive differentiation of individual or collective structures and of the ensuing inability to attach a specific meaning to the environment.[10] Accordingly, the following analysis of assimilation and accommodation in the educational context must be interpreted in relative terms. When I write about the use of assimilation, I am examining the conditions under which this particular mode of adaptation prevails, by relative terms, over the use of accommodation.

The Distinction between Actors' Perspectives. The current usage of the concept of assimilation neglects a necessary differentiation of the perspectives. The sentence by Price, "Although few [migrants] assimilate completely," has a variety of meanings. It evokes a reduction of the differences opposing the perceptive, cognitive, and ethical structures of these migrants and those of the dominant categories of the host society. Nevertheless, such a reduction may involve different processes. It could mean that, regardless of the patterns of action followed by migrants, the dominant social categories of the host society refuse to sanction the contrasts that oppose their own values, practices, and ideas to those of the migrants. Accordingly, they treat such migrants as if they shared the same perspectives as those of the dominant groups. For instance, assimilation requires the English teacher in Puerto Rican schools to act as if his or her students were native English speakers and as if they were learning their mother tongue. In this case, assimilation is a process of generalization unilaterally decided by the dominant group regardless of what migrants do or do not do.

However, the sentence "Although few assimilate completely" may refer to the process I call accommodation. In this sense the sentence means: "although few [migrants] transform their preexisting system of ideas and values to adapt it to the norms and practices of the dominant social categories of the host society, regardless of what these categories do or do not do". Puerto Rican students "assimilate" English language when their use of the English vocabulary and grammar ceases to betray their origin and when, in fact, they have successfully accommodated to the requirements of the language of the host society.

Thus Price refers to a particular *end product* of the interaction between migrants and nonmigrants and thus to their growing *equality* as well as to the declining *disparities* between them. But this does not say anything about the processes by which such an end is obtained. Is there a systematic complementarity between the modes of adjustment used by the two poles of a communication system? In the educational context, what are the conditions under which the modes of adaptation used by teachers and pupils are complementary to one another or parallel?

Styles Characterizing Content and Forms of Teaching. The use of assimilation by teachers as a mode of adjustment to the teaching situation rests upon the generalization of a predetermined uniform treatment to all their students, who are in the role of passive receptors and are exposed to a complete depersonalization of their role. Many teachers are prone to compare their activities to those of a gardener who must "seed" intelligence in the uncultivated brains of his pupils; who must, depending on his own theoretical orientations, "water" carefully the frail buds of their curiosity or, conversely, "weed out" the undisciplined twigs of their imagination; who must also "whip" the white horses or conversely "tame" the black horses of their minds. In fact, the pedagogies that invoke metaphors derived from horticulture or husbandry and rely upon a generalized conception of nature are assimilation oriented.[11]

Assimilation is also associated with the generalization to a current cohort of students of educational treatments deemed appropriate in the past and frequently appropriate for the cohort to which the teacher himself belonged as a student. "What was good enough for me should be good enough for you."

Assimilation also involves the generalization to other groups of the educational treatment initially accorded a particular segment of the society at large. For a long time religious missions in the Gold Coast gave to their African students the same curriculum they believed to best fit the needs, aspirations, and orientations of the British working class.[12] After all, the assimilation of the Third World to the Third Estate is not so new a phenomenon. Later on, as British colonial authorities became aware of the kind of educational amenities made available to black peoples in the United States, schools in British colonies developed curricula along the same lines as those suggested and promoted by Booker T. Washington in this country.[13] Insofar as it evokes a generalized view, the concept of "Negritude" is highly assimilation oriented.

Finally, assimilation may rest upon a generalized stereotypic view of the particular category of students. The definitions of the form and the content of the courses may evolve around the image of an *ideal* student, as is the case in traditional societies, or of an *average* student, as is the case in technocratic social systems. In both cases, nevertheless, the strategies underlying curricula and pedagogy rely upon a preexisting and stable framework and lead to a generalized treatment.[14]

The patterns of attitudes and behavior characteristic of assimilation and of accommodation independently affect the ideological orientations of an educational system, its curriculum, and the teaching style of its personnel.

A study of commencement day speeches in French high schools shows marked contrasts in the choices of the speakers and in the themes they stress.[15] During periods characterized by a high degree of political and economic mobilization such as the Gaullist era following the political crisis engendered by the war in Algeria (1961–1966), the postdefeats eras (such as the years following 1871 or 1940), or the phases of intense political and economic development, speakers tend to be chosen outside of the school personnel, and they tend to stress the necessity for students to learn the values, norms, and practices that will enable them to transform their environment, to redeem the "sins" committed by their predecessors, to restore a threatened political or economic equilibrium, or to gain access to elite positions. Educational activities are viewed as contingent upon the needs and the orientations of the society at large, which acts as the generalized and preexisting framework around which curricula and teaching styles should be articulated.

During other historical periods, however, speakers tend to be chosen within the school itself, and they tend to underline the potential contribution of high schools to the cognitive growth of individual students and to the refinement of their values and initial orientations. Insofar as they define educational activities as being student centered, they stress the necessity for both curricula and teaching styles to be differentiated and to take into account the differential cognitive, emotional, and normative structures of individual pupils.

Insofar as we can evaluate various educational systems or a same system over time in terms of the extent to which their ideologies mirror assimilation- or accommodation-based modes of adaptation to their students, we can also differentiate their curricula along similar lines.

In general terms, the adoption of an accommodation-based curriculum involves a differentiation in the sequence of courses offered to individual students and in the choices made available to them. In contemporary Germany or Sweden, for instance, students are not only allowed to choose their program of instruction among a number of disciplines but, in addition, their progresses in each discipline are evaluated separately; they can simultaneously follow advanced courses in mathematics and elementary elements of literature. A number of American colleges have been recently adopting an accommodation-based mode of adaptation; they allow students to broaden the fields of their interests and to rank the various fields so chosen by taking some courses for full credits and others under the Pass/No Pass (P/N) option.

Within the broad context of a given curriculum, certain disciplines may be defined as assimilation rather than accommodation based; for their teaching rests upon the transmission of a body of knowledge deemed to be fixed and immutable, through techniques of communication which should be both *uniform* and *permanent*. European laws and humanities offer examples. The incorporation of legal decisions into a system of codes rests upon the postulate that the law has an external and universal meaning, independent of the perceptions held by individual students or of the specific circumstances of the cases they are asked to solve. Under such conditions these students are expected only to memorize legal items and adapt themselves to a preexisting and generalizable framework. Similarly in the case of Latin, it is clear that grammar, syntax, and vocabulary are viewed as having a universal and permanent meaning. Student activities in such a field are viewed as evolving around a generalizable and preexisting frame of reference.

The situation is obviously different in physical and social sciences.

The corresponding bodies of knowledge are deemed to change and there are variations in the rules underlying the definition of the relevant activities; so the teaching of these disciplines must favor research and must rely upon differentiating, accommodation-based strategies and techniques.

Assimilation and accommodation also pertain to two opposite types of teaching style. In effect, the manifestations of assimilation as a teaching style are quite diverse. Regardless of the fields of knowledge examined, the stress teachers place upon the memorization by students of rules or items (for instance, through the use of multiple-choice questions) is assimilation oriented: it stresses the preeminence of a preexisting universal and permanent framework of action or of analysis. Teachers whose style relies upon "self-fulfilling prophecies" offer another case in point. Studies like *Pygmalion in the Classroom* illustrate the frequency and the significance of this particular style; often enough, the communication style of teachers is markedly influenced by *a priori* judgments passed on the abilities or motivations of groups of students.

Of course, the relationship between curriculum and teaching style is indeterminate, and there may be variations in the degree to which various teachers of a same discipline rely upon assimilation or accommodation in their dealings with their students. For instance, although the teaching of history tends to be assimilation based since it views the meaning of history to be fixed and corresponding to a preexisting frame of interpretation, there are still variations in the interpretation and the functions that various teachers assign to this particular field. Early interpretations of the American Revolution by American and English teachers, for instance, tended to be uniformly assimilation based, since their respective views of the significant events of that period were incorporated within two generalized preexisting frameworks developed around culturally relative needs.[16] Yet these interpretations have varied over time, depending on the tensions developed between the two nations and on their respective levels of political development. Changes in the meaning attached to historical events currently oblige teachers to make a greater use of accommodation as a mode of adaptation. Because of such changes, certain teachers differentiate the content and the form of their courses in terms of the perceived needs and aspirations of the student populations to whom they are attached.

The ideologies attached to the educational activities of a particular school system, its curricula, and its prevailing teaching styles are not necessarily evenly influenced by assimilation or accommodation based processes. Ideologies, curricula, and teaching styles do not indeed evolve concurrently, nor do they necessarily converge since their respective logics may be distinct. For example, the vocational nature of the courses initially offered to lower classes or to minorities in this country was accommodation oriented insofar as educational authorities stressed the specific nature of the needs, abilities, and orientations of these people. But the underlying ideology was assimilation oriented since this kind of training program aimed clearly at perpetuating and generalizing over time the existing hierarchy of social and ethnic groups. The corresponding teaching styles were also assimilation oriented insofar as they presupposed a generalized notion of the cognitive and normative orientations of the black or lower class populations.

More recently, the perceived relationship between formal schooling and upward mobility has induced educational authorities to offer the same curricula to all segments of society, making these curricula more assimilation oriented. However, the same authorities have begun to acknowledge the implications of cultural differences in cognitive styles and to recommend the adoption of accommodation-based teaching styles. The teaching of English to migrants offers a case in point. While the content of English courses is generalized—assimilation oriented—a number of educators argue that the teachers working in Puerto Rican or Mexican neighborhoods, for instance, should be bilingual and should accommodate to the cultural and linguistic peculiarities of their clientele. In fact, their stance has been recently legitimized by the courts. In July 1973 a judge in New Mexico instructed local school systems to "develop bicultural programs in as many areas as practical."

Functions of Educational Institutions. The use of assimilation or accommodation by teachers is dependent upon the cultural and structural functions assigned to schools. Insofar as such institutions aim primarily at ensuring a proper transmission of a cultural inheritance, teachers are expected, both in the content and in the form of their courses, to minimize the significance of the variations in the needs, motivations, and perceptions of their individual students. This is particularly so when the social definition of this cultural heritage is both fixed and monolithic. Contrasts between Catholic and Protestant cultures come easily to the mind. The long-established emphasis of so many Catholic countries upon the permanent and central nature of "revealed truths," induces many educators to generalize to current cohorts of students the same messages as those handed to their predecessors. Conversely, the stress placed upon the immanent rather than transcendental nature of religious truth by Protestant theologians is necessarily conducive to a greater differentiation of pedagogical messages and tools.

Yet the use of assimilation or accommodation by teachers is also influenced by the relationships existing between educational institutions and the various components of the society at large. Thus the generalization to a current cohort of students of a past curriculum or pedagogy can be regarded as a form of conspicuous consumption and might help, as such, to differentiate the status of a stable leisure class from that assigned to less privileged segments of society.[17] Past-oriented pedagogies symbolize the preeminent position of the classes placed at the apex of the social hierarchy. And while the creation of boarding schools in a rural or bucolic setting facilitates a higher control of students by teachers and administrators, it also symbolizes the notion that education should be removed from the ever-changing contingencies of an urban environment. Similarly, the stability of leisure classes enables them to be oriented toward liberal arts rather than sciences, and it is not surprising, as Piaget notes, that in the field of liberal arts both the content and the form of the relationships between students and teachers have been most stable over time.[18]

More broadly speaking, the use of assimilation-oriented curricula and teaching styles depends upon the perceived contributions of formal schooling to a *stable* social hierarchy. Variations in the importance attached to upward mobility tend to be accompanied by parallel contrasts in the place assigned to assimilation-oriented disciplines in the curriculum. In the early British elite schools, when upward mobility was limited to narrow segments of the population, preeminence was given to Latin over modern languages and to basic over applied sciences, since the teaching of Latin and of basic sciences was believed to foster a detached orderly cognitive approach which could be easily generalized to solve a variety of problems. For instance, in 1884, Eton employed 26 teachers of classics, six mathematics instructors, no modern language teacher, and no science teacher.[19] As economic development proceeds, however, and as upward mobility becomes more diffuse, there is naturally a decline in the importance attached to the most assimilation-oriented disciplines. In France, for instance, the teaching of classics, which represented 37 percent of the major subjects offered by the secondary institutions during the period of industrial takeoff, constitutes only 26 percent of the major courses offered by the schools of the postindustrial era. The difference is even more startling in Germany. During the period of economic takeoff, classics represented no less than 50 percent of all courses offered by secondary schools, but the corresponding percentage is only 30 percent now.[20]

Similarly, as the social hierarchy becomes more stable and as political integration becomes more evident, there is a corresponding development of assimilation oriented boarding schools. This is evident in France where 44 percent of secondary school students were boarders at the eve of the Industrial Revolution and where the corresponding percentage remained at 25 percent in 1956. In the French context, the system of boarding schools is, in effect, assimilation oriented for at least two reasons. It represents a generalization of the pedagogical framework developed by earlier religious institutions and reflects the concern that the State has, to impose a centralized culture which would eliminate or at least lower discrepancies in the life styles of various categories of the population able to claim the status of elites. In contrast, since patterns of access to elite positions remained differentiated for longer periods of time in Great Britain, boarding schools emerged relatively later and did not attract large sections of middle class populations before the middle of the nineteenth century.[21]

In addition, whenever a society is deemphasizing upward mobility, teachers are likely to stress the ascriptive qualities of grace and elegance to the achievement-oriented qualities of hard work and diligence. French schools have long enough favored gifted students at the expense of hard-working individuals.

While the development or the perpetuation of assimilation- or accommodation-oriented curricula and pedagogies depends upon patterns of social stratification, it also depends upon the status assigned to children and to the various age groups constitutive of childhood and adolescence. Yet changes in social views about the status of children follows a modification of the general social organization. Aries, for example, has shown how French children who were initially deprived of a distinctive social status have been successively recognized as the miniature copies of adults and have been ultimately granted a highly distinctive position.[22] Only after the Industrial Revolution and the corresponding accentuation of individualistic ideologies, could educators begin emphasizing the value of a curriculum and a pedagogy more tailored to the needs, aspirations, and motivations of each individual child.

Stress upon accommodation as an appropriate educational strategy also results from developments in the psychology of learning. Accommodation-based teaching strategies developed only after it was demonstrated that childrens' modes of learning are initially based upon assimilation. Only recently, long after the researches of Piaget, have educators recognized the necessity of adapting their strategies to the psychological development of the child and have, for example, modified the teaching of one particular discipline to make it more consistent with the cognitive structures and processes characteristic of a specific age group. The differentiation of students into distinctive groupings within separated facilities (such as elementary, junior high, and high school) aims at making both curricula and teaching styles more consistent with the perceived needs and orientations of differing age groups. The introduction of modern algebra in early grades is another example.

The stress placed upon accommodation in the educational field is also a by-product of research conducted in other fields. Research about the industrial environment has often been applied to the educational context; since the studies of Mayo and his associates on the influence exerted by the physical environment on workers' performances, significant changes have been introduced in the layout of schools and classrooms.[23] In addition, to isolate the conditions under which accommodation of teachers is most effective seems to stem from the research of sociologists on the consequences that competition or cooperation and group cohesiveness exert on individual performance in small groups. Undoubtedly such researches were initially aiming at changing industrial rather than educational organizations. In all these cases, the human and material organizational patterns of schools have accommodated to changes affecting other processes and structures.

The use of assimilation or accommodation by teachers, however, depends upon variations in the perceptions that differing subcultures hold toward the educational process and more specifically upon the degree to which these subcultures perceive schooling as *mediating imitative adjustment* on the part of students. Teachers of rural schools are more likely to maintain an assimilation-based curriculum and style than urban teachers. Rural school populations are more homogeneous, and thus teachers have less incentives and fewer means to differentiate their pedagogical tools and methods.

In the urban context, assimilation-based strategy is likely to be maximal in the schools of slums and decaying neighborhoods, for lower-class parents often view the formal schooling of their offspring as an unavoidable and mitigated "bliss" on which they have no control. An assimilation-based teaching style tends to prevail because parents and children have not enough resources to challenge the existing system.

However, the situation is analogous at the opposite end of the social-class continuum because parents and children have no incentives to change the existing pedagogical order.[24]

Varying with the social class of school populations, teaching strategies should also vary with the differing orientations of such populations toward the problems of mobility. Miller and Swanson have suggested a meaningful distinction between bureaucratic and entrepreneurial families.[25] The first type has been settled for a long period of time in the urban environment, and its adult members are employed in large-scale organizations with at least two levels of supervision. Entrepreneurial families come from a rural environment, and their adult members are engaged in small-scale salaried work or are self-employed. Insofar as this distinction is associated with differing child rearing practices, we can suggest that schools located in communities dominated by bureaucratic populations are more prone to use assimilation-based strategies than those in areas where the population is predominantly "entrepreneurial." Insofar as "entrepreneurial" families stress the significance of self-reliance and autonomy as values, they attach more importance to the adaptation of teaching styles and curricula to the needs of their children. Conversely, adaptation to a bureaucratic order requires the teaching of cognitive and normative behaviors to be "standardized." The importance of "getting along with others" legitimizes a maximal dependence of students upon the particular teaching style of their teachers, which should be assimilation-oriented.

The use of assimilationist strategies is also determined by the interaction between the characteristics of the community and those of the teacher himself. Limited contrasts between the background of a teacher and of his students' parents make the use of assimilation less problematic. Conversely, since an increase in this contrast leads a teacher to be more aware of the disruptions that occur in his interactions with students, he feels obliged to rely more frequently upon accommodation. This is probably why the middle-class teachers of the Chicago school systems observed by Becker tend to perceive both upper- and lower-class students as the most difficult to deal with.[26]

The effects of similarities between teachers and students' background are probably not alike at the various levels of an educational system. Becker notes that residents in medical schools tend to teach along the lines desired by medical students (accommodate to their needs and orientations) when they all share the same training and educational experiences. The sharing by both categories of analogous professional goals and similar educational histories facilitates a greater differentiation of teaching methods and tools. In this instance, a "teacher" is sure of the legitimacy of his role, which enables him to cater more directly to the differentiated needs structures and orientations of his clients.[27]

Organizational Principles of Educational Institutions. The use of assimilation and accommodation by teachers depends upon both the dominant ideological orientations and organizational patterns of educational institutions.

Both the curricula and teaching styles of schools are affected by historical processes. Undoubtedly, older educational systems tend to be prisoners of their own pasts, and the assimilation-based preeminence attached by French schools to aristocratic qualities of elegance and grace results from the fact that, anxious to develop formal schooling, the French bourgeoisie was equally concerned with the legitimation of the new enterprises. Such a legitimation had to depend upon explicit references to the earlier definition that French nobility and the Jesuit mentors gave of the national culture. The same need for legitimacy induces newer educational systems to look for historical precedents that will justify their current outlook and profile. The perceived absence of educational traditions in the United States has made many American colleges persistently dependent upon German influences; this results not only from the contributions of German immigrants to the formation of the American middle class, but also from the fact that the cultural models the German bourgeoisie imposed upon its own school systems were particularly "assimilable" by the American middle class.[28] The positions occupied by these two types of bourgeoisie in their respective social and educational structures were comparable, and so were the roles that they played in the development of educational institutions. In Africa, the same perceived absence of alternative educational objectives and goals accounts for the fact that a country like the Ivory Coast follows every French educational change.

Despite their differing functions and historical origins, both traditional and technocratic educational systems induce their teaching force to rely upon similarly generalizing principles. The teachers of traditional systems address perhaps themselves to an "ideal" student; those of mass-serving institutions are perhaps concerned with an "average" student. Teaching in the first case may be viewed as a sacred form of activity, while it is often defined in terms of a closed system of cybernetic interactions in the second one. Yet, whether they rely upon a "sacred" view of teaching or upon a deification of science, these two models do not facilitate a greater differentiation of educational strategies. For example, in *Coming of Age in America,* Friedenberg notes that the essential function of many mass-oriented American schools is to protect society from subjectivity and normalize and standardize their educational outputs.[29] In the current bureaucratic context, authority based on superior competence or insight must defer to more popularly acceptable social formulations, and conformity is preferred to creativity. Many institutions scrutinize the personality of their students to make sure that they meet the standards of normality defined by the society at large. The use of assimilation-based strategies in this particular technocratical context is manifest in the fact that teachers and educators work *on* students rather than *with* them—to use the terminology of Friedenberg. To work *on* students represents a generalizing strategy at variance with the accommodation based principles underlying interaction *with* students.

The use of assimilative strategies also varies with the degree of centralization of the system. Centralization increases the difficulties that individual instructors encounter in their potential endeavors to depart from socially approved norms of teaching, and their desire to innovate depends upon the directives of central authorities who, due to their very position, tend to be insensitive to the aspirations and orientations of local constituencies.[30] Further, the effects of centralization along these lines vary in intensity with the stratification or hierarchy of the teaching force. Distinctions between statuses in the system enhance the pressures exerted toward the development of a uniform, hence "assimilation-based," teaching style, and newcomers are prone to use the pedagogical tools that have made the fortune of their elders. Indeed, as the number of alternative channels of upward mobility within the educational system declines, the greater are the pressures toward conformity and the more likely teachers are to articulate their activities around the one socially acceptable preexisting framework.

Alternatively, stress upon accommodation seems to increase with educational decentralization, for decentralization fosters competition among institutions, which aim at satisfying the specific needs and aspirations of their clientele. Teachers are obliged to change both the content of their courses and their techniques of communication when their fate is dependent upon their acceptance by the community in which they are working. For example, missionaries in Africa were obliged to accommodate to certain demands of the public for both religious and economic reasons. Since proselitizing rather than educating was their ultimate end, the achievement of this goal often obliged them to sacrifice to the educational aspirations of their clientele. In areas controlled by Great Britain, for example, to satisfy the academically broader aspirations of an emerging bourgeoisie, certain missions early abandoned the narrow vocational curriculum initially exported from lower-class institutions.[31] In French-controlled areas the same stress placed upon proselitization induced missionaries to study local languages in depth in order to determine the conditions under which they could print religious documents in such languages. They were accommodation oriented, for their practices departed markedly from the prevailing colonial ideology. Yet the flexibility, and thus the "accommodation-based," strategies used by missionaries was also the result of their economic dependence upon local populations. Their survival was indeed a function of the degree to which their parishioners were satisfied with their roles.[32]

In addition, the use of assimilation- or accommodated-based curricula and teaching styles depends upon the relative importance of the selective and certifying functions carried out by the school. The greater the influence exerted by examinations on the fate of both faculties and students, the more teachers are prone to base their teaching upon the method or curriculum proven to be most effective with past cohorts of students or other segments of society.[33] French educators call this *bachotage;* their American counterparts call it *cramming.* It is of course likely to become more frequent as the number of alternative tracks decreases and as the educational system becomes more "assimilationist," generalizing to a variety of social groups the curriculum and the pedagogy initially used for the benefit of the social groups who owe their current social preeminence to earlier overall educational achievement. Teachers ultimately generalize to lower-class students the curriculum and the pedagogy that made the fortune of middle classes, even though they may be considered irrelevant by lower-class standards. In *The Way It S'pozed To Be* Herndon illustrates, for example, the extent and the nature of the feelings of irrelevance experienced by slum children in the context of their academic career.[34]

The dependence of teachers upon their clientele also varies with the informal authority and power structure prevailing in the educational organization itself. Frequently enough, the principals of American primary and secondary schools are unwilling to intervene in the conflicts between teachers and students. Under such conditions these two categories of actors are obviously obliged to look for compromises in the tensions between them, to differentiate their initial principles of action, and to accommodate to one another.[35]

Naturally, teaching styles also depend upon the pedagogical means available to teachers. We have often laughed about French teachers who taught young Africans that their ancestors were called the Gauls and had blue eyes and blond hair, but one forgets too easily that, at least in the early days of colonization, the choice of this particular type of lesson was dictated by the very nature of the scarce written material that these educators could use and that it was directly borrowed from metropolitan institutions.[36]

Space has the same effect. With overcrowding, teachers enjoy less flexibility and are obliged to accord their student population a uniform and generalized assimilation-based treatment—as much the result of a lack of alternative opportunities as of a concerted ideology. For the same reason, assimilationist teaching styles are often the by-products of the topographical arrangement of the classroom. Although the teaching policies recommended by administrators may have changed, their implementation remains blocked by the rigidity of the pedagogical space. Corresponding to an obsolete model, the use of a podium located above the fixed chairs of the students still symbolizes the preeminence of the teacher. Most important, it limits alternative patterns of interaction and condemns the instructor to use a uniform teaching style which makes the emergence of differentiated pedagogical strategies more difficult.[37]

Finally, both curricula and teaching styles reflect variation rates of change both in the society at large and in the educational system itself. Since high rates of change are often associated with accentuated disparities between the resources made available to educators and the needs they experience to keep the institution running, teachers are obliged to depart from traditional approaches. In French-speaking Africa, for example, the resistance initially displayed by many traditional authorities against the diffusion of formal schooling induced many administrators to reward regular school attendance and academic progress with monetary and material premiums, a practice which has never been used in Metropolitan France itself.[38] Similarly, high rates of change in the educational field usually imply an increased heterogeneity in the patterns of recruitment of the teaching force. This increased heterogeneity leads in turn to accentuated disparities in individual teaching styles. Accordingly, there comes a time when the maintenance of the system as a whole requires these disparities to be socially accepted.[39] As a result, accommodation becomes an approved practice.

Organization of the Disciplines. Dependent upon the overall organization of the system, the use of assimilation or accommodation by teachers is also a function of the organization of their discipline. In *Boys in White* Becker shows how the content and the method of medical studies are more determined by the organization and the hierarchical articulation of the profession than by the aspirations and orientations of students. The presentation to students of a standardized and fixed (high assimilation-based) package increases the time that medical residents can devote to research activities, which they deem to be the most rewarding.[40]

The preference of these residents toward assimilation-based teaching methods is shared by other types of teachers as well. Whenever teaching and research are performed by separate classes of personnel, teachers may have few incentives to depart from methods based upon their own experiences as trainees. Symmetrically, however, whenever teaching and research are carried through by the same persons, assimilationist methods of teaching tend to prevail when research is more rewarded than teaching.[41]

Thus the relative importance of assimilation-based methods depends also upon the stability of the power structure of the discipline examined. The medical profession is able not only to control the number and the dominant quality of their new members but also to prevent changes in their training.[42] In spite of the absence of relevant studies showing the usefulness of Latin and Greek, medical doctors have been able to maintain these two subject matters in the curriculum of medical schools, even in countries as different from one another as Japan and Poland. Similarly, the preeminent position acquired and maintained by sociology professors in the power structure of this discipline probably explains why the training of sociologists remains more oriented toward teaching than toward research activities.[43]

Probably the same stability of power structures accounts for the profile of "normal science" as described by Kuhn in the *Structure of Scientific Revolutions*. Indeed, normal science is assimilation-based in the sense that it makes the history of science look linear and that it renders scientific revolutions invisible. Most often students are prevented from becoming aware of the variety of problems to which the members of the scientific community have addressed themselves in the past. Rather, they learn through textbooks, (assimilation-based devices because of their generalizing orientations) the bases necessary for "puzzle-solving" activities (which aim at the *replication* of already identified generalized principles). "The student discovers, with or without the assistance of his instructor, a way to see his problems as *like* a problem he has already encountered. Having seen the resemblance and grasped the analogy between two or more theoretical problems, he can interrelate symbols and attach them to nature in ways that have *proved effective before.* . . . Scientists solve puzzles by modeling them on previous puzzles solved." [44]

Characteristics of Teachers.   The extent to which educators use assimilation as a teaching strategy varies first of all with the position that they occupy in the educational system. University professors are legitimately expected to use this teaching strategy more frequently than primary school teachers, although they enjoy a larger number of choices in the content and the style of their teaching. In effect, since university professors are subjected to a more limited number of external controls in the exercise of their activities, the decline in the importance or the incidence of pedagogical courses as one moves up in the educational ladder reflects the differential legitimacy of assimilation. In French one says of a primary school teacher that *il fait la classe* (an activity that precludes the exclusive use of assimilation), whereas one refers to the *cours magistral* of the university professor (which legitimates the use of assimilation, since it eliminates any feedback on the part of students).[45] Similarly, in English, the assimilation-oriented concept of *lecture* refers to the activities of a university professor but not to those of the primary school teacher, which is why most pedagogical innovations take place at the primary school level.[46]

Increasing as one moves up in the educational ladder, the use of assimilation is also most frequent among teachers who have obtained tenure and are thus protected against demands external to the system. Kuhn suggests that in the field of science, for example, accommodation-based scientific revolutions are likely to be made by individuals for whom allegiance to the scientific community is of little significance, hence by those with little seniority.[47] This observation can probably be generalized to other disciplines. As a newcomer into the system, Herndon has been willing to accommodate and hence to depart from the traditional stereotypes used by his colleagues in their dealings with slum children. It is also because the teachers of Peyrane studied by Wylie were not full members of the community and were occupying junior positions in the primary school hierarchy that they were willing to accommodate to the needs and aspirations of their students.[48] They had nothing to lose.

The relationship between the social status of teachers and the stress that they place upon accommodation as a mode of adjustment is in fact one of the main paradoxes with which educational institutions are confronted. While the internalization of the proper values by new students and hence their accommodation to the system presupposes them to be taught by the most experienced teachers, the very position of these teachers makes them often unwilling and unable to adjust to the needs and orientations of incoming students. Conversely, while young and new teachers are more frequently able to accommodate to such needs and aspirations due to the marginal position that they occupy in the system, the very marginality of their position induces them to maintain a minimal level of allegiance to the educational organization. Correspondingly, educational institutions are confronted with serious dilemmas along these lines. Among colleges and universities the question is to determine whether freshmen should be taught by full professors or by teaching assistants. Among primary schools the parallel problem is to decide whether first graders should be taught by beginners or by the most experienced staff.

Responses to such dilemmas are determined by the intensity of the crosspressures associated with the particular hierarchical organization of the school and with the demands of the public. On the one hand, teachers compete with one another for students deemed to be the most rewarding. Student populations of terminal classes occupy a particularly strategic position because their impending graduation is likely to be attributed to the efforts of the educators who taught them *last* and also because such educators are necessarily in a position to negotiate the future fate of their clients with parents or with representatives of institutions of higher learning. Accordingly, teachers with an already high status are tempted to enhance their power both within and without the institutions by asking to teach exclusively at the terminal level.

On the other hand, a marked increase in the level of criticisms addressed to educational institutions often leads their administrators to place their most experienced staff at the lowest educational rungs. The presence of such teachers in lowest grades serves in fact two functions. It prevents parents from being overcritical, and the expertise of these teachers enables them to blame the students themselves for their poor performances; hence they act as gate-keepers and eliminate the weakest elements from their classroom. This of course cannot but improve the future standards of the student population as a whole and lower the level of the outside pressures exerted on the institution itself.

Finally, the use of assimilation or accommodation depends upon the psychological make up of individual teachers. Assimilation should prevail among teachers characterized by bureaucratic rather than by professional orientations, for the latter have a more powerful sense of the concept of *clientele*.[49] Similarly, the use of assimilation should also depend upon past experiences. In *The Way It S'pozed To Be* Herndon suggests that previous failures to establish satisfying lines of communication with students leads certain teachers to use generalizing models in their systems of interaction with their class. The principal, the substitute, the language and social studies consultant, keep reminding Herndon that there is only one way of dealing with "them," since their traits, shortcomings, and peculiarities are all alike. "Mrs. Z. didn't talk to the kids. She only talked to ladies and gentlemen. These kids were not. Therefore she did not talk to them." As the years pass by, Mrs. Z. becomes probably more convinced than ever that "to discuss an instruction with 'them' is only admission that there could be some disagreements about whether the rule or the assignment is proper." Assimilation and authoritarianism are certainly related, and the reluctance of Herndon to use the same generalizing principles as those used by his colleagues eventually leads him to be dismissed from the system.

Conclusions.   Undoubtedly schools are a mechanism of assimilation; their function is to merge the values and practices of the oncoming generation with those of the adult population and to merge the values and practices of marginal segments of society with those prevailing in the mainstream of the social system under study.

The concept of assimilation, however, is problematic. In its current usage, it does not distinguish the end result of the interaction between students and teachers, from the processes underlying such an interaction. Neither does it separate the relevant processes of adaptation used by teachers from those used by students. Given the fact that educational processes aim at a decline in the disparities opposing the cognitive, emotional, and normative styles of teachers and students, is this goal attained only when these two categories of actors use complementary modes of adaptation?

The initial meaning of the word *assimilation* refers to one particular pattern of adjustment used by a specific actor. Indeed assimilation is an *inwardly* oriented generalizing pattern of adaptation, which induces the actor to reinterpret the current relationship in which he is engaged in terms of a preexisting stable frame of reference. It must therefore be contrasted with accommodation which represents a process of differentiation, that is, a modification of that preexisting frame of reference to make it meet the specific properties of the stimulus to which the actor is currently exposed.

Assimilation as a mode of teaching prevails when responses to an immediate stimulus are influenced by "jurisprudential" considerations, that is, by a reinterpretation of the current relationship in terms of the structures of analysis derived from the past experience of the subject. Assimilation is more likely to characterize the curricula and teaching styles of schools located in societies with centralized and stable systems of values, stratification, and organizational patterns. The use of this particular mode of adaptation is also likely to prevail among educational institutions which have rigid links with other societal institutions and have limited resources. Depending upon the orientations and the organizational patterns of the society at large as well as of the school itself, the use of assimilation is also contingent upon the background of teachers, their occupational history and their social and psychological vulnerability to outside influences. In fact, I hope to have shown that accommodation is relatively rare and corresponds most often to the initial stages of a political, economic, or educational "revolution." The preeminence of assimilation as a mode of adaptation characterizing both curricula and teaching style suggests that to a large extent, educational activities tend to duplicate existing patterns and processes in the structure of the society at large.

NOTES AND REFERENCES

1. For a full discussion of the findings of such a survey, see C. A. Anderson, "The International Comparative Study of Achievement in Mathematics," *Comparative Educational Review,* Vol. 11, 1967, pp. 182–196.

2. See E. Halsall, "A Comparative Study of Attainment in French," in M. Eckstein and M. Noah, eds., *Scientific Investigations in Comparative Education* (London: Macmillan, 1969), pp. 97–112.

3. For a further examination of the characteristics of ideologies, see J. Piaget, "Pensee égocentrique et pensee sociocentrique," *Cahiers internationaux de sociologie,* Vol. 10, 1951, pp. 34–49.

4. As quoted by C. Price, "The Study of Assimilation," in J. Jackson, ed., *Migrations,* Social Studies 2 (Cambridge: Cambridge University Press, 1969), pp. 181–237.

5. Although assimilation aims at an abolition of the *valued* differences between subordinates and superordinates, it can take place only after these differences have been recognized as valued. For a further discussion, see

R. Clignet, "Damned If You Do, Damned If You Don't, The Dilemmas of the Colonizer-Colonized Relations," *Comparative Educational Review,* Vol. 15, 1971, pp. 296–312.

6. M. Gordon, *Assimilation in American Life* (New York: Oxford University Press, 1964).

7. C. Price, *op. cit.,* p. 204.

8. I am using here the definition of assimilation as suggested by J. Piaget in *La psychologie de l'Intelligence* (Paris: Armand Colin, 1956).

9. Thus in this context all authority figures are assimilated into the perceived roles of fathers.

10. Experimental neuroses, produced by the random punishment of *all behaviors* developed by the subject, are good illustrations of this second type of neurosis. Indeed, learning cannot be exclusively based upon mechanisms of positive feed-back.

11. For a discussion of the use of these metaphors in the French pedagogical system, see J. Chobaux, "Un système de normes pédagogiques," *Revue Francaise de sociologie,* Vol. 8, 1967, pp. 34–56. For a pessimist use of the references made by American teachers to husbandry as a pedagogical model, see J. Kozol, *Death at an Early Age* (New York: Houghton Mifflin, 1967). See also J. Herndon, *The Way It S'pozed To Be* (New York: Bantam Books, 1969). "Teaching these children is like training animals" says the consultant (Chapter XIII).

12. For a presentation of this theme see, for example, P. Foster, *Education and Social Change in Ghana* (Chicago: University of Chicago Press, 1964), Chapter 2.

13. *Ibid.* See also R. Heyman, "The Initial Years of the Jeanes Schools in Kenya, 1924–1931." Mimeographed. No date.

14. See A. Linares, "Evolution de l'ecole et des ideologies scolaires en Espagne," R. Castel and J. C. Passeron, eds., *Education Development et Democratie* (Paris: Mouton, 1967), pp. 151–180.

15. See V. Isambert Jamati, "Permanence et variations des objectifs pour suivis par les Lycées Depuis Cent Ans," *Revue Francaise de sociologie,* Vol. 8, 1967, pp. 57–59.

16. For an illustration, see A. Walworth, *School Histories at War* (Cambridge: Harvard University Press, 1938), pp. 3–20, as quoted by B. Clarke in *Educating the Expert Society* (San Francisco: Chandler, 1962), pp. 17–18.

17. The importance of the mechanisms by which leisure classes distinguish themselves from lower classes have already been stressed by T. Veblen in *The Theory of the Leisure Class* (New York: The Viking Press, 1965), Chapter XIV.

18. See J. Piaget, *Psychologie et pedagogie* (Paris: Denoel, 1969).

19. T. Wilkinson, *The Prefects* (Oxford: Oxford University Press, 1964). In addition to the examples of assimilation given in the main text, uniform dresses and rituals are as important symbols of the generalized treatment accorded to the students in these British elitist schools.

20. These figures are derived from J. Armstrong, *The European Administrative Elite* (Princeton: Princeton University Press, 1973), pp. 139–149.

21. *Ibid.,* Chapters VI, VII.

22. See P. Aries, *Centuries of Childhood* (New York: Knopf, 1962).

23. For a general account of the studies undertaken along these lines in the field of industrial sociology, see F. Roethlisberger and W. Dickson, *Management and the Worker* (Cambridge: Harvard University Press, 1939).

24. For a demonstration of the assimilationist tendencies of the schools catering to upper classes, see T. Veblen, *The Theory of the Leisure Class,* Chapter XIV. For a demonstration of the assimilationist tendencies of schools catering to lower classes, see J. Herndon, *op. cit.,* or H. Gans, *The Urban Villagers* (New York: The Free Press, 1963).

25. D. Miller and G. Swanson, *The Changing American Parents* (New York: Wiley, 1958). Our proposition remains problematic, for it has been suggested that entrepreneur families are conformist and tradition oriented in their childrearing practices. If this is so, they are assimilationist in their teaching strategies.

26. See H. Becker, "The Teacher in the Authority System of the Public School," *Journal of Educational Sociology,* Vol. 27, 1953, pp. 128–141. See also H. Becker, "Social Class Variations in the Teacher Pupil Relationship," *Journal of Educational Sociology,* Vol. 25, 1952, pp. 451–465.

27. H. Becker et al., *Boys in White,* (Chicago: University of Chicago Press, 1961), p. 357.

28. For a development of this theme, see P. Bourdieu and J. C. Passeron, *La reproduction* (Paris: Minuit, 1970), Chapter 2. For a discussion of the same theme in the United States, see V. F. Calverton, *The Liberation of American Literature* (New York: Scribner's, 1932).

29. E. Friedenberg, *Coming of Age in America* (New York: Random House, 1963).

30. For a discussion of this theme, see M. Crozier, *The Bureaucratic Phenomenon* (Chicago: University of Chicago Press, 1964). Yet it could be counterargued that centralization also protects teachers from the retaliations that are likely to result from their innovating practices.

31. For an account of these changes see, for example, P. Foster, *Education and Social Change in Ghana, op. cit.* See also F. Ade Ajayi, "The Development of Secondary Grammar Schools in Nigeria," *Journal of the Historical Society of Nigeria,* Vol. 2, 1964, pp. 516–535.

32. For an example of the dependence of missionaries upon the local environment in French-speaking Africa, see D. Bouche, "Ecoles Francaises au Soudan," *Cahiers d'Etudes Africaines,* Vol. 6, 1966, pp. 225–262.

33. For an examination of the similarities and differences between French and American systems along these lines, contrast P. Bourdieu and J. C. Passeron, *op. cit.,* with D. Mechanic, *Students under Stress* (Glencoe: Free Press, 1962).

34. Of course Herndon is not the only author to stress this viewpoint. For another example of the illustrations of this theme of irrelevance see J. Kozol, *Death at an Early Age, op. cit.*

35. This informal dependence between teachers and students is stressed, for example, by C. W. Gordon in "The Role of the Teacher in the Social Structure of the High School," in R. Bell and H. Stub, eds., *The Sociology of Education, A Sourcebook* (Homewood: Dorsey, 1968), pp. 288–297.

36. For a full presentation of the details concerning this question, see D. Bouche, "Les ecoles Francaises au Soudan 1886–1900," *op. cit., loc. cit.* It is, in fact, only recently that French publishers have decided that the markets of African new nations were broad enough to justify the differentiation of textbooks and pedagogical material.

37. This point is made by Bourdieu, *op. cit.* For a more general discussion of the effects that the size of a group exerts on the functioning of a group, see P. Hare, E. Borgatta, and R. Bales, eds., *Small Group Studies in Social Interaction* (New York: Knopf, 1965), notably Chapter IX. Experiments on small groups show that the patterns of communication within a group vary with the shape taken by the network and that a "sun-like" network is more assimilation oriented than a "chain," for example; linear communication flows in one direction in the first case *only.*

38. See D. Bouche, *loc. cit.* Thus students in Mali were provided with a uniform. In the same way they were given some tips, the value of which was dependent upon their attendance and their academic progress.

39. This would suggest then that in this case ideology is nothing but a rationalization of new patterns of behavior.

40. See H. Becker et al., *op. cit.,* pp. 351–363.

41. Thus it appears that distinctive organizational traits are associated with similar attitudes and patterns of behavior on the part of teachers. Truly enough, for distinctive reasons and through distinctive mechanisms, both American and French teachers do not accord a considerable attention to the needs of their students.

42. See J. Piaget, *Psychologie et pedagogie, op. cit.,* p. 92.

43. This is, as I read it, one of the leading themes of the article of B. Beck and H. Becker, "Modest Proposals for Graduate Programs in Sociology," *The American Sociologist,* Vol. 4, 1969, pp. 227–234. Indeed, they see the

teaching of sociology as being insufficiently geared toward research activities defined as the most significant part of the current sociologist role.

44.   T. S. Kuhn, *The Structure of Scientific Revolutions* (Chicago: University of Chicago Press, 1970), p. 189.

45.   See P. Bourdieu and J. C. Passeron, *op. cit.* Indeed, the expression *faire la classe* suggests a fair amount of give and take—differentiated modes of adaptation.

46.   To the innovations made at the primary school level by Montessori in Italy, Freinet in France, Decroly in Belgium, etc., do not correspond parallel trends at the level of institutions of higher learning.

47.   T. S. Kuhn, *op. cit.,* Ch. IX.

48.   *Village in the Vaucluse,* pp. 62–63.

49.   See R. Corwin, *Militant Professionalism,* (New York: Appleton-Century-Crofts, 1970). In addition, the monopoly of "professionals" on appropriate techniques and knowledge minimizes their accommodating power.

9

ASSIMILATION AND ACCOMMODATION AS OPPOSITE LEARNING STYLES

If an assimilation-oriented mode of teaching reflects the liberty teachers enjoy in the exercise of their activities, it also makes a difference on the ultimate cognitive, emotional, and normative liberty of student populations. Yet students are like their teachers in the sense that while they may rely upon assimilation as a mode of adaptation and integrate the messages they receive into a preexisting framework, they may also rely upon accommodation and modify their preexisting framework to have it fit the characteristics of the stimuli to which they are exposed in school. The first part of this chapter is devoted to an analysis of variations in learning style.

However, the outcome of the interaction between teaching and learning styles is highly problematic, and the influence teachers may exert on their students is probably less significant or less universal than educational authorities would like it to be.

To be sure, we would like to believe that educational experiences enhance the liberty students enjoy in their systems of familial, political, economic and religious interaction, and that, as a result of their schooling, they translate the dilemmas of their familial, economic, political, and religious life into educational terms. Thus we expect them to assimilate their familial, economic, political, and religious problems into the framework they have built during their stay at school. The last part of the chapter is devoted to an examination of this problem. Do students assimilate the various facets of the problems that confront them during their adult life into a fixed generalizing framework built as a result of formal schooling, or do they accommodate such a framework to the realities of the various situations in which they participate?

An Overview of the Determinants of the Two Learning Styles. Like teachers, students are prone to incorporate the stimuli to which they are exposed at school into a preexisting framework; that is, they are likely to generalize the structures and processes of the experiences undergone outside of school to the pedagogical communication. As a result, the meaning of such a communication is reinterpreted in terms of values, norms, and practices that are alien to the educational context. This use of assimilation by students takes a variety of forms.

First, assimilation pertains to cognitive patterns and involves the reintegration of the words, ideas, and concepts presented to students into their own cultural framework. Assimilation entails the reinterpretation of current stimuli in terms of a fixed and preestablished frame of reference. As such, it involves heavy reliance upon deduction and memorization.

This mode of adaptation may also involve the generalization of one particular mode of analysis to other fields of knowledge of discipline. In *Boys in White* Becker shows how medical students carry over their methods of learning anatomy to other fields such as physiology and biology, thus suggesting that there is, in the mind of students, an explicit hierarchy of courses and disciplines, with their reactions to the highest influencing their responses to the lowest.[1] This generalization may result from the fact that students perceive that anatomy constitutes the most significant requirement to become a medical doctor. It may, however, result from the fact that the ways of learning anatomy carry more visible payoffs than those of other disciplines, since the boundaries between right and wrong anatomical answers are easily identifiable. In this sense, learning anatomy does not differ from prior modes of learning in primary or secondary school. Homans has proposed that the more rewarding a unit of particular behavior in the past, the most an individual will tend to repeat this unit over time.[2]

However, assimilation may also involve the translation of the emotional and normative experiences acquired at school into an alien general system of references. For example, Clignet and Foster show that in the Ivory Coast students with the same amount and form of formal schooling but with differing ethnic backgrounds hold dissimilar atti-

tudes toward their immediate academic experiences or toward their occupational future.[3] The significance attached to similar educational experiences varies along ethnic lines and may be reinterpreted in terms
of differing cultural contexts. Similarly, the fact that up to a certain
point, formal schooling in Africa is associated with an increase in the
frequency of polygynous marriages suggests that the experiences undergone in a westernized school are reinterpreted in terms of the generalized traditional prescriptions regarding the ideal forms of marriage.

Friedenberg draws similar conclusions in his analysis of the functions
and the significance of homecoming games in American high schools.
Such games tend to be reinterpreted in terms of the economic values of
the environment rather than in terms of the collective purposes of the
schools.[4] A similar conclusion is reached by Coleman when he identifies
the variety of subcultures existing among American high schools. The
"fun" and "delinquent" subcultures of high school populations stress
themes that are alien to the overt purposes of educational institutions.[5]
As such, these themes are assimilation-oriented.

However, formal education is also associated with changes in the initial cognitive, emotional, and normative framework of students—with
accommodation-based activities. These changes may be determined by
interaction with peers as much as by interaction with teachers. Furthermore, accommodation is not necessarily global. It may affect cognitive
modes of adjustment to a greater extent than emotional and social patterns of adaptation. In *Student Culture* Wallace shows how freshmen in
a traditional American college change their initial system of values and
expectations as they become increasingly exposed to students with
greater seniority in the environment. Initially influenced by their social
and educational pasts, the behavior and attitudes of these freshmen
are increasingly conditioned by their interaction with sophomores,
upper-class students and faculty.[6]

These two sources of influence are not necessarily consistent. Faculty
members induce freshmen to place a greater emphasis upon cognitive
accommodation symbolized by higher grades, while interaction with
peers pushes them away from such an emphasis. Furthermore, the influence of interaction with peers is more diffuse and is based upon the
powerful rewards and sanctions of social integration. The mechanisms
underlying the accommodation of the individual student toward his external environment are also functionally differentiated. Because individuals accommodate life style to close friends and organizational problems to more distant acquaintances, it is necessary to identify the

conditions under which these various types of accommodation are mutually exclusive.

In the classroom itself, the responses of students to "assignments" illustrate the difficulties they encounter in their attempt to obtain a proper mix between assimilation- and accommodation-based modes of adaptation. The very choice of the word *assignment* suggests that the task demanded of them remains external to their concern. Further, the initial requests for clarification of such a task often deal with external criteria such as the format of the paper, its length, the character of footnotes, and references. Students make clear that they want to minimize the importance of accommodating to a particular teacher and that they prefer rather to depend upon the preexisting and generalized framework they have built as a result of their educational experiences. Yet they also complain that their scholarly production is hindered by the fear of the grade; and although they recognize thereby the need of adapting to the specific expectations of a particular teacher, they are often at a loss over the strategies most appropriate for "psyching out" instructors.

Learning styles reflect a variety of forces related to (a) the general cultural orientations prevailing in the environment in which they participate, (b) their relative position in the academic hierarchy, (c) the composition of the educational milieu, and (d) their own social and psychological characteristics.

The Cultural Environment.   Assimilation-based teaching styles and curricula tend to prevail not only in cultures dominated by religious orientations but also in cultures that stress the transcendental over the immanent nature of religious revelations. Whenever learning is culturally defined as a religious ritual primarily based upon memorization, this memorization tends to ensure a perpetuation of the individual's preexisting framework. Far from transforming the existing cognitive or normative structures of the student, memorization reinforces them and limits the importance of changes. Assimilation as a learning style, prevails in societies (such as the Kpelle of Liberia) with strong traditional orientations, and where teaching activities are assimilated into religious and authority roles.[7] This style prevails also in social systems that treat information as "real" rather than as constructs, and develop systems of analysis based upon deductive rather than inductive principles.

Relative Positions of Students on the Academic Ladder.   At the individual psychological level, Piaget has demonstrated that the use of assimilation as a particular mode of adaptation tends to characterize the early stages of development of the child. This assimilation manifests itself in the cognitive and normative "egocentrism" of young children: Objects cease to exist when they are located out of the spatial or temporal framework of the individual. Similarly, moral rules are reinterpreted in terms of the prior needs and expectations of the individual. Prevailing in early grades, the use of assimilation should decline further up the academic ladder, not only because of psychological forces such as maturation but also because of the social psychological processes associated with the organization of schools. In early grades assimilation as a learning style is facilitated by the fact that the child has only one teacher. Later on this learning style is made problematic by the increased exposure of the individual to a greater number of instructors and by changes in the norms underlying interaction between students and teachers. Both the emergence of emotionally neutral relations and the growing importance attached to grades lower the immediate gratifications students derive from their activities. The ensuing progressive differentiation they establish between their familial and educational roles or between their present and future academic experiences leads them to see the limits of assimilation as a mode of adaptation and to accommodate to the value system of the school.[8]

The declining importance of assimilation is confirmed by the performances on verbal achievement tests of American students of differing ages. The percentage of variance related to the characteristics of teachers and schools increases as the student moves from first to twelfth grade. As teachers increasingly influence the quality of the pupils' performances, there is a corresponding decline in the use of assimilation as a learning style. Further, the payoff of this learning style should decline, as the destination of students in adult structures becomes clearer and more specific and as the orientations of these students must fit with those of their future environment.

Thus, one can expect assimilation-based learning styles to be less frequent

1. Among college students then among high schoolers.
2. Among final-year graduate students than first-year students.[9] Becker, for instance, suggests indirectly that the assimilation-dominated "academic perspective" declines as medical students get closer to graduation, experience therefore more intensely elements of anticipatory socialization and have more intense contacts with medical procedures and realities.[10]

3. Among male students, since the academic experience of girls has less immediate occupational consequences than that of males. This is indeed what comes out of the analysis of male and female college students conducted by W. Wallace in *Student Culture.*[11]

Composition of the Educational Milieu.   The extent to which students may rely upon assimilation as a mode of adjustment varies with the general characteristics of schools and classrooms. The use of assimilation in this context prevails among schools where students originate from markedly different background, do not share similar life conditions, and do not aim at the same occupational goals and where, therefore students' communities of fates are minimal. This is the case in institutions which, because of their limited traditions, and hence of their limited requirements, enable students to "assimilate" their educational experiences into another framework. This is also the case in schools where students do not share common residential facilities and participate in highly distinctive substructures. In the French context, Bourdieu shows how assimilation is more frequent among the heterogeneous student populations attending the University of Paris than among their counterparts enrolled in provincial universities.[12] There are fewer dormitories in Parisian than in provincial universities and the population of the former institutions enjoys a more diversified life style. In a parallel approach, Becker notes that students perspectives are less easily acquired by independent students than by those loving in fraternities and sororities.[13] For similar reasons assimilation should be most frequent among the population of large-scale institutions, whose size impedes systematic interaction among students or between them and their teachers.

Finally, the use of assimilation as a learning style does not only depend upon the structural characteristics of the school system or of the classroom, but also upon the dominant orientations of the student population. Coleman distinguishes between the fun, the delinquent, and the academic subcultures.[14] The first two subcultures are oriented toward assimilation insofar as they entail a reinterpretation of pedagogical communications and educational activities in terms that are alien to the demands of the school milieu. In other words, they are assimilation oriented insofar as they lead to a generalization of preexisting "fun" or "delinquent" principles of action and analysis to the educational scene. Alternatively, the academic subculture limits the use of assimilation as a mode of individual adjustment since it incites individual students to make an outward adjustment to the expectations and demands of the faculty. Of course, the degree to which an "academic" subculture entails the use of accommodation varies with the background of the individuals examined: In the context of this particular subculture, children of teachers are more likely to rely upon assimilation than the children of other occupational groups.

Depending upon the characteristics and orientations of the student population, the use of assimilation as a mode of learning also depends upon the variety of teaching styles to which students are exposed. An increase in this variety might prevent students from establishing frequent and significant contacts with each educator and hence from making an outward adjustment to the particular demands of each one of them. Under such conditions, a student cannot help but be tempted to retranslate each pedagogical communication he receives into a preexisting framework.

This is illustrated in the reactions of Herndon's students in *The Way It S'pozed To Be*. These students were obliged to accommodate to the demands and the expectations of a system whose culture was entirely alien to their own. After having made the necessary adjustments, they were naturally mystified by the new and "strange" orientations of Herndon, whom they perceived as challenging their sense of the "educational order." "All other teachers made us get to work. Why didn't you make us work yesterday?" Hence their reactions to the innovations of Herndon were negative: "No man, Mrs. A. [Herndon's substitute] was a better teacher [than you were]. They were learning, spelling and writing sentences and doing all *they was s'pozed to do*." [15] The expression "all they was s'pozed to do" is highly assimilationist, since it represents the generalizing principle around which these students organized their educational experiences.

Sex Characteristics of Students.   The use of assimilation as a learning style varies first along sex lines and should be maximal among girls. This of course is not the result of genetic factors, but it reflects the particular position women occupy in familial groups and the roles expected from them during their adult life.

First, the processes underlying sex-role identification are not the same for boys and girls.[16] Typically, females are consistently exposed to same-sex parental models for longer periods than males. Further, while for girls the process of identification is based upon a direct imitation of the model and is immediately rewarded (reinforced), the corresponding processes for a boy involve indirect and more abstract mechanisms. Both his mother and his female teachers tell a boy he should not be a sissy but cannot give him positive clues as to what he should be. Given the unavailability of positive models to imitate, he is induced to experiment (accommodate) to discover the principles that constitute the proper masculine role behavior. These differences in the identification processes of girls and boys are associated with parallel contrasts in their respective cognitive styles. Field dependence, that is dependence upon an *a priori* generalizing principle is more marked among girls.[17] Girls are more likely to imitate a model in problem-solving activities. Boys are more interested in tackling problems that are not yet solved, but girls are more inclined to continue working on problems they have already solved.[18] The importance girls are induced to attach to *imitation* leads them to *repeat* and hence to generalize certain patterns of behavior.

Second, the use of assimilation by girls in the school context reflects the particular roles expected from them during their adult life. Their participation in educational structures results from social and psychological considerations at variance with the purported functions of educational institutions. In this country, high schools, colleges, and universities constitute socially approved marketplaces for finding suitable marriage partners. The studies of Coleman about high schools, or of Wallace and Becker about colleges, show how the "dating" system acts as a generalizing preexisting framework around which education activities and experiences are reinterpreted.[19] For example, the perceived function of grades is not to evaluate the individual relative level of academic achievement but rather to determine who dates whom and under what circumstances. Under such conditions, the pursuit of academic excellence is not an end in itself but a means facilitating immediate access to scarce valuables. Girls assimilate their academic activities into a romantic framework, and Wallace confirms this point when he observes that the academic behavior of female students is markedly influenced by their romantic status. Girls who are chiefly interested in finding suitable partners are more likely to use assimilation-based modes of adaptation and tend to have a lower academic commitment than those who are already engaged or married.[20]

Social and Ethnic Origins of Students. The use of assimilation as a learning style also depends on social class and hence on the relative distance separating the sets of norms or values proposed by the schools from those prevailing in the familial environment. Bourdieu suggests that in France the esthetic, cognitive, and social values of students are more intensely influenced by familial rather than by educational factors

as one moves up the social ladder. Teachers only reinforce the pedagogical communications given upper-class students at home, and thus
school experiences are easily assimilated by the student into the preexisting framework already provided by his home environment.[21] In contrast, French lower-class university students are more likely to owe their
definition of cultural activities to their teachers and hence to adopt accommodation-based adaptation, but this holds true only for individuals
who have reached the top of the academic ladder.

In lower grades, there is probably a curvilinear relationship between
the use of assimilation as a mode of learning and student position in
the social structure. Students coming from the opposite ends of the
social hierarchy are especially likely to use assimilation, either because
of the maximal degree of consistence between the information made
available to them by their families and by the school or because of the
maximal degree of discordance between these two sources of learning.

Learning styles seem also to depend upon ethnicity. Indeed, their
cultural origin leads individuals to adopt different kinds of classification under different circumstances. Correspondingly, there are intercultural variations both in modes of adaptation to a same stimulus and
in the outcome of such an adaptation. This is evidenced in a study conducted by Lesser and his associates on the patterns of ability characteristic of six- and seven-years-old children from different social-class and
ethnic backgrounds.[22] The study aimed at isolating the differential distributions of four mental abilities (verbal, reasoning, numbering, and
space conceptualization) and showed that while social class may be a
leading determinant of individual level of achievement, the patterns of
distribution of the four abilities also vary along ethnic lines. Regardless
of social class, Chinese and black children do better in space conceptualization than in verbal skills, while the opposite is true of Jews.
Puerto Rican children perform at their best in verbal tests, but their
weakest point is numbering. These ethnic divergences in the relative
clustering of mental abilities illustrate the double-edged nature of assimilation as a cognitive style. The existence of ethnically distinct patterns in the distribution of abilities shows that tasks are translated into
an *a priori* and generalizing principle subsumed under the concept of
ethnicity. However, the application of this principle has a variable degree of consistency with the requirements of the variety of tasks expected from children in the educational context. For the Jews, for instance, the use of assimilation proves to be successful in the case of
verbal skills, but leads to failures in the conceptualization of space.

These data also suggest that ethnic particularisms tend to be more pronounced for lower than for upper classes.[23] The offspring of the upper strata of ethnic minorities successfully perform the cognitive tasks demanded of them by the American school system, only insofar as they lose their ethnic specificity and accommodate to the requirements of the prevailing cognitive style. In fact, the role played by accommodation in the academic achievement of minorities is underlined by the analysis of J. S. Coleman and his associates.[24] The differential performances of black and white students on verbal tests suggest that these two groups do not make the same use of accommodation or assimilation as learning styles; it also suggests that these two modes are not uniformly rewarded. Among twelfth graders, contrasts in the characteristics of the teaching force account for a larger part of the variance in the distribution of results obtained by black than by white students (9.52 percent compared to 1.82 percent). Alternatively, parental cultural variables account for 2.17 percent of the variance in the case of white students but for only 0.11 percent for blacks. The importance of home environment among whites suggests that their success depends more upon the relevance of *assimilation* as a mode of learning than upon their differential accommodating power. In contrast, white *assimilation* does not explain the differential performance of black students, variations in accommodation (both on the part of teachers and students) affect the relative achievement of this particular population. Indeed teachers can make a difference only insofar as students are willing and able to *accommodate* to them.

Personality Factors. Friedenberg suggests that the preeminence of assimilation as a mode of individual adjustment varies with personality characteristics. Showing that populations with high IQs can be distinguished in terms of their relative subjectivity, he proposes that subjective people have very little use for the school, since they want to learn who they are and how to live with themselves, a search that is most often based upon assimilative principles.[25] While the school wants to help them get somewhere, they want primarily to live with themselves. In fact, the experiences of Holden Caufield, Salinger's hero in *Catcher in the Rye* not only illustrates the characteristic responses of a subjective personality, but also show how his mode of adjustment based on assimilation diverges from that expected from him in the educational context.[26]

However, background variables interact with one another, and their combined effects on the attitudes that students adopt toward the merit of assimilation and accommodation as modes of adaptation to the classroom situation can be measured. Thus we may examine variations in the proportion of undergraduate students positively attracted toward a particular job in view of the opportunities it offers to be creative and original, for we may assume that "originality" and "creativity" consist in mirroring a preexisting framework (Table 21). Indeed, what are originality and creativity if not the desire of generalizing to our immediate environment the dreams and desires that we have already built in ourselves? Insofar as this assumption is valid, the data presented reflect both the value attached by students to assimilation and the use they make of this particular mode of adaptation in their immediate environment.

As we could expect, the popularity of assimilation tends to be greater among girls than boys; in addition, this popularity tends to decline as one moves down in the social and academic ladder and as one compares intellectually gifted students coming from cosmopolitan homes (from families with a high socioeconomic status living in large urban centers) with the less-gifted individuals originated from more provincial backgrounds. Obviously, the first populations are more favorable to

Table 21. Percentage of United States Undergraduate Students Who Value the Fact of Being Original and Creative [a]

Socioeconomic and Academic Status	Protestant		Catholic		Jewish	
	Men	Women	Men	Women	Men	Women
Maximal [b]	64	62	53	52	66	74
Minimal [c]	35	40	36	41	26	86

[a] Derived from J. Davis, Undergraduate Career Decisions (Chicago: Aldine, 1965, p. 220.
[b] *Maximal* refers to individuals who have jointly a high socioeconomic background, an urban origin, and a high level of academic performances.
[c] *Minimal* refers to individuals who have jointly a low socioeconomic background, a rural origin, and a low level of academic performances.

assimilation because their privileged position makes the use of this particular learning style less risky. Finally, the value attached to assimilation as a mode of learning is higher among Protestant and Jews than among the Catholics whose religion emphasizes the merits of an adaptation to an external truth.

However, Catholic students tend to be more assimilation oriented in their modes of adaptation than Protestants or Jews, for their evaluation of assimilation is more independent of environmental variations or of variations in level of attainment. Thus, the influence of religion on prevailing modes of adaptation follows conflicting patterns. The belief in a transcendental Truth (as in Catholicism) emphasizes the importance of conforming to an external set of principles and minimizes the value individuals assign to assimilation, but the same belief leads the same individuals to rely upon an *a priori* frame of reference in their evaluations and to follow an assimilation-oriented mode of adaptation. The influence of sex in this regard is more consistent. Girls are not only more likely to assign a positive value to assimilation, but this evaluation is also more independent of their educational attainment or of their socioeconomic origin.

Pedagogical Implications of Assimilation and Accommodation as Differing Modes of Learning

Pedagogical Value of Assimilation. Assimilation introduces many equivocations in the dealings between teachers and students. At the end of a lecture a teacher often asks his students whether they have assimilated the material presented to them. However, it is not clear whether he expects students to alter their preexisting framework of analysis in view of the new stimuli presented to them, so that they can meet his own expectations or whether he expects them to assimilate this material, that is, to integrate it into their own preexisting frames of analysis. Most unfortunately, many teachers expect the former while their students hope for the latter. "I want to be free and organize my work according to my own wishes and methods" report many French students in the study of Bourdieu.[27]

The use of strategies allowing students to assimilate the pedagogical communication into their own framework seems to exert positive effects on learning. In *Teacher,* for example, Sylvia Ashton Warner shows how the learning of reading and writing is facilitated by the use of the key vocabulary of the child, that is, the vocabulary derived from his past emotional experiences.[28] The author suggests that learning of reading and writing skills is facilitated when it is easily incorporated into the preexisting frame of reference of the child. The study of Baratz and Shurz confirms this proportion; they conclude that the "ease with which one learns to read a language is largely contingent upon the degree of consistency between the written language and the spoken language of the learner." [29] There is a high consistency between these two languages among middle-class students, who are therefore in a position to use assimilation as an *effective* mode of learning.

In addition, since middle-class families perceive language as a vehicle for the transmission of information rather than as a means of social control, middle-class pupils are more often able to assimilate legitimately the pedagogical communication into the familial context. Disposing of an "elaborated" code, middle-class students use a wider range of nouns, adjectives, and verbs, and they are likely to use more abstract and more differentiated linguistic structures than their lower-class counterparts who are accustomed to deal primarily with a "restricted code." [30] In the first case assimilation is successful because of convergences in familial and educational communications; in the second case, assimilation is a failure because of conflicts and divergences between such communications.

At a higher level of abstraction, Clignet has suggested that the performances of sampled Ivory Coast postprimary students on the test of the Kohs blocks (which requires the translation of two dimensional patterns into a three dimensional space) vary with the color of the patterns used.[31] Performances are better when the colors used are red and white, colors that are differentiated in local languages, than when the colors are blue and yellow, colors that have no direct translation in such languages. This is because assimilation of the Kohs blocks problems into traditional frames of analysis appears to be easier and more effective in the first than in the second case.

In another context Gay and Cole reach similar conclusions when they observe that Kpelle students do better than Americans on tests involving problems of disjunctions because Kpelle language deals less ambiguously than English with this type of logical argument.[32] They indirectly suggest that Kpelle students are more likely to use assimilation for solving this particular problem than their American counterparts and, at least in the short run, this mechanism of adaptation accounts for a higher level of success.

Thus far I have shown the conditions under which assimilation exerts positive effects on learning. It is easy enough to reverse my stand and to isolate the conditions under which the generalization associated with assimilation may in fact lower the students' level of comprehension of the material with which he is confronted.

For example, memorization does not serve the same functions in the context of African and European schools. In the latter case memorization is supposed to lead to an automatization of basic skills and hence to prepare students for more abstract and complex tasks. This, however, is not what happens in African schools. The following example presented by Gay and Cole: "A teacher gave the problem 'six is two times what number?' When the children had heard the words 'six,' 'two,' and 'times,' they shouted 'twelve.' Their experience with the teacher showed that he was always asking the time table and they guessed he was asking again." [33] Clignet has also suggested that memorization of the computation formula for the area of triangles leads African students to commit many more errors and to be slower when they are asked to compute the base of the triangle than when asked to compute its surface. African students are tempted to assimilate the formula into a religious ritual instead of limiting the generalization of its use to strict mathematical problems.[34]

Similarly, the past experiences of Herndon students lead them to assimilate into their preestablished frame of reference the new roles allocated to them by the author, which makes their behavior incongruent with Herndon's explicit purposes. "Virgil hadn't *changed* any since the first day which makes it obvious how his own group [of reading] went. . . . While this was going on, he advised them not to consult me because I was still trying to figure out ways to get them into troubles. . . . This kept them where *he* wanted them to be. . . . For one thing having had to take everybody's crap *for so long* about her looks, Judy was not going to hold back pointing out their lack in the area of brains." [35]

Finally, assimilation lowers students' performances when it is the result of fears and anxieties. Bourdieu, for example, shows how French students transform their preparation for examination into magical rites. Following the principles of magical repetition—based on assimilation—certain students remain faithful to the objects or the strategies which had led them previously to success.[36] Similarly, Becker shows how medical students often prefer the generalizing principles of the textbook to the more specific recommendations of their teachers and irrationally attach more credence to the former than to the latter, probably because the outcome of the relationship with a book is deemed to be more predictable than that of the dealings with a teacher.[37]

Pedagogical Value of Accommodation. The interaction between the use of accommodation-based learning styles and the heterogeneity of the population of a classroom or of a school (the contrasted profiles of the students and their teachers) follows a curvilinear pattern. Up to a certain point, the heterogeneity of students seems to have positive effects on their learning. Thus the international study of achievement in mathematics shows that lower-class pupils enrolled in classes where the majority of the population has a higher social origin, are obliged to accommodate to the situation, and do in fact outscore in mathematics all students enrolled in socially homogeneous classes except those where the majority of students originate from high status-homes. Similarly, Clignet has shown that the performance of black African students in French improves as they are exposed to an increasing number of French students. The sons of African farmers perform better both in French and in mathematics when they have a large number of class-mates with an urban origin than when they constitute the majority of their own classes.[38]

The effect of heterogeneity on the influence exerted by accommodation on learning remains equivocal, however. First it varies with the nature of the "imported group." For instance, does the presence of African students in metropolitan French institutions have the same effect on their cognitive performances as that resulting from the presence in Africa of European students? In this country does the busing of black students to white-dominated schools have the same implications as the busing of white students to the schools of the black ghettos?

Second, the effects of heterogeneity, and hence of accommodation, on learning may vary with the proportions of the mix between the various social categories represented in the classroom. One could expect that heterogeneity exerts positive influences on learning only within certain limits and that both an excess and a shortage of "privileged students" impedes the progress of a classroom population.[39]

Third, the effect of heterogeneity on the relationship between accommodation and learning probably varies with the social distance separating the various social groups from one another. Perhaps ethnic heterogeneity enhances the positive effects of accommodation only when social class is held constant; or symmetrically, social mixing may have the same positive effects only when it takes place within ethnically homogeneous populations.

Finally, the positive effects of heterogeneity on the relationship between accommodation and learning probably vary with both the nature and the functions of each institution. This is suggested by Testaniere in a study concerned with the distinctive types of *chahut* (acts of disruption by students) taking place in various French educational institutions.[40] In traditional schools, students come from the same type of family, share similar life styles, have clearly designed educational goals, and have common academic and cultural perspectives. This "community of fates" enables them to pattern the organization of *chahut* activities that involve the performance of clearly defined and routinized pranks and practical jokes. This patterning is evident in the allocation of roles to individual pupils, for *chahut* involves the best as well as the weakest elements of a particular class. In this sense the organization of *chahut* activities has nothing to do with the academic performances of individual students. This patterning also concerns the objects of *chahut* activities, which are systematically directed against poor teachers or against educators whose discipline marginally affects the final destination of these students. In this particular case students accommodate in the sense that they differentiate not only the various demands imposed upon them, but also the relative positions of the teaching staff with which they are interacting as well as the various facets of their roles. In this sense accommodation is a factor of integration since this particular form of *chahut* reconciles the obligations of solidarity that students owe one another with the invidious comparisons that their differential performances may generate. It is also a factor of integration in the sense that the selective nature of the targets chosen by these students symbolizes and thus reinforces the hierarchy of roles defined by the educational environment itself.

At the opposite end of the continuum, however, another form of *chahut,* called *anomique* by Testaniere, takes place predominantly in institutions where students have not yet internalized occupational or educational ambitions and owe their presence to the laws regulating compulsory attendance. Such schools, which are usually located in the urban environment, have few boarders, and their populations have a heterogeneous origin. In such schools disruptive acts are directed indiscriminately against all members of the educational staff and classmates. They also are associated with low academic performances. Thus, students acquire all the characteristics of a captive audience since they are unable to focus both on the main targets of their frustrations and on their academic efforts. The very nature of the institutions they attend makes them unable to integrate their experiences into a meaningful framework or to differentiate among the distinctive types of demands imposed upon them. Far from being an asset, heterogeneity becomes a liability which leads individuals to reduce their academic efforts into irrelevant sets of categorizations and thus to return to assimilation as a mode of adaptation. Indeed, accommodation is defined as an inappropriate learning style, since it does not yield any significant and immediate rewards.

The effects of accommodation on learning, however, are not exclusively dependent upon the dominant features of the classroom. They are also affected by the characteristics of the students themselves. Middle-class children are more often able to meet the demands of the school than their lower-class peers because the "elaborate" code expected from students in the classroom corresponds to the language used in the middle-class familial environment. The assimilation of their academic experiences into their familial framework is academically successful because both milieus stress the significance of accommodation as a mode of adjustment to the external world.

There is a time, however, at which this stress constitutes a handicap rather than an asset. Thus, Entwistle shows that slum children enrolled in the first grade are better able to manipulate certain categories of verbal stimuli than middle-class children.[41] This is perhaps because the stress placed by middle-class mothers on accommodation as a mode of learning induces them to use models of action that are too complex for the understanding abilities of their offspring. Such models also conflict with the restrictions that both parents and teachers impose upon the explorative behaviors of their children at this stage of their development. Correspondingly, slum children are more successful not only because the "restricted code" to which they are exposed corresponds more closely to the initial demands of their teachers, but also because these children enjoy a real sense of autonomy within the limits to which they are subjected.

Finally, the positive effects of accommodation as a mode of adjustment on learning activities vary with the age of the student. These effects increase with his sense of identity and integrity. As this sense becomes more affirmed, the differentiation of the frameworks of analysis and action that accommodation requires becomes less threatening.

Interdependence between Teaching and Learning Styles. Teachers may wonder whether through their own strategies they can modify the prevailing modes of adaptation of their pupils. More concretely, they may wonder whether the use of assimilation as a teaching style facilitates the adoption of assimilation or of accommodation as learning styles or whether alternatively the modes of adaptation of teachers and students tend to remain independent of one another.

In his study of the French system of higher education, Bourdieu suggests that the large distance separating university professors from their students lead both to rely primarily upon assimilation as a mode of interacting. To the magistral monolog delivered by the teachers from their podium corresponds the "regurgitating" of students in their examination copies, which is assimilation-based since the material presented to students is often enough modified and integrated into a framework that is irrelevant to the purposes of the teacher. Bourdieu calls the pedagogical communication a form of replication.[42] In its content as well as in its form, this communication not only repeats the organization of existing cultural patterns; it also constitutes a replication of the frameworks developed by teachers and students outside of their interaction in the classroom.

The use of assimilation by American middle-class teachers in slum schools has the same effects. The lesson to be drawn from books such as *The Blackboard Jungle* [43] or *The Way It S'pozed To Be* is that the majority of teachers and students in slum schools tend to engage primarily in exercises of assimilation, repeating endlessly the specific cognitive emotional and normative patterns of attitude and behavior attached to their distinctive social affiliations and their differential position in the school system. This pattern is referred to by Ryan as "blaming the victim." [44] Obviously, this pattern also characterizes all experiences modeled after *Pygmalion in the Classroom.* Both teachers and students engage in self-fulfilling prophecies; and while the former justify their assimilation-based teaching style by stressing the intrinsic strengths or weaknesses of their pupils, the latter rationalize their assimilation-based learning style by emphasizing the labeling processes initiated by their instructors. [45] However, this does not mean that all self-fulfilling prophecies have undesirable outcomes. After all, students and teachers of "elitist" school systems rely predominantly upon assimilation in their dealings, which enables them to legitimately perpetuate the existing social hierarchy.

At the other end of the continuum, rapid conditions of change in either political or educational structures or both, lead teachers and students to rely more heavily upon accommodation as a mode of adaptation. An examination of the history of the educational endeavors of religious missions in Africa offers cases in point. As a result of their contacts with British traders and administrators, Ghanaian populations modified their initial definition of social stratification to make it more consistent with the British model, and this accommodation obliged their instructors to follow suit and to adopt a new curriculum since their survival was contingent upon the satisfaction of their parishioners. The immediate aftermaths of May 1968 in France offer another case in point. Both teachers and students were obliged to depart from their socially acceptable repertoire of interactions and had to accommodate to new, albeit insufficiently explicit, models. On the whole, however, situations where both teachers and students make greater use of accom-

modation than of assimilation are temporary. Further, the outcome of
such situations is not always desirable. An excess of accommodation
prevents both teachers and students from making sense of the situations in which they are participating and is conducive to a series of
successive crises, and hence of high resignation as well as of high drop-
out rates.

To examine situations where learning and teaching styles are parallel
is insufficient. In most cases, educational processes rely upon the assumption that whenever assimilation is used in teaching methods and
curriculum, students automatically are more likely to use accommodation, and hence to respond with a complementary mode of adaptation. Of course, this assumption is often unwarranted. This situation
obtains perhaps in the case of professional boarding schools, for instance in the case of the *Ecole Normale Superieure* in France or of British
public schools, where the effects of a centralized and autocratic system
of teaching were reinforced by the continuous exposure of students to
the particular life style characteristic of the institution. This situation
tends also to prevail among medical students already involved in the
routines of a hospital since their conformity or lack of conformity is
easily and immediately sanctioned in terms of their prospective career.
Finally, this type of complementarity probably characterizes the interaction between teachers with a large amount of seniority acquired in
the context of a centralized system and their lower-class students with
high aspirations to upward mobility. Most often, however, this type of
model does not work.

Another type of complementarity where the accommodation-based
style of teachers elicits an assimilation-based learning style tends to
characterize the primary schools of decentralized system. In the United
States it probably prevails in affluent suburbs. However the outcome of
this interaction is not always positive. Herndon emphasized the importance of an accommodation-based teaching style under the assumption
that it would lead his students to rely upon the same mode of learning.
Yet his students felt that Herndon's innovations were deviances from
the expectations of the majority of the school personnel, and they continued to rely upon assimilation in their adaptations to his particular
classroom. In fact both the author and his students seem to have been
disappointed by the results of their communication.[46] In more general
terms, the effects of teaching are not independent of the prior learning
experiences of students. Lippitt and White have shown that the influence on children of a democratic as opposed to an authoritarian teach-

ing style is not the same when the democratic style precedes authoritarianism and when it follows it.[47]

Up to this point, I have identified overall parallels and complementarities between learning and teaching activities, as they occur in natural settings.[48] However, this description should not prevent us from examining whether teachers may consciously choose a particular strategy to elicit a particular learning style. Before we answer this question, we must of course be aware that insofar as these strategies are based upon ideologies, they are necessarily assimilation oriented. And this naturally characterizes conservative as well as "progressive" ideologies.

In *Summerhill* A. S. Neill, a British psychologist, stresses the necessity of adapting the discipline of educational institutions to the needs and aspirations of individual students and of introducing psychoanalytic concepts and techniques to facilitate and enhance the learning activities of children. He is arguing both that the best form of learning is assimilation based and that it is facilitated by accommodation-based teaching methods.

Yet his plea for methods based on accommodation is also somewhat ideological, hence based on assimilation, when he displays a complete contempt for pedagogical methods (i.e., when he argues that, regardless of the method used, *all* children can learn how to make divisions) or for the pedagogical value of work. Correspondingly, while he encourages the use of assimilation as a learning style, this use might have a limited beneficial effect, insofar as his students are often allowed to enjoy artificially a greater number of choices than most adults, notably in work experiences. In fact, the benevolent attitudes that the author displays toward assimilation as a learning style tend to perpetuate rather than to change the existing social order. It is only the individuals from the upper segments of society who are rewarded in their use of assimilation as a learning style.[49]

Thus it is insufficient to analyze the ideological stance of an educator to determine whether his teaching style will elicit a particular learning style. This is not only because the actual behavior of a teacher may differ from his ideological posture but also because both his orientations and his behaviors will be differentially perceived and acted upon in a variety of contexts.

In fact, the effects of teaching strategies on learning activities do not seem to be direct or linear. Thus, available evidence shows that teaching in large-sized classes (which is assimilation based rather than accommodation based) is not always detrimental to the learning activities of

students. Similarly, instructor-centered strategies (by definition highly
assimilation oriented) do not yield results that are necessarily systematically inferior to student-centered (accommodation based) teaching
methods.

Under these conditions, it is important to assess the factors affecting
the desirability and the outcome of a particular teaching style. The normative interaction between teaching and learning styles varies by discipline and activity (Table 22). Teaching strategies based upon accommodation are particularly effective with regard to noncognitive activities (more specifically, group therapy or group dynamics) since this
style should elicit an accommodation-based learning style and the goal
of the enterprise is to enable *all* participants together to acquire the
skills of "give and take." [50] Alternatively, the teaching of law and engineering should be assimilation oriented since the practice of both law
and of engineering relies upon the accommodation of the individual to
a set of rules defined as external and immutable. After all, to state the
law is not to change it, and successful legal minds tend to have a narrow definition of the limits within which jurisprudence may be creative.
While the double use of assimilation-based teaching and learning styles,
does not seem to be desirable, the use of accommodation-based teaching
techniques is probably more suited to the teaching of disciplines like
art, the practice of which requires the esthetic translation of an external
stimulus in the preexisting framework of the artist. As art becomes a
highly individualized mode of expression, good painters cease to be
good teachers, for they operate themselves within an assimilation-cen-
tered framework and are not therefore interested in the development
of the assimilation-based abilities of their pupils. Yet the use of accommodation as a teaching style in art is particularly important when students come from a background which minimizes the value of assimilation as an expressive style. Herndon's students, for example, did not
want their drawings to look original but were rather keen to make
them look like posters, that is, like the universal models proposed by
mass media. As such, they believed that esthetic activities should be accommodation rather than assimilation oriented. This goes against the
socially acceptable definition of successful art.

There are even stronger evidences to support the hypothesis that the
effectiveness of assimilation or accommodation as teaching styles varies
with each discipline. In Antioch an experiment showed that independent small groups learned more subject matter in physics than students
working independently, whereas students working independently in art
performed better than those in small groups. This is because the per-

Table 22. *Normative Complementarity between Teaching and Learning Styles, by Discipline*

		Teaching style	
		Assimilation	Accommodation
Learning style	Assimilation	—	Art Individual sport
	Accommodation	Law, engineering Collective sports	Group therapy Scientific revolution

formance of scientific activities precludes the adoption of learning activities based exclusively upon assimilation and because students who learn by themselves encounter more difficulties along these lines than those subjected to the discipline of a group placed under a single instructor. By contrast, the activities of an art student are more assimilation based, and the effectiveness of learning by oneself is therefore higher than that of learning with a group or *a fortiori* under the close supervision of a teacher.[51]

Of course the validity of varying teaching methods is not independent of the nature of the criteria used to measure their differential effectiveness. Following the models provided by industrial sociology or social psychology, certain researchers have suggested that the effectiveness of a teaching style should be evaluated in terms of its impact on both the *performance* and the *morale* of the students to whom it is applied. Yet a high correlation between these two variables is uncertain, and effective learning is often associated, at least initially, with the emergence of certain hostile feelings toward the teacher. In fact, a study conducted before World War II on 66 history teachers and 1,275 students suggests a significant negative relationship between student ratings of these teachers' permissiveness and mean gains on information on a history test.[52]

That the morale and the performance of students evolve within similar temporal frameworks is also uncertain. While students tend initially to like friendly teachers better, they may learn more from demanding ones, and in the long term, these students possibly resolve this particular "dissonance" by modifying their ratings and more specifically by evaluating their instructors in terms of the degree to which they have successfully internalized the requirements of the particular discipline.

Finally, the effectiveness of a particular teaching style is not independent of the social context within which it is practiced. Thus Guetskow, Kelly, and McKeachie have suggested that the assimilation-based lecture method of teaching helps psychology students to attain higher levels of performance in final examinations and to develop stronger interests in the field than the use of accommodation-based discussion groups or group tutoring.[53] These results, however, might reflect the fact that the structures of a final examination are more consistent with those of the lecture method than with the main outlook of the two other accommodation-based teaching methods. In the first case, individual students are able to channel their anxieties in a positive way, but they are prevented from doing so in the second context because of the conflicting requirements of the learning and of the examination situation.

To conclude, the validity of a teaching method and its effect on learning styles tend to be relative. This seems to be too easily forgotten by ideologists, such as John Holt, who are so keen to criticize the American education system that they forget that the impact of the strategies allegedly used uniformly by American educators is not the same on all American students.[54]

Assimilation as an Effect of Educational Processes.   The liberation of students from the cognitive emotional and normative constraints of their environment requires them to generalize their academic experiences and apply them to other facets of their adult lives. In short, it requires them to *assimilate* these facets into the framework built from academic experience.

While formal schooling is aimed at enabling individuals to rely upon general and abstract principles of explanation to cope with particular problems, its influence in this regard is culturally relative.[55] In the United States individual performance on tasks such as free associations, free recall, conjunctive and disconjunctive rules, and inferences improves regularly from kindergarten on, since students learn how to use the same principle of generalization in an increasing number of situations. By contrast, the gains the Kpelle children derive from their formal schooling are more uneven and more differentiated.

Barbichon has shown that even in industrialized countries, assimilation of adult occupational roles into an educational framework remains limited.[56] Individuals are usually able to segregate their various fields of experience; they do not connect their theoretical and technical knowledge nor their occupational and extraoccupational practices. This absence of linkage is particularly manifest whenever individuals shift too rapidly from a theoretical to a technical type of training and whenever this theoretical training is not reinforced by the diffusion of appropriate scientific information within the occupational environment. In addition, formal schooling does not necessarily eliminate the coexistence of conflicting modes of analysis or of interpretation. Moscovici and Rialan have noted the frequent absence of cultural norms pertaining to contradictory modes of analysis. They have observed, for example, that individuals having completed their secondary formal education argue simultaneously that things tend to fall because of the weight of air but that these things also fall in the vacuum. At another level the two authors note that many individuals tend to recommend as highly moral the use of psychoanalytical techniques in the context of dramatic and specific situations but judge this use to be immoral when the purpose of the corresponding types of investigations is theoretical in nature.[57] In short, inconsistencies between the formal and informal aspects of educational and occupational experiences limit the extent to which the knowledge acquired at school serves as a framework around which an individual organizes his occupational or social life.

Determinants of the Assimilation of Occupational Activities into an Educational Framework

Role of cultural models. The assimilation of occupational experiences into an educational framework depends on the number and the nature of the models of cognitive exploration adopted in the society at large. The absence or the irrelevance of such models reinforces the discontinuities opposing the variety of arenas in which an individual participates. Similarly, the existence of a *deductive* model of cognitive exploration, as it is proposed in the educational environment, may be irrelevant to or at variance with the occupational activities of the subjects investigated. Thus, Wilkinson shows that while the educational experiences of the British elite facilitate its leadership under normal circumstances they prevent individuals from coping with certain types of political or economic crises.[58] This is to be expected, for the type of generalization engendered by a classical education is only operative in the context of clear-cut patterns of interactions. British elitist education is often irrelevant in times of social crises, when new solutions have to be invented.

Role of teaching strategies.   Assimilation may be inhibited by the restrictive nature of pedagogical techniques. There may be limitations in the volume or in the character of knowledge and information transmitted. Bourdieu stresses the charismatic image that French teachers have of their role and their preference for noble schemes of explanation. These limitations may also result from the fact that the material taught is presented out of sequence or according to a sequence that cannot be internalized by students. Teachers are confronted with perennial dilemmas since they must choose between a logic deemed to be heuristic and the logics underlying the specific development of their own individual system of analysis. "Inflationary" techniques have the same effect, and students may be unable to integrate the material presented to them because of the overflow of informations to which they are subjected. This condition is often met among the enterprises of "mass education," when the goal is to transmit a maximal knowledge in a minimal period of time. It is also met whenever rapid changes in the social definition of knowledge occur, for instance, in the case of developing nations, where young teachers are eager to demonstrate that wisdom is not an exclusive trait of old age, and whenever there are strong discrepancies between the models of learning activities and those underlying the performance of adult roles. Whatever their form, these restrictions do not necessarily prevent the student from adapting to the requirements imposed upon him in educational context but they may prevent him from seeing the "relevance" of the material presented to him in the educational context to his new political, occupational, or social environment.

Role of learning strategies.   If the assimilation of adult activities into an educational framework depends upon the models used by professors, it also depends upon the perceptions students hold of their teachers and of the norms that they use for integrating the informations communicated to them. Becker shows, for example, how the cognitive style of medical students is mainly affected by their perspective; that is, by the *immediate* opportunities and restrictions associated with their current role (i.e. by their definition of what the faculty wants them to learn) as well as by their culture of origin (in particular with regard to their professional dealings with women or persons of another social class).[59] Despite the fact that the manifest function of medical schools is to ensure a proper internalization by students of the values, norms, and practices of the corresponding occupational group, the socialization of these students develops around the more immediate goal of graduating; there is correspondingly a certain doubt as to what is transmitted from learning activities in medical schools into the exercise of the profession.

In brief, cognitive socialization is effective only when a mode of knowledge is transmitted from the educational to the non-educational context. This condition is fulfilled only when there is a certain congruence between the origin and functions of schools and of other institutions and when educational experiences are not exclusively determined by assimilative processes. The more teachers and students assimilate their interrelationships into an extraneous and *a priori* framework, the more disruptions there are in their dealings and the less generalizable the knowledge and information communicated within school systems.

Limitations of the transferability of educational experiences. In the previous section, I have identified some of the obstacles preventing an effective transmission of cognitive messages acquired within the educational environment. Despite the limitations of the generalization of the cognitive experience acquired by students in schools to other contexts, many observers of the educational scene are still eager to stress the role of schools as agents of political and social change. Yet the efficiency of educational institutions in this area remains equivocal.

In the political field many studies conducted in American colleges show that students become more liberal as they get closer to their graduation. Yet a study conducted on the students of Sarah Lawrence College by Lois Murphy and E. Raushenbush shows not only that relatively few individuals perceive themselves as having changed, but also that the majority of them do not perceive themselves as having adopted views that differ markedly from those of their parents.[60] Further longitudinal studies of college graduates political attitudes tend to indicate that although there is no "regression to the mean of their family" among students in the initial postcollege years, the effects of college education are not necessarily permanent.

In the social and economic field many planners have been anxious to believe that changes in curriculum and teaching of educational institutions could modify the occupational and economic orientations and aspirations of their populations. Thus, a careful study conducted in Nigeria by M. Armer suggests that variations in the length and the nature of studies undertaken are associated with variations in the level of "modern" orientations acquired by individuals. More specifically, Armer shows that accommodation to modern values is more frequent among students enrolled in western institutions than among their counterparts attending Muslim schools.[61] But it is not certain that the adoption of these modern attitudes persists after graduation. Clignet and Sween note that among the older residents of African cities a higher level of education is frequently associated with the restoration of polygynous ideals. Similarly, Clignet and Foster find that in the Ivory Coast, the graduates of vocational schools do not often perform the job for which they have been prepared.[62]

The influence of formal schooling does not necessarily remain constant across a variety of arenas of participation. The further one moves away from cognitive activities, the more problematic becomes the influence of academic experiences.

Conclusions. Undoubtedly the effectiveness of communications between students and teachers depends upon their "matching," that is upon the *complementarity* rather than upon the *similarity* of their respective patterns of adaptation or feed-back to pedagogical stimuli.[63]

The conditions under which this matching takes place remain to be identified. This has been a constant preoccupation of educators, and indeed it was already a major concern of a philosopher like Plato. Schools have often been accused of offering both too little and too much to their pupils, generating irretrievable losses in the pedagogical communication. The reduction of these losses depends upon the emergence of relevant social movements and upon the pressures that such movements are able to exert on school administrators. Educational changes cannot take place without a mobilization of the public and a widespread commitment to a new educational ideology. Yet the effectiveness of such changes also necessitates a maximal congruence between the ideological stances taken by the movement's leaders and a scientific examination of the alternative solutions available to them. Often enough, however, educational ideologies present internal contradictions, which I would like to explore further in this closing section.

Educational ideologies often involve generalizing propositions that jeopardize any other form of change. The first generalization in which many American ideologists seem to indulge frequently consists in attributing to all social classes the same motivations, orientations, and preoccupations as those prevailing in the particular social group to which they belong themselves. Many ideologists in the United States condemn current educational systems for preventing students from being creative and acquiring an appropriate sense of inquiry and purpose.[64] Such a condemnation presupposes that educational administrators are powerful enough to go against an ideal uniformly shared by all segments of society. Yet, while individual creativity is a value mostly stressed by current upper-middle classes, other social categories are more likely to view this creativity as a quality to be acquired by means other than formal schooling. Whereas they deem individual creativity to be a luxury accessible to high-class individuals only, they believe in the merits of conformity with the values, norms, and practices of the educational environment, since this is the key to upward mobility. The belief that schools act as privileged loci to teach individuals how to occupy various slots of the occupational structure and to drill pupils toward a perfect performance of a particular role, is shared both by the "educational establishment" and by a part of the current school's clientele. Any rational attempt to change pedagogical communications requires therefore an initial assessment of both variations in the views that all social categories hold of the "ideal school" and of the determinants of such views.

To argue, as many ideologists do, that lower classes are "alienated" and therefore adopt irresponsible attitudes toward such problems is not a sufficient reason for imposing one's life style and one's own value system as the best one and the only socially acceptable one. Such an approach remains elitist and is much too often based upon a naive and reactionary use of historical precedents. Thus, when Illich writes that "during medieval times an apprentice, even though he did not become a master or a scholar, still contributed to making shoes or to making church services solemn," he seems to experience a definite nostalgia for a time when things had a convincing meaning and when "education was complex, lifelong, and unplanned." This nostalgia is naive insofar as it stresses the strengths of the medieval social system but too easily neglects its weaknesses. Furthermore, it is reactionary because it does not take into account the fact that, far from being poetic, the spontaneous, irrational, character of medieval education much too often facilitated a gross manipulation of individual needs and aspirations by religious and political leaders.

Ideologists, however, are not only likely to assimilate other social groups into their own system of values and expectations; they are also likely to generalize unduly the processes by which they deem that educational ideals may be achieved. Although they often argue that the pursuit of individual creativity requires the development of alternative educational means, their proposal does not take enough account of the patterns by which these new institutions recruit their clientele. This recruitment is not likely to take place randomly. Insofar as ascriptive forces remain significant determinants of individual placement in adult structures, upper-class children take no risks in indulging in educational innovations.[65] Their fortunate circumstances enable them to gain access to the most rewarding types of adult roles, regardless of what they have learned at school and outside of school. Further, while the very participation of elites in new educational activities legitimizes such activities, such a legitimation is jeopardized whenever educational innovations are initially offered to the lowest strata of society. In other words, the apparently "democratic" concern of opening alternative schools frequently turns out to be a reactionary enterprise since it minimizes the consequences attached to the differential access of social groups into the existing variety of educational amenities.

Worse, however, the "assimilationist" tendencies manifested by many ideologists in their proposals seem often to result from ethnocentric analyses. Thus when Illich writes that "most people who learn a second language do so as a result not of sequential teaching, but of odd circumstances, that is as a result of their going to live with their grandparents, their travels or their falling in love with a foreigner," he is implicitly and unconsciously indicating that most people who learn a second language are children of the elites since the elites only are able to enjoy "odd circumstances" and capitalize on them. The few poor children who learn a second language owe its acquisition to the school and its teaching methods.

Another example of the ethnocentrism characteristic of too many educational ideologists pertains to their confusion of the means and the ends associated with educational changes. Thus Illich illustrates his idea of the "intellectual match" by asserting that "each man at any given moment and at a minimum price should be able to identify himself to a computer with his address and telephone number indicating the book, article, film, etc. on which he seeks a partner for discussion." Although necessary for the emergence of a more satisfactory educational program, this condition is far from sufficient. It presupposes that individuals have *already* the desire to do so and that such a desire is a by-product rather than a determinant of the revolution the author is so anxious to produce. The same confusion between means and ends characterizes the positions of Paul Goodman when he writes that "the present day preoccupation with careful methodology is academically praiseworthy but it does not lead to intensely interesting propositions. . . . There is a good deal of sharpening of tools but not much agriculture." [66] Yes, methodological cautiousness is often used as an excuse for not doing anything, and as pointed out convincingly by Illich, it is too often the mask that teachers wear to "monopolize their license and protect their trade interest." But experimentation, as the word is often used by "radical ideologists" refers to mere sloppiness and to change for the sake of change. These ideologists tend to forget too easily that the costs attached to the failures of new educational programs do not carry uniform implications and are higher in the context of institutions catering to the needs and aspirations of the poor than in the context of curricula designed to enhance the creativity of middle- and upper-class children.

Although schools and universities are often the cradles of revolutionary activities, they tend also to be the last institution to be affected by the new social order resulting from these activities. Educational ideologies may therefore serve only two functions. Either they constitute the mechanisms by which revolutionaries attempt to mobilize the energies necessary for changing *all* societal structures, but it remains necessary to determine whether focusing popular discontent on schools and hence on superstructures is an appropriate strategy. Or they aim at changing educational institutions regardless of their relationships with other institutions, which tends to be Utopia. To induce effective educational changes, to state that schools are the "killers of the dreams" is not sufficient; it is equally necessary to determine whose dream is killed and by whom or to take into account the variety of definitions that various social groups give of educational activities. Similarly, it is insufficient to stress teaching rather than learning (or vice versa) as a cause of the current malaise, for this is to forget that pedagogical communication, like all forms of communication, involves emittors and receptors and that there are two categories of actors with perhaps distinctive reference groups but whose universe is not exclusively that described by Pirandello in "to each one one's own truth."

NOTES AND REFERENCES

1. See H. Becker et al., *Boys in White* (Chicago: University of Chicago Press, 1961) pp. 108–110, 118–120.
2. See G. Homans, *Social Behavior, Its Elementary Forms* (New York: Harcourt, 1961), p. 53. Hence the importance of stressing an effective pedagogy at an early stage of the academic career.
3. R. Clignet and P. Foster, *The Fortunate Few*, Chapter 6, 7.
4. E. Friedenberg, *Coming of Age in America* (New York: Random House, 1963) Chapter 4.

5. J. Coleman, *The Adolescent Society* (New York: The Free Press, 1961).

6. W. Wallace, *Student Culture* (Chicago: Aldine, 1966), Chapter 5.

7. See J. Gay and M. Cole, *An Old Culture and the New Mathematics* (New York: Holt, Rinehart and Winston, 1962), pp. 88–89.

8. For a general discussion of what children are supposed to learn in school, see R. Dreeben, *On What Is Learned In School* (Reading, Mass.: Addison-Wesley, 1968). The author, however, suggests more what should be than what is.

9. Similarly, in France the use of assimilation is more frequent among university students than among the individuals enrolled in *grandes ecoles*. The former entertain vague occupational projects and tend to translate their educational experiences into their own myths. See P. Bourdieu and J. C. Passeron, *Les Heritiers* (Paris: Editions de Minuit, 1964), for example, Chapter 3.

10. H. Becker et al., *op. cit.*

11. W. Wallace, *op. cit.*

12. P. Bourdieu and J. C. Passeron, *La reproduction* (Paris: Editions de Minuit, 1970), Chapter 1. This results of course from the fact that Paris is at the very center of cultural innovations. See also P. Bourdieu and J. C. Passeron, *op. cit.*, p. 73. "Insofar as the number of teachers is greater in Paris than in the province, Parisian students are more frequently able than their counterparts in the province to belittle the prestige of the university environment and to treat accordingly their academic experience as a personal adventure."

13. See H. Becker et al., *op. cit.*, pp. 137–157. See also H. Becker, B. Geer, and E. Hughes, *Making the Grade* (New York: Wiley, 1968), Chapter 8.

14. J. Coleman, *op. cit.*, Chapter VII.

15. J. Herndon, *The Way It S'pozed To Be* (New York: Bantam Books), p. 101.

16. For a more thorough discussion, see D. Lynn, "The Process of Learning Parental and Sex-Role Identification," in R. Winch and L. Goodman, eds., *Selected Studies in Marriage and Family* (New York: Holt, Rinehart and Winston, 1968), pp. 281–288.

17. See D. Lynn, "Sex-Role and Parental Identification," *Child Development*, Vol. 33, 1962, pp. 555–564.

18. See V. Crandall and A. Ratsun, "Children Repetition Choices in an Intellectual Achievement Situation Following Success and Failure," *Journal of Genetic Psychology*, 97, 1960, pp. 161–168.

19. See J. Coleman, *op. cit.*, H. Becker, B. Geer, and E. Hughes, *op. cit.*, pp. 10, 51; or W. Wallace, *op. cit.*, Chapter 5, 6.

20. W. Wallace, *Ibid.*, Chapter 5.

21. See P. Bourdieu and J. C. Passeron, *Les Heritiers, op. cit.*, Chapter 2.

22. See G. Lesser, G. Fifer, and D. Clark, "Mental Abilities of Children from Different Social Class and Cultural Groups," *Monographs of the Society for Research in Child Development,* Vol. 30, 1965; as quoted by L. Fein in *The Ecology of Public Schools* where the author shows the relevance of cognitive abilities on the problem of community control and hence on decentralization. For another discussion of the effects of assimilation on performance, see P. Renaud, *Les fautes de Francais en ème: Etude typologique et statistique* (Yaounde: Université Fédérale du Cameroun, section Linguistique Appliquée, 1969), or G. Camus, *Le Francais écrit dans les classes de ème* (Yaounde: Université Fédérale du Cameroun, section Linguistique Appliquée, 1969). Both authors stress that the differential performances of African students in French reflect variations in the relative differentiation of sounds in African languages, in the semantic characteristics of pers nal pronouns, and in the definition of verbs.

23. This constitutes the basis on which F. Fanon justifies his criticisms of African bourgeoisies who do not remain faithful to their cultural inheritance. See F. Fanon, *Les Damnés de la Terre* (Paris: Maspero, 1961), Chapter IV.

24. J. S. Coleman et al., ed., *Equality of Educational Opportunities* (Washington, D.C.: Office of Education, 1966).

25. J. D. Salinger, *Catcher in the Rye* (New York: Franklin Watts, 1951).

26. See E. Friedenberg, *op. cit.,* Chapter 5.

27. P. Bourdieu and J. C. Passeron, *op. cit.,* Chapter 3.

28. S. Ashton Warner, *Teacher* (New York: Simon and Schuster, 1963). Such pedagogies are, of course, based upon the increased recognition of the regularities observed in patterns of cognitive development.

29. R. Shurz and J. Baratz, *Teaching Black Children To Read* (Washington: Center for Applied Linguistics, 1969).

30. These distinctions are suggested by B. Bernstein in "Social Class and Linguistic Development," in A. Halsey, J. Floud and C. A. Anderson, eds., *Education Economy and Society* (New York: The Free Press, 1963). Examples of concrete studies testing the propositions of B. Bernstein are reported in W. P. Robinson, "Social Factors and Language Development in Primary School Children," in M. Matthiejsen and C. Verwoort, eds., *Education in Europe: Sociological Research* (Paris: Mouton, 1969), pp. 50–66.

31. R. Clignet, "Reflexions sur la psychologie en Afrique noire," *Bulletin de l'INOP,* Vol. 18, pp. 86–94. Of course the problem remains to isolate the cultural components of the frame of reference used by children. The results suggested in the article mentioned here do not match exactly with those reported by P. Greenfield et al. in "On Culture and Equivalences," J. Bruner et al., eds., *Studies in Cognitive Growth* (New York: Wiley, 1968), pp. 270–318. In fact, Greenfield suggests the importance to distinguish cultures both in terms of the richness of their vocabulary at one level of its structure and of the numbers of levels of generality they use.

32. For a development of this theme, see J. Gay and M. Cole, *op. cit.*, Chapter 10.

33. *Ibid.*, p. 33.

34. See R. Clignet, "The Legacy and Meaning of Assimilation, West African Education System, Its Meaning and Ambiguities," *Comparative Education Review*, Vol. 12, 1968, pp. 56–57.

35. J. Herndon, *op. cit.*, pp. 92–93.

36. P. Bourdieu and J. C. Passeron, *Les Heritiers, op. cit.*, p. 97.

37. H. Becker et al., *op. cit.*, pp. 116–121, 169–174.

38. See R. Clignet, "Bilan de l'orientation des eleves de la classe de 5eme," (Abidjan, 1959) Mimeographed. However, the classes where the two populations were the most mixed were the "best" classical and modern sections of the institution. As a result it is difficult to determine whether the higher achievement of African students in this context was the result of their greater interaction with European pupils or of their initial self selectivity. We are once more confronted with the problem of deciding whether pedagogical communication is the mere product of the differential recruitment of actors or follows a logical development of its own.

39. For a more systematic discussion of this theme, see G. Cain and H. Watts, "Problems in Making Policy Inferences from the Coleman Report," *American Sociological Review*, Vol. 35, 1970, pp. 228–241 and the rejoinder of Coleman himself, pp. 242–248.

40. C. Testaniere, "Chahut traditionnel et chahut anomique," *Revue Francaise de sociologie*, Vol. 9, 1968, pp. 25–37.

41. See D. Entwistle, "Developmental Socio Linguistics of Inner City Children," *American Journal of Sociology*, Vol. 74, No. 3, 1968, pp. 37–49.

42. See P. Bourdieu and J. C. Passeron, *La Reproduction, op. cit.*, most specially Chapter 2.

43. E. Hunter, *Blackboard Jungle* (New York: Simon and Schuster, 1954).

44. W. Ryan, *Blaming the Victim* (New York: Vintage, 1971).

45. R. Rosenthal and L. Jackson, *Pygmalion in the Classroom* (New York: Holt, Rinehart and Winston, 1968).

46. J. Herndon, *op. cit.*, Chapters 44 and 45.

47. R. Lippitt and R. White "An Experimental Study of Leadership and Group Life," in W. W. Charters and N. Gage eds., *Readings in the Social Psychology of Education* (Boston: Allyn and Bacon, 1962), pp. 141–52.

48. Of course this analysis remains incomplete, for the various aspects of learning and teaching activities are not necessarily internally consistent. The orientations underlying the content of a curriculum and those underlying what students learn effectively may be parallel while teaching and learning styles are complementary. The teaching of history could offer a case in point in this regard. What teachers teach and what students

learn in this discipline may both be dominated by assimilation-based principles. Yet the procedures used by teachers in their style may be still accommodation oriented.

49. A. S. Neill, *Summerhill* (New York: Hart, 1960).

50. For a summary of the findings of the researches undertaken in this field, see W. J. McKeachie, "Procedures and Techniques of Training: A Survey of Experimental Studies," in N. Sanford ed., *The American College* (New York: Wiley, 1962), pp. 312–364.

51. See R. Churchill and S. Baskin, "Experiment of Independent Study," as quoted by W. J. McKeachie, *op. cit.,* p. 340.

52. As quoted by R. Anderson, "Learning in Discussion: A Resume of the Authoritarian Democratic Studies," in W. W. Charters and N. Gage, eds., *op. cit.* 1962), pp. 153–161.

53. H. Guetzkow, E. Kelly, and W. McKeachie, "An Experimental Comparison of Recitation Discussion and Tutorial Methods in College Teachings," *Journal of Educational Psychology,* Vol. 45, 1954, pp. 193–209.

54. As an example of how ideologies lead authors to rediscover America, see J. Holt, *How Children Learn* (New York: Putnam, 1957); and *How Children Fail* (New York: Putnam, 1966). Indeed Holt does not seem to realize that his conclusions have been reached before by educators who had a better sense of experimentation and were thus able to propose more differentiated solutions.

55. See M. Cole et. al., *The Cultural Context of Learning and Thinking* (New York: Basic Books, 1971), Conclusion. In this interesting study, however, the authors argue that almost *all* experimental situations are nonsocial in the sense that their successful solution requires manipulations of objects or words abstracted from context rather than relating with people (p. 22). Yet, this assertion is perhaps more characteristic of a western trained objective scientist than of his subjects. There is, after all, a serious amount of literature to suggest that even in the west, social interaction between experimenters and subjects affects the outcome of experiments.

56. See J. Barbichon, "La diffusion des connaissances scientifiques et techniques, dans le public," *Journal of Social Issues,* Vol. 24, 1968, pp. 135–155.

57. See S. Moscovici and B. Rialan, "La diffusion des connaissances scientifiques et techniques," (Paris: CERP, 1962). Mimeographed.

58. See R. Wilkinson, *The Prefects,* (Oxford: Oxford University Press, 1964) p. 122. See also D. Ward, "The Public School and Industry in Britain After 1870," *Journal of Contemporary History,* Vol. 2, pp. 37–52.

59. H. Becker et al., *op. cit.,* Chapter XVI.

60. See L. Murphy and E. Raushenbush, *Achievement in the College Years* (New York: Harper, 1962). See also M. Freedman, "Studies of College Alumni," in N. Sanford, *op. cit.,* pp. 847–886.

61. See M. Armer and R. Yontz, "Western Education and Modernity," *American Journal of Sociology*, Vol. 76, 1971, pp. 604–626.

62. R. Clignet and P. Foster, *op. cit.*, Chapter 5, 6.

63. All the following discussion is, in effect, derived from a critical evaluation of I. Illich's piece, "School Must Be Abolished," *The New York Review of Books*, Vol. 15, No. 1, July 1970.

64. J. Holt and P. Goodman are the most vocal representatives of this school.

65. The history of many progressive schools offers a case in point. For example, Montessori schools, which are initially designed for lower-class children, did not become legitimized before they changed their clientele and catered primarily to the needs of intellectual middle classes as they do now in this country.

66. Quotation given without reference at the end of the article of B. Beck and H. Becker, "Modest Proposals for Graduate Programs in Sociology," *The American Sociologist*, Vol. 4, 1969, pp. 227–234.

10

GRADES, EXAMINATIONS, AND OTHER CHECKPOINTS AS MECHANISMS OF SOCIAL CONTROL

The occupational liberty of teachers affects not only their ability to define the content and the form of the communication they establish with students, but also their legitimized power of evaluating the effectiveness of such a communication. The certifying functions that enter into the definition of teaching activities limit and shape the liberty individual students may derive from their academic experiences.

These functions are increasingly challenged, and administrators as well as teachers are frequently accused of being insensitive to the distinctions that should be entered between schooling and education, or between drilling and education.[1] The use of examinations, for instance, is said to minimize the relationships between the individual qualities or efforts displayed by students and the roles for which their formal schooling prepares them. A century ago Marx protested against the fact that "examinations were nothing but a bureaucratic form of christening knowledge and endowing it with sacred characteristics."[2]

Before undertaking a systematic criticism of the functions currently served by examinations, we must determine how the mechanisms by which teachers evaluate their students vary with the characteristics of an educational system and with the profile of the society at large. We must also examine how the conflicting interpretations that teachers and students make of grades and examinations tend to create an "anomic" system of interaction and to induce patterns of behavior and interaction analogous to those that the use of money generates among individuals and social groups in the context of the society at large.

Determinants of the Growth and the Differentiation of Evaluation Systems. Institutionalization of academic evaluation systems does not emerge before societies and their educational institutions reach a certain level of complexity. Ancient Greece, with its collection of autonomous schools and independent teachers, had no examination system. Although examinations did exist during the Middle Ages and some of them were reputed to be tough (Robert de Sorbon in France complained that university examiners were tougher than those of the Last Judgment), they were not institutionalized before the end of the thirteenth century.[3] Not until the end of the Napoleonic reign in France did the higher Council of National Education define professions to which access should be determined by examinations. For obvious reasons the first profession to be affected by such regulations was teaching itself.[4]

In brief, the emergence of examinations follows the institutionalization of the teaching force and its differentiation from other occupational categories. As soon as this differentiation takes place, educators are in a position to regulate school outputs. The institutionalization of examinations, however, does not necessarily eliminate variations in the functions they serve and in the techniques by which they are administered. With increases in the size of the student population and with growing divergences in the purposes served by varying types of educational institutions, there is a parallel increase in the differentiation of the mechanisms of social control schools use to evaluate the relative socialization of their students. These mechanisms are two-fold: certification systems and guidance and counselling activities.

Distinction between Guidance and Certification Activities. The purposes of guidance and certification activities are different, and they are supported by varying organizational structures. First, although the function of certification is merely to allow or prevent the entry of an individual into the higher rungs of a particular branch of the academic system, guidance eventually ensures the redistribution of school populations among a variety of educational or occupational enterprises. The model underlying certification is anthropological, of the "yes–no" type; that corresponding to guidance activities is sociological, of the "more-

or-less" variety, since it aims at adjusting eventual disparities between educational demand and supply or between individual educational orientations and relevant societal expectations.

The forms of evaluation pursued by examiners and counsellors are also different. The former are concerned with an assessment of the absolute knowledge or the ability of candidates in a particular discipline or set of disciplines. The latter are expected to take into account the variety of differential abilities, knowledges, motivations, and general level of information of their clients. Certification is specific and school-centered since it minimizes problems posed by the differing motivations, attitudes, or cognitive skills of individual students. Guidance and counselling are diffuse since they are supposed to reconcile potential strains between individual educational orientations and the various requirements of school systems.

Although the population subject of examinations is defined according to universalistic criteria, the clientele of counsellors is selectively recruited among subpopulations most likely to experience conflicts between their own orientations and those of the educational milieu. At least in the early stages of the development of the profession, counsellors work only with "problem students."

Contrasts in the functions of certifying and guidance activities are associated with parallel disparities in their organizational structures. While certifying is usually not performed by a specialized personnel, counsellors constitute a particular category of personnel whose patterns of recruitment and socialization differ from those of other segments of the educational environment. The emergence of counselling as a legitimate full-time activity is relatively recent. It does not occur as long as tensions between the educational aspirations of the school populations and the corresponding societal sets of expectations remain low. Tensions reach a critical point because of political factors and, for instance, because of conflicts among social classes over the current system of allocation of educational amenities. In France, for example, counselling became recognized as a full-time educational activity during the Popular Front in 1936 when the prevailing ideology stressed the significance of the equalizing functions that French schools should perform. Tensions also reach a critical point because of specific economic and technological developments. In the United States counselling has become more salient as a result of the frustrations experienced by political elites after the launching of the first Russian satellite. Although it was initially a concrete enterprise of talent hunting, modes of interaction among

social classes or between classes and educational institutions trans-
formed this hunt for talent into a hunt for academic failures and shortcomings.

Affected by the recent character of the distinction introduced among
guidance, teaching, and certifying activities, the recruitment of full-
time counsellors is equally influenced by the marginal character of the
subpopulations they are supposed to serve. Because the status attached
to a bureaucratic role declines as it is more recent and as its clientele is
more marginal, the prestige attached to counselling is often limited.
Most often recruited in the ranks of primary school teachers, French
counsellors, for example, have a limited influence on the educational
decisions of the secondary school personnel. In fact, the low position
frequently occupied by counsellors in the educational power structure
affects the significance of their functions. The desire to be recognized
as professionals and to achieve a status comparable to regularly accre-
dited teachers induces American counsellors to view their activities as
school-centered rather than as client-centered.[5]

Determinants of Variations in the Forms of Examinations. Because both
certifying and guidance activities depend upon academic grades, distinctions between internal and external examinations become indispensable. Administered within the school, internal examinations are
based upon the syllabus, sanction the dependence of students upon
particular teachers, and are eventually instrumental in the definition of
the counsellor's clientele. External examinations are more universalistic
in content, and they are more likely to sanction the dependence of
students upon educational institutions taken *in toto*.[6]

Mobility, examinations, and guidance. The significance of external examinations depends upon the extent and the forms of mobility available in
the society at large. As a social system is more rigid and as it offers
fewer alternative patterns of mobility, the access to higher education or
to the most rewarding status of the occupational structure becomes
more dependent upon the certifying functions of its schools and hence
upon external examinations.

These certifying functions are particularly visible in countries characterized by sponsored-mobility systems such as Great Britain, France
and its satellites, or traditional China. The monolithic character of
elites limits the number of channels of upward mobility. Correspondingly, occupational placement is almost entirely determined by
individual performances on examinations administered by the educa-

---

tional institutions themselves, and results obtained to a particular examination are frequently more significant determinants of occupational achievement than performance on the job. Such examinations determine the level at which an individual not only enters but also moves in the labor market. For example, many French collective-bargaining agreements define the various skill levels of a particular branch of activity as much in terms of the diplomas acquired by an individual as in terms of what he is able to do in his firm. Similarly, in traditional China civil servants remained under the control of schools during their entire career, and the hierarchy of academic successes commanded the hierarchy of occupational achievements.[7]

The significance of the certifying role performed by educational authorities is enhanced by the competitive nature of most examinations. Often the number of successful candidates is predetermined and authorities are entitled to pass a number of students lower than this "ideal," should they think that the quality of candidates is actually below their expectations. In addition, the competitive nature of French examinations traditionally introduces a rather elaborate system of rankings, with a number of coefficients varying with disciplines and a broad range of grades (the basic scale of grades used to vary from 0 to 20 instead of 0 to 4 in the United States), the ultimate result being to make individual occupational fates dependent upon minimal academic differences. The social importance thus accorded to academic competition is the translation of the Noble tradition of "heroism" that Jesuits imposed upon early French schools. This heroism manifests itself in the institutions of the Concours general, a purposeless competition opposing the best students of all *lycées*.[8]

The nature of examinations given in the context of sponsored-mobility systems is often more diffuse and pervasive than intended. In France, for example, examinations constitute opportunities for assessing not only the knowledge and the understanding of the candidates in specific fields of knowledge but also to evaluate their moral and aesthetic qualities against the relevant criteria established by the elites. "In seminaries," said Stendhal, "there is a way of eating cooked eggs which reveals the progress made by the candidate in his pious life" (and hence in his clerical career).[9] In this sense the examinations given by sponsored-mobility systems seem likely to reflect the existing social hierarchy, for differences in academic results constitute the symbolic translation of the rank ordering of the cognitive and cultural styles of groups occupying differing positions in the social ladder.

Students are expected to internalize sets of values that recognize the existence of a double hierarchy (that is of a hierarchy of students within rank-ordered educational institutions). To a large extent, individual self-esteem becomes a function of the position achieved by individuals within the various branches defined by academic authorities. Correspondingly, the sharing of successful examination experiences is conducive to marked forms of solidarity. French voluntary associations concerned with educational matters tend often to be weak and ineffective, but associations regrouping successful candidates to a particular examination are not. Regardless of age and occupational differences, the individuals who have successfully gone through this modern form of ordalie use the personal *tu* in their interaction instead of the most distant *vous*.[10] More important, the power of these associations affects both the life style of their members and the changes governments would introduce with regard to examinations.[11] For example, the *société des Agrégés* is able to define both the number of candidates to be admitted to this examination and the procedure by which they will be evaluated.

In contrast, the social structure of countries characterized by contest-mobility systems is more flexible and allows for a greater variety of channels of upward mobility. Guidance fulfills as significant an educational function as certification, at least at the intermediate rungs of the academic ladder. A more thorough investigation of guidance activities shows them, however, to serve primarily "cooling out" purposes.[12] Although prevailing ideologies tend to enhance individual aspirations toward higher education, the implementation of such aspirations is made problematic by the way in which they are interpreted and reinterpreted by counsellors. In fact, counsellors shape academic fate by allocating individuals to a particular form of training.[13]

Contrasts in extent and forms of mobility are associated with differential mechanisms of individual, educational, and occupational placement. In one case, accent is placed upon selectivity; in the other it is placed upon guidance. In France the elitist nature of prevailing educational philosophies and the lack of an ideology stressing mobility also leads guidance activities to be mostly concerned with the search of a "mechanical" fit between individual abilities and specific occupational slots. In the United States the emphasis placed upon mobility and upon a more diffuse mode of adaptation to the prevailing types of bureaucratic organizations induces counsellors to view mental health and personality factors as crucial elements of their diagnosis of their clients' academic future.[14]

Social classes and examinations.   The form of examinations tends often to advantage the upper segments of society. This is particularly true of oral examinations since the manipulation of language follows class lines quite closely and the criteria for success at such examinations reflect all the "ideal" qualities of the elite. Teachers rationalize the importance attached to verbal communication by arguing that it is less fragmentary and less specific than a written examination and that it facilitates a deeper understanding of the candidate. "It is a personality who tries to understand another personality," writes Bougle.[15] Yet this form of communication also induces a number of misunderstandings related both to differences in the social background of the examinee and the examiner and to the image of the elite the system imposes them.[16]

The hierarchy of the disciplines included in a curriculum may be the symbolic translation of the hierarchy of social groups. In French society "upper class" is deemed to be synonymous with natural grace, elegance and inborn gifts while "lower class" means hard and graceless work. This belief is paralleled by the preeminence accorded to the "noble" disciplines over those deemed to be more "pedestrian." Natural sciences, history, and geography belong to the latter category and count much less in the final destination of a candidate than "aristocratic" disciplines as French and mathematics. Candidates for teaching positions in "pedestrian" disciplines tend to be recruited from among the lower segments of society; noble and non-utilitarian disciplines such as mathematics are more likely to attract individuals originated from more fortunate circumstances. In mathematical examinations themselves educators often insist on the grace of the final report to be handled by the candidate. Professors and inspectors recommend: "It is perfectly acceptable to spend as much time writing the report on your problem as finding the solution." [17]

Access to the higher rungs of the academic ladder formally depends upon success in a prior examination, and success in such an examination is itself conditioned by the social background of the candidate. N. Bisseret observes that the rates of success to the examination sanctioning the end of the first year of liberal arts studies at the University of Paris vary with (*a*) whether the student is full time or parttime, (whether he is gainfully employed or not), (*b*) his age (whether he has been retarded in his academic progress), (*c*) his previous studies (more specifically, whether he has attended a classic *lycée*), and (*d*) whether he has ended his secondary studies with or without laude.[18] The more positive traits a student presents in terms of these four variables, the more likely he is to be admitted in the second year of the program. Three-quarters of the students having a positive trait on all four of these variables have been successful compared to only one-fourth having none or only one positive characteristic.

Although the percentages of success for individuals having a maximal number of these traits do not vary along social class lines, the distribution of these traits themselves is markedly influenced by the social background of the populations investigated. Only 15 percent of the lower-class students have all favorable traits against compared to more than 33 percent of their classmates coming from upper-class origins. Reciprocally, over 50 percent of students in the first category have none or only one of these traits compared to less than 25 percent of the upper-class students.

This is not a surprise, for upper-class students are more likely to gain access to the prestigious *lycées* and to begin their career at an early age. Similarly, the advantages accorded full-time students reflect the consummatory nature of academic experiences, indicating once more the privileges upper classes enjoy with regard to academic experiences. Further, the organization of academic work and of examinations is not independent either of a system of norms and values characteristic of limited segments of society. The academic calendar, although originally influenced by agricultural activities, currently corresponds more closely to the wishes of the leisure class than to those of less fortunate segments of an urban society. All these privileges present psychological implications that reinforce the effects of the differing positions occupied by students within the educational and social system. Thus students' self-evaluations tend to be more influenced by social class variables than by past academic performances, and lower class individuals internalize the handicaps resulting from their condition by underestimating their abilities as well as their chances of success.[19]

Insofar as in their current form, systems of examinations are often the academic translation of the existing system of social stratification, the validity of examinations is often dubious. In Kenya, for example, sharp contrasts have recently been observed not only in the overall performances of students derived from high- and low-cost Nairobi schools in the examinations concluding the cycle of primary studies but also in the relative discriminating power of the questions used in such examinations.[20]

About one-third of the items used to test mathematic abilities discriminate strongly the good from the poor male students enrolled in the high-cost schools of Nairobi, but the corresponding proportion drops to 8 percent for the population attending the low-cost institutions of that city. In other words, the nature of examinations provides the students of the best institutions with two distinct privileges: They are more likely to pass the tests than those of less fortunate institutions; the principle of justice is more frequently respected in the first than in the second instance. In short, the greater the psychological and social distance between the demands of an examination system and the cognitive or normative orientations of a student population, the more randomly, and hence the more unfairly, distributed will be the results of such a population.

Degree of centralization in educational institutions. The centralization of an educational system enables examiners to control the quantity and the quality of educational outputs by introducing deliberate variations in the severity both of the questions used in examinations and of the notations employed to assess individual performances. In addition, centralization enlarges the number of candidates and induces the development of impersonal and anonymous examination systems which allegedly facilitate the use of universalistic and objective criteria in the evaluation of students. In fact, educators aim at establishing "rational" parallels in the rank ordering of individuals and of occupations. This aim characterizes types of bureaucracies as different as those prevailing in traditional China and in modern France.[21] In both cases the centralized nature of educational institutions has enabled teachers to maximize the value socially assigned to the normative and cognitive skills they provide and sanction. The additional power educators derive from centralization helps them to convince elites that the "qualities" to be demonstrated by individuals in the educational and occupational contexts are identical. Thus in traditional China as in modern France, access to the top echelons of the elite depends upon the demonstration of literary skills whose relevance to strictly administrative tasks remains problematic. The social definition of these tasks emphasizes the importance of writing documents in a style analogous to that used in written examinations. In France, for example, the value depends upon the degree to which their authors follow the ideal logic inspired by the Hegelian plea for a thesis, followed by an anti-thesis, reconciled in a synthesis.

In contrast, decentralization is accompanied by marked variations in the forms and the techniques of examinations as well as by a constant increase in the number of these examinations. Thus certain American universities use both written and oral examinations. Others use only written evaluations with variations in the degree of openness in the questions and in the time allowed to candidates or in the documents they can consult. Decentralization also implies a more limited student-teacher ratio, which leads to the use of diffuse and particularistic criteria in the evaluation of candidates. Indeed a low student-teacher ratio induces patterns of intense social interaction between students and faculty, among students or among teachers. The limited contacts of French students with the faculty prevents them from sharing the viewpoint of their American counterparts who often seem to believe that "the faculty is favorably impressed by students who seem anxious about examinations." [22]

The particularistic value of the criteria used for evaluating candidates enhances the vulnerability of the decentralized teaching force to public pressures and makes examinations easy to challenge, for example.[23] Further, criticisms of examinations in a centralized organization pertain more to the administration than to the principle of the evaluation, and they vary in intensity with the degree of "protectionism" displayed by educational authorities and hence with the severity of the notation systems in usage; by contrast, it is more the principle of examinations itself which is likely to be at stake in a decentralized self-supporting educational system. This situation results from the role conflicts experienced by teachers who act both as professionals and as clients of their students.

This role conflict is particularly manifest as there is a rise in the demand for education and therefore in educational aspirations. Since their survival depends in part upon the satisfaction of their clientele, "decentralized" teachers are tempted to comply with the aspirations of their students and to process them toward higher educational and occupational positions. As they do so, however, they may jeopardize the standing their school occupies in comparison with similar educational institutions, or the influence they claim to exert on the labor market, which may lower the quality of the student population they will attract later on.

Responses to these role conflicts are oblique; for example, the recent increase in the American graduate school population seems to be often associated with an increase in the number of master's degrees delivered but with a correspondingly sharp decline in the symbolic significance attached to this examination, which becomes a "cooling out" mechanism at a higher level.[24] The dilemmas experienced by the teachers of centralized systems are different since they recruit their own graduates or leave to their students themselves the difficult task of selling the skills acquired during their academic experience. But French educators have become more overtly concerned with the dangers of what they call "academic inflation." After the events of May 1968 the former dean of the Law School of Paris, Georges Vedel, compared the newly planned types of examination to the worthless paper money of 1793 and argued that the new plan would transform universities into factories of unemployment, reinforcing the existing privileges of the upper classes.[25]

Finally, contrasts between centralized and decentralized institutions affect the form of academic competition experienced by students. While French individuals tend to evaluate themselves according to a single monolithic hierarchy, their counterparts in decentralized countries are more prone to compare the institutions from which they graduate. This leads them to try their chances in the context of an ever increasing number of institutions. By 1955 the average male student who tried to secure a place in a British university was estimated to have applied to 2.1 institutions, and for his female counterpart the corresponding figure was 2.5. The constant increase in the number and variety of examinations presented by British secondary pupils may exert a negative effect on the intellectual progress of sixth-form students, who earlier and earlier in the academic year begin to revise and polish the variety of subject matters demanded by the various institutions into which they wish to be admitted.[26]

Organization of academic institutions and examinations. Institutions can be distinguished from one another in terms of their "feeding" functions. In a highly selective country like France certain schools are known as *boîtes à bachot* or *boîtes à concours,* and their overt aim is to push as large a number as possible of candidates over specific academic hurdles, which obliges them to screen carefully incoming students since their own standing depends upon their success rates. The situation is the same in the United States where certain public or private high schools derive their status from the fact that they act as regular feeders to the most prestigious colleges of the country. Such functions lead these schools to accept "low-risk" candidates and to use guidance as the mechanism appropriate for enhancing or at least maintaining their reputation. This is achieved through a manipulation of the information given to students about the variety of courses offered to them as well as through an interpretation of their personality and academic profiles by counsellors.[27] To sum up, in the French, as in the American context, the purpose of examinations and guidance is perhaps to control the information, the knowledge, or the abilities of individual students, but it is also to improve the bargaining positions that educational institutions occupy vis-a-vis one another.

Second, the importance of examinations depends upon the hierarchies of academic functions, as defined by the teaching force itself. Thus it can be argued that the separation of research and teaching activities and the specialization of personnel into either one of these branches reinforces the prestige attached to the certifying functions of the school. Variations in the occurrence and duration of examinations reflect the relative stress placed upon certifying functions. In France examinations at the end of secondary studies usually take place twice a year, and candidates are expected to write on four disciplines for four hours each. As one moves up the ladder, examinations last longer and are less frequent. The highest examination in the law school takes place every other year, and the written parts last several full days.[28] Further, close records are kept of past examinations in order to enable teachers and students to have a "jurisprudence" of the questions asked and to enable the top of the hierarchy to pinpoint the strengths and weaknesses of candidates as well to measure the changes that have occurred over time in this respect.

Conversely, whenever research is more highly evaluated than teaching because it offers better payoffs in terms of obtaining grants, pay raises, and promotions, certifying functions tend to be minimized, particularly in countries where the majority of educational institutions are self-supported. For example, American colleges accord a low symbolic value to examinations, as witnessed by their high frequency and short duration as well as by the limited amount of feedback informations given to students on their performance.

Third, the form of the examination is related to the history of educational institutions. The ideal form of the examination in the French system is influenced by both scholastic and Hegelian philosophies, and the model form of outline often influences the final evaluation of the copy more than its content.[29] The influence of the scholastic and hence dogmatic philosophy is also apparent in the high dependence upon the teacher viewed both as an exclusive source of information and as an absolute and particularistic judge. The use of library facilities in France has been long enough a privilege exclusively reserved for individuals who have reached the highest rungs of higher education, and students could only repeat the information they had obtained from their particular instructor. Thus the highly assimilationist type of teaching which goes with a French type of centralization induces a similarly assimilationist type of examination. The dissertation on a predefined theme prevents an adequate measurement of the independent learning activities of the candidate. Because they are unable to assess the efficiency of the pedagogical communications, teachers tend to evaluate a large number of papers as mediocre; that is, as "not very wrong." [30]

By contrast, the multiplicity of forms of examinations practiced by American schools probably reflects the relatively strong historical development of educational psychology in that country, with its critical evaluation of classic forms of examination. Thus, the use of sentence-completion materials or of case studies reflects the preference given by psychologists to objective tests over essay examinations.

The strong influence historical factors exert on the forms of examination probably accounts for the discrepancies between the style of interaction prevailing in evaluation situations within the educational sphere, and that which characterizes other institutions. While the Protestant ethic has affected patterns of economic organization through its stress upon individualism, it has failed to penetrate Catholic-oriented educational institutions. Indeed, Catholic orientations still underlie examinations that require a strong dependence of students toward examiners; they are symbolically equivalent to confessions. As Protestant values pervade an increasing number of institutions, the Catholic aspects of educational activities are increasingly vulnerable to criticisms.

In fact, criticisms of examinations have occurred earlier and been more intense in Protestant than in Catholic countries. Many current reforms of grades and examinations are "protestant" in their orientations in that they aim at a transfer of the burden of proof from students to teachers and propose that students should choose not only their evaluators but also the subject of the examination and its form.[31] These reforms, however, are suggested at a time when economic organizations become more bureaucratic, more centralized and tend to be "Catholic" again. One might wonder accordingly whether the effects of the dialectics between Catholicism and Protestantism, as they take place in the educational setting, are strong enough to overcome functional links between schools and other basic societal institutions. In short, one might speculate about the chances of examination reforms since the direction and the timing of the specific changes at which they aim, conflict with the evolution of other institutional contexts.

Reactions of School Actors to Examinations. The manipulation of grades induces teachers to evaluate themselves *vis-a-vis* peers and in certain cases, such as the oral examination of the doctoral dissertation, the formulation of questions by evaluators facilitates the probing of colleagues as much as the assessment of the candidate himself. More generally teachers are sometimes prone to use "flunking" for bringing back deviant colleagues in the mainstream of the organization, for the massive failure of *his* candidates cannot but induce a professor to be more sensitive to the expectations and orientations of his peers. This sensitivity will be particularly manifest in cases where the pay of individual teachers is made dependent upon the academic performances of his students. Such a situation existed in England between 1863 and 1897. It also characterized certain educational scenes in English-speaking Africa. Thus the educational code of Sierra Leone in 1870 provided for a "result" grants of sixpence for each pass in an examination in the three "R's." [32] For similar reasons examinations enable entire schools to evaluate their relative standing in the educational marketplace. [33]

It is, however, on the fate of students that examinations exert the most powerful influence. [34] They condition the basic nature and the skill level of the occupations in which students ultimately enter, and this function becomes more manifest with the bureaucratization of the society at large. Grades also condition how long a student remains in the system. This of course, results from the close association between the social value allocated to a particular occupation and the length of studies required to be admitted into that occupation. In the United States academic performances in college determine not only whether an individual will enter graduate programs but also the specific field he may enter. Although 44 percent of seniors beginning graduate studies in English belong to the top fifth of the college population academically, only 13 percent of their counterparts entering graduate schools of business fall into such a category. [35] Examinations also condition the perpetuation of the student status because the allocation of fellowships and scholarships depends upon academic criteria. This seems to characterize all societies regardless of their political organizations. Thus, no later than 1969, the Chinese journal *pa-yi pao* complained "the struggle for grades is the fate of the student. Texts and examinations are the Bibles of the teachers. The grades have become the center of all educational work."

Grades and examinations influence student participation in academic voluntary associations. In the United States the hierarchy of fraternities and sororities is not independent of the hierarchy of academic grades, and access to the most prestigious of these associations necessitates highest grade point averages. [36] Recruitment into student political office is also determined at least partly by grade average. Although student participation in university government is more limited in a country like France, it is similarly affected by academic success. Student self-evaluation influences the range of their choices with regard to leisure activities and is therefore a crucial determinant of their timetables. Similarly administrative and political roles are often enough ascribed to *majors,* students who pass an examination with the highest grade point averages.[37]

Examinations affect the choices a student can make in his emotional life. In the United States grades and examinations determine the range of partners available to an individual in the context of dating activities. A number of sanctions may be exerted on students who date "irresponsible" partners.[38] In France, where the delimitation of a student's field of eligible partners is less institutionalized or socially sanctioned, the severity of academic competition still determines the amount of time and energy a student can spend in the pursuit of a better romantic status. The severity of the competition underlying access to the most rewarding *Grandes Écoles* forbids candidates from having any kind of emotional involvement. This repression probably accounts for the highly romantic nature of many novels dealing with adolescent sentimental attachment. The "ideal" character of Yvonne de Galais in *The Wanderer,* of *Fermina Marquez* in the novel of the same name, of Florence in *Comme le temps passe* reflects the repression of feelings experienced by many French students.[39] Because of the limitations imposed upon them by their academic life, the love stories of French students have often the nostalgic flavor of past summers and sunny seasons.

Through examinations and grades educators are able to exert a diffuse control over their students, which is often reflected in the very vocabulary they use to describe the performances of examinees: in France failing students are reported to "corrupt," to "destroy," to "rape" the language or ideas taught.[40] This reflects the overall subordinate position of students who tend correspondingly to evaluate their academic experiences by reference to examinations rather than by reference to their occupational future. This attitude persists even at the highest rungs of the ladder when ultimate occupational choices are made. Becker shows how freshmen medical students in the United States are unable to relate their professional aspirations and expectations to their daily routines and are ultimately obliged to retreat from an unspecific and idealistic perspective into a pragmatic short-term approach. They define their learning activities in terms of "what they think the faculty wants them to learn." [41]

Examinations and Teacher-Student Relations. Like other subordinate groups, students want the exercise of power and authority exerted upon them to be predictable. They want a certain rationality in the distribution of rewards to which they aspire and a clear definition of the interaction between their behavior and the rewards they can legitimately expect—hence the considerable amount of time and energy that they spend to guess the "real" nature of the criteria used by teachers to evaluate them. This search implies frequent contacts with previous cohorts of students already exposed to a particular teacher or to his peers. This search also implies incessant bargaining processes to obtain from the teacher a clearer definition of his criteria for evaluating one particular examination; for example this search frequently involves material details and pertains to the number of pages to be covered in which book and to the bonuses or penalties associated with concrete aspects of a performance such as spelling, bibliography items, etc.

This quest for predictability is in effect an attempt at limiting the control of one particular examiner, for students are always confronted with the problem of choosing a variety of alternative rewards and of adjusting their productivity in such a way that their efforts in a particular field yield the highest returns. Students attempt to limit the control of one examiner not only because examiners compete with one another in their demands but also because they are unable to systematically reward each increment of effort by a commensurable increment in their own rewards (the range of grades is predetermined). Correspondingly, while teachers expect their students to entertain an unlimited appetite for additional knowledge and skills, the system of examinations limits the investments a student is willing to make in a particular field. Not only must the student learn how to satisfy the succession of demands developed at different times by differing examiners, he must also adjust his production to the grades that he needs.

Examinations and Interaction among Students. The dependence that binds student to teacher through examination systems affects as well the network of interaction among students themselves. In the United States the dependence of individuals' educational fate upon academic achievement leads groups of students to build mechanisms to hold their members in line. Such groups keep archives of examinations, have informal tutoring techniques to help their members achieve a reasonable level of performance, are likely to exert negative sanctions on "rate busters" or on those who cannot reach a minimal level of performance. Indeed, students are afraid that deviations from the norms they establish will modify the implicit contract imposed upon them by their teachers. This fear leads the relationships established between students to be ambivalent. In the United States, students are eager to communicate with one another only insofar as the outcome of the interaction is likely to enhance individual self-esteem and deplete that of others. "The reason individual C was telling individual B how much he had read was to make him anxious rather than to tell him about his own accomplishment." [42] It is in this sense that students are less optimistic than their teachers as to the effect of socialization by peers.[43]

Such mechanisms are less likely to develop in the context of the French system. The greater dependence of students on teachers compartmentalizes the competition among pupils and is compensated for by a strong intraclass solidarity. First, good students are often expected to be the leaders of *chahut* (hazing), which enables them to demonstrate that their academic abilities do not necessarily make them stooges of the system.[44] Second, the most competitive examinations are followed by dionysiac rites which forge anew the solidarity of students and divert their potential frustrations against the society at large. The novel *Les copains* by Jules Romain illustrates the amount of ingenuity French candidates to a *grande ecole* can display to ridicule established institutions and make fun of themselves.[45] Third, dependence on teachers is often counteracted by the elaboration of a show in which teachers themselves are caricatured and ridiculed to demonstrate the egalitarian character of the institution and to induce distinctions between teachers as roles and as persons.

To sum up, I have suggested that educational systems are comprised of differing subcultures that have their own specific definition of the goals to be achieved through academic experiences and of the means that may be used to attain such goals.

Anomic Tendencies of Examination Systems.   Examinations involve anomic aspects, which are associated with the emergence of particular patterns of adjustment corresponding to the typology established by Merton.[46] Examination systems are often anomic mainly because there is no consensus among the main actors of the educational scene as to the definition of the most "valuable things" of the system.

Differentiation of disciplines induces marked contrasts as to what deserves a maximal grade. In the social sciences, teachers seem to base their evaluation on the learning activities of a student but their counterparts in physical sciences seem to base their evaluation on his performance. In the first case the value of the "basic grade unit" is rarely

The School as a Microcosm

fixed and predetermined, whereas it tends to have a more "universalistic" significance in physical sciences.[47] Within a same discipline varying systems are used; some teachers give preeminence to critical skills, others stress the importance of erudition. "Every year, there is a fashion and one finds in the examination papers the dummy caricature of the ideas taught by such or such a professor."

Anomie may also be precipitated by conflicts in the manifest and latent demands of teachers. In the *Red and the Black*, Julien Sorel as a future priest is expected to know how to speak and write Latin fluently. Yet, Sorel is trapped by his examiner, who takes advantage of his skill in Latin to induce him to discuss the merits of Horace's poetry, which is considered to be immoral. Instead of passing the examination as the best student of the seminary (a position to which he should be entitled in view of both his skill in Latin and the display of his general culture), Sorel is ultimately admitted with the lowest rank of his entire class.[48]

Cleavages opposing teachers to students in this respect are even

Table 23. Student and Faculty Perceptions of the Functions of Examinations (Percentage Distribution) [a]

Function	Respondents Reporting Functions as Very or Fairly Characteristic of Examinations	
	Students	Faculty
Objective evaluation of ability	67	73
Objective evaluation of knowledge	77	86
Attempt to make student organize thinking	73	82
Attempt to get student to study intensively	82	95
Method of weeding out incompetents	59	77
Method of weeding out undesirable personalities	36	9
Initiation rite	41	41
Attempt to depersonalize evaluation of students	55	73
Test of student's ability to handle stress	55	45

[a] Derived from D. Mechanic, *Students Under Stress* (Glencoe, The Free Press, 1963) p. 54.

greater. Students often view the valuable things offered by examiners as inaccessible in view of the rules of the game imposed upon them. Further, their potential frustrations in this respect are reinforced by the very institutionalization of learning and teaching models. As it is, teachers do not interpret the failure of their students in terms of their own shortcomings. Rather, they view all disruptions in pedagogical communication (as revealed by bad examination papers) as produced by the deficiencies of students.[49] Students know this and conclude that their own success requires a narrowly defined pattern of behavior.

There are, however, more specific manifestations of the cleavages between these two groups of actors. Table 23 shows that while students are more likely to view examinations as mechanisms designed to get rid of individuals having personality problems (i.e., undesirable or unable to cope with anxiety), faculty is more likely to redefine examinations as attempts to evaluate more objectively the abilities and knowledges of candidates.

Discrepancies also pertain to the definition of the means most likely to yield the highest rewards. While professors attach a greater importance to intelligence and organization, students are more likely to emphasize the influence exerted by the appearances of being hard working, by "throwing the bull," or simply by the amount of preparation (Table 24). In fact, teachers tend to evaluate examinations in terms of

Table 24. Student and Faculty Perception of the Most Significant Determinants of Individual Failure or Success to Examinations (Percentage Distribution) [a]

	Students	Professors
Ability to deal with anxiety	32	36
Ability to deal with knowledge	73	86
Ability to deal with intelligence	14	27
Well-liked personality	14	0
Amount of preparation	55	41
Ability to convey a hard-working image	27	14
Ability to "throw the bull"	23	0
Demonstration of research competence	23	18
Organization	41	73
Other	—	9

[a] Derived from D. Mechanic, *Students Under Stress* (Glencoe, The Free Press, 1963), p. 63.

the external qualities of the "finished product" presented to them, since these qualities determine the amount of time spent on each copy.[50] In contrast, students attach more significance to the real or apparent efforts invested in the venture. For example, they believe that "they want you to write lengthy and pedantic answers, to drop names, etc." The students interviewed by Mechanic are also likely to attribute a high importance to the role of nonobjective factors in the outcome of examinations. Three-quarters of his respondents argue that the faculty is favorably impressed by candidates who seem anxious about examinations. They also tend to believe that candidates well liked by teachers have more chances than their less fortunate peers and that examinations results are predetermined.[51]

However, the anomic nature of the academic examination situation is also related to the external functions of schools, that is, to the problematic nature of the linkage of academic experience with occupational and more generally adult roles.[52] As modernization proceeds the structure of the labor market is increasingly universalistic and the ideology underlying universalistic achievement-based orientations stresses the significance of equality in job opportunities. Insofar as there is still a rank ordering of occupations and "truck driving is not defined as another kind of success that potential nuclear physicists are likely to prefer," the functioning of the labor market is obviously dominated by conflicts and inconsistencies in the definitions of successful individual roles.[53] Thus students adopt a cynical view of examinations, for they realize that good grades are necessary but insufficient determinants of occupational success.

The ensuing vulnerability of schools to inconsistencies in the values assigned to occupational achievement is reinforced by the fact that the rewards derived from success to examinations belong to the future and are therefore more symbolic than real. As a result students are tempted to shift their attention away from the achievement symbols of grades and examinations each time they do not give them a satisfactory self-evaluation. Correspondingly, they become attracted by ascriptive symbols of adulthood such as owning a car, frequent dating, smoking. However, schools also hold inconsistent positions since, exalting the values of youth, they still equate the inferiority of students (viewed as necessary for the transmission of knowledge) with the inferiority of the young.[54]

Responses to Educational Anomie.   The patterns of deviant adjustment to educational institutions tend to be similar to those observed by Merton in the society at large. *Innovation*, the first of these patterns, occurs when the individual has assimilated the cultural emphasis upon the goal without internalizing the institutional norms governing means for its attainment. Innovation manifests itself in the variety of cheating forms displayed by students. Many medical students, for instance, cut short certain procedural tasks expected from them and report in their final results what they are supposed to find, either by taking their samples from classmates or by looking for materials outside the official source.[55] Innovation also entails the manipulation of the examiner's judgment either by catering to his prejudice or by getting to know him personally. In the students' culture this is known as "brown nosing," with the notion that it is a real art and as such might carry positive as well as negative effects on the desired goal.

Ritualism involves the abandoning or scaling down of the lofty cultural goals while one continues to abide almost compulsively by institutional norms. As indicated by Merton, it is a response to a situation that appears threatening and induces distrust. In the educational context, Bourdieu and Mechanic note that students often transform seemingly rational procedures into magical rites.[56] Such are the revisions of the material during the entire night preceeding the examination, and note-taking activities which are more frequently, in Bourdieu's words, a technique of spiritual comfort than a rational accumulation of knowledge and information. In the same vein, an informant of Becker reports: "I have gone into classes where that's all you do, memorize and memorize . . . and then you go in and take the final, everything you have memorized, and then you forget it. You walk out of class and your mind is purged perfectly clean. Someone asks you the next week what you learned in the class and you could not tell them anything because you did not learn anything." [57]

Even more obviously ritualistic is the behavior of some students who seek a private escape from the dangers and frustrations inherent in the competition for highly scarce good grades and cling all the more closely to the safe routine of presenting a paper with the most refined external appearances (superb script, titles underlined). Of course, the uttermost form of ritualism along these lines is displayed in the highly religious rites which precedes or follow examinations. Bourdieu notes the presence of many *exvotos* in French cathedrals which ask for the assistance of the Holy Virgin or thank her for their contributions.[58] Similarly, Mechanic indicates the importance that candidates to examinations attach to the possession of "fetishes." "Older students enclose three red rocks in the envelope, saying that these were good luck charms. . . . I lost mine . . . and went running around the house trying to find some. . . . I realized how superstitious and idiotic this was and yet, I still persisted." [59]

The third type of deviant pattern of adjustment to examinations is *retreatism.* Even though Stinchcombe labels the relevant forms of behavior as rebellion rather than as retreatism, he still shows how exclusion of the classroom, truancy, and flunking out of college programs are all closely related to feelings of academic alienation and notably to the beliefs that work in class is not rewarded and that grades are not important. Thus only 7 percent of the upper-class men of a Californian high school who have never skipped a class, have never been sent out of the class, and have not received a college flunk notice, believe that work in the classroom is not rewarded as against no less than 32 percent of their counterparts who have missed a class, have been sent out, and have been eliminated from college programs. Similarly, while 80 percent of the first category perceive academic grades as important to their personal satisfaction, this characterizes only 36 percent of the second group. [60]

Dropping out of the institution before the examination itself is of course the most extreme form of *retreatism.* It is usually preceeded by certain symptoms such as ceasing to do assigned work. "There just seems no point in studying. I mean I don't feel that I can learn anything and if I did it would not be worth it so the hell with it." [61] Students who start thinking that they cannot win resign themselves to losing. [62]

Finally, the last type of adjustment, *rebellion,* does emerge when individuals or groups of individuals strive toward a sharp modification of the cultural standards of educational success and regard accordingly the institutionalized system of grades as the barrier to the satisfaction of a definition of learning deemed to be more legitimate. Rebellion may characterize teachers, and in Great Britain, for example, some teachers of modern secondary schools themselves came to challenge the current system of control and allowed their pupils to come back into the competitive world of educational and social advancement from which they had been excluded at the age of 11. [63] Similarly, regardless of their specific origin, current student revolts in the United States have induced specific demands about existing grade and examination systems. [64]

Of course, the distribution of strategies is likely to vary with the relative position school populations occupy in the social structure. Thus Stinchcombe suggests that regardless of their social-class affiliations, girls are less likely to be "alienated" from the examination scene and more generally from their educational experiences taken *in toto,* since they are able to substitute matrimonial to occupational aspirations whenever their self-respect is jeopardized by academic failures. In short, they are less likely to "retreat" from the system. Similarly Stinchcombe also indicates that this alienation is more pronounced among lower-middle-class high school students than among their lower- or upper-class counterparts. It is indeed the former who are the most intensely subjected to the conflicting pressures resulting from a high committment to success and from actual failure. In contrast, upper-class parents are more able than their lower-middle-class counterparts to delay the pressures they exert on their offspring. Further, their better knowledge of the educational process enables them to select for their children an anxiety level nearer the optimum that is more likely to help them to succeed than to fail. Academic failure is more expected among working-class parents and their children than among lower-middle-class strata.[65] This latter subgroup is most sensitive to "anomic" experience and hence most likely to "retreat" from the school scene.

Crosscultural Variations in Responses to Anomie.   The emergence of any one of these strategies depends upon the dominant characteristics of the specific functions and structures of examination systems attached to the types of schools under study. For a long time, the centralized nature of French schools has made students more sensitive to what they consider to be the excessive scarcity of rewards offered to them than to conflicts between the goals and the means of academic institutions. The ensuing form of anomie induces both students and teachers to adopt two specific kinds of deviant patterns of innovation. There has been an increasing "black market" of examination subjects which are often sold to students before the examination. In addition, the dependence of the French teacher upon the success rates of his class leads him to adopt discriminatory treatments both toward his students and toward the various disciplines to be treated. Frequently, depending on their perceived ultimate educational status, French students do not get from their teachers the same amount of attention. Nor do they occupy comparable seats in the classroom.[66] Before the examination at the end of primary studies the teacher in *Village of the Vaucluse,* like most of her colleagues, stresses the mathematics curriculum much more than French, since it is possible to obtain the maximal amount of grade points for mathematics.[67] There is indeed an old motto which says that "20 [the maximum] is given only to God, 19 to his saints, 18 to the

professor's professor, 17 to the professor himself" which means that
students can at best obtain 16 in French composition.

By contrast, the anomic tendencies of the American system have obviously other origins and are consequently associated with other patterns of deviance. Thus, different subjects tend to be equally weighted,
and students are therefore exposed to a variety of equally strong conflicting pressures, in contrast to the French scene where there is an institutionalized hierarchy of disciplines and subdisciplines. The absence
of hierarchy among various disciplines, the particularistic nature of the
relationship established between students and teachers, and the vulnerability of teachers to public pressures induces many American students
to bargain over the grade. This follows naturally from the belief that
examinations are predetermined and that failures reflect the dislikes of
the faculty rather than the objective weakness of the candidate.[68] This
form of "innovation" has only begun to emerge recently in France, as a
result of the decline in the relative position occupied by teachers in the
French society. Its use, however, remains limited because of the anonymous character of most examinations.

Finally, the differential stress attached by French and American
schools to competition and equality should be associated with parallel
contrasts in the incidence of ritualism and retreatism among their respective student populations. In France the high importance attached
to competition should maximize the incidence of ritualistic patterns of
behavior and minimize the importance of retreatism. Since this last
form of deviance lowers competition, it is not necessarily viewed as
problematic, for it does not threaten the functioning of the system. In
the United States, conversely, retreatism and thus dropping out of
school has a more salient meaning since it challenges directly the egalitarian assumptions of the local educational system.

Examination Reforms. The main definition of educational institutions remains to mediate the socialization of students to cognitive skills,
and many critics attack examinations for interfering with this main objective.

The first type of examination reform consists in the mere abolition of
grades, which are deemed to have little relevance to the demands of a
particular job. But this is perhaps to forget a little too easily that employers often use particularistic criteria for hiring their employees. Initially at least, the purpose of examinations was in part to protect individuals from the abuse of power that any Establishment is likely to
commit.[69] Another argument advanced to support the abolition of aca-

demic grades is that the anxiety experienced by students prevents them from performing to the best of their abilities. Yet available evidence shows the effects of anxiety on examinations to be vague and contradictory.[70] Further, one of the functions of examinations is perhaps to socialize anxieties and to teach individuals how to use the corresponding energy for creative purposes.[71] The critical remarks made about examinations in this respect could very well reflect the anxieties of teachers, particularly so in Protestant countries where stress is placed upon individual responsibilities rather than upon dependence *vis-a-vis* others' judgments or in countries where the decentralized nature of educational institutions makes teachers vulnerable to public criticisms.

More valid seems to be the proposition that examinations should be disposed of because unsuited candidates tend to eliminate themselves from the competition without action on the part of the faculty. The French educational system tends to confirm in cultural terms the social privileges of the dominant segments of society, and this confirmation takes place as much through the choices of individual students themselves as through their academic performances. Lower-class pupils are unlikely to attend the most prestigious *lycées,* not because they have failed the corresponding examinations but because they have not taken them.[72] Yet auto-elimination from the educational scene may reflect a lack of proper information and may lead to the perpetuation of the existing social hierarchy, hence to dysfunctions in the distribution of elite roles.

A second type of reform consists of achieving a greater rationalization in the administration of grade systems. While certain educators have advocated the replacement of examinations by objective tests wherever possible, others (particularly in France) have been initially anxious to analyze the determinants of grade distributions and have proposed the development of a new science designed to deal with this particular problem.[73] This science, called *docimologie,* consists of examining the variance of such distributions in a variety of disciplines and of determining what factors are likely to enhance the homogeneity of grade curves. From the efforts of such scientists, have emerged systems of multiple examiners (whose optimal number varies by discipline) and attempts to decompose the performance of a student in a number of smaller cognitive units to diminish the halo effect observable among so many examiners. Docimologists, however, have hardly been involved in the examination of the influence exerted on grades by the interaction between the social characteristics of students and examiners. Nor have they been involved in the analysis of the influence exerted along similar lines by the relative position occupied by individual examiners in the educational structure. (Do young new Ph.D.'s grade harder than old timers, and what forces account for the corresponding differences?) In short, docimologists are only concerned with a greater rationalization of the system as it exists currently. Similar are the orientations of those who recommend a simplification of the grading procedure (using the pass/fail system) which ultimately meets the same problems.

A third type of reform advocates a greater personalization of grades and examinations systems. This personalization is twofold. First, it entails its "privatization," and in their real form grades are not communicated to university or college administrators.[74] Second, it also implies that examiners pay more attention to variations in the efforts and motivations of individual students. Yet this last type of reform would remain vain if it is not accompanied by a greater corresponding personalization of teaching procedures or at least by a greater "accommodation" in the classroom. Although in this perspective, schools should be more prone to accept the existence of variations in cultural cognitive styles and integrate these variations in their pedagogy, the corresponding reforms are doubtful as long as they are perceived as leading to "double-standard" rules both in teaching and evaluating.[75] But perhaps the time has come to recognize that the "reception" of the pedagogical communication varies along sex, cultural, and social lines and that single-standard rules perpetuate social inequalities rather than reduce them as they claim to do.

To conclude, examinations are not only means to control the knowledge or the information of the student population but also are the instruments by which a superordinate group attempts to impose its power upon a subordinate group. Examinations serve latent functions: they are a means of socializing individuals to power relations and to subsequent bargaining processes that exist in the society at large. The rule of the game is perhaps not so much to learn certain types of information as to learn how to cope with the adult power structure. The very definition of knowledge itself is social and its possession is closely related to the exercise of power.

NOTES AND REFERENCES

1. For a further discussion of this point, see I. Illich, *Schools Must be Abolished.*

2. K. Marx, "Kritik des Hegelschen Staatsgerecht," as quoted by P. Bourdieu and J. C. Passeron, *La Reproduction* (Paris: Editions de Minuit, 1970) p. 166.

3. As quoted by P. Bourdieu and J. C. Passeron in *Les Héritiers* (Paris: Editions de Minuit, 1966) p. 46.

4. For a general treatment of this history of examinations in the French educational system, see A. Leon, "Le rôle des examens," *Bulletin du groupe d'etudes de psychologie de l'Université de Paris,* Vol. 6, 1952, pp. 31–39.

5. For a discussion on the development of guidance counselors in the United States and of the functions that they perform, see J. Kitsuse and A. Cicourel, *The Educational Decision Makers* (Indianapolis: Bobbs-Merrill, 1963), Chapter 4.

6. For a further discussion of the distinction between internal and external examinations, see the "The 15–18: A report of the Great Britain Central Advisory Council for Education," (London: Her Majesty's Stationery Office, 1959), Chapter 8.

7. See P. Bourdieu and J. C. Passeron, *La Reproduction, op. cit.,* notably Chapter 3.

8. *Ibid.*

9. As quoted by P. Bourdieu and J. C. Passeron; *ibid.,* p. 150.

10. For an elaboration of the implications attached to the distinction between *vous* and *tu,* see R. Brown, *Social Psychology* (New York: The Free Press 1965) pp. 58 ff.

11. The *Société des Agrégés,* for example, has been able to resist quite victoriously all the changes brought about by the agitation of May 1968. For a description of the arguments invoked by the *Agreges,* to resist the efforts of the government to broaden the recruitment of French secondary school teachers, see P. Bourdieu and J. C. Passeron, *La Reproduction, op. cit.,* pp. 183–184, footnote 19.

12. See J. Kitsuse and A. Cicourel, *The Educational Decision Makers, op. cit.,* particularly Chapter 5. See also B. R. Clark, "The Cooling Out Function in Higher Education," *American Journal of Sociology,* Vol. 65, 1960, pp. 565–576.

13. See J. Kitsuse and A. Cicourel, *op. cit.,* notably Chapter 3.

14. The function of counselors has changed in the same direction as that initially taken by the function of counselors in the United States, but the stress still remains placed on economic and opportunity factors in the former country.

15. As quoted by P. Bourdieu and J. C. Passeron, *La Reproduction, op. cit.,* p. 200.

16. *Ibid.,* Chapter 3.

17. *Ibid.* for the rich documentation collected by Bourdieu in this respect and notably all the critical assessments of higher education examinations made by Bougle.

18. N. Bisseret, "La naissance et le diplome; les processus de selection au debut des etudes universitaires," *Revue Francaise de sociologie,* Vol. 9, 1968, pp. 185–205.

19. See P. Bourdieu and J. C. Passeron, *Les Héritiers, op. cit.*, p. 29. The author notes that while the objective performances of lower-class students are better than those of their classmates derived from upper strata, the latter consider themselves to be better students. Whereas 18 percent of middle-class students report to be above average compared to only 10 percent of their lower class counterparts, 58 percent of the latter group have passed a prior examination *cum laude* compared to only 39 percent of the middle-class pupils.

20. See *Employment, Incomes and Equality: A Strategy for Increasing Productive Employment in Kenya* (Geneva: ILO, 1972), pp. 522–523.

21. This point is made by Bourdieu and Passeron in *La Reproduction, op. cit.*, Chapter 3. Wilkinson makes the same comparison between the examination structures of British elite schools and of traditional Chinese institutions. See R. Wilkinson, *The Prefects* (Oxford: Oxford University Press, 1964) notably Chapter VI. See also D. Ward, *The Public School and Industry in Britian After 1870.*

22. See D. Mechanic, *Students Under Stress* (Glencoe: Free Press, 1963), Chapter IV.

23. The principles underlying current systems of examinations have been criticized by P. Goodman, J. Holt, P. Illich. See also B. Beck and H. Becker, Some Modest Reform Proposals for Graduates Studies in Sociology, *American Sociologist*, Vol. 4, 1969 pp. 227–234.

24. There have been changes along these lines. When I initially came to Northwestern University, the Master was a significant *rite de passage* toward the obtention of the Ph.D. Some time later it became the mechanism by which the department got rid of undesirable elements. It is now automatically granted after 36 hours of credit and serves therefore as a sort of minimal guaranteed diploma.

25. See G. Vedel, "Assignats universitaires," *Le Monde*, No. 7522, March 21, 1969.

26. "The 15–18," *op. cit.*, Chapter 8.

27. J. Kitsuse and A. Cicourel, *The Educational Decision Makers, op. cit.*, notably Chapter 2, 3.

28. P. Bourdieu and J. C. Passeron have noted that originally the grading of examinations was the only obligation incumbing upon French professors, R. Castel and J. C. Passeron eds., *Education Developpement et Démocratie* (Paris: Mouton 1967). The high importance of the Law Aggregation was symbolized by the complexities of the rituals underlying the examination situation. Candidates were supposed to work for one another for the preparation of their oral examinations, the candidate himself paying all the expenses incurred by his competitors who acted temporarily as his assistants. The attempt of playing deliberately on cooperation and competition among candidates was an important feature of this examination. The

growing stress placed upon the need for accountability measures in American schools is likely to have similar effects and to change both the teaching techniques used by American high or primary school educators and more generally the attitudes they hold toward their students. More specifically, the sanctions attached to the number of "successes" or "failures" in their classroom could very well lead these actors to attach a higher significance to the recruitment patterns of their pupils.

29. The importance attached to the organization of the examination paper may lead the examinee to take dangerous risks with regard to his knowledge or absence of knowledge of the problem posed. For example, Bourdieu in *La Reproduction, op. cit.,* p. 142, explains that a candidate to *Ecole Normale Superieure* who, ignoring the meaning of the question asked to him about "Krach boursier a Vienne," decided to believe that the words meant "Krach got a scholarship in Vienna" whereas they meant "Collapse on the stockmarket in Vienna" and organized a systematic comment on his interpretation of the question. Very clearly the decision to take such risks results from the assumption that organization of knowledge is more important than the knowledge of the facts themselves. As shown in this anecdote, these risks are sometimes real.

30. See, for example, P. Bourdieu and J. C. Passeron, *La Reproduction, op. cit.,* Chapter 3, 4. In addition, Bourdieu in *Les Heritiers, op. cit.,* notes that the whole pedagogical communication in the French system consists in the circulation of "gifts" from teachers to students and vice versa. In this context gifts are assimilationist in this sense that their exchange does not constitute a dialogue but a succession of monologues. Further, as pointed out by Bourdieu, gifts can only be given by gifted persons. Once more the confusion between passive and active forms betrays the assimilationist characteristic of the communication.

31. For an illustration of these reforms see, for example, B. Beck and H. Becker, *op. cit.*

32. M. C. Sherman, "Accountability Not New," *Phi Delta Kappan,* Vol. 52, 1970, p. 253.

33. Reports in the mass media of the overall level of performances obtained by the students of various metropolitan areas offer as many cases in power.

34. See, for example, H. Becker, B. Geer, and E. Hughes, *Making the Grade: The Academic Side of College Life* (New York: Wiley, 1968), Chapter IV.

35. See J. Davis, *Great Aspirations* (Chicago: Aldine, 1964), p. 168.

36. See H. Becker et al., *Making the Grade, op. cit.,* p. 51.

37. Academic excellence is thus treated as a favor conceded by the Establishment who expects thus a return of the favor by the student to whom this favor has been given.

38. For illustrations of this phenomenon, see H. Becker et al., *Making the*

Grade, op. cit., Chapter 4. See also W. Wallace, *Student Culture* (Chicago: dine, 1966), notably Chapter 5.

39.   Alain Fournier, *Le Grand Meaulnes* (Paris: Emile-Paul, 1936); Valery Larbaud, *Fermina Marquez* (Paris: Plon, 1920); R. Brasillach, *Comme le temps passe* (Paris: Plon, 1963).

40.   For illustrations of this phenomenon see P. Bourdieu and J. C. Passeron, *La Reproduction, op. cit.,* p. 200, footnote.

41.   H. Becker et al., *Boys in White* (Chicago: University of Chicago Press, 1961); see the subtitle of Chapter X.

42.   See D. Mechanic, *op. cit.,* p. 75.

43.   *Ibid.,* p. 90. See, for example, Table 18 which shows that whereas only 32 percent of the students interviewed think that to talk to individuals who already took the examination is a good way of preparing oneself to the examination, this view is held by almost half of the faculty. Of course individuals competing with one another do not have the same philosophy as the judges of the competition itself.

44.   See C. Testaniere, "Chahut traditionnel et chahut anomique," *Revue Francaise de sociologie* Vol. 9, 1968, pp. 25–37.

45.   J. Romains, *Les copains* (Paris: Gallimard, 1922).

46.   R. Merton, *Social Structure and Anomie, Social Theory and Social Structure* (New York: Free Press, 1964), pp. 131–60.

47.   Z. Gamson, "Performances and Personalism in Student Faculty Relations," *Sociology of Education,* Vol. 40, 1967, pp. 279–301.

48.   Stendhal, *The Red and the Black* (Paris: Gibert, 1942), pp. 202–203.

49.   P. Bourdieu and J. C. Passeron, *La Reproduction, op. cit.,* who stresses that this is related to the charismatic definition of teaching. See, for example, pp.151–154.

50.   The importance attached to the organization of the paper results, it seems to me, from the fact that it shortens the amount of time necessary both to absorb and evaluate the informations offered by the candidates. The importance attached thus implicitly to time saving factors reflects the lack of rewards associated with a reading of examination copies.

51.   For a further discussion of this point, see D. Mechanic, *op. cit.,* p. 56 and Table 9, 10.

52.   A. Stinchcombe, *Rebellion in a High School* (Chicago: Quadrangle, 1965), pp. 56–57.

53.   *Ibid.,* p. 179.

54.   *Ibid.,* pp. 181–194.

55.   H. Becker et al., *Boys in White, op. cit.,* p. 171.

56.   See for example P. Bourdieu and J. C. Passeron, *Les Heritiers, op. cit.,* pp. 94ff. See also D. Mechanic, *op. cit.,* pp. 136–138.

57. H. Becker et al., *Making the Grade, op. cit.,* p. 59.
58. P. Bourdieu and J. C. Passeron, *Les Heritiers, op. cit.,* p. 97.
59. D. Mechanic, *op. cit.,* p. 137.
60. A. Stinchcombe, *op. cit.,* pp. 202–22.
61. H. Becker et al., *Making the Grade, op. cit.,* p. 102.
62. To use here the framework that Merton coined to describe retreatism. See R. Merton, *op. cit.,* notably pp. 141–140.
63. See R. Taylor, *The Secondary Modern School* (London: Faber, 1963).
64. The main outcome of the strike started in May 1970 at Northwestern University to protest against the death of four students at Kent State University was the introduction of new and temporary grades (T) and the promise of introducing a more systematic revision of the entire evaluation procedure.
65. A. Stinchcombe, *op. cit.,* p. 153.
66. Indeed physical distance is used as the symbolic translation of cognitive distance. Best students sit close to the teacher while dummies *(cancres)* are concentrated at a distance.
67. See L. Wylie, *op. cit.,* pp. 91–97.
68. See D. Mechanic, *op. cit.,* pp. 56–57.
69. A good illustration of this is provided by the differential approaches followed toward adult education by the Chamber of Commerce of Abidjan (Ivory Coast) and the French Federation of Mechanical Industries that opened a training program in the Ivory Coast in the early 1960s. The first organization prepared workers for examinations defined and sanctioned by the Ministry of Education and success to these examinations enabled individuals not only to claim a higher position in their firm but also to move to another one if they were unable to obtain the promotion to which they were entitled by local collective bargaining agreements. The second organization gave examinations, the validity of which was limited to each specific enterprise. In the first case examinations protected individual workers against the arbitrary power of French manager. In the second case the examinations were the translation of this arbitrary power.
70. D. Lavine, *The Prediction of Academic Performances* (New York: Russell Sage, 1965) Chapter 5.
71. Indeed it can be argued that a lack of exposure to anxiety-raising situations does not necessarily facilitate the cognitive and emotional growth of an individual. After all, from an impressionistic viewpoint, it seems that although or because less repressive, the American university system does not necessarily prepare its students to be independent and write a dissertation, for example, as easily as its French counterpart. I am personally puzzled by the intensity of the inhibitions experienced by some gifted American students at the time of writing their dissertation.

72. For a discussion of this point, see P. Bourdieu and J. C. Passeron, *Les Heritiers*, Chapter 1, Conclusion. See also P. Clerc, "Nouvelles données sur l'orientation scolaire au moment de l'entreè en 6'eme," *Population*, Vol. 13, 1966, pp. 830–872.

73. See H. Pierron, "La technique des examens et la nécessité d'une docimologie," *L'enseignement scientifique*, Vol. 17, 1928, pp. 133–196.

74. For a discussion of this proposal, see B. Beck and H. Becker, *op. cit.*

75. Once more this point brings us back to the ambiguities underlying the relationship between liberty, and equality. While a stress placed on equality through standardization is often alienating, a stress placed upon liberty through differentiation of curricula and pedagogies is often considered as forms of discrimination.

11

ECONOMIC AND POLITICAL IMPLICATIONS OF FORMAL SCHOOLING

With the previous chapter, I have completed the analysis of the differing moments of the *life cycle* of both educational institutions and their students. This analysis has enabled me to examine the various facets of the conflicts between equality and liberty as they result from educational experiences. The meaning attached to such experiences is however relative insofar as they do not constitute ends in themselves, but rather means of gaining access to rewarding adult roles. Thus it becomes important to examine in greater detail the patterns of interaction between academic experiences and occupational choices and histories. This chapter is accordingly devoted to an examination of the degree to which academic experiences really "liberate" the individual from major economic constraints and contribute to enlarge his occupational choices. This leads to an examination of the political behavior of students, for their own activism can be assumed to reflect their disillusioned responses to the disparities between the rewards they expect to gain and the rewards they actually derive from the educational process.

Schooling and the Labor Market. The analysis of the interaction between academic and occupational experiences requires a number of preliminary analyses. In the perspective of a liberal economy, an additional amount of schooling is associated with a commensurate increase

359

in productivity and with a commensurate increase in the rewards that individuals derive from their occupational activities.[1] Since, in this perspective, schools are expected to inculcate the skills and values most consistent with productivity, occupational choices and aspirations should be predominantly affected by educational experiences. Yet we can also assume that teachers only repeat the messages parents want their children to internalize. Contrasts in the occupational choices of individuals with differing amounts of schooling do not necessarily parallel their differential patterns of socialization but rather the differential position that their parental background enables them to occupy in the social structure. Insofar as the length of educational experiences reflects the socioeconomic and cultural origin of students, contrasts in productivity do not result from varying amounts of training but from varying backgrounds. Indeed, productivity may be looked upon as the criteria that elites use to justify their preeminence and that of their offspring.

Even if formal schooling increases individual productivity, the problem remains to ascertain the mechanisms by which job seekers identify the most productive and hence the most rewarding parts of the labor market. In the perspective of a liberal economy, one may expect that an additional amount of schooling widens the networks of information individuals use to gain access to the labor market and enables them to be more geographically and socially mobile after they have joined the labor force.

Finally, the influence of productivity on rewards remains problematic. We may assume that variations in productivity within a particular occupational category result from contrasts in levels of educational attainment and are associated with differential incomes. Yet we may also assume that the most significant variations in productivity occur *between* rather than *within* occupational categories. In this latter case we are confronted with the task of determining the factors that make certain occupations more productive than others. These differences may be the result of the differential skills associated with the performance of specific activities; yet, they may be also the result of the differential bargaining power of the variety of occupational categories present in the labor force.

Schooling and Occupational Aspirations.   Evidence shows that peoples accord differential values to a number of occupational roles and that the ranking of a particular occupation depends upon the number of highly educated individuals it attracts.[2] From this observation we may infer that individual level of educational attainment determines individual levels of occupational aspirations. Clignet and Foster have shown that the level of occupational aspirations in the Ivory Coast varies markedly not only with the cycle of studies followed by students, but also with self-reported academic performances measured in terms of the incidence of repeating in prior classes or of ranking in the classes currently attended.[3] *Lycée* students with the best academic rankings are those with the highest educational and occupational aspirations. Similarly, Gouveia and Havighurst report that in Brazil, students enrolled in scientific secondary studies tend to have higher levels of occupational aspirations than their counterparts enrolled in commercial institutions.[4] These results are analogous to those observed in the United States where Sewell, Haller, and Portes report relatively high zero-order correlations between occupational aspirations and educational attainment (.43) or between the first variable and educational aspirations (.70).[5]

In addition, the specific type of studies undertaken also influences occupational expectations and motivations, regardless of the level of such studies. Thus a recent study of the aspirations and orientations of the graduates of French *Grandes Ecoles* shows marked contrasts in this respect between the individuals who have attended business schools and those who have attended engineers schools.[6] The former are mostly attracted by consultant and advertising firms, the latter by state-owned economic organizations or public research outfits. The former expect their first employer to allow them to gain a further occupational qualification, but the latter tend to look primarily for a stable type of employment. The majority of business school graduates consider their first employment as a bridge between educational and vocational training, and they view their future horizontal mobility (or change in employment) as a determinant of their future upward mobility (or access to higher skill level). They see a change of employers as leading to greater opportunities. In contrast, over 40 percent of the future engineers want to spend all their work life with the same employer, and they equate change of employer with occupational instability.

While the first population is willing to participate in the risks of commercial enterprises, the second one refuses to share the risks of an industrial venture. These contrasts cannot be accounted for by the differing modes of recruitment of these two types of institutions of higher learning, since their students have the same origin. Rather, such contrasts result from the differential expectations that these populations entertain toward their future occupational environment. While business school students are trained to view their future employers as stressing the value of innovations and risk-taking activities, those of engineering schools are trained to perceive their future employers as conservative and hostile to innovations.[7]

However, the influence of academic experiences on the nature and the level of occupational aspirations is contaminated by other factors. Parents often prefer their children to attend institutions whose population share the same social status and the same life style as their own. They suspect (and rightly so) that the social psychological environment of the school contributes to shape the academic, occupational, and matrimonial fate of their offspring. Their suspicions are validated by the results of the American study mentioned above, which shows that the influence of significant others, that is, parents, teachers, and peers, considered jointly, markedly influence academic attainment or occupational aspirations (the relevant zero order correlations are .57 and .53, respectively).

Of course, the nature of these significant others reflects the social position of students and tends to be independent of educational processes and of prior educational attainment. In Brazil 82 percent of the upper-class students enrolled in the schools of Porto Allegre have high levels of occupational aspirations against only 66 percent of those derived from lower social categories.[8] Similarly in the Ivory Coast a high level of occupational aspirations characterizes 86 percent of the students coming from families with a maximal level of acculturation compared to only 56 percent of those whose parents have a minimal level of acculturation.[9] Furthermore, in this latter country specific occupational choices are more frequently influenced by socioeconomic than by academic factors, and attraction toward teaching agricultural and military careers is more closely related to social origin than to academic performances.

The significance of the association between formal training and occupational choice is affected by a number of other factors.[10] For example, family background affects cognitive skills and hence both academic performances and preferences toward jobs that stress the significance of cognitive skills. In addition, family background also affects the range of institutions to which an individual might gain access and the degree to which his actual academic socialization will reinforce the relationship between his cognitive skills and his occupational aspirations and orientations. Finally, the magnitude of the association between academic experiences and occupational aspirations is not independent of the ascriptive characteristics attached to family background, and this association, for instance, differs necessarily for white and nonwhite populations in this country. Correspondingly, formal schooling often serves as a way of keeping the distribution of aspirations in balance with the distribution of actual opportunities. It enables various students to take a differential advantage of the existing occupational structures rather than to create new ones.

Schooling and Occupational Status.　The length and the nature of the studies undertaken by an individual and his academic successes affect both the mechanisms he uses to join the labor force and his point of entry into the labor market. In Kenya, the number of years completed have been shown to constitute adequate predictors not only of migratory patterns but also of the relative importance attached to kin and friends networks as means of entering the modern labor market.[11] Similarly, in a study of 384 workers employed by seven firms in Abidjan in 1963, Clignet observes that the use of formal channels (employment agencies, newspaper ads, etc.) to gain access to current employment is more characteristic of individuals with higher educational qualifications. While 34 percent of the individuals who had completed the first cycle of their postprimary studies entered their current position by making use of such devices, this characterized only 18 percent of those individuals who had only completed their primary studies, and 7 percent of those individuals who had never attended any institution. Perhaps formal schooling enlarges the number of contacts that individuals can use to find a job, and it also makes these contacts more likely to be universalistic.

Educational attainment and occupational status are usually highly correlated. In the United States three-quarters of the long-term unemployed persons during the 1960s came from half of the population who had not completed high school. Further, the overall association between level of schooling and occupational status was .65.[12] In this sense occupational aspirations tend to be "self-fulfilling prophecies." The magnitude of such an association, however, varies with educational and economic development. In new nations increases in the length of studies undertaken are not necessarily associated with parallel increases in chances of being gainfully employed. This reflects the intervention of two forces. First, high school or university enrollments may be disproportionate to the growth rate of the economy. In other words, the number of jobs both newly created in the labor market (and resulting from the development of new industrial activities) or vacated by their present holders (because of age or of sickness) are smaller than the number of school leavers. Second, while the initial scarcity of educational facilities enabled older age groups to entertain high occupational aspirations with some realism, the occupational rewards anticipated by the current cohorts of school leavers diverge from the opportunities actually offered to them by the labor market. As a result, many individuals refuse to participate in the labor force as long as they cannot find jobs that correspond both to their aspirations and expectations.

This situation can be observed in many contemporary African nations. A study by Sween and Clignet in Douala (Cameroons) suggests we may distinguish jobless populations in that particular urban center in terms of those who are *unemployed* and of those who are *deemployed*.[13] The first group includes persons who have never been able to enter the labor market, while the second is comprised of persons who have been obliged to leave the labor market. The social and cultural profiles of these two subgroups are different. Members of the first subgroup are younger and are characterized by higher educational attainment. They are jobless because the economic conditions of the country introduce distortions between what the market offers and what educated individuals expect to do when they are in a position to join the labor force. By contrast, members of the second subgroup are jobless because a lack of formal education prevents them from adapting to the technological changes that have affected local economic organizations. There are also variations in the length of time during which these two groups of jobless persons are out of the labor force. Unemployed individuals tend to be jobless for longer periods of time than deemployed persons, mirroring the differential psychological factors underlying their respective plight: Older, deemployed individuals must find jobs quicker to support their families or must leave the urban environment and return to the hinterland.

Many emerging nations have perhaps invested a lot of financial and human resources in educational development with the hope that a rise in the size of educational outputs would improve the profile of local economic situations, but the results of these educational investments have been disappointing. They have not only induced a rise in the educational level of jobless populations but have also accentuated tensions between age groups. Although better educated, younger individuals have often been unable to replace their predecessors at the top of the occupational structure because seniority continues to affect access to rewarding economic roles. The situation begins to change, and in the Ivory Coast, for example, school leavers begin to anticipate lower occupational rewards. They are willing to take unskilled manual positions, at least temporarily. They can use a "wait-and-see" strategy and negotiate later on the academic hurdles that will enable them to gain access to more rewarding occupational positions.[14] Similarly, in the Cameroun, while the highly educated segments of the older age groups tended to be predominately attracted by the better payed nonmanual occupations, their counterparts in younger age cohorts enter the manual sector of employment in large numbers, and differences in the educational attainment of manual and nonmanual workers have correspondingly declined.[15]

Occupational placement, however, does not only depend upon the *length* of the studies undertaken but also upon their *content*. In the context of developing nations, planners have often asserted that both economic development and individual mobility should be enhanced by the development of vocational rather than academic schools. This assertion is faulty on a number of counts. First, the linkage between educational and occupational markets is never perfect, and there is always a gap between the time at which industrial and commercial enterprises experience a need for particular skills and the time at which schools are able to offer the desired workers on the labor market. Second, patterns of competition are not alike for educational and occupational enterprises. Many vocational schools are still under the control of expatriate teachers and administrators. Insofar as they are competing with the personnel of similar institutions in highly industrialized countries, they want to use the most sophisticated technology. This does not necessarily prepare their students to fill positions in the local economy where many enterprises derive their profit from the use of a cheap labor force and obsolete machinery. Finally, the products of vocational schools consider themselves to be professional and have more rigid expectations than the students graduating from schools with a more academically oriented curriculum. In effect, one can suspect that in societies with a low level of division of labor, the individuals most likely to adapt to the simple, albeit changing, requirements of industrial tasks are those with the least specific and most flexible skills and motivations. For instance, Clignet and Foster have shown in the Ivory Coast that the students most likely to be unemployed are not those graduating from the regular high schools but those from the vocational training centers. They also show the latter experience the lowest rates of upward mobility on the job and the least degree of occupational satisfaction.[16]

The fit between vocational training and occupational placement is not necessarily higher in industrial countries. Indeed, the destination of individuals is not so much affected by their educational experiences as by the perceived hierarchy of occupations. Thus in France a study by

Baudot and Vimont shows that no less than 40 percent of males with a technical diploma do not fill the job for which they were initially prepared and that interoccupational migrations are clearly patterned, certain occupations being definitely preferred to others regardless of variations in types of training.[17] Similarly, studies of occupational mobility in Switzerland also show that the incidence of upward mobility varies as a direct function of the length of general academic experiences, regardless of the nature of the vocational training followed; is greater when this vocational training is acquired in a school than on the job itself; and is greater when this training takes place in an institution of higher learning than in a vocationally oriented school.[18] The most general type of curriculum seems to yield the largest number of occupational choices.

Depending on the length and the nature of the studies undertaken, modes of access into the labor market are probably also influenced by the proprietorship status of the institution attended. The schools of centralized countries are able to adjust their output to the variations characterizing the labor market, but this is more difficult to achieve in decentralized school systems. Certainly, there is often a higher solidarity among the alumni of private institutions, and current graduates may use a more diffuse network of social relations to enter the labor force. Certainly, many private institutions also feel responsible for the placement of their graduates. But administrators of decentralized and private school systems have less information about the trends prevailing in the labor market than their counterparts operating in centralized institutions. Further, the administrators of private schools experience two kinds of diverging pressures from their clientele. Students want both to find employment, and to be graduated from the institution, independently of their performance. Correspondingly, administrators must find compromises between the expectations of future employers and the aspirations of their current students.[19] To satisfy all of the latter is probably to deceive most of the former.

Finally, formal schooling influences not only entry into the labor market but subsequent moves within and across occupational categories. As time passes, however, the relative role of education in this regard declines. A study conducted in 1957 on a random sample of seniors in Wisconsin high schools revealed a high aggregate correlation between aspirations and the status of the job occupied four years after graduation. Yet when specific individuals were considered, the absolute difference between aspirations and actual status seven years later were much higher. About 42 percent of these seniors were engaged in occupations that ranked above the one to which they aspired, whereas 58 percent were holding positions ranked lower than the one they should have entered.[20]

In short, educational credentials act perhaps as necessary conditions for occupational placement but they are certainly not sufficient alone, and there are in fact enormous differences in the occupational status of peoples with the same amount of education. These differences reflect partly ascriptive characteristics and ethnic status, for example. For a black man in this country, to have both the right parents and an additional amount of formal schooling is still of little relevance in determining his occupational status. In fact, his status depends as much on the composition of the student body of the school attended as on the number of years of schooling.

Further, differences in the degree to which individuals move from employer to employer, among branches of activity, among occupations, or among skill levels within a same-job category reflect contrasts not only in educational attainment and ascriptive characteristics (sex, age and ethnicity), but also in the organizational structures of varying sectors of employment. In a developing country like Cameroun, for instance, the experience acquired in the job itself or in the firm compensates for a lack of educational qualifications. Yet the trade-off between occupational and educational experiences is not the same for blue- and white-collar populations, and the latter market seems to be more universalist and to stress more strongly the significance of educational background. Similarly, the influence of education on mobility is not the same for the two categories of wage earners. Change of occupations is more closely associated with years of formal training in the case of white collar workers, and these changes enable nonmanual workers to experience upward mobility more frequently than their manual counterparts.[21]

Despite variations in the form and the magnitude of the relationship between academic experiences and entry into the labor force and subsequent occupational histories, a large number of individuals continue to hold strong beliefs about the effect of schooling on mobility. The development of night courses, adult education, and generally occupational upgrading programs rests on such beliefs. The functions of these programs are quite diverse, and while they constitute primarily mechanisms of upward mobility, they also tend to be used by individuals who try to prevent the incipient processes of downward mobility resulting from their earlier academic failures.

The differentiation of the functions performed by these programs should be paralleled by contrasts in the social and psychological characteristics of their respective student populations. More specifically, such programs should be attended not only by individuals with low educational qualifications but also by individuals who have dropped out of the institution to which they should be naturally attached. But what are the characteristics of such dropouts? One might suspect that dropping out of the relatively most rewarding rungs of the academic ladder reflects not only a lack of resources or of abilities but also insufficient motivations. Thus studies on dropouts from colleges in the United States indicate that while performances in college are determined by performances in high school, no less than 48 percent of a sample of "discontinued" college students did drop college because of a reported lack of interest in further studying.[22]

Thus, it seems apparent that the individual dropouts more likely to take advantage of promotion or upgrading courses are those who are exposed to status inconsistencies. A study of the population attending the night courses offered by the Chamber of Commerce in Abidjan shows that a substantial number of students come from ethnic or socio-economic groups with an already high level of participation in modern structures. Such students take advantages of the courses offered to them because an initial academic failure prevents them from holding occupational positions consistent with those to which they could aspire in view of their backgrounds and of the status achieved by their "normal" peers.[23] Likewise, a study in France shows that students attending adult education courses and occupational upgrading programs were able to do their military services as junior officers and hence were able to achieve military ranks yielding more prestige and income than the positions into which they were supposed to enter in the civilian occupational market, often had parents and spouses with a higher educational achievement than their own, and tended to associate with friends with higher socioeconomic status than their colleagues on the job.[24] In short, participation in upgrading courses depends upon the particular reference groups of dropouts. The higher the status of such groups, the stronger will be the motivations of these individuals to reduce the gap between the position they occupy in the social structure and that achieved by significant others. Correspondingly, upgrading courses prevent downward mobility as often as they facilitate upward mobility.

Schooling and Occupational Rewards.   In a first perspective, we may assert that schooling primarily affects productivity *within* one particular occupational category. From this assertion we may infer that contrasts in the income of individuals performing the same job result from their differential exposure to educational structures or educational attainment. Insofar as differential educational experiences are deemed to influence individualistic values and orientations, the impact of such experiences on income should be maximal in the case of economic activities that stress the significance of entrepreneurship—hence in the case of self-employment. Yet the available evidences suggest that correlations between educational attainment (as measured by grades) and success in careers such as engineering, medicine, and teaching remain limited and that individuals who received high grades in professional schools do not necessarily enjoy higher earnings than those who did poorly in such institutions.[25] In addition, both economic and educational developments are associated with a decline in the numerical importance of self-employed activities and hence with a decline in the significance of entrepreneurship. As a result, the influence of formal schooling on income should decline.

In a second perspective, we may assert that formal schooling affects the productivity of distinct occupations. The task remains to determine the criteria that are used to establish the corresponding hierarchy of occupations. First, we may believe that there is a marked *consensus* in the definition of the tasks and responsibilities attached to a variety of jobs and that this consensus facilitates the institutionalization of a hierarchical arrangement of disciplines in the educational context, which duplicates the hierarchy of occupations. Because everybody agrees that the tasks performed by an engineer involve more responsibilities than those performed by a technician, the additional years of schooling demanded of future engineers correspond to the additional skills and qualities expected from them in the exercise of their activities. In short, if an additional year of schooling yields an additional amount of income, it is because this additional year of schooling entails the acquisition of qualities that are not taught previously. Second, we may also believe that the hierarchy of occupations results from their differential social composition and that contrasts in the income of various categories reflect the varying political and economic power they muster in the society at large. In this latter case the influence of schooling on productivity and hence on income is only a social convention, and variations in the amount of educational experiences acquired by distinct social groups are used as a mechanism designed to *legitimize* over time the differential income and prestige of these groups. To perpetuate themselves, elites maintain their children in educational institutions for longer periods of time than other social groups and they use this contrast as a legitimizing device to justify the fact that their children should and do earn more than those coming from more modest circumstances.

In more general terms, the liberal economy states that there is a high relationship between schooling, productivity, and income because the labor market is perfect. Conversely, the opponents of such a theory emphasize the fact that such a market is fragmented and imperfect. Certain categories of employers are likely to use formal schooling as the main criteria underlying their hiring practices because it constitutes a cheap and convenient way of screening job seekers. Alternatively, certain categories of workers are able to use educational experiences as a "union card" preventing the most vulnerable employers from lowering the salaries they offer below certain unacceptable limits. Correspondingly, the association between schooling and income should not be the same in all parts of the labor market, for the definition of "scarcity of skills" is socially relative and differs as between sectors of employment. Neither should this association be alike in countries characterized by differing levels of technological, economic and educational development.

In an analysis of the modern sector of the Camerounian economy Clignet has compared the annual salaries earned by manual and nonmanual Camerounian workers and has examined what percentages of the variance of the corresponding distributions are explained by (*a*) the formal training of these two populations, that is, their formal educational achievement, the forms of vocational training to which they have been exposed, and the number of jobs for which they have been trained either before or after entering the labor force; (*b*) their occupational history defined in terms of the seniority acquired with their current employer and on their current job and in terms of the mobility that they have experienced since their entry in the market; and (*c*) the characteristics of their employers defined in terms of the branch of activity for which they currently work, the size, the legal status, and the location of the headquarters of the firms that have hired them.[26]

The results of this analysis show educational antecedents to be more significant predicators of the annual earnings of nonmanual than of manual populations. They explain 25 percent of the variance of the first distribution but only 15 percent of the variance of the second one. In addition, although the rewards derived from an additional amount of formal education do not remain constant at various points of the educational continuum, they tend to be higher for nonmanual than for manual wage earners. By contrast, the *relative* weight of occupational history is greater for blue-collar than for white-collar populations, since the overall educational and occupational antecedents of individual workers account for 27 percent of the variance of the distribution of annual manual salaries and 31 percent of that of the distribution of nonmanual earnings. Last, considered independently of other factors, the characteristics of the employers explain no less than 18 percent of the variance of the distribution of manual annual earnings but only 8 percent of the corresponding variance for white collar populations.

Such results therefore indicate differences in the structures of the two markets of employment. The perceived influence of education on occupational performance varies between industrial and commercial tasks. Thus the rewards derived from education are higher in the case of nonmanual work because the definition of white-collar work is more universalistic than that of blue-collar activity. There are less variations in the definition of the requirements imposed upon typists or accountants than in the definition of the tasks to be performed by mechanics.

The same imperfections characterize as well a more developed and complex labor market such as that of the United States.[27] First, evidence shows that constituting three-quarters of all disposable income in the country, earnings differ markedly among the various segments of the working population. Clearly, such contrasts reflect differential amounts of formal schooling (Table 25). As was the case for Cameroun, however, the influence of formal schooling on earning does not

Table 25. Incomes of Full-time, Year-round Workers over 25 with Different Amounts of Schooling (As a Percentage of the 1968 Average) [a]

Amount of Schooling	Male	Female
Didn't finish elementary school	70	40
Finished elementary school but no high school	85	47
Entered high school; did not finish	96	51
Finished high school; no college	111	61
Entered college; did not finish	129	71
Finished college; no graduate school	120	84
At least one year of graduate school	188	106
N (in thousands)	34.422	12.575

[a] Derived from Christopher Jencks et al., *Inequality: A Reassessment of the Effect of Family and Schooling in America* (New York: Basic Books, Inc., 1972), p. 222.

remain the same for the variety of occupational roles present in the current American economy. In addition, the returns from an additional year of schooling vary both across the educational ladder and over time.

If the returns derived from educational investments vary with the nature of the tasks performed and the studies undertaken, they also depend upon the social class affiliations of the individuals examined. Such returns are naturally higher for upper- and middle-class wage earners than for their lower-class counterparts, and the corresponding contrasts are in fact magnified when one takes ethnicity into consideration; middle-class black persons, for instance, gain hardly any advantage from an additional amount of formal schooling. In effect, family background, cognitive skill, educational attainment, or occupational status do not explain much of the variations in men's incomes, but they will affect the variety of particularistic factors that account for the major part of the variance in the corresponding distribution. Jencks insists on the role of "good luck," but to the extent that this luck implies social know-how and the appropriate usage of social networks at the proper time, it is not independent of familial background.

The "liberating" effects of formal schooling are in fact moderate. This is because schools tend to certify individuals who are different from one another to start with and because educational institutions and processes tend to replicate rather than to modify what goes on in other sectors of society. This is also because the logics underlying the constraints and the choices operating in the economic and educational fields are independent. The efforts that economic and social planners devote to educational enterprises are often vain, and students as well as parents know the limits of the equalizing role assigned to educational activities. The consciousness of these limits is often at the origin of educational crises and malaises.

The Crisis of Educational Institutions.   Both the internal and external functions of educational institutions are increasingly challenged. This challenge accentuates the dilemmas with which schools are confronted. Teachers and administrators are caught between the views of the segments of society who view educational institutions as conservatories of existing norms and techniques and of those who believe that schools should act as centers aiming at the creation of new modes of action. The intensity of this first dilemma is a function of the rates of changes in the technological and social organization of economic structures. As such rates increase, attitudes toward social change become polarized.

Although universities were traditionally deemed to be the seedbeds of potential elites and provided their students with the general kind of education suitable to the needs and aspirations of the ruling classes, they have been increasingly considered to be higher centers of vocational trainings, specialized in the recruiting and the training of the variety of professionals needed by changing economic structures. These two functions require varying curriculum and forms of selectivity. The choices available to educational institutions along these lines are limited by the increasing tensions opposing professionals to technocrats in large-scale economic organizations, and bureaucracies to more classical and more limited types of economic enterprises.

Universities are also confronted with the problem of determining whether they aim at the training of various categories of professionals and technocrats or at the identification of new models of knowledge and action. We hope to have sketched strongly enough in previous pages the dimensions of the conflicts between teaching and research activities and, more specifically, to have suggested the variety of difficulties associated with the differentiation of these two functions as well as with their continuing presence amidst similar organizational contexts.

The intensity of these dilemmas is aggravated by a variety of forces. Originally perceived in consummatory terms, formal education is increasingly treated as an economic investment. Most nations in the world have been eager to increase the size of their educational facilities and to enhance the number of individuals potentially entitled to exert activities of communication and coordination in economic organizations. Whatever their nature, the performance of the functions currently fulfilled by educational institutions are consistently hindered by the resulting changes in the size and the composition of their population. While the political and economic orientations of most contemporary nations call for a democratization of educational institutions (i.e., for the emergence of recruitment patterns likely to minimize the waste of human capital), the same societies have been more reluctant to change the terms of the relationships between these elites and the remaining of the population. Yet the democratization of recruitment patterns becomes necessarily disruptive when it is not accompanied by parallel changes in the organization and the teaching system of schools, in the relationship between schools and labor markets, and in the model of relationships between school graduates and less fortunate segments of the population at large.[28] An increasing heterogeneity of teaching styles and pedagogical objectives must correspond to the increasing heterogeneity of the school populations. However, the introduction of this diversity has been at odds with the increasing bureaucratization and standardization of educational and other societal institutions.

More important, the negative effects of bureaucratization have been enhanced by the increasingly marginal status allocated to intellectuals and more specifically to teachers. Changes in occupational structures have been associated with a consistent erosion of the prestige accorded to intellectual and teaching careers. Further, the increasing division of labor and corresponding specialization of the fields of knowledge have reduced the subjective sense of control intellectuals originally believed they exerted on their occupational fate. Clinging to the splendors of a lost past because of the conservative nature ascribed to their role, teachers have also been increasingly isolated from the other segments of the working population and are correspondingly alienated from the society at large.

However, the dilemmas that confront educational institutions are also aggravated by the ever-increasing contradictions plaguing the society at large. Thus the lack of political and economic independence of many developing nations limits both the number and the nature of the position to be offered to the graduates of their institutions of higher education. For this reason student movements in Latin America or in Africa are probably closer to European political movements of the nineteenth century than they are to student movements among highly industrialized nations. To the extent that nationalism and political independence affect the fate of an entire polity, the agitation of students in Latin America forewarns deeper crises and cleavages, and such students act as the avant garde of the entire societies in which they participate.[29]

Current cleavages take more complex forms among highly industrialized nations. The classical forms of class struggle between working and owner classes are increasingly superseded by conflicts between professionals and technocrats. As a result, tensions arise not only in the secondary sector of the economy and in factories, but also in the context of large-scale organizations, where they mainly pertain to the control to be exerted over activities of coordination and communication. Indeed, in the same way that capitalists view individual profit as being the key factor of economic growth, technocrats perceive the systematic programming of all activities to be the most significant factor of social and economic development. As a result, the technicians of coordination and communication occupy a position analogous to those of the workers of the nineteenth century, while the fate of university students can be compared to that of the Lumpen proletariat of the past century—both groups being expected to replace current cohorts of workers in case of conflict with the established order.

Contemporary tensions cannot but lead to a political challenge of the functions exerted by universities, since they contribute both to the elaboration of new models of programming social and economic activities and to the training of individuals who feel increasingly deprived of the plums that have traditionally accompanied higher forms of formal schooling. The heydays of engineers, and for that matter of the whole gamut of professionals (lawyers, architects, physicians), trained by universities are gone. No longer able to exert full control and responsibility over their activities, they are in fact increasingly reduced to the roles of technicians and are exclusively expected to elaborate programming activities on the finality of which they have little to say. Student agitation has been most warmly received among the occupational groups that have a professional status. This is certainly not random, because students merely tend to anticipate the kind of frustration currently experienced by their elders.

Finally, the emergence of systematically programmed societies is associated with a decline in the autonomy of all daily activities or (to use here the terminology of G. Lefebvre and other philosophers) with an accentuation of the exploitation mechanisms based upon consumption. Students are particularly vulnerable to this type of alienation.[30] Like all young people, they are treated as objects of consumption insofar as advertising stresses the significance of *obsolescence* (and hence *a contrario* of youth) and uses images of youth as yielding additional status. They are also treated as subjects of consumption activities, as they participate in the special markets for young people that mass consumption has developed. At the same time, however, students remain economically and politically marginal and probably more so than their counterparts already employed in agricultural, industrial, or commercial activities. As a result, they are often the first ones to claim a new definition of liberty and, for instance, to argue that, under the present system, educational and occupational activities not only prevent the longing for privacy and independence from being satisfied but prevent this very longing itself. They are the first ones to reject both the implications of the scarcity underlying the functioning of current society and the assumptions on which this scarcity relies.[31]

Student Responses to the Crisis. Because of the variety of educational tensions, the nature of student agitation is difficult to analyze. With the growing malaise of educational institutions, there has been a marked increase in the number of studies that aim at accounting for student unrest. These studies might be divided into three groups.

Some studies are based on the assumption that student agitation is but one particular manifestation of a broader intergenerational conflict.[32] A critical assessment of these studies requires an examination of:

1. The *extent* of differences between age groups, that is, of the number and the significance of the arenas of social participation within which varying age groups enjoy differential rights and duties.

2. The *novelty* of such differences. There may be sharp variations over time both in the definition of the roles assigned to varying age groups and in the ideological justifications of the relevant differentiation.

3. The *permanence* of such differences. Either these differences correspond to the various phases of one individual's life cycle and the problems encountered by a young person are uniformly solved as he or she reaches the threshold socially defined as social maturity and enters the adult population; or differences between generations are specific to each historical period, in which case the scope, the intensity, and the implications of intergenerational differences cannot be compared over time, for individual and social times are systematically distinct.

In this particular perspective, it has been proposed for instance, that student rebellion is a direct translation of Oedipal conflicts and more specifically of the revolt of the youth against the authority socially invested in the fathers' image.[33] While this proposition disregards variations in the extent of generational differences and sees such differences as recurrent and constant, it raises a number of questions. Despite the diffuseness of the educational malaise throughout the world, there are still marked crosscultural variations in patterns of familial organization as well as in the salience of familial groups. Should we then infer that feelings between generations develop regardless of the social context within which they take place? Further, although these feelings might be permanent, they are not "acted out" with the same intensity or in the same form in different places and at different times. Therefore it remains necessary to identify the social mechanisms facilitating the overt expression of the hostility that children feel toward their fathers. Does this expression vary as a direct function of the absolute deprivation undergone by young people, and does it correspond to an accentuation of the gerontocratic nature of the power structure; or is it rather a by-product of insufficient improvements in the rights that young people enjoy in the society at large and hence a result of their feelings of being relatively deprived? To reduce student unrest to intergenerational conflicts does not in fact explain why participation in such conflicts tends to be selective and is more likely to involve young students than young workers or farmers.

The second type of studies aims at establishing a sociopsychological typology of student activists. Narrower in scope, these researches tend to explain unrest in terms of the childrearing practices prevailing among the particular social groups or classes from which the majority of the population enrolled in institutions of higher learning is originating. There are nevertheless some contrasts among these studies. Initially many of the researches relied upon the assumption that activism tends to prevail among students coming from an authoritarian and oppressive familial background. More recently, however, a number of authors have reversed this particular stance and argue that there is marked continuity between the value systems of radical students and those of their parents. They conclude that the "radical" students of today are the offspring of the "liberal" students of yesteryear and that the demands of the former only reflect the high level of expectations that they have internalized as a result of their rearing.[34] Whether they emphasize continuities or discontinuities in the orientations of "educated families," these researches raise a number of problems analogous to those evoked in the previous section. An examination of childhood experiences constitutes an assessment of the conditions that are *necessary* for the emergence of student activism. But are such conditions also sufficient? If childhood experiences are such a key variable in this regard, is it true that individuals derived from a particular background will be activist, independently of the social environment in which they participate currently? If this is so, it means that activism should take place not only within universities but within other contexts as well. Similarly, this also implies that the individual students who do not come from an "activism-prone" family will not be likely to participate in the same form and with the same intensity in student agitation. In brief, the weakness of this type of research is twofold: It does not explain how educational environments may trigger activism, and it treats the manifestations of student unrest within a monolithic framework.

The third type of research stresses the significance of the particular role played by students both in the society at large and within the university itself. In the society at large, students occupy the position of "marginal elites."[35] They are elites insofar as they participate in the elaboration of collective goods, "the need for which is keenly felt by political and spiritual leaders." Yet they are also marginal in that they "live off the community," are not sanctioned according to the principles governing other segments of the population, and are often physically separated from the rest of the community. Obviously, this marginality varies with the political and educational development of the society under study. Furthermore, it is not likely to be similarly experienced by individuals engaged in different types of studies. Depending on the form and the intensity of the marginality they experience, various categories of students will tend to oscillate differentially between elitist attitudes that enable them to protect their own distinctiveness and populist orientations that will help them reduce their feelings of being alienated from the "idealized" majority of the population.

As student roles differ across cultures and across disciplines, there are corresponding variations in the meaning and the form of student agitation. Indeed the tensions prevailing at one particular time within the educational milieu are not uniformly experienced or dealt with. In France in 1968, for example, Touraine distinguishes between the frustrations and the goals of French graduate students or teaching assistants and those of their counterparts still engaged in undergraduate work.[36] While the former are most likely to fight against the overall orientations of universities and their linkage with other economic, social, or political organizations, the former are more concerned with the problems raised by their future unemployment or their underemployment. Comparing the former to the skilled workers and artisans and the latter to the unskilled labor force of the nineteenth century, Touraine shows how the alliance of these forces first developed, then died during the month of May 1968.

In a parallel manner there is no doubt that the extent and the direction of student movements in the United States has varied with the composition of both the student body and the faculty of American institutions. While students movements have been uniformly started by student "elites" and hence by the elements the most likely to experience relative rather than absolute deprivation, they have evolved in three distinctive directions, depending on the structures of the educational milieu and of its linkages with outside agencies. In France, as in the United States, the movement has been split into three distinctive subgroups. While the first one perceived educational problems as secondary and aimed therefore at a drastic overall political change and while the second one has only been concerned with educational reforms, the third one is that of an Utopian communism in which individuals hope to reconcile their spontaneity as persons and their actions in groups.

The extent of the split and the actualization of student protests seems also to have been affected by the nature of the linkage between educational and other societal institutions. Thus Weinberg and Walker underline the role played in this respect by variations in political systems, and more specifically by the degree of centralization of political institutions and of educational facilities.[37] Classifying these two forms of variations in a fourfold table, these authors show how combinations of such variations may affect student movements (Table 26).

Table 26. *Institutionalized Forms of Students' Politics* [a]

Recruitment to Political Careers through Party Sponsorship of University Student Aspirants	Government Control over University Structure and Financing	
	Strong	Weak
High	Factional competition among political parties branches (Latin America)	Political parties branches of clubs (Great Britain)
Low	National student unions (France)	University student government (USA)

[a] Derived from I. Weinberg and K. Walker, "Student Politics," *American Journal of Sociology,* Vol. 75, No. 1, pp. 77–96. By permission of the University of Chicago Press, 1969.

When the centralization of both educational and political institutions is low as in the case in the United States, student activities are hardly linked to adult political structures and tension-reducing mechanisms tend to be built at the level of each specific campus in the form of student governments. Social distance between educational and noneducational institutions as well as among educational institutions themselves pushes noninstitutionalized forms of student movements toward extremism. The progression toward extremism of such movements results in the formation of splinter groups with limited membership and highly ideological orientations. Called retreatists by Weinberg and Walker, these groups are often in favor of the variety of Utopian solutions.

The second situation is obtained wherever both educational and other societal institutions are highly centralized, and it characterizes nations with one-party systems. In such a context most universities are highly politicized and student movements play a significant role in shaping national politics. If centralization of political institutions leads to the formation of student unions with significant powers, such unions are in turn willing or able to confront the government, as has been the case in Cuba or more recently in Czechoslovakia. Influences between schools and other basic institutions are reciprocal. While governments are able to affect university politics through student unions and through the cooperation of student leaders, the broad orientations of student unions enable their leaders to beat governments at their own game.

There are, however, variations in the relative centralization of social systems. At one end of the continuum is France, which is characterized both by the centralization of its institutions and the diversity of its political parties. The conflict between centripetal and centrifugal forces fostered by the French type of centralization and the ensuing fear of face-to-face contacts gives to student organizations a profile similar to those of other French political or social institutions. Thus students are regrouped into a national and centralized organization since bargaining processes in the educational sphere necessarily take place in Paris. The diversity of political parties, however, prevents them from penetrating effectively in universities, and the powerless diversity of political orientations limits both the size and the effectiveness of the student movement. Indeed, student activists often are both unwilling and unable to negotiate concrete and specific issues at the local level. While radical ideological orientations have helped labor unions to maintain their *raison d'être*, these orientations may hardly take roots in the university in view of the social composition of its population and of the diversity of its occupational trajectories. Yet student movements gain a strong impetus in times of national crisis, as during the war in Algeria when it became clear that all students shared a common fate and were threatened with a similar danger. Their gains in power may also result from the acute crises fostered by an excessive centralization. Mobilization of students was helped, for instance, in 1968 by the complete inability of educational authorities to cope immediately with specific issues raised by students in a variety of institutional arenas. In both cases national union of students has become temporarily an autonomous political force with which both the government and political parties had to reckon. In both cases, however, the political capital so acquired has been rapidly eroded by the social distance opposing French social categories to one another and by the autistic radicalism that so often colors the ideological orientations of French political and social movements in times of crisis.

At the other end of the continuum is the case of Great Britain where the relative centralization of political institutions is to be contrasted with the decentralization of universities and other schools of higher education. For a long time student movements in Great Britain have been articulated around the existing political parties that were able to maintain strong clubs and sections in universities and to use them as agencies of recruitment and socialization for adult politics. As noted by Weinberg and Walker, however, increases in university enrollments, and the ensuing increased disparities in the quality of educational facilities as well as the resulting accentuation of types of government control has led to the obsolescence of previous institutional arrangements. The formation of the Radical Students Alliances, for instance, has jeopardized the traditional mechanisms by which tensions between students and adult organizations used to be reduced.

Conclusions.   The schools constitute the privileged locus of current societal tensions.

As a society increases in scale, there is a corresponding rise in the educational prerequisites underlying access to the most rewarding slots of the occupational structure and a subsequent rise in the importance that all individuals attach to formal schooling. Formal schooling acts as an increasingly *necessary* condition for economic and social success but it does not act as a sufficient condition along these lines. As a society becomes more complex, and as social processes become subjected to the conflicting forces of universalism and particularism, there are increased discrepancies between the actual rewards that individuals derive from their educational investments and the aspirations they entertained while they were at school. These discrepancies concern differences between the nature and the income of the jobs that school graduates were striving for and those of the occupations they ultimately enter.

Further, since increase in scale is accompanied by a growing differentiation of residential, occupational, and educational structures, the various segments of a society tend to be exposed to differing types of training and educational programs. As a result the form and the magnitude of the discrepancies between educational dividends and educational aspirations vary with the type of school population considered and the type of curriculum to which they are exposed. Correspondingly, these populations have an increasingly difficult time communicating with one another.

Since increase in societal scale induces maximal tensions between centripetal and centrifugal forces, such tensions are most likely to express themselves on the educational scene. In spite of the stress placed upon the communication and coordination functions to be performed by schools, contrasts in the characteristics of the population they serve, disparities in the objectives at which they aim, increased social distance between teaching forces and remaining parts of the adult societies—all these forces cannot but erode the consensus-building functions that many peoples would like to see attached to educational enterprises. Under these conditions it is important to identify the conflicts plaguing the educational scene and its linkage with other institutional arenas. Such conflicts might reflect rearguard reactions against unavoidable changes and against the abolition of certain privileges slowly acquired by certain segments of society but they might also prefigure the emergence of a new social order. In other words, the actions of the actors involved in such conflicts may be retrospective or prospective.

NOTES AND REFERENCES

1. See M. Blaugh, *Education and the Employment Problem in Developing Countries* (Geneva: International Labor Office, 1972), pp. 27–39.

2. C. Jencks et al., *Inequality: A Reassessment of the Effect of Family and Schooling* (New York: Basic Books, 1972), Chapter 5.

3. R. Clignet and P. Foster, *The Fortunate Few* (Evanston: Northwestern University Press, 1966), Chapters 6, 7.

4. See A. Gouveia and R. Havighurst, *Ensino medio e desenvolvimento* (São Paulo: Edicies Melhioramentos, 1969), Chapter 7.

5. See "The Educational and Early Occupational Attainment Process," *American Sociological Review,* Vol. 34, 1969, pp. 82–92. See also J. Spaeth, "Occupational Attainment Among Male College Graduates," *American Journal of Sociology,* Vol. 75, 1970, pp. 632–644.

6. See C. Bommelaer, "A quoi revent les grosses tetes," *Expansion* (Juillet: Aout, 1970), pp. 101–105.

7. This results probably from the fact that traditionally the best students of engineering schools were supposed to join the public sector of the economy.

8. A. Gouveia and R. Havighurst, *op. cit.,* Chapter 7.

9. The group of highly acculturated students was comprised of individuals whose parents had at least completed primary school, were engaged in modern nonmanual occupations, and were from an urban origin. Their low counterparts comprised individuals with a rural background and illiterate parents engaged in subsistence farming. See R. Clignet and P. Foster *loc. cit.*

10. C. Jencks et al., *op. cit.*, Chapter 6.

11. See H. Rempel, *Labor Migration into Urban Centers and Urban Unemployment in Kenya* (unpublished Ph.D. dissertation, University of Wisconsin, 1970).

12. C. Jencks et al., *op. cit.*, p. 181.

13. See R. Clignet and J. Sween, "Urban Unemployment as a Determinant of Political Unrest," *Canadian Journal of African Studies,* Vol. 3, 1969, pp. 463–488. This situation is not specific to Cameroun. A similar study conducted earlier in Brazzaville by R. Devauges, *Le chomage à Brazzaville* (Paris: Orstom, 1959), tends to yield similar results. As in Douala the educational characteristics of jobless populations varied significantly with their age, and the higher educational attainments of younger jobless populations accounted for their differential reaction to their current plight; as in Douala the unemployment of young school leavers reflected disparities between levels of aspirations and levels of opportunity offered by the local economy.

14. For example, I have observed that in 1963 a substantial number of unskilled manual workers employed by an Abidjan textile firm were individuals with one or two years of postprimary education and had failed to be admitted in the next grade. They reported to choose deliberately an unskilled job in order not to commit themselves to that current job and to be ready to go back to school as soon as they would pass an examination into one of the training programs sponsored by the government.

15. Thus while the proportion of nonmanual workers over 45 years of age and with more than 12 years of education is 20 times greater than the corresponding percentage for their manual counterparts (11 percent versus 0.6 percent), the differences between these populations is less marked among younger age groups, for example, for those less than 20 years old. No less than 13 percent of the manual workers in that age group have more than 12 years of formal schooling against 29 percent of the white-collar individuals.

16. R. Clignet and P. Foster, *op. cit.*, Chapter 8.

17. C. Baudot and J. Vimont, "Les titulaires d'un diplôme d'enseignement technique ou professionel dans la population active," *Population,* Vol. 20, 1965, pp. 751–786. For a narrower study of the same phenomenon, see also J. Vimont and G. Gontier, "Enquete sur les femmes fontionnaires," *Population,* Vol. 20, 1965, p. 2152, where the motivations of security are shown to decline with level of educational attainment.

18. See C. Bartholdi, "De la donnee profession du père dans les recherches de sociologie de l'éducation," in M. Matthijsen and C. Vervoort, *Education in Europe* (Paris: Mouton, 1969), pp. 30–66.

19. Of course the distinction between centralized and decentralized institutions in this regard is probably culturally relative. First, it varies with the relative incidence of public and private schools. In addition, it also varies with historical patterns of educational development. As already argued, a French type of centralization implies that students of public institutions are deemed to be more qualified than their counterparts attending private institutions, but the pattern is reversed in the British-dominated decentralized school systems.

20. W. Sewel, A. Haller, and C. Ohlendorf, "The Educational and Early Occupational Status Attainment Process," *American Sociological Review,* Vol. 35, 1970, pp. 1014–1022.

21. R. Clignet, *Blue and White Collar Workers: the Modern Labor Force in the Cameroun,* (forthcoming).

22. See J. Summerskill, "Drop Outs of Colleges," in N. Sanford, *The American College* (New York: Wiley, 1962), pp. 627–657. Of course we are aware of the fact that the motivational factors that are important in this case decline in importance as one considers drop-out populations at the level of high or of primary schools. For a discussion of the findings at this latter level, see R. Dentler and M. Warshauer, *Big City Drop Out and Illiterates* (New York: Praeger, 1968).

23. Personal communication of H. Benoit, former director of these courses.

24. See C. deMontlibert, "Promotion et reclassement; Les élèves d'un centre d'enseignement par cours du soir à la recherche d'une promotion par un diplôme," *Revue Francaise de Sociologie,* Vol. 8, 1967, pp. 208–212.

25. C. Jencks et al., *op. cit.,* Chapter 6.

26. R. Clignet, *Blue and White Collar Workers, op. cit.*

27. See C. Jencks, *op. cit.,* Chapter 7.

28. For a discussion of this theme, see J. Scott and M. El-Assel, "Multiversity, University Size, University Quality and Student Protest: An Empirical Study," *American Sociological Review,* Vol. 34, 1969, pp. 702–709. The authors found that large, complex, high-quality schools had higher rates of demonstration than small, simple, low-quality institutions.

29. See A. Touraine, "Le Communisme Utopique ou le mouvement de mai" (Paris: Le Seuil, 1968), Chapter 1.

30. G. Lefebvre, *Sociologie de la vie quotidienne* (Paris: Gallimard, 1967), Chapter 2.

31. P. Slater, *The Pursuit of Loneliness* (Boston: Beacon Press, 1970), Chapters 5, 6.

32. For a systematic review, see V. Bengtson, "The Generation Gap: A Review and Typology of Social Psychological Perspectives," in P. Altbach and R. Laufer, eds., *The New Pilgrims* (New York: McKay, 1972), pp. 195–213.

33. L. Feuer, *The Conflict of Generations, The Character and Significance of Student Movements* (New York: Basic Books, 1969).

34. See V. Bengtson, in P. Altbach and R. Laufer, *op. cit.,* p. 208.

35. See F. Pinner, "Students: A Marginal Elite in Politics," in P. Altbach and R. Laufer, *op. cit.,* pp. 281–296.

36. See A. Touraine, *op. cit.,* Chapters 5, 6, and Conclusion. See also A. Zijderveldt, *The Abstract Society,* (Garden City: Doubleday, 1970).

37. See I. Weinberg and K. Walker, "Student Politics and Political Systems, Toward a Typology," *American Journal of Sociology,* Vol. 75, 1969, pp. 77–96.

12

FINAL CONCLUSIONS

At the end of this long journey, it is probably relevant to return to the point of departure of this enterprise and to evaluate what has been accomplished. Clearly enough, educational institutions around the world experience a growing malaise. As this malaise proliferates, there is an ever-increasing number of pamphlets written both to explain the sad condition in which schools have fallen and, more important, to propose remedies and solutions to the current crisis. The first underlying preoccupation of this book is to challenge the legitimacy of most of these quests.

> If we ask ourselves some questions about the nature of ideal education, regardless of variations in space and in time, we are implicitly positing that an educational enterprise is not real. We are not seeing in it a sum of practices and institutions that have evolved slowly through time, that are linked to the remaining social institutions and mirror them, and cannot as such be changed more freely than the very structure of society. . . . Often enough, we believe that men develop schools and educational enterprises in order to achieve a particular goal. And we believe that insofar as the underlying organizations of such enterprises are not everywhere the same, it is because individuals and social groups have made mistakes either as to their goals or as to their means. From this viewpoint, the schools of the past appear to be as many total or partial errors. . . . We feel that we must therefore disregard them and that the teaching of history only helps us to avoid

repeating the mistakes of the past. . . . Yet it is vain to believe that children can be educated the way their parents
wish. . . . Whether children are reared according to obsolete
or futuristic principles, it does not matter, they do not grow
under normal conditions since within each period of time and
unit of space there is a regulatory type of socialization from
which it is impossible to deviate without creating many resistances which in turn give way to corresponding dissidences.
. . . The fact is that the ideas and customs on which this regulatory type of education is based is not made by us as individuals. Rather, they are the product and the reflection of
our social life and in a large part they are the outcome of
the organization and ideas of preceding generations. . . .
Under such conditions, is it possible for the individual to
reconstruct through his own personal mode of thinking what
is not a result of individual thought? Indeed the individual
does not confront a tabula rasa on which he can build anything he wants. Rather he is confronting realities that he cannot create nor destroy nor transform at will. . . .[1]

The first stone on which this book is built pertains therefore to the
notion that an assessment of current educational problems requires the
use of a particular theoretical and methodological framework, hope-
fully provided by sociology. Insofar as educational institutions result
from both present and past aspects of a social structure, the primary
task of the sociologist is to isolate and identify the form, the magnitude,
and the universality of the various patterns of interaction among
schools and societies. But where does this particular quest begin and
end? And how does the sociologist take into account what the actors of
the particular scene studied say they do, rather than to analyze directly
what they do?

**Summary of the Contradictions between Liberty and Quality in the
Educational Process.** In the introduction I suggested that the current
malaise results from the dilemma experienced between equality and
liberty, and I have shown that the first step toward a sociology of education consists in examining the conscious rationalizations, expectations, and hopes that teachers, parents, students, and other members of
a community entertain with regard to this dilemma. This is both the
beginning and the end of the sociological approach, for the social scientist must not only derive his work from the conscious models used by
the various groups present in the situation, but he must also ultimately
enable such groups to modify the initial models underlying their ac-

tions and enlarge the number of choices they perceive as available to cope with the situation.

Thus the initial task is to determine whether the forms and the intensity of the dilemma vary among types of educational institutions and among the distinct categories of actors involved in the educational process or whether, alternatively, they pervade an entire social structure. The first part of the book, accordingly, has been devoted to an evaluation of variations in the relative autonomy enjoyed by schools and their actors *vis-a-vis* other societal basic institutions. I hope to have shown the importance of conscious and unconscious models in the patterns of interaction between familial, economic, political or religious organizations, and educational structures.

At the conscious level, educators are still expected to act as *in loco parentis*. Further, their duties are also often defined by reference to religious prescriptions, and in both cases this tells us something about the educational history of mankind. Since specialized educational institutions appear only after social systems have reached a certain level of complexity, they are most likely to borrow specific images, symbols, and values from the family and the church, the very organizations from which they stem. With the secularization of society and the growing importance attached to economics, teachers and school administrators have also begun to borrow their vocabulary from industrial and commercial organizations. In short, the conscious models used to account for and justify educational enterprises reflect the successive moments of educational, political, and economic development and differentiation.

At the unconscious level there is a full set of influences of family structures on school attendance or educational behavior; variations in the political and economic organization of a society are associated with parallel contrasts in the structure of its educational institutions; and cleavages in religious orientations are accompanied by parallel differences in types of academic behavior. Reciprocally, however, variations in educational attainment are associated with corresponding contrasts in (a) patterns of mate selection, conjugal relations, and child rearing practices; (b) patterns of economic behavior both in terms of consumption and of production; (c) forms and nature of political participation; and (d) attitudes toward religion. These variations affect the limits within which educational experiences liberate individuals from the constraints imposed upon them in a number of areas of social participation.

Thus, equality of educational opportunities does not constitute an end in itself but provides the means necessary for enhancing the liberties individuals might enjoy in other arenas of social participation. The limits under which the influence of this equality operates depend first on the social value attached to formal schooling. In the United States Jefferson wrote in 1816 in a letter to Colonel Yancey "If a nation expects to be ignorant and free in a state of civilization, it expects what never was and never will. . . . I know of no safe depository of the ultimate powers of a society but the people themselves; and if we think them not enlightened enough to exercise their control with wholesome discretion, the remedy is not to take it from them but to inform their discretion by education." [2] However, nation-states do not necessarily equally subscribe to such views, and even those that formally attach an equally high value to this particular ideal still differ in terms of the linkage that exist between educational structures and political, economic, and religious institutions. Thus the nature and the effectiveness of the mechanisms likely to facilitate equality of educational opportunities differ between decentralized and centralized systems. Further, the definition of educational opportunities depends upon the forms and the extent of the principle of stratification operating in the cultures under study.

However, the very concept of educational opportunities is equivocal, since the term may refer to the necessity of (a) providing all individuals with the same chances of gaining access to educational structures; (b) correcting the imbalances that characterize the cognitive and social skills of various social groups before they enter the educational process; and (c) providing individuals who have enjoyed equal amounts and forms of schooling with identical rewards in the familial, economic, political, and religious arenas of participation. Although in this latter perspective, we intend willy-nilly to substitute a meritocratic stratification to the preexisting principles of social hierarchy, new forms of inequality in educational achievement do not necessarily have more beneficial effects on the sentiments of justice and dignity experienced by individuals. Nor is the establishment of a meritocracy, absolutely independent of preexisting principles of social stratification.

Similarly, there are also equivocations in the concept of educational liberty. Education enables individuals to adapt more easily to the social system in which they participate and to gain the maximal amount of advantages from the position they occupy in the social structure. While this concept of liberty supposes a stable social order, the second conception stresses the fact that education enables individuals to change the structure and the dynamics of the institutions to which they belong.

In brief, the first definition of liberty minimizes the importance of the interaction between schooling and conflict, while the second definition stresses both the significance and the variability of this interaction.

To summarize the entire first part of this book, the initial chapters aim at establishing that the definition of educational activities and their liberating and equalizing effects are not independent of past and present social structures and processes. Because the dilemma between liberty and equality concerns the interaction between schools and other basic social institutions, its own forms and the forms of this interaction are culturally relative and should be treated as distinct. This provisional conclusion serves as a background to the second part of my enterprise which is concerned with a more thorough examination of the multifaceted aspects taken by the dilemma in the educational context.

As soon as educational activities become distinctive and require the services of a skilled personnel operating in a specialized locale, social groups are obliged to relinquish part of the power they are entitled to exert upon their young members and to delegate the corresponding responsibilities to teachers. The extent and the form of this delegation vary both in time and in space, and schools and their personnel are subjected to varying forms of control. At one end of the continuum this control is exerted in a centralized and *generalizing* framework, and this organizational pattern rests upon the postulate that formal schooling is a *right* uniformly guaranteed to school age populations. At the other end of the continuum are schools whose organization reflects a decentralized and hence *differentiating* pattern. The corresponding mechanism of control rests upon the notion that formal schooling is a *privilege* to be privately acquired and is hence subjected to constant negotiations between teachers and parents.

Clearly the nature, the form, and the intensity of the pressures exerted on school personnel are different in these two contexts. While decentralization is *always* initially based upon the belief that parents should enjoy a maximal amount of liberty in determining the educational fate of their offspring, the implications of this organizational pattern on the autonomy of teachers are variable. Wherever schooling is defined in elitist terms and wherever teaching activities are to be exerted by individuals who share the same characteristics as current elites, decentralization refers to the autonomy that each school enjoys both *vis-a-vis* other educational institutions and *vis-a-vis* the public at large. In contrast, wherever schooling is only one mechanism of upward mobility and wherever teaching remains therefore an activity that yields low prestige, decentralization refers to the control that local communities are able to exert on school personnel and their activities. Although local communities have the *legitimate authority* to supervise educational activities, they differ from one another in their actual power along these lines. Thus, there are inequalities in the control that various social groups exert on school personnel, and correspondingly, there are parallel differences in the effective restrictions decentralization imposes upon the occupational liberty of teachers and administrators.

Far from being uniform, the effectiveness of the mechanisms of social control exerted on schools varies both with historical precedents and with the current profile of the various basic institutions of a particular society. While decentralization aims at stressing the liberty parents should enjoy toward teachers and administrators, its effectiveness depends both upon the value historically assigned to formal schooling and upon the relative integration of political, economic, educational, and religious institutions. As a result, there are variations in the degree to which parental liberty operates against the occupational liberty of teachers.

Regardless of the pressures that parents intend to exert on school personnel, teachers and administrators strive to obtain a professional status and hence to control the recruitment and the socialization of new practitioners, in order to enjoy a maximal amount of autonomy in the exercise of their activities. The relative professionalization of teachers (and hence their claim to a maximal occupational liberty) depends upon the relative political and economic development of a country (and hence upon the number of alternative channels for upward mobility and occupational success) and upon the mechanisms of social control exerted on schools. Indeed, while decentralization exposes individual teachers to conflicting pressures and prevents them from forming an autonomous and powerful subculture, centralization is a necessary but insufficient condition for enhancing the solidarity of this particular occupational group and its autonomy. In addition, the professional status of teachers varies not only across cultures but also across educational institutions. University professors occupy a better position than primary school teachers, both because their clientele is not "captive" and because they affect more immediately the ultimate occupational destination of their students. Thus some teachers are more professional than others.

Insofar as the liberty that teachers and communities enjoy in the educational realm are both relative and mutually exclusive, there are variations in the form and the intensity of the conflicts that oppose them to one another. Whenever school personnels define themselves as professionals, one would expect them to use strategies that reflect their autonomy and their differentiation from other segments of society. Conversely, whenever they perceive their activities as those of the employees of a bureaucratic organization, they should be more likely to use the strategies common to all working classes and, more specifically, to resort to unionization and strikes to obtain satisfaction in their demands. Such expectations are not necessarily valid, and striking may simultaneously characterize teaching forces afraid of losing their professional status and teaching forces that desire such a status. Thus, once more, the implications attached to particular organizational patterns are not universal, and the generalizing framework of a centralized bureaucratic organization is not always conflicting with the differentiating framework that underlies the activities of an occupational group viewed as professional. In other words, the fit between the means and the ends of such groups varies both through space and time.

The fact remains, however, that schools concern primarily children and students. While such institutions are supposed uniformly to liberate all segments of the school-aged population from the constraints imposed upon them in their social surroundings, it is not sure that all segments of society enjoy equal access to the most liberating educational experiences. If the concept of equality of educational opportunity means equal access to the liberating effects of formal schooling, "equality of access" is problematic because of the differential distribution of abilities, motivations, and informations across various segments of the society at large. More important, the forms and the extent of patterns of inequalities of access into schools are conditioned by the profile of educational enterprises and hence by the distinction between centralization and decentralization as well as by the status accorded to teachers. In effect, all the data analyzed in this book suggest that the effects of centralization or decentralization on the status of educational actors are not necessarily convergent. While centralization or national integration might enhance the professionalization of the teaching force by facilitating its formation as a homogeneous and autonomous subculture, it might also be associated with declines in educational inequalities and hence in the differential access of various social and cultural groups to educational institutions. The effects of centralization may be internally inconsistent, since professionalization of teachers and equality in patterns of access to schools tend to be mutually exclusive ideas. Indeed, the preeminence of the status assigned to teachers is often enough a function of the preeminence of the status of their clientele. Centralization is perhaps a necessary but not a sufficient condition to the professionalization of teachers or to the equalizing functions of schools.

The conflicts between liberty and equality affect *access* to crucial educational roles, but they also pertain to the modes of interaction between teachers and students. The outcome of this interaction is problematic and depends in effect upon the prevailing modes of adaptation used by these two groups of actors. Both teaching and learning styles oscillate between assimilation and accommodation or between generalization and differentiation. Assimilation-based curricula and teaching styles emphasize perhaps a particular type of equality among students who are subjected to a same treatment. Yet such a type of curriculum and of teaching style reflects primarily the occupational liberty of educators, since this mode postulates the preeminence of the framework of action and analysis preestablished by such actors and, by implication, their power over students. In contrast, the adoption of accommodation-based curricula and teaching styles reflects a more crucial concern over educational equality, since this mode of adaptation entails a differentiation of the frameworks of action and analysis used by a teacher and the legitimation of the perspectives adopted by individual students. In addition, the relative use teachers make of either one of these modes of adaptation is not the product of chance but is contingent upon the composition of the student body (and hence upon patterns of access), upon the status of teachers in their community (and hence their professionalization), and upon the organizational patterns of the school (and hence its relative centralization).

Alternatively while assimilation as a mode of learning facilitates perhaps the perpetuation of the initial framework of analysis and action of the individual, it may thereby prevent students from reaping later on the liberating rewards that go with the educational process. In other words, there may be conflicts between the short- and long-term influence that educational activities exert on the liberty of students. Further, the influence of assimilation or accommodation-oriented modes of learning on the liberation of students varies with their social position (and hence the form and extent of social stratification operating in the society at large) and also with the disciplines they study (and hence the form and the extent of the stratification operating among the various disciplines involved in the educational process).

Yet the liberating effects of formal schooling are always conditional and are socially sanctioned by examinations. Examinations symbolize the liberty that teachers enjoy vis-a-vis students, but the exercise of this liberty varies with the prevailing organizational pattern of educational institutions (and hence their degree of centralization or decentralization), the relative professionalization of the teaching force, and the characteristics of the student body. As a result definitions and interpretations of this particular type of liberty conflict with one another and may create an anomic climate, that is, a climate "where the individual derides the values of others and loses his sense of integration." [3] In other words, examinations may lead the contradictions underlying the liberties of individual teachers and individual students to become "activated," and as such they threaten the integrity of the whole educational process.

To emphasize once more the main focus of this book, the exercise of liberty evokes decentralization, professionalization, differentiation in the academic career of students, assimilation as learning and teaching styles, and divergences in the occupational choices and histories of students. Yet, these various facets of liberty are often conflicting and the most "liberated" populations acquire their privileges at the expense of other groups in the society at large or in the educational scene. Conversely, equality implies centralization, bureaucratization of teachers, access of all categories of the school-aged population to the most rewarding types of educational institutions, accommodation as teaching and learning styles, and convergences in the occupational placement or rewards of individuals with a similar level of educational attainment. Yet, these various aspects of equality are not necessarily consistent and certain categories of actors involved in the educational process tend always to be more equal than others.

Insofar as the modes of interaction among and between the components of educational liberty and equality vary through space and time, one of the tasks of the sociologist is to examine the cultural relativeness of the relevant dilemmas. This cultural relativeness results from the fact that an educational institution has not rigorously systematic properties, and that its functioning, its profile, or the behavior of its main actors are simultaneously influenced by specific historical precedents and by the current organizational patterns and tensions operating in educational and other institutions of a particular society. Under these conditions, the purpose of the sociological enterprise is to identify the limits within which centralization, professionalization, representation of various groups in educational institutions, teaching and learning styles, and examinations interact with one another, that is, the conditions under which their effects are reinforcing one another or alternatively tend to cancel one another.

The comparative method and its strategies have often enabled us to identify such conditions. For example, it is often tempting to interpret laws on compulsory education within a contemporary and generalizing framework and to read them as a mechanism by which the bureaucracies characteristic of postindustrial societies oppress the younger segments of the population and prevent them from enjoying both educational and occupational liberties. This, however, is to neglect the differentiating influence of history and, more specifically, to forget that originally at least, these laws were primarily aimed at protecting youth.

Passed at a time when ideologies and political structures facilitated a ruthless employment of workers under age, these laws were derived from the postulate that it was necessary not only to prevent employers from hiring children, but also to define the place where the latter population should spend their days. Under such conditions, the role of the sociologist is to examine whether intercultural differences in the dates at which such laws are passed and in the degree to which they are enforced reflect varying social arrangements. His role is also to ascertain the degree to which laws on compulsory attendance are still enforced because of a mere "time lag" and of the rigidity of legal organizations or because of deliberate attempts to subvert the initial intentions of lawmakers. Before deciding that such laws are oppressive and must be abolished, we must assess whether current social patterns differ from those prevailing at the time when the law was passed and hence to assess whether the abolition of such laws might foster the same type of exploitation as that existing before the law.

A study of the historical development of the controversies surrounding the policy implications of the notion of educational equality offers another illustration of the conflicting effects of historical and social forces on educational activities. Because of the conservative nature of such activities, the elite-oriented ideology stressing the contribution of academic experiences to liberty persists long after the first phases of industrialization.[4] It is indeed long after the increase in scale of economic enterprises that the majority of the public at large recognizes the fact that changes in economic structures require schools to facilitate individual social and geographic mobility and that an ideology emerges, which emphasizes the contribution of formal schooling to equality.

The concrete implications of these ideological changes vary, however, with the value attached to centralization and decentralization as organizational patterns. As long as all social processes continue to be perceived as legitimately decentralized, the recognition of the equalizing functions of schools tends to remain purely formal. Indeed, since equality involves comparisons in the educational treatments accorded to

all individuals within a social system, it requires a process of centralization. Insofar as this process is at variance with the highly decentralized nature of most American institutions, the federal government has
never been in a position to assess directly whether local communities
and school districts really allocate equal human and social resources for
the education of *all* segments of the school-aged population. Whatever
the definition of the equalizing functions assigned to schools, the ensuing conflicts between centralization and decentralization make the implementation of equalizing policies dependent upon the interventions
of the courts.[5]

Divergences between the dynamics of economic and political forces
and historical legacies affect not only the time lag between structural
and ideological changes but also the significance of the tensions between ideologies and practices as well as the nature of the specific
mechanisms by which such tensions are reduced. Whenever there is a
high degree of consistency in the relative pattern of centralization characterizing political, religious, economic, and educational institutions,
educational changes are more likely to be uniform and pushed forward
by executive and legislative interventions. Conversely, whenever these
patterns are highly inconsistent, educational changes occur more
frequently on a piecemeal basis, and they require furthermore the intervention of the judiciary.

Sociological analysis consists not only in examining the cultural relativeness of the evolution of the concept of equality of educational opportunities but also in identifying the relevant strategies currently
adopted by the major actors of the educational scene. In the United
States, the federal government has pursued two distinct policies in this
regard. It has pushed programs of compensatory education for the
"underprivileged" segments of the population, and it has also tried to
develop programs of educational integration and hence of educational
centralization. Clearly the results of the first policy have been limited for
a number of reasons. Because of the decentralized nature of the political process, federal authorities cannot exert a tight control on the
mechanisms by which the administrators of individual school districts
reallocate effectively human and social resources to minorities. Since
compensatory programs require the commitment of individual school
districts, their development remains limited both in space and over
time. Insofar as this restricts the evaluation of such innovative measures on a standardized and uniform scale, it also minimizes their contributions to a policy of equality and centralization.

The second policy, educational integration, rests upon the premise that the mixing of privileged and underprivileged school-aged populations has both short- and long-term beneficial effects. It is supposed to enhance the educational attainment of minorities without lowering the performances of their white counterparts, and it is expected to be associated with a growing uniformity in the major social and psychological outlook of the American population and hence to facilitate the further development of centralization. In fact, this expectation is based upon three sociological assumptions, the validity of which is culturally relative.

The first assumption states that changes in behavior should induce change in attitudes. Yet an examination of the differential modes of adoption of integration across the various parts of the United States shows the limits within which changes in behavior can effectively take place. Clearly integration has been more frequently implemented in the South than in the North for a number of reasons. The segregation of southern schools was *de jure* and corresponded therefore to a centralized legal pattern. In addition, the *de jure* nature of southern segregation often facilitated the coexistence of black and white schools in a same territory.[6] Thus integration was technically easier to achieve than in the North, where educational segregation is *de facto,* has no legal basis, and is more systematically paralleled by patterns of residential segregation. Because southern educational activities are more directly financed by the federal government, they were also more vulnerable to a direct central mode of control. Pressures toward integration and hence educational centralization are heightened when the financial and legal structures of local educational institutions are already themselves centralized. While this facilitates a *uniform* rather than a piecemeal attack on the problem at hand, we may infer that changes in behavior are not evenly easy to bring about and hence that their effects on attitudes are not necessarily alike.

The second assumption underlying educational integration is that increased contacts between individuals makes them more likely to like one another.[7] Unfortunately, an examination of patterns of social interaction prevailing in schools where part of the population is bussed, shows the limits of this particular proposition which does not take into account variations in the circumstances underlying the initiation of social contacts. The desirability of interracial contacts is often defined from *without* rather than *within* the groups of students affected by this particular innovation. For white people, these contacts may be viewed negatively insofar as they are superimposed by the *fiat* of a central authority and are at variance with the traditional ideals of decentralization. For black people, these contacts, as desirable as they may look, are still a manifestation of the control that white people would like to impose upon the functioning of black communities.[8] In addition, this assumption does not take into account other social psychological propositions that have stressed that differences in the perceived status of interacting individuals or groups of individuals are associated with parallel contrasts in their patterns of communication and hence with a reinforcement of the differences in the status of individuals participating in the interaction process.[9] Given the fact that white students occupy a preeminent position not only because of their station in the society at large but because of their role as hosts, the chances are they will not interact in an egalitarian manner with their new classmates.[10] As a matter of fact, integration and bussing may lead segregation *within* schools to succeed to segregation *between* schools, and the disruptive effects of segregation are not necessarily minimized when physical proximity becomes combined with social distance.

Finally, although less frequently and explicitly stated, the last assumption underlying educational integration is that the exposure of black students to a uniform white-dominated curriculum and teaching style will always facilitate their upward mobility. This mobility may be the result of three differing educational strategies. Upward mobility may be defined as the result of the lonely efforts undertaken by each individual student, in which case the obligations of educational institutions are primarily assimilation oriented. These obligations involve the elimination of particularistic criteria in the processing of students, and schools are expected to attract and process their pupils on the basis of academic abilities alone. Even though these expectations may imply the award of financial aid to gifted but poor students, they are without consequences on the recruitment of teachers and on the teaching styles demanded of them. There are two limitations in this particular view of formal schooling. First this assimilation-oriented policy favors the upward mobility of a *restricted* number of individuals. Second, the approaches adopted by educators do not necessarily affect the attitudes of employers toward hiring.[11]

A second strategy for satisfying the aspirations toward upward mobility of lower classes requires both accommodation-based teaching and learning styles. This second strategy also requires individual students to have exceptional abilities and motivations in order to adapt to the demands of the dominant surroundings. In contrast to the first strategy, however, this one also requires the teaching force to be particularly sensitive to the cultural style of marginal social groups. A marked per-

sonalization of the relations between teachers and pupils is necessitated; its implementation depends on the professionalization of teachers.
However, this professionalization is made problematic by the very nature of the student body, and the specific nature of the teaching skills
appropriate to enhance the performance of lower-class students prevents educators from achieving a high status in the community.
Teachers base their claim to the status of professional on the premise
that their activities parallel those of a medical doctor and consist in
bringing back the marginal elements of the population into the main
stream of social skills, practices, and values.[12] Yet the labeling of lower
classes as "deviants" contaminates the status ascribed to teachers who
cannot be entitled to be treated as professionals. In addition, while a
personalization of pedagogical treatments necessitates the professionalization of teachers, this professionalization is not a sufficient condition for a greater personalization of the pedagogical communication.
Finally, the personalization of the relations between teachers and students in this regard raises two major questions: Is this personalization
functionally specific and should it concern exclusively the transmission
of cognitive skills? But is it possible to affect cognitive styles without simultaneously influencing individual values and orientations? Although
teachers may be universalistic in their activities, does this automatically
guarantee that employers are likely to adopt the same set of values and
orientations?

The third strategy for satisfying the aspirations toward upward mobility of the lower classes involves their partial or total mobilization in
order to obtain drastic changes in the distribution of educational resources. This revolution threatens the legitimacy of the entire educational enterprise, for this legitimacy is based upon the postulate that
formal schooling is both a necessary and sufficient condition for obtaining access to the scarce rewards that the social system offers to individuals. As a result, the revolution is liable to fail whenever educational
changes are not accompanied by parallel changes either in the value
system of the society at large or at least in the linkage between educational and occupational experiences.

The current fate of black students enrolled in white dominated universities offers a case in point. Thus far, these students are hardly exposed to a differentiated pedagogical treatment. This results from a
number of factors. University officials want to pay a minimal price for
integration, which leads them to minimize the difficulties eventually encountered by minorities. And although these officials often believe that
an individualization of the pedagogical treatment applied to black stu-

dents is likely to induce a political mobilization of the individuals involved, and hence an acceleration in the ongoing process of change,
black activists are sometimes hostile toward this individualized pedagogy, for they fear that it will bring about a lowering in the very pressures that enabled them to obtain an increase in the share of the "educational pie." For these black leaders, special courses are not only a
recognition of their low level of adaptation to the norms of the institution but they also represent activities that will prevent political activism.
Correspondingly, since changes in the composition of student populations are not accompanied by changes in the teaching or in the evaluation styles of the institutions of higher learning, there is a devaluation
of the certifying functions these universities are expected to perform.

As this devaluation becomes more apparent, a shift to the third strategy is more likely to occur, and the risks of both political revolutions
and counterrevolutions are correspondingly heightened. White individuals may begin to feel "victimized" by the declining value of their
education, and this might lead them to reaffirm directly or indirectly
the supremacy of their "race." Or black individuals may become aware
of the illusory nature of the "plums" offered to them, and they may
decide to demand simultaneous and drastic changes in the distributive
system of *all* economic and social assets, while they will continue to advocate a curriculum and a pedagogical technique more relevant to their
own needs and orientations. In this process, however, they risk losing
their credibility and risk jeopardizing the functioning of revolutionary
institutions.[13]

Because various groups do not enjoy the same resources, nor the
same orientations, it is illusory to believe that equality of educational
opportunities requires uniformities in recruitment patterns and in pedagogical treatments. To impose such uniformities, at best, mediates a
perpetuation of existing inequalities. Does the implementation of equality rely, after all, upon differentiation? Of course, the answer is not
so easy, since differentiation is also used for facilitating the emergence of liberties.

The conclusions of the controversial study of Jensen illustrate the
ambiguities attached to the linkage between equality and diversity
(rather than uniformity) of educational facilities, techniques, and
aims.[14] To plead in favor of a diversity of educational facilities and
techniques does not seem problematic in the sense that they facilitate
greater justice and rationality. The diversity of educational aims, however, remains a troublesome concept. Who is to legitimize "diverse educational aims?" The technocratic expert? The economic and political es-

tablishment? And which criteria should be used to make the relevant decisions? Even though Jensen makes reference to *diverse* patterns of ability rather than about *uneven* levels of ability, the fact remains that diverse patterns of ability are not evenly valued and that, in their definition of diverse educational aims, "experts" may prevent social change and greater equality. Of course, it could also be argued that the responsibility to legitimize diverse abilities should not incumb upon experts, but should be a privilege exerted by individual students themselves or by their families who should be allowed to experiment and find by trial and error the goals they assign to educational activities. But who is going to pay for the costs resulting from the potential mistakes that individuals could make in this regard? The costs of these mistakes might be as high for the remaining parts of society as for the individuals concerned.

To conclude, the cultural relativeness of dilemma between equality and liberty reflects variations both in the relative importance to be attached to individual as opposed to societal goals, and in the relative importance to be attached to the past, the present and the future. But does the task of the sociologist consist only in the analysis of this relativeness? Observer and analyst of a situation, he is also an actor of this situation and as such he is interested in proposing an answer to the educational dilemma between liberty and equality. Correspondingly, his contribution consists also in making a critical assessment of the range of the responses offered to solve these dilemmas.

The Variety of Utopian Responses to These Contradictions. These responses are, in effect, ethical, ideological, or Utopian, and the first step in this assessment consists in distinguishing these responses from one another. Ethical responses concerned with the identification of the ideal norms with which individual actions are supposed to comply, are bidimensional insofar as they must reconcile the demands of an absolute and the requirements of the "here and now." [15] They become, however, ideological as soon as the historical and social structures of a system change intensely enough to make ethical prescriptions and proscriptions irrelevant and unreal. [16] To give an illustration of this point, while the taboo against taking interests on loans is *ethical* as long as the social structure involves intimate relations between neighbors who are functionally interdependent, it becomes *ideological* as soon as the scale of social and economic exchanges increases and economic development becomes articulated around the notion of capitalism and the notion of retributed loans. Indeed this taboo is unworldly in the sense that it is

circumvented and disobeyed. Similarly, the *ethical* view that the school
should be the locus where children learn to find for themselves the nature and the limits of their creativity becomes *ideological* whenever the
current system of social stratification prevents all forms of creativity
from being *equally* valued and increases the dependence of the rewards
attached to creativity upon social status. In turn, ideologies become
Utopias as soon as individuals and social groups embody the corresponding wish-images into actual patterns of behavior.

The main characteristics of an educational Utopia remain to be determined. Clearly Utopia presuppose idealistic philosophies, for the importance attached to socializing activities relies upon the preeminence
attached to free will. Such philosophies are likely to prevail at times
when gross contradictions emerge between various aspects of the existing social structure and when men aim at making more sense of their
surroundings and at regaining control over their own fates.

Historically, such philosophies were particularly numerous during
the Renaissance, when changes in patterns of economic organization
made the scholastic models of thought increasingly obsolete. The writings of both Rabelais and Montaigne, for instance, offered two independent models to build a more individualistic system of ethical prescriptions and proscriptions. Similar ideas emerged again during the
eighteenth century, when it became clear that the economic power of
the bourgeoisie was in conflict with the political and religious influences
retained by the nobility and the Church. The same ideas seem to have
been again particularly alive at the end of the nineteenth century as a
result of the contradictions fostered by industrialization between the
demands of liberty and equality, to blossom once more today, when
such contradictions take new forms as a result of the conflicting pressures brought about by the emergence of postindustrial patterns of
social organization.[17] In brief, the idea of Utopia is likely to appear easily in the field of educational activities, for the retrospective nature of
schooling (and its ensuing sensitivity to influences of the past) mag-
nifies current social contradictions.

Utopia in education takes a variety of forms. Following the distinctions proposed by Mannheim, it is possible to establish the subsequent
typology.

1. *Chiliasm.* This type of Utopia sees the revolution as a value in itself.
Coupled with radical anarchism, it sees the revolution as the only creative principle operating in the immediate present. Obviously the
schools of thought that view the educational process as aiming at a per-

manent liberation of individual creativity are salient in this particular category. All the free schools that do not accept the view that education is a preparation for life might be considered as chiliastic. Such schools conceive the revolution as being experienced through patterns of daily interaction. Correspondingly, children and students are defined as occupying the same positions and hence enjoying the same rights as teachers, parents, and adults. The main purpose of this Utopia is the reconciliation of individual and collective spontaneities, the reconciliation of individual and collective intelligences and emotions, deemed to be arbitrarily separated by the oppressive mechanisms of the current social order.

> There are these free school leaders who make a virtue of the capacity to start and stop things in response to sudden impulse and who [forget] about English grammar and the preparation for the Mathematics College Boards but get into "group talks and encounters." Thus [like the original chiliasts], the leaders of these Free Schools expect "a union with the immediate present" and stress the importance of "communicating," "touching," and "opening up." [18]

However, while the established elites of the existing social order do not differentiate between various types of Utopia, the educational "chiliasts" are often equally blind to the existing varieties of social order.

2. *Liberal humanitarianism.* This particular Utopian framework serves as a measuring rod by means of which the course of concrete events may be theoretically evaluated. In this "progressive" perspective, individual and collective goals are seen as interchangeable, and the schools are defined as the instrument by which both individuals and groups will reconcile simultaneously the conflicts that arise from the dilemmas between liberty and equality. This double reconciliation is viewed as possible because the ultimate function of education is to "enlighten." Thus the educational process is deemed simultaneously to facilitate processes of individual upward mobility and of creativity. Most important, it is also supposed to minimize the antagonisms that result from the differential privileges distinct groups can claim. Specifically, the liberal humanitarian argues that sharing a same educational experience will lead black and white upper- and lower-class children to share the same values and ideals of fraternity. It will enable them to alter the dynamics underlying the current existing social order. On the whole, this kind of Utopia seems to characterize the schools that "run skirmishes on the edge of the functions and priorities of domestication without undermining them. As they fly the flag, they are still accountable to it

and to the power or values that it represents." [19] In effect, such a Utopia constitutes a basic extension of the ideology of public schools.

3. *Conservatism.* The conservative mentality is not Utopian insofar as its very structures are in complete harmony with the reality it has mastered. It becomes Utopian only insofar as the counterattack of opposing classes causes conservatives to challenge the basis of their own current dominance. Like the liberal humanitarians, conservatives use a privileged segment of time to make a theoretical evaluation of the current concrete events, but whereas the former stress the role of the future in this respect, conservatives emphasize the significance of the past. A conservative Utopia is likely to prevail in the schools of the established elite and notably of the leisure class. The setting of private exclusive schools and the etiquette and the courses they impose upon their students celebrate the ideals of a defunct nobility. They also characterize the

> Free Schools which justify their escape in the country by pointing out that they have retired from the North American system as a whole. They do their thing, which is sun, good food, and fresh water, old battled XVIIIth century houses and a box of baby turtles. . . . Some of these Free Schools build the core of their life style around competence in those areas of basic handiwork and back-to-nature skill in which there is no competition from the outside world in as much as there is neither functions, use nor application in the social interlock in which we are obliged to live.[20]

4. *Socialo-communism.* Like the liberal model, this particular Utopia emphasizes the role of the future. Whereas the former assigns an absolute value to it, this form stresses its relativeness. Like chiliasm, a socialo-communist Utopia emphasizes the significance of revolutions in historical processes. Against chiliasm, however, this Utopia invites us to perceive the discontinuities corresponding to revolutions as privileged and hence scarce moments of historical developments. Like the conservative Utopias, finally, the socialo-communist Utopia stresses determinateness. Yet, while in the former case this determinateness results from the absolute value assigned to the past, such a determinateness is attributed in the latter case to the conflicts underlying the social structure.

Insofar as this particular Utopia is materialistic in its orientations, it treats educational phenomena as "superstructures" and tends to minimize the significance of the changes to be brought about by educational activities per se. Yet, insofar as it stresses the preeminent role to be performed by a particular class or social group in the revolutionary process, the educational activities of this particular Utopia will address themselves to the group supposed to own "historical consciousness." While the majority of the free schools enter in the chiliastic or the liberal humanitarian categories, "community schools" are more likely to be in this particular class. Many of these schools tend only to alleviate the negative consequences attached to the neglect displayed by the society at large toward marginal ethnic or social groups, but their purpose is also to mobilize the political energies of local populations and hence to induce drastic changes in the allocative and normative patterns of social organization. Thus Kozol shows that the function of these community schools is not only to alert the public against the failures of the public education system but also to "radicalize" parents, teachers, and students as well, against the fire and building departments and municipal courts, against, in effect, all the institutional mechanisms that the dominant power structures use to harass minorities.

Although different in their outlooks, these Utopias share a number of common properties. Clearly they tend to involve the same categories of actors. In the United States their personnel is recruited from among the ranks of the subgroups who have been intensely engaged in civil rights activities and anti-war manifestations. For some of them, educational militancy represents a deliberate strategic choice and results from the belief that their political failures have been brought about by an insufficient mobilization of the masses. Thus, their educational militancy still reflects the pervasive American creed that education is the key determinant of social organization. For others, however, this educational militancy is only a tactical withdrawal, justifiable by the fact that circumstances do not facilitate direct action. Similarities in the characteristics of their personnel lead free schools to experience analogous problems. Their marginality tends to make their teachers "tormented and vindictive people whose energies are turned toward power struggles and more likely to 'devastate' than to care about children." [21]

Sharing the same type of personnel, all Utopias serve similar functions in the society at large. Insofar as they transcend the immediate societal context and orient individual attitudes and behaviors toward elements that the situation does not contain, they facilitate the building up of pressures toward changes in institutionalized educational structures. Indeed the proliferation of laboratory schools attached to universities or to regular primary school systems results from the comparisons that discontented parents establish between Utopian and institutional schools. Yet they also tend to block further educational change. This is because the current social order is able to incorporate for its own survival some of the demands symbolized in the existence of Utopian school movements, and hence to erode their dynamic power. However, this is also because these Utopias accentuate existing contradictions in patterns of social organization but do not in fact cope with them. The chiliast utopia, for instance, rejects the entire existing social order without realizing that it is a by-product of it and that its survival is the result of the wealth accumulated by such a system. Similarly, liberal humanitarians do not address themselves to the problems raised by the current system of interaction among social groups and classes, while communism in its present educational forms operates at a scale too low to facilitate a complete restructuring of educational systems.

The existence of the idea of an educational utopia reminds human actors of the contradictions implicit in the concepts of liberty and equality. While the sociologist stresses the aspects of liberty that are based on the acceptance of necessities and constraints, the Utopian mentality stresses those aspects that are based on creativity. Similarly, while the sociologist underlines the actual uniformities that underlie the processes of equality, the Utopian accentuates the differentiating requirements that accompany the fulfillment of this ideal. There is a time for Utopia and a time for sociological analysis. Although these times appear to be conflicting, individual morality consists in learning how to reconcile these diverging times and to experience them as complementary rather than as mutually exclusive. Both sociologists and Utopians must keep their "sense of wonder." Their quest is an endless one.

NOTES AND REFERENCES

1. E. Durkheim, *Education et sociologie* (Paris: Alcan, 1922), pp. 40–43.

2. See S. Padow, ed., *Democracy by T. Jefferson* (New York: Appleton Century, 1939), pp. 137–138.

3. R. Merton, *Social Theory and Social Structure* (Glencoe: The Free Press, 1957).

4. If we take the example of the writings of Voltaire on education, it is clear that he recognizes the fact that prejudices are related to ignorance and that academic experiences will enable middle-class individuals to escape the negative implications attached to ignorance. Yet it is equally clear that the same Voltaire was not in favor of diffusing formal schooling to all strata of society. In this sense the concern over educational liberties seems to precede the concern over educational equalities. Yet the preeminence of educational liberty has lasted longer in Europe than in this country.

5. However, the importance of the courts symbolizes the very preeminence of decentralization since it implies that federal goals and policies do not

have necessary and automatic priority over state decisions and practices. This of course results from the fact that educational matters are in the hands of the state rather than in those of the federal government.

6. Indeed patterns of residential segregation are not necessarily alike in traditional southern communities and in northern metropoles. In the former case, there has been a persistence of the slavery-type of residential arrangement.

7. See G. Homans, *Social Behavior: Its Elementary Forms* (New York: Harcourt Brace, 1961).

8. For a discussion of this point, see L. Fein, *The Ecology of Public Schools* (New York: Pegasus, 1973).

9. See R. Brown, *Social Psychology* (New York: Free Press, 1965), Chapter 2, 3.

10. In most cases bussing implies the transportation of black students to white schools. The transfer of white students to black schools, it is argued, is likely to destabilize white communities. Are we then infering that black neighborhoods are "destabilized?" See P. Peterson, "The School Busing Controversy: Distributive or Pluralistic Politics," *Administrators Notebook,* Midwest Administration Center, Vol. 20, 1972, pp. 1–13. See also L. Rubin, *Busing and Backlash* (Berkeley: University of California Press, 1972).

11. Many novels illustrate the misfortunes of young gifted lower-class individuals who have to accept an occupational position by far inferior to their merits. Julian Sorel is a good illustration of this phenomena. See Stendhal, *The Red and the Black* (Paris: Gibert, 1942).

12. For a development of this point, see T. Parsons, *The Social System* (Glencoe: Free Press, 1951), pp. 249–325.

13. In the Third World such "revolutions" induce the emigration of skilled professionals and technicians, and this emigration is often feared by local politicians.

14. A. Jensen, "Environment Heredity, and Intelligence," *Harvard Educational Review,* Reprint Series No. 2, 1969.

15. See H. Marcuse, *One-Dimensional Man* (Boston: Beacon Press, 1968).

16. K. Mannheim, *Ideology and Utopia* (New York: Harcourt Brace, 1935), Chapter IV.

17. For a brief review of current educational Utopias in the United States see *The Chicago Guide,* Vol. 21, January 1972, pp. 8–22.

18. See J. Kozol, *Free Schools* (New York: Houghton Mifflin, 1972), pp. 22–23, 44.

19. *Ibid.,* p. 15.

20. *Ibid.,* pp. 9, 59.

21. *Ibid.,* p. 22.

AUTHOR INDEX

409

SUBJECT INDEX